외투기업의 No.1 노무법인
KangNam Labor Law Firm
Second Edition

Practical Manual
on Labor Law (5/20)

Wage Manual

실무자를 위한
임금 매뉴얼

Dr. Bongsoo Jung
Ph.D. in Law / Labor Attorney
법학박사/공인노무사 **정 봉 수**

- Labor Law Practical Manuals
① Work Force Restructuring
② Foreign Employment and Immigration
③ Lawful Dismissal
④ Labor Union
⑤ Wage
⑥ Working Hours, Holidays and Leave
⑦ Irregular Employment and 'Employee' Status
⑧ Employment Contract
⑨ Industrial Accident Compensation
⑩ Preventing Workplace & Sexual Harassment
⑪ Labor Inspection Preparation
⑫ Rules of Employment

실무자를 위한 노동법 실무 매뉴얼 시리즈
① 구조조정 매뉴얼
② 외국인 고용과 비자 매뉴얼
③ 해고 매뉴얼
④ 노동조합 매뉴얼
⑤ 임금 매뉴얼
⑥ 근로시간, 휴일, 휴가 매뉴얼
⑦ 비정규직과 근로자성 판단 매뉴얼
⑧ 근로계약 매뉴얼
⑨ 산재보상 매뉴얼
⑩ 직장 내 괴롭힘과 성희롱 예방 매뉴얼
⑪ 근로감독 준비 매뉴얼
⑫ 취업규칙 매뉴얼

강남노무법인

Preface

I visited a large bookstore while sightseeing in Kyoto, Japan in June, 2018. While there, I was surprised and in awe about two things: one was the number of labor management books in the Labor Law section, while the other was that those labor books were divided into practical guides and volumes on research & theory. In Korea, not only are there few books on labor management, but most are simply academic and do not lend themselves well as practical guides.

The articles and books I have written have not been directly related to actual application of labor laws, and so I have made work-related manuals to help companies make such real-life applications. In this practical manual, I have selected 20 themes in which I make detailed references to related law and court rulings, case studies, and guidelines for application.

Wages play the most important role in labor law. This Wage Manual consists of a definition of wages, classification of statutory wages, method of paying wages and remedies for unpaid wages, and the retirement benefit system. First of all, this manual explains the theory of wages by category and provides related practical labor cases that have frequently occurred in relation to wages.

Wage systems in Korea have had two major changes in recent years, the first of which is the place that fixed bonuses have in ordinary wages and the second regarding the illegality of a comprehensive wage system.

In the first case, an important court ruling in the classification of statutory wages is the determination that bonuses paid on a regular basis are included in ordinary wage, which was the decision by all judges on the Supreme Court in December 2013. This ruling led to reorganization of the distorted wage structure and, above all, set consequences that limited the overtime working hours of production workers. Secondly, a change expected as much as the above ordinary wage judgment was the one on comprehensive wage systems, which refer to the practice of including any overtime in pre-determined fixed wages for office workers. Since 2007, such comprehensive wage systems for office workers whose working hours can be calculated, have been judged as illegal in the courts. This text includes such cases explained in detail.

I hope this manual will be of assistance to HR managers in giving them an opportunity to better understand the legal concept of wages and see how wage-related matters in labor law apply in practice.

I would like to thank Labor Attorney Cheny Park, Instructor Hyun-jin Lee, and Publisher Young-cheol Jung who edited and published the book so that it might see the light. In particular, I thank my longtime friend and proofreading editor, Dave Crofton. This manual, which has been made possible by the efforts of many people, is a collaborative work and is not a product of the author alone.

October 10, 2023
Bongsoo Jung
Labor Attorney, PhD in Law

머리말

2018년 6월, 일본 교토 관광을 하면서 대형서점을 들렸다. 거기서 노동법 섹션에 꽂혀있는 노무관리 책들이 참으로 다양하다는 것과 실무 서적과 연구 서적을 구분하여 저술활동이 이루어지고 있다는 것을 보고 느낀 바가 많았다. 한국의 경우 노무관리 책들이 많지 않을 뿐만 아니라, 그나마 나와 있는 책들도 학술서적이 대부분이기 때문이다.

그동안 내가 저술해왔던 기고문이나 서적 등이 실무 활용부분에서 동떨어져 있던 것이 사실인지라 이번에는 기업실무에서 바로 도움이 될 수 있는 업무처리 매뉴얼을 작성하고자 하였다. 실무에서 특히 중요한 노무관리 부분 20선을 테마로 선정하여 관련근거, 사례연구, 적용지침까지 자세히 정리해서 실무자들의 업무처리 지침서로 만들고자 하였다.

임금은 노동법의 여러 내용 중 가장 핵심이 되는 부분이다. 임금 매뉴얼은 임금의 정의, 법정 임금의 구분, 임금지급 방법과 임금체불의 구제방법, 그리고 퇴직급여제도로 구성되어 있다. 우선, 해당 부분에 대한 이론을 설명하고, 이와 관련된 현장 사례를 설명한 실무서적이다.

우리나라의 임금제도는 최근 두 개의 커다란 변화가 있는데, 첫 번째는 고정 상여금의 통상임금 판례이고, 두 번째는 포괄임금제의 위법성이라 할 수 있다. 첫 번째의 경우를 살펴보면, 법정 임금 구분에 있어 중요한 판례사례가 2013년 12월에 나온 매년 정기적으로 지급하는 상여금의 통상임금 판결이다. 이 판결로 인해 왜곡된 임금구조를 개편하는 계기가 되었고, 무엇보다 생산직 근로자의 연장근로를 제한하는 결과를 가져오게 되었다. 두 번째로, 위 통상 임금 판결에 못지않게 예상되는 변화가 사무직 근로자들을 중심으로 연장근로를 시키면서 고정임금을 지급해 온 관행인 포괄임금제이다. 2007년 이후 판례는 근로시간 산정이 가능한 사무직 근로자에 대한 포괄임금제를 부정해 오고 있는데, 이 부분에 대해서도 본문에서 자세히 설명하고 있다.

이번 매뉴얼을 통해 실무자들은 노동법에서의 임금 관련내용이 실무에서 어떻게 적용되는지 사례를 접하고 임금을 더 잘 이해할 수 있는 기회가 되기를 바란다.

본서 출간에 있어 문맥 교정과 더불어 전반적으로 내용을 감수해 주신 안태욱 법무팀장님, 이현진 강사님, 그리고 이 책이 빛을 볼 수 있도록 편집과 출판을 해 주신 정영철 사장님께 감사드린다. 특히 나의 오랜 친구이자 영문 교정을 맡고 있는 Dave Crofton에게도 고개 숙여 감사드린다. 여러 사람의 노력이 배어있는 본 매뉴얼은 공동의 작업이지 결코 저자 혼자의 산물이 아니라고 생각한다.

2023년 10월 10일
정봉수 / 공인노무사 / 법학박사

Chapter 1 — Understanding Wages

Ⅰ. What is Wage Management? 6
Ⅱ. Employers' Duties regarding Wages 10
Ⅲ. Determination of Employee Incentives Are Wages 14
Ⅳ. Related Labor Cases 20
 <Case 1> Whether Retention Bonus (or Signing Bonus) is deemed as Wages 20
 <Case 2> Labor Inspection over Unpaid Wages for Temporary Workers 26
 <Case 3> Case related to Hiring Academy Instructors as Freelancers 32

Chapter 2 — Statutory Wages

Ⅰ. Ordinary Wages 37
Ⅱ. Supreme Court Decision on Ordinary Wage 43
Ⅱ-2. Precedents Following the Supreme Court's Unanimous Decision on Ordinary Wages 51
Ⅲ. Average Wages 60
Ⅳ. Minimum Wage 70
Ⅴ. Shutdown Allowances 78
Ⅳ. Additional Allowances 85
Ⅶ. Related Labor Cases 88
 <Case 1> Occupational Accident Compensation 88
 <Case 2> Branch Manager's Severance Pay 90

차 례

제1장 임금의 이해

Ⅰ. 임금이란? ·· 6
Ⅱ. 임금관련 사업주의 의무 ·· 10
Ⅲ. 인센티브가 임금인지 임금이 아닌지 판단 ············· 14
Ⅳ. 실무사례 ··· 20
    <사례 1> 리텐션 보너스와 사이닝 보너스 ············· 20
    <사례 2> 지방의회의 일급직 사무보조자(위촉직)의 임금체불 ····· 26
    <사례 3> 원어민 강사를 프리랜서로 고용한 노동사례 ··········· 32

제2장 법정기준임금

Ⅰ. 통상임금 ··· 37
Ⅱ. 통상임금 관련 대법원 합의체 판결 ······················· 43
Ⅱ-2 통상임금 대법원 합의체 판결 이후 판례 경향 ··········· 51
Ⅲ. 평균임금 ··· 60
Ⅳ. 최저임금 ··· 70
Ⅴ. 휴업수당 ··· 78
Ⅵ. 가산임금 ··· 85
Ⅶ. 실무사례 ··· 88
    <사례 1> 업무상 재해자의 산업재해보상금 계산 ············· 88
    <사례 2> 지사장 퇴직금 진정사건 ·························· 90

Chapter 3: Payment of Wages

- I. How to Pay Wages 96
- II. The Principle of Complete Payment of Wages & Exceptions 99
- III. Procedures for Wage Adjustments (Increases, Reductions, Freezes, Returns) and Related Cases 104
- IV. Annual Salary Systems 111
- V. Inclusive Wage System 114

Chapter 4: The Protection of Wages

- I. Preventive Measures for Delayed Payment of Wages 124
- II. Alternative Payment System for Resolving Unpaid Wages 126
- III. Small-Scale Alternative Payment System for Resolving Unpaid Wages 130
- IV. Statue of Limitations 134
- V. Related Labor Cases
    - <Case 1> A Claim for Insolvency Payment 141
    - <Case 2> Petition for Unpaid Weekly Holiday Allowance 142
    - <Case 3> Whether Compensation Should be Given for Unused Annual Leave 144

Chapter 5: Retirement Benefit Plan

- I. Severance Pay System 148
- II. The Retirement Pension Plan 155
- III. Severance Settlement-related Taxation Issues 161
- IV. Key Issues: The Confusing Administrative Interpretation from the Ministry of Employment and Labor on Calculating Severance Pay 168

제3장 임금지급

Ⅰ. 임금 지급 원칙 ··· 96
Ⅱ. 임금 전액지급의 원칙과 예외 ································· 99
Ⅲ. 임금조정 (인상, 삭감, 동결, 반납) 절차와 관련사례 ············ 104
Ⅳ. 연봉제 ·· 111
Ⅴ. 포괄임금제 ··· 114

제4장 임금채권 보호

Ⅰ. 임금체불 예방조치 ··· 124
Ⅱ. 체불임금 해결을 위한 대지급금 제도 ··················· 126
Ⅲ. 소액대지급금제도 ··· 130
Ⅳ. 소멸시효제도 ·· 134
Ⅴ. 실무사례
    <사례 1> 대지급금사건 ··· 141
    <사례 2> 주휴수당 미지급사건 ································ 142
    <사례 3> 미사용 연차휴가수당 미지급사건 ············ 144

제5장 퇴직급여제도

Ⅰ. 퇴직금제도 ··· 148
Ⅱ. 퇴직연금제도 ·· 155
Ⅲ. 퇴직합의금의 과세문제 ·· 161
Ⅳ. 주요쟁점: 이상한 퇴직금 계산법을 안내하는 고용노동부의 행정해석 ·· 168

Ⅴ. Related Labor Cases

    <Case 1> Failure to Pay Severance Pay to Foreign Teachers 173

    <Case 2> Failure to Pay Severance Pay to Company Directors 175

Chapter 6 — Premiums for the Social Insurances

Ⅰ. Social Insurances 179

    1. Industrial Accident Compensation Insurance 179

    2. Employment Insurance 180

    3. National Health Insurance 181

    4. National Pension 182

Ⅱ. Social Insurances for Foreign Migrant Workers 183

Ⅲ. Insurances Exclusive to Foreign Migrant Workers 188

Chapter 7 — Wage-related Personnel Systems

Ⅰ. Motivation Systems 193

Ⅱ. Gain Sharing System 198

Ⅲ. Welfare System Operation 199

Ⅴ. 실무사례
    <사례 1> 원어민 교사 퇴직금 미지급 사건 ················· 173
    <사례 2> 회사 임원 퇴직금 미지급 사건 ··················· 175

제6장 사회보험료

Ⅰ. 사회보험 ·· 179
  1. 산업재해보상보험 ·· 179
  2. 고용보험 ·· 180
  3. 국민건강보험과 노인장기요양보험 ························ 181
  4. 국민연금 ·· 182
Ⅱ. 외국인근로자의 사회보험 ···································· 183
Ⅲ. 외국인근로자의 전용보험 ···································· 188

제7장 부록: 임금관련 인사제도

Ⅰ. 동기부여제도 ·· 193
Ⅱ. 성과배분제도 ·· 198
Ⅲ. 복리후생제도 ·· 199

Chapter 1 Understanding Wages

I. What is Wage Management?
II. Employers Duties regarding Wages
III. Determination of Employee Incentives Are Wages
IV. Related Labor Cases

⟨Case 1⟩ Whether Retention Bonus (or Signing Bonus) is deemed as Wages

⟨Case 2⟩ Labor Inspection over Unpaid Wages for Temporary Workers

⟨Case 3⟩ Case related to Hiring Academy Instructors as Freelancers

제1장 임금의 이해

Ⅰ. 임금이란?

Ⅱ. 임금관련 사업주의 의무

Ⅲ. 인센티브가 임금인지 임금이 아닌지 판단

Ⅳ. 실무사례

〈사례 1〉 리텐션 보너스와 사이닝 보너스

〈사례 2〉 지방의회의 일급직 사무보조자(위촉직)의 임금체불

〈사례 3〉 원어민 강사를 프리랜서로 고용한 노동사례

Chapter 1 Understanding Wages

Ⅰ. What is Wage Management?

1. The Characteristics of Wage Management

Wage management is classified into ① level management, for total amount management, and ② system management, for the distribution of wages to employees. Level management is concerned with the exterior market balance, whereas system management maintains interior balance.

Wage management has two distinct characteristics: labor costs in the form of a company's production costs, and an employee's living costs. Accordingly, the principle of the least amount is applied to the former, while the principle of the greatest amount is applied to the latter. This brings about many conflicts in finding mutual interests. However, extremely low wages make it impossible to recruit or maintain capable manpower, while extremely high wages burden the company and hinder stable growth.

There are three separate working conditions. These are wages, working hours, and the work place (or work environment), which become the criteria by which new employees choose a company for which to work. Accordingly, the wage level must be determined considering working hours and the work place.

2. Determining Wage Level[1]

The company's ability to pay, the employees' living costs, and the market price of wages are major factors considered when determining the wage level.

(1) Company's ability to pay

The company's ability to pay is not the financial capability of the company to pay the maximum, but its encompassed ability to pay within the limits of business operation.

Ability to pay is decided and disclosed by economic indicators of physical productivity such as value added, increased sales, and product productivity.

---

[1] Jung, Bongsoo, 『The Korean Labor Law Bible』, 6th ed., 2021. Jungang, pp. 591-592.

Ⅰ. 임금이란?

1. 임금관리의 특징

임금제도는 크게 임금 총액 관리로서의 임금수준관리와, 그 인건비 총액을 어떻게 근로자에게 분배할 것인가의 임금체계관리로 나눌 수 있다. 임금수준은 대외적 형평의 문제이고 임금체계는 대내적 형평에 관한 문제라는 관점에서 이해할 수 있다.

임금은 회사 측면에서는 제조원가 구성요소의 인건비가 되는 동시에 직원의 입장에서는 가계의 원천으로서 생계비가 되는 양면성을 가지고 있다. 전자에게는 최소화의 원칙이, 후자에게는 최대화의 원칙이 작용하여 상호 상반관계로 이해되기도 한다. 지나친 저임금은 우수한 인력의 확보 유지를 어렵게하게 하고 지나친 고임금은 기업의 부담을 증가시켜 기업의 안정성장을 저해하게 되는 것이다.

임금, 근로시간, 작업장소(또는 작업환경)를 3대 근로조건이라 하며 근로자 직장 선택의 기준이 되고 있다. 따라서 임금수준을 대비할 때에는 근로시간과 작업장소를 감안할 필요가 있다.

2. 임금수준의 결정[1]

임금수준의 결정에 영향을 주는 요인은 회사의 지불능력, 근로자의 생계비와 노동시장의 임금수준이다.

(1) 회사의 지불능력

회사의 지불능력이라고 하는 것은 단순히 기업의 보상으로 지불할 수 있는 최대한의 재정적 능력이 아니라, 기업이 안정된 운영을 계속할 수 있다는 전제조건 하에서 지불할 수 있는 회사의 능력을 말한다.

지불능력은 부가가치 향상, 매출액증가, 제품생산성 등 물적생산성과 같은 경영지표에 준거해서 파악된다.

---
[1] 정봉수, 「한국노동법 영문해설」 제6판, 중앙경제사, 2021, pp. 591-592.

(2) Living costs

Living costs are the employee's general living expenses, including child education fees, as well as all other necessities of life. Direct living costs are difficult to calculate and so a model of the standard living costs including economic, social, and cultural conditions often serves as the common method adopted by the Life Cycle of a household model.

(3) Market prices of wages

Wages are directly related to manpower acquisition and employee morale. Even if wages are decided reasonably in terms of general considerations, it is usually impossible to hire the necessary employees if the company's wage level is lower than that of other companies in the same industry or if the company is unstable. Accordingly, the social wage level is highly considered when determining the wage level.

3. Wage System Management[2]

The wage system is designed to keep internal balance through a reasonable distribution of limited labor costs. In practice, it depends on how the portions are divided among the items. The wage system is divided into basic pay and miscellaneous pay.

(1) Basic pay

Basic pay is the wage paid for labor under ordinary working hours and ordinary working conditions. Not only does it account for calculating standards for miscellaneous pay, but it is also the core of the wage system, revealing the company's wage policy.

Basic pay consists of seniority-based pay centered on human factors, job-based pay centered on job factors, and combined job-ability pay. Most companies use seniority-based and job-based pay schemes to varying degrees.

---

[2] Jung, Bongsoo, 『The Korean Labor Law Bible』, 6th ed., 2021. Jungang, pp. 592-598.

(2) 생계비

생계비라 함은 근로자의 의식주뿐만 아니라 자녀교육비 등 생활 전반에 필요한 경비를 말한다. 어느 정도가 직접생계비인지는 단정하기 어려우나 그 나라의 경제·사회·문화적인 여건을 고려하여 매년 표준생계비 모델을 작성하게 되는데, 근로자의 연령별 세대모형에 의한 Life Cycle에 따른 작성이 통상적인 방법이다.

(3) 노동시장 임금수준

임금은 인력의 확보 및 근로자의 사기 향상과 직결되어 있기 때문에 다른 제반 요건을 충분히 감안하여 합리적으로 결정되었다고 하더라도 같은 지역 같은 업종의 임금수준, 즉 노동시장 임금수준과 균형을 취하지 못하고 그보다 낮은 수준에 머물러 있다면 필요한 종업원을 구하기도 어려울 뿐더러 생산성의 향상은 더욱 기대하기 어려울 것이다. 따라서 임금수준의 결정에 있어서 사회적 임금수준을 충분히 고려해야 한다.

3. 임금체계 관리[2]

임금체계는 한정된 인건비 총액을 합리적으로 배분하여 대내적 형평을 유지하기 위한 것이다. 실무적으로 살펴보면, "임금항목간의 구성비를 어떻게 할 것인가?"의 문제인 것이다. 임금체계는 일반적으로 기준임금과 기준외임금으로 구분한다.

(1) 기준임금

기준임금이라 함은 통상적인 노동시간 및 작업조건 하의 노동에 대해 지급되는 임금으로 기준외임금의 계산기준이 될 뿐만 아니라 기업 임금체계의 핵심이 되는 부분이다.

기준임금은 인적요소 중심의 연공급과 직무요소 중심의 직무급이 있으며, 양자를 절충한 직능급이 있다. 대다수의 기업이 정도의 차이는 있으나 연공급과 직무급적 요소를 절충하여 사용하고 있다.

---

[2] 정봉수, 「한국노동법 영문해설」 제6판, 중앙경제사, 2021, pp. 592-593.

1) Seniority-based pay

Seniority-based pay, which is also known as human-based pay, is the typical wage system in accordance with the criteria of human factors. This is a wage increase system along with the regular promotion system according to the number of service years in terms of individual education, age, etc. and is widely adopted in Asian cultures.

2) Job-based pay

Job-based pay is a type of wage structure that determines individual wages according to the respective value of each evaluated job. This means to say that the system is a wage structure designed by the principle of "equal pay for equal work." Therefore, job-based pay is one of the most general ability-centered wage structures.

3) Job-ability based pay

Job-ability based pay is a wage structure that combines seniority-based pay for human factors and job-based pay for job factors. That is, job-ability based pay classifies job skills, defines office organization (e.g., in-charge, part leader, section manager, etc.) and equates hobong (service year) level with seniority-based pay, which includes seniority factors. Therefore, the wages are determined by job content and individual job ability.

(2) Miscellaneous pay

Miscellaneous pay is wages paid as a reward for labor service, which has been provided additionally and for job performance as an additional pay structure. Miscellaneous pay includes technology allowances, title allowances, and legal allowances (overtime, day-off, and night allowances).

4. Wages and the Labor Standards Act[3]

(1) Concept of wage

> Article2 (5) of the LSA (Definition of Wages)
> The term "wages" means wages, salary, and any other money or valuables, regardless of its title, which the employer pays to a worker as remuneration for work.

---

[3] Jung, Bongsoo, 『The Korean Labor Law Bible』, 6th ed., 2021. Jungang, pp. 71-72.

1) 연공급

연공급은 속인급이라고도 하며 인적요소 기준에 의한 대표적인 임금형태로 개개인의 학력, 연령 등을 감안하여 근속연수에 따른 임금체증제도와 함께 정기승급제도가 마련되어 있으며 동양 문화권에서 주로 채택되고 있다.

2) 직무급

직무급이란 직무평가에 의하여 평가된 각 직무의 상대적 가치에 따라 개별 임금을 결정하는 임금체계의 형태를 말하는 것으로 "동일노동·동일임금(equal pay for equal work)"의 원칙에 입각한 임금체계를 말한다. 그러므로 직무급은 능력주의적 보상체계의 가장 전형적인 형태라 할 수 있다.

3) 직능급

직능급은 인적요소 기준의 연공급과 직무요소 기준의 직무급을 절충한 임금체계이다. 직능급은 먼저 직능을 등급화하여 직제(예 : 주임, 계장, 과장 등)를 정하고 이를 다시 세분하여 호봉의 등급을 정하는데 호봉에는 근무연수 등의 연공적 요소가 포함된다. 이처럼 직능급은 직무의 내용과 개별적인 직무수행 능력에 따라 임금을 결정하는 형태이다.

(2) 기준외임금

기준외임금은 기본임금에 대한 부가급의 형태로 직원의 정상적인 근로이외의 근로에 대한 대가와 작업의 성과에 대한 대가로 지급되는 임금을 말한다. 기준 외 임금으로 기술수당, 직책수당, 법정수당(시간외 수당, 휴일, 야간) 등이 있다.

4. 근로기준법상 임금[3]

(1) 임금의 개념

> 근로기준법 제2조 제5항 【임금의 정의】
> "임금"이란 사용자가 근로의 대가로 근로자에게 임금, 봉급, 그 밖에 어떠한 명칭으로든지 지급하는 일체의 금품을 말한다.

---

[3] 정봉수, 「한국노동법 영문해설」 제6판, 중앙경제사, 2021, pp. 71-72.

(2) Wage requisites

1) Paid by the employer

Given that wages are what the employer pays to the employee, the service charge that a worker receives from customers in a hotel or restaurant cannot be considered as wages in principle.

2) Remuneration for work

As wages are paid as remuneration for work, they cannot be deemed wages if the employer renders payment under friendly and favorable terms outside of work, or if the employer provides pay as part of welfare, or if the employee receives reimbursement for actual expenses.

3) Any payment regardless of label

Wages are paid in forms of salary or allowance in general. If the employer is paying remuneration for work to a subordinate employee, it is considered wages, regardless of what label the payment is given. Accordingly, we shall not estimate information allowance and welfare fees as wages just by their titles, because wages are differentiated by payment conditions.

(3) Concrete criteria of wages

1) Money paid under friendly and favorable terms is not considered wages

Money is not considered to be wages if paid for optional, courteous, and friendly reasons including congratulatory and consolation allowances, awards for quality control activities, or money paid favorably to celebrate special occasions such as the Company's foundation day.

2) Money paid for actual expenses is not considered wages

Money paid to reimburse the actual cost of purchasing production instruments such as security equipment is not wages. Reimbursements for purchase of work uniforms, tools and materials, business trip expenses, travelling expenses, account expenses, confidential expenses, and information fees are also not considered wages.

3) Welfare fees are not considered wages (in principle).

The welfare fee in its true meaning is not a wage because it cannot be treated as remuneration for work. However, if paid regularly to all workers in accordance with the collective agreement, rules of employment, or a repeated precedent, it is considered to be wages under the Labor Standards Act.

(2) 임금 요건
1) 사용자가 지급할 것
임금은 사용자가 근로자에게 지급한 것이므로 호텔, 식당 등에서 손님이 직접 근로자에게 지급하는 봉사료는 원칙적으로 임금이라고 할 수 없다.

2) 근로의 대상일 것
임금은 근로의 대가로 지급하는 것이므로 근로의 제공과는 상관없이 사용자가 호의적·은혜적으로 지급하는 경우나 복지후생의 일환으로 제공하는 경우 또는 실비 보상적으로 지급하는 경우 등은 임금으로 볼 수 없다.

3) 명칭을 불문한 일체의 금품
임금은 봉급 또는 수당이라는 명칭으로 지급되는 것이 보통인데, 사용자가 종속관계에 있는 근로자에게 근로에 대한 대가로 금품을 지급하면 그 명칭과 관계없이 임금으로 간주된다. 따라서 정보비, 복리후생비 등 명칭만을 가지고 임금의 해당 여부를 판단하여서는 안 되며 지급실태에 따라 달라진다.

(3) 임금 판단기준
1) 은혜적·호의적으로 지급되는 금품은 임금이 아니다.
경조금, 위로금 등 임의적, 의례적, 호의적 의미에서 지급되는 금품, QC 활동 등에 대한 포상금이나 회사 창립일 등 경축일에 호의적으로 특별히 지급되는 금품과 같이 은혜적으로 지급되는 금품은 임금이 아니다.

2) 실비 보상적인 금품은 임금이 아니다.
보안장비 구입비 등과 같이 생산수단 구입을 위한 실비 보상적인 금품은 임금이 아니다. 작업복구입비, 작업용품 대금, 출장비, 여비, 판공비, 기밀비, 정보비 등도 마찬가지이다.

3) 복리후생비는 임금이 아니다(원칙적).
순수한 의미의 복리후생비는 근로의 대가로 볼 수 없으므로 임금이 아니나, 수당의 이름이 복리후생비라 하더라도 단체협약, 취업규칙 등에 의하거나 또는 관례나 관행에 따라 정기적으로 전 근로자에게 같은 금액을 지급하는 경우에는 순수한 의미에서 복리후생비로 볼 수 없으므로 근로기준법상 임금이다.

Wages	Non-wages
· Regular and continual bonuses and grants · Severance pay (post-paid wage) · Benefits paid for paid holidays or paid monthly/annual leave · Allowances for suspended work · Monetary payment for employee benefit, such as a price-linked allowance, a commuter allowance, or a family allowance whose payment is a general and established practice.	· Monetary payment made as a token of courtesy, goodwill, or favor, such as an allowance for congratulations or condolence · Monetary payment made to reimburse expenses for business trips · Dismissal allowances · Compensation for damage, such as suspended work compensation

Ⅱ. Employers' Duties regarding Wages

1. Payroll

(1) According to Article 48 of the Labor Standards Act, employers must prepare a wage ledger whenever wages are paid. (Fine for negligence) Article 116 of the Labor Standards Act: Fine for negligence up to 5 million won
(2) The wage ledger includes information that can identify the worker, such as name, date of birth, and employee number, date of employment, work performed, matters that are the basis for calculating wages and family allowances, number of days worked, number of working hours, overtime, night work, or holidays. In the case of work, the number of hours, basic wage, allowance, amount of other wages by detail, part of the wages in accordance with laws or collective agreements should be included in the amount (health insurance premium, national pension, employment insurance premium, income tax, etc.). (Fine for negligence) Article 116 of the Labor Standards Act: Fine for negligence up to 5 million won

2. Payment of Various Money and Goods such as Wages

임금에 해당하는 경우	임금에 해당하지 않는 경우
• 정기적·계속적으로 지급하는 상여금, 생산장려금, 능률수당 • 퇴직금(후불성 임금) • 유급휴일, 연월차휴가 미사용 수당 • 휴업수당 • 정기적·일률적으로 지급하도록 명시되어 있거나 관례적으로 지급되는 물가수당·통근수당·가족수당·월동수당 등의 복리 후생적 성격의 금품	• 경조금·위로금 등의 의례적 호의적으로 지급되는 금품 • 여비·출장비 등의 실비 보상적으로 지급되는 금품 • 해고예고수당 • 휴업보상등의 재해보상금

Ⅱ. 임금관련 사업주의 의무

1. 임금대장

(1) 근로기준법 제48조에 따라 사용자는 임금을 지급할 때마다 임금대장을 작성하여야 한다. (과태료) 근로기준법 제116조 500만 원 이하의 과태료
(2) 임금대장에는 '① 성명, 생년월일, 사원번호 등 근로자를 특정할 수 있는 정보, ② 고용 연월일, 종사하는 업무, 임금 및 가족수당의 계산기초가 되는 사항, ③ 근로일수와 근로시간수, ④ 연장근로, 야간근로 또는 휴일근로를 시킨 경우에는 그 시간 수, ⑤ 기본급, 수당, 그 밖의 임금의 내역별 금액, ⑥ 법령 또는 단체협약에 따라 임금의 일부를 공제한 경우에는 그 금액(건강보험료, 국민연금, 고용보험료, 소득세 등)'이 포함되어야 한다. (근로기준법 제116조) 500만 원 이하의 과태료

2. 임금 등 각종 금품 지급

(1) In case of death or retirement, wages, compensation, and all other money and valuables must be paid within 14 days from the occurrence of the reason for the payment. However, in special circumstances, the period may be extended by agreement between the employer and the worker. (Article 36 of the LSA). (Penalty - Article 109: Imprisonment for up to 3 years or a fine of up to 30 million won

(2) All money and valuables include not only compensation for the work provided by the worker, but also money and valuables to be paid by the employer based on the labor relationship.
(Penalty) Article 109: Imprisonment for up to 3 years or a fine of up to 30 million won

(3) Exceptionally, in special circumstances, the payment date can be extended by agreement between the parties. In this case, the agreement between the parties must be made within 14 days from the date of occurrence of the reason for payment. (Penalty) Article 109: Imprisonment for up to 3 years or a fine of up to 30 million won

(4) In principle, unpaid wages and severance pay must be paid, including delay interest (20% per annum) for the number of delayed days until the payment date. However, delay interest does not apply if the cause of Article 18 of the same Enforcement Decree, such as the commencement of corporate rehabilitation procedures or a decision to declare bankruptcy, etc. (Penalty) Article 109: Imprisonment for up to 3 years or a fine of up to 30 million won

3. Payment of wages

(1) Wages must be paid in convertible currency under the Korean Bank Act, except where the law or collective agreement stipulates that wages be paid in other ways. However, in cases stipulated by the collective agreement, part of the wages may be paid in kind, stocks, or commodity exchange vouchers only to union members (Article 43 of the LSA).
(Penalty) Article 109: Imprisonment for up to 3 years or a fine of up to 30 million won

(2) Wages must be paid directly to workers.
It is also not permitted to pay wages to workers' parents or legal representatives.
It is possible for workers to deposit money into a bank account at a designated bank and withdraw it on payday. (Penalty) Article 109: Imprisonment for up to 3 years or a fine of up to 30 million won

(3) Part of wages cannot be deducted from wages, except when there are special

(1) 사망 또는 퇴직한 경우 그 지급 사유가 발생한 때부터 14일 이내에 임금, 보상금, 그 밖에 일체의 금품을 지급하여야 한다. 다만, 특별한 사정이 있을 경우에는 사용자와 근로자 사이의 합의에 의하여 기일을 연장할 수 있다 (근로기준법 제36조). (벌칙 제109조) 3년 이하의 징역 또는 3천만 원 이하의 벌금
(2) 일체의 금품이란 근로자가 제공한 근로에 대한 대가뿐 아니라 근로관계에 기초하여 사용자가 지급해야 할 금품이라면 모두 포함된다. (벌칙 제109조) 3년 이하의 징역 또는 3천만 원 이하의 벌금
(3) 예외적으로 특별한 사정이 있는 경우에는 당사자간 합의로 지급기일을 연장할 수 있는데, 이 경우 당사자간 합의는 지급사유 발생일로부터 14일 이내에 해야 한다. (벌칙 제109조) 3년 이하의 징역 또는 3천만 원 이하의 벌금
(4) 원칙적으로 미지급된 임금 및 퇴직금 등에 대하여 지급하는 날까지 지연일수에 대한 지연이자(연20%)를 포함하여 지급하여야 한다. 다만, 회생절차개시, 파산선고의 결정이 있는 경우 등 동 시행령 제18조의 사유에 해당하면 지연이자는 적용되지 않는다 (근로기준법 시행령 제17조). (벌칙 제109조) 3년 이하의 징역 또는 3천만 원 이하의 벌금

3. 임금지급

(1) 임금은 법령이나 단체협약에 다른 방식으로 지급하기로 정한 경우를 제외하고는 강제통용력이 있는 「한국은행법」에 의한 화폐로 지급해야 한다. 다만, 단체협약으로 정한 경우에는 조합원에 한하여 임금의 일부를 현물, 주식, 상품교환권 등으로 지급할 수 있다 (근로기준법 제43조). (벌칙) 제109조 3년 이하의 징역 또는 3천만 원 이하의 벌금
(2) 임금은 근로자에게 직접 지급해야 한다. 근로자의 친권자나 법정대리인에게 임금을 지급하는 것도 허용되지 않는다. 근로자가 지정한 은행의 은행예금 계좌에 입금하여 임금지급일에 인출할 수 있도록 하는 것은 가능하다. (벌칙 제109조) 3년 이하의 징역 또는 3천만 원 이하의 벌금
(3) 임금은 법령이나 단체협약에 특별한 규정이 있을 때를 제외하고는

provisions in laws or collective agreements, and the full amount must be paid to workers.

Therefore, deductions are possible when there are legal grounds (income tax, local tax, four major insurances) and when collective agreements stipulate deductions for labor union fees and welfare facility usage fees. However, in principle, wage deduction based on the provisions of the employment rules or the contents of the labor contract is not permitted. On the other hand, since wages must be paid in full to the worker, even if the employer has a claim for damages from the worker, the full wage must be paid without the worker's consent. However, when wages are overpaid due to a calculation error, wages can be offset, but even in this case, the timing of offset is reasonable enough to be seen as an adjustment to the wages paid in excess, and the amount and method of offset are disclosed to the worker. It must be a case where there is no fear of harming the lives of workers by giving advance notice. Penalty (Article 109) Imprisonment for up to 3 years or a fine of up to 30 million won

(4) Wages must be paid on a fixed date at least once a month. Employment rules must specify the wage payment period, and even if a worker joins the company midway through the month, part of the wage must be paid on the first wage payment day following the month of joining. Penalty (Article 109) Imprisonment for up to 3 years or a fine of up to 30 million won

4. Pay Slip

(1) When paying wages, the employer must issue a wage statement that includes the statutory details to the worker. (Applied to all workplaces with at least one full-time worker)
Penalty (Article 116) Fine for negligence up to 5 million won

(2) The pay slip is a written statement (including electronic documents pursuant to Article 1, Article 2 of the 「Framework Act on Electronic Documents and Electronic Commerce」) stating matters prescribed by the Presidential Decree, such as the composition of wages, calculation method, details of cases in which a part of wages are deducted pursuant to the proviso of Article 43 (1) of the Labor Standards Act. Penalty (Article 116) Fine for negligence up to 5 million won

임금의 일부를 공제할 수 없고 전액을 근로자에게 지급해야 한다. 따라서, 법령에 근거가 있는 경우(소득세, 지방세, 4대 보험)와 단체협약에 노동조합비, 복리후생시설 이용비 등에 관한 공제를 규정하고 있는 경우에는 공제가 가능한다. 그러나, 취업규칙의 규정이나 근로계약 내용을 근거로 한 임금공제는 원칙적으로 허용되지 않는다. 한편, 임금은 근로자에게 전액 지급되어야 하므로 사용자가 근로자에게 손해배상을 청구할 일이 있다 하더라도 근로자의 동의가 없다면 임금전액을 지급해야 한다. 다만, 계산의 착오로 임금이 초과 지급되었을 때에는 임금을 상계할 수 있으나, 이 경우도 상계하는 시기가 초과 지급한 임금에 대한 조정으로 볼 수 있을 만큼 가까워 합리성이 있고, 상계 금액과 방법을 근로자에게 예고하여 근로자 생활을 해할 염려가 없는 경우이어야 한다 (근로기준법 제43조). 벌칙 (제109조) 3년 이하의 징역 또는 3천만 원 이하의 벌금

(4) 임금은 매월 1회 이상 일정한 날짜를 정하여 지급해야 한다. 취업규칙에는 반드시 임금지급 시기를 명시하여야 하며, 월도중에 근로자가 입사해도 입사한 달에 도래하는 첫 임금 지급일에 임금 일부가 지급되어야 한다 (근로기준법 제43조). (벌칙 제109조) 3년 이하의 징역 또는 3천만 원 이하의 벌금

4. 임금명세서

(1) 사용자는 임금을 지급할 때 근로자에게 법정 기재사항이 포함된 임금명세서를 교부하여야 한다. 이 규정은 상시근로자 1인 이상 사업장 전체 적용된다 (근로기준법 제48조 제2항). (벌칙) 제116조 500만 원 이하의 과태료

(2) 임금명세서는 임금의 구성항목, 계산방법, 제43조 제1항 단서조항에 따라 임금의 일부를 공제한 경우의 내역 등 대통령령으로 정하는 사항을 기재한 서면(「전자문서 및 전자거래 기본법」 제2조 제1호에 따른 전자문서를 포함)으로 교부하여야 한다 (근로기준법 제48조 제2항). (벌칙 제116조) 500만 원 이하의 과태료

Chapter 1 Understanding Wages

5. Wage payment for subcontracting

In the case where a project is carried out under a subcontract, if the wages of workers hired by a subcontractor are in arrears due to reasons attributable to the immediate upper-level contractor, the immediate upper-level contractor shall be jointly and severally responsible for the payment of wages with the subcontractor. If the immediate upper-level contractor pays wages in arrears to workers hired by the sub-contractor, the immediate upper-level contractor may exercise the right to indemnity against the sub-contractor. With the revision of the Labor Standards Act, this provision applies even if a contract has been made once, so it is also applied in case of non-payment of wages to workers hired by the contractor due to reasons attributable to the contractor. Penalty (Article 109) Imprisonment for up to 3 years or a fine of up to 30 million won

6. Shutdown allowance

(1) 'Suspension' refers to a case in which a worker tries to provide work but is unable to provide work against his or her will, or the employer refuses to accept the work. In the case of suspension of business due to reasons attributable to the employer, the employer must pay workers an allowance of at least 70/100 of the average wage during the period of suspension. However, if the amount equivalent to 70/100 of the average wage exceeds the ordinary wage, the ordinary wage may be paid as a suspension allowance. In addition to intention and negligence, management failures that occur within the scope of the employer's power are regarded as causes attributable to the employer, but force majeure such as natural disasters or wars, and other circumstances outside the company that do not fall within the scope of the employer's power are not considered to be attributable to the employer. not. Penalty (Article 109) Imprisonment for up to 3 years or a fine of up to 30 million won

(2) Average wages means the amount obtained by dividing the total amount of wages paid to the worker for the three months preceding the date on which the reason for calculating them occurred by the total number of days in that period.

(3) The 'Employment Maintenance Subsidy System' is a system to prevent workers from losing their jobs by providing support to employers who are forced to adjust their employment due to business crises such as declines in sales and production, and take measures to maintain employment, such as temporary shutdowns or layoffs.

5. 도급사업에 대한 임금지급

사업이 도급계약으로 이루어지는 경우 직상 수급인의 귀책사유로 하수급인에게 고용된 근로자의 임금이 체불된 경우에는 직상 수급인은 그 하수급인과 연대하여 임금지급의 책임을 진다. 직상 수급인이 하수급인이 고용한 근로자에게 체불 임금을 지급한 경우에는 직상 수급인은 하수급인에게 구상권을 행사할 수 있다. 근로기준법 개정으로 도급이 한 차례 이뤄진 경우에도 이 규정이 적용되므로 도급인의 귀책사유로 수급인에게 고용된 근로자에 대한 임금체불이 발생한 경우에도 적용된다 (근로기준법 제44조). (벌칙 제109조) 3년 이하의 징역 또는 3천만 원 이하의 벌금

6. 휴업수당

(1) '휴업'이란 근로자가 근로를 제공하려 하지만 그 의사에 반하여 근로제공이 불가능하거나, 사용자에 의하여 노무수령이 거부된 경우를 의미한다. 사용자의 귀책사유로 휴업하는 경우 사용자는 휴업기간 동안 근로자에게 평균임금의 100분의 70 이상의 수당을 지급하여야 한다. 다만, 평균임금의 100분의 70에 해당하는 금액이 통상임금을 초과하는 경우에는 통상임금을 휴업수당으로 지급할 수 있다. 고의, 과실 이외에도 사용자의 세력범위 내에서 생긴 경영상 장애까지 사용자의 귀책사유로 보지만, 천재지변이나 전쟁 등과 같은 불가항력, 그 밖에 사용자의 세력범위에 속하지 않는 기업 외적인 사정은 사용자의 귀책사유로 보지 않는다 (근로기준법 제46조). (벌칙 제109조) 3년 이하의 징역 또는 3천만 원 이하의 벌금

(2) '평균임금'이란 이를 산정하여야 할 사유가 발생한 날 이전 3월간 그 근로자에 대해 지급된 임금의 총액을 그 기간의 총일수로 나눈 금액을 말한다.

(3) 매출액, 생산량 감소 등 경영상 위기로 고용조정이 불가피하게 된 사업주가 휴업, 휴직 등 고용유지조치를 실시하는 경우 이를 지원함으로써 근로자의 실직을 예방하기 위한 제도로 '고용유지지원금제도'가 있다.

III. Determining Whether Incentives Qualify as Wages

Many companies still incorrectly include employee incentives in calculating the total amount of wages. The following analyzes reviews whether employee incentives should be included when calculating wages under administrative guidelines, Labor Ministry Guidelines, and/or judicial rulings.[4]

1. Characteristics of Bonuses in the Wage System

(1) Calculation Rules for Wages: Whether bonuses are included when calculating wages[5]
 (i) Bonuses to be included as wages
   In cases where payment conditions, amounts, and payment rates are regulated in the rules of employment, or where employees are paid habitually and naturally expect to get paid: regular bonuses, exercise subsidies, etc.
 (ii) Bonuses not included as wages
   In cases where payments are not paid habitually, but paid temporarily or definitely based on company profits at the employer's discretion: employee incentives, production bonuses, reward bonuses, incentive allowances, etc.

(2) Bonuses/benefits paid temporarily or indefinitely are excluded when calculating the total wages.[6]

Among the incentives based on business performance, bonuses/benefits which have never been paid annually but have been paid temporarily based on corporate profits (or where the purpose is not specific) shall be excluded when calculating total wages for determining the Industrial Accident Compensation Insurance premium.

(3) Criteria for Business Performance Bonuses[7]

The Employee Welfare Corporation has regulated the "Criteria for Business Performance Bonuses" as follows: 1) if the condition for payment is related to business performance, the bonus is not to be considered wages; 2) business performance is acceptable in various areas such as corporate profits, output, total sales, cost-saving measures, quality assurance targets, accident ratio, market share, labor disputes, and so on; and 3) if the payment was decided by the results of business performance (such as sales, profits, etc.), even though the bonus has been paid regularly for a certain period due to good business performance, payment is not

---
[4] Jung, Bongsoo, 『Major Labor Issues and Related Cases』, 3rd ed., 2014. Jungang, p. 212.
[5] Article 476 of Regulations of the Ministry of Employment and Labor.
[6] Ministry of Employment and Labor (MOEL) Guidelines: Jingsu 68607-285, on Jun. 9, 1994.
[7] MOEL Guidelines: Kongdan Jingsu 6510-52, on Jan. 23, 2003.

Ⅲ. 인센티브가 임금인지 임금이 아닌지 판단

　많은 기업에서는 아직도 경영성과금을 임금으로 판단하여 임금총액에 삽입하고 있는바, 여기에 대하여 행정지침, 판례, 행정해석을 살펴보고자 한다.[4]

1. 상여금의 임금성 여부

(1) 임금산정지침에 따라 상여금의 임금 여부[5]
(ⅰ) 상여금이 임금인 경우
　　취업규칙 등에 지급조건, 금액, 지급시기가 정해져 있거나 전 근로자에게 관례적으로 지급하여 사회통념상 근로자가 당연히 지급받을 수 있다는 기대를 갖게 되는 경우 : 정기상여금, 체력단련비 등
(ⅱ) 상여금이 임금이 아닌 경우
　　관례적으로 지급한 사례가 없고, 기업이윤에 따라 일시적, 불확정적으로 사용자의 재량이나 호의에 의해 지급하는 경우 : 경영성과배분금, 격려금, 생산장려금, 포상금, 인센티브 등

(2) 일시적으로 지급되거나 불확정적인 금품[6]
　경영성과에 따른 성과금 중 관례적으로 지급한 예가 없고 기업이윤에 따라 일시적으로 지급되거나 그 지급사유의 발생이 불확정적인 금품은 평균임금 산정의 기초가 되는 임금총액에서 제외된다.

(3) 근로복지공단의 경영성과 배분금의 판단지침[7]
　지급조건이 경영성과와 연계되어 있다면 임금으로 보기 어려울 것이다. 이때 경영성과라 함은 기업이윤, 매출액, 비용절감, 불량률, 재해율, 시장점유율, 노사분규상황 등이 폭넓게 인정한다. 경영성적(매출액, 이익금 등)의 평가 결과에 따라 지급여부가 결정되었다면 결과적으로 경영성적이 좋아 일정기간 계속 지급하였다 하더라도 근로의 대상이라고 볼 수 없다. 회사가 퇴직금

---
[4] 정봉수, 「노사문제별 사례별 대응방안」 제3판, 중앙경제사, 2014, p.212
[5] 노동부예규 제476호, 2002.1.22
[6] 행정해석: 징수 68607-285 1994.06.09
[7] 근로복지공단의 경영성과배분금의 판단지침, 2003.1.23., 공단징수 6510-52

usually recognized as a general practice regulated as remuneration for work. Even though the company has included the business performance bonus into average wages to calculate severance pay, or the company has stipulated in the rules of employment, 'the bonus is paid according to the results of company business,' a business performance bonus whose payment and amount is determined by business results is not wages regardless of whether or not there is repeated payment. However, regular bonuses with no connection to business performance shall be included in total wages.

2. Cases where incentives are included when calculating wages

(1) If employee incentives and production promotion bonuses of the same amount are paid periodically and given to all employees pursuant to the collective bargaining agreement(CBA), they are characterized as wages.[8]

A certain company claimed that employee incentives and production promotion bonuses were not calculated as wages because they had been an indefinite amount of money paid at the discretion of the employer for the purpose of preventing labor disputes or bringing about early termination of wage negotiations with employees. However, although there had been slight changes in bonuses since 1996, the above bonuses/benefits had been paid uniformly in regards to payment amount, payment period, etc. It was a burden for the employer to pay employee incentives and production promotion bonuses to all employees uniformly according to the wage CBA. In terms of formal items such as payment rules, purpose, etc., the payment was also definite and scheduled, so these bonuses were not paid annually and were temporary in nature. When the above incentives and promotion bonuses are analyzed totally and substantively, they were wages determined to be as remuneration for work.

(2) Individual sales incentives that have been paid regularly and periodically shall be included in average wages.[9]

A company's salary system consists of the basic annual salary and annual incentives. The basic annual salary is paid monthly, and the annual incentive is paid in January as a lump sum payment based upon the valuation of sales targets and outcomes for the fiscal year. The amount of severance pay the company gives reflects the basic annual salary without including the annual incentive. An employee requested that the company re-calculate his severance pay, insisting that the annual incentive should be included in the calculation of average wages because the annual incentive belongs to the wage concept. When his request was rejected, he filed a suit against the company. In determining whether individual items of pay may be

---

[8] Seoul Appellate Court ruling on Sep. 18, 2003, 2002Na18697.
[9] Seoul District Court ruling on Jun. 21, 2007, 2006Na20978.

기초인 평균임금에 포함시켰다던가, 취업규칙에 '경영성과에 따라 지급한다'고 규정하더라도, 경영성과와 무관하게 주기적으로 지급한 정기상여금 등은 임금총액에 포함되나, 경영성과에 따라 지급액이 결정되는 배분금은 비록 반복 지급되었다 하더라도 임금이 아니다.

2. 경영성과금이 임금인 경우

(1) 경영성과금과 생산장려격려금이 지급액과 지급시기가 일정하고 협약에 의해 모든 근로자에게 일률적으로 지급되도록 규정되어 있다면 임금의 성질을 갖는다.[8]

피고회사는 경영성과금 및 생산장려격려금이 노동쟁의를 방지하거나 임금협상을 신속하게 마무리하기 위한 목적으로 무쟁의 내지 임금협상의 조기타결을 조건 삼아 근로자들에게 은혜적으로 지급하는 불확정적인 금원이어서 임금에 포함되지 않는다고 주장하나, 위 금품은 1996년 이후에는 그 명칭만 조금 달리할 뿐 그 지급액, 지급시기 등이 일정한 점에 비추어 보면, 경영성과금 및 생산장려격려금은 임금협약에 의하여 피고회사가 모든 근로자에게 일률적으로 의무적으로 지급하도록 규정한 것으로 그 지급규정이나 명목 등 형식적인 사항만을 고려하여 그 지급사유의 발생이 불확정적이고 일시적으로 지급되는 것이라거나 의례적, 은혜적 급부라고 볼 수 없고, 위 성과금 및 격려금을 전체적, 실질적으로 파악해 보면 근로의 대가로 지급되는 임금의 성질을 갖는다고 할 것이다.

(2) 근로의 대가로 정기적으로 지급된 개인 영업성과 연봉은 평균임금에 포함한다.[9]

이에 대한 사례를 살펴보면, 회사의 임금체계는 기본연봉과 성과연봉으로 구성되어 있고 기본연봉은 매월 기본급으로 지급하고, 성과연봉은 해당 연도 영업목표 및 경영성과를 평가해 익년 1월에 일괄해 지급했다. 회사는 갑에게 퇴직금을 지급하면서 위 성과연봉을 포함시키지 않고 기본연봉을 기초로 평균임금을 산정해 퇴직금을 지급했으나, 갑은 위 성과연봉이 임금이기 때문에 평균임금 산정 시 포함해야 한다면서 퇴직금 재산정을 요구했고 회사가 이를

---
[8] 서울고등법원 2003.09.18 선고 200218697 판결.
[9] 서울중앙지방법원 2007.06.21 선고 2006나20978 판결.

identified as wages reflected in the calculation of average wages, the following criteria is considered: 1) the items are paid regularly and periodically; 2) they are mandated by the employer according to collective bargaining agreement, rules of employment, salary regulations, the labor contract, or habitual practice; or 3) employees identified under general conditions are paid uniformly. If individual items of pay meet any of these criteria, the items of pay shall be considered wages regardless of their titles. The annual incentive was ruled as wages.

(3) The performance-based pay of public institutions corresponds to wages.[10]

The performance-based pay for public institution management evaluation is provided based on the 'Public Institutions Operation Act,' according to the evaluation results of the Minister of Planning and Finance's management performance. Article 48, Paragraph 10 of the Public Institutions Operation Act specifies matters necessary for the procedure of management performance evaluation, measures based on management performance evaluation results, and the composition and operation of the management evaluation committee by presidential decree. Article 27, Paragraph 4 of the Enforcement Decree of the Law on the Operation of Public Institutions states that "The Minister of Planning and Finance may make recommendations and requests for personnel or budgetary measures based on the evaluation results through the deliberation and resolution of the operating committee, as well as determine the performance pay rate based on subsequent measures." The annual budgeting guidelines for public enterprises and quasi-governmental agencies announced by the Minister of Planning and Finance include information on budgeting for public institution management evaluation performance pay, and the budget execution guidelines for public enterprises and quasi-governmental agencies include specific methods for calculating and paying public institution management evaluation performance pay according to established criteria. Therefore, most public enterprises and quasi-governmental agencies specify in detail in collective agreements or employment regulations the timing, calculation method, and payment conditions for management evaluation performance pay based on the results of management performance evaluations.

The wages that form the basis for calculating the average wage are payments made by employers to employees as compensation for labor, which are continuously and regularly paid to employees and are obligatory for employers, as specified in collective agreements, employment rules, salary regulations, labor contracts, labor practices, and the like. If the public institution's management evaluation performance pay is continuously and regularly paid, and the recipients, payment conditions, and other details are determined, it should be considered as part of the wages paid as compensation for labor.[11]

---

[10] Supreme Court ruling on December 13, 2018, 2018da231568
[11] Supreme Court ruling on October 12, 2018, 2015du36157.

받아들이지 않자 소송을 제기했다. 어떤 금품이 평균임금 산정의 기초가 되는 임금에 해당하는지 여부를 가늠할 수 있는 구체적인 사안으로 근로자에게 계속적·정기적으로 지급되며 단체협약, 취업규칙, 급여규정, 근로계약, 노동관행 등에 의해 사용자에게 그 지급의무가 지워져 있고, 또한 일정한 요건에 해당하는 근로자에게 일률적으로 지급하는 것이라면, 그 명칭 여하를 불문하고 임금이라고 볼 수 있을 것이라면서 영업성과연봉을 임금으로 판단했다.

(3) 공공기관의 경영성과급은 임금에 해당된다.[10]

공공기관 경영평가성과급은 공공기관운영법'에 근거하여 기획재정부장관의 경영실적 평가결과에 따라 지급되고 있다. 공공기관운영법 제48조제10항은 경영실적 평가의 절차, 경영실적 평가 결과에 따른 조치와 경영평가단의 구성·운영 등에 관하여 필요한 사항을 대통령령으로 정하도록 하고 있다. 공공기관의 운영에 관한 법률 시행령 제27조제4항은 "기획재정부장관은 운영위원회의 심의·의결을 거쳐 평가결과에 따른 인사상 또는 예산상의 조치에 대한 건의 및 요구, 성과급 지급률 결정 등의 후속조치를 할 수 있다."라고 정하고 있다. 기획재정부장관이 매년 발표하는 공기업·준정부기관 예산편성지침에는 공공기관 경영평가성과급의 예산 편성에 관한 내용이, 공기업·준정부기관 예산집행지침에는 경영실적 평가결과의 후속조치로서 확정된 기준에 따라 공공기관 경영평가성과급을 산정·지급하는 구체적인 방법이 포함되어 있다. 이에 따라 대부분의 공기업과 준정부기관은 단체협약이나 취업규칙 등에 경영실적 평가결과에 따라 경영평가성과급을 지급하는 시기, 산정방법, 지급 조건 등을 구체적으로 정하고 있다.

평균임금 산정의 기초가 되는 임금은 사용자가 근로의 대가로 근로자에게 지급하는 금품으로서, 근로자에게 계속적·정기적으로 지급되고 단체협약, 취업규칙, 급여규정, 근로계약, 노동관행 등으로 사용자에게 지급의무가 있는 것을 말한다. 공공기관 경영평가성과급이 계속적·정기적으로 지급되고 지급대상, 지급조건 등이 확정되어 있어 사용자에게 지급의무가 있다면, 이는 근로의 대가로 지급되는 임금의 성질을 가지므로 평균임금 산정의 기초가 되는 임금에 포함된다고 보아야 한다.[11]

한편 2012년부터는 공공기관 경영평가성과급의 최저지급률과 최저지급액이

---

10) 대법원 2018. 12. 13. 선고 2018다231536 판결.
11) 대법원 2018.10.12. 선고 2015두36157 판결 등 참조

On the other hand, since 2012, there has been no minimum payment rate or minimum payment amount set for performance-based pay for public institution management evaluation. Therefore, depending on the results of the management performance evaluation of the affiliated institution, individuals may not receive performance-based pay. However, even in cases where performance-based pay is not received, considering the proportion of performance pay in the total salary, the actual payment situation, and the purpose of the average wage system, it should be regarded as wages paid as compensation for labor.

3. Cases Where Incentives are Not Calculated as Wages

(1) Whether profit-sharing bonuses paid on the basis of business performance are considered wages.[12]

According to Article 2 of the Labor Standards Act, the term "wages" means wages, salary, and any other kind of money or valuables (regardless of title), which the employer pays to a worker as remuneration for work. In cases where employee incentives were previously determined in regards to the method of payment, amount, and payment period in the rules of employment, the employee incentives were paid customarily to all employees. This repeated payment led employees to expect a bonus. Accordingly, these bonuses shall be regarded as a part of wages.

However, without regulating this working condition, which was previously provided in the rules of employment, the company management and labor determined the business profit target. In the event that the employer makes a decision to pay a fixed amount (e.g., a certain incentive rate or a one-time bonus), then if that target is achieved, such bonuses will not be treated as wages, because what they received is dependent upon the result of business performance. Whether a payment condition is met or not determines the actual payment, that is, the amount being disbursed based on an evaluation of the company's performance. Therefore, since the condition for the payment is variable, temporary, and based on the company's performance, this payment cannot be regarded as part of wages.

That company's rules of employment stipulate that "the bonus can be paid in consideration of yearly corporate performance. If business performance is good, as in the case of company profit, the company may, through internal decision-making, determine whether to pay special incentives, the amount and conditions required for payment for each department." Accordingly, this type of profit-sharing bonus is paid according to whether a business surplus is achieved or not. Therefore, in consideration of the payment conditions and purpose, it is difficult to deem this payment as wages according to Article 2 of the Labor Standards Act.

---

[12] MOEL Guidelines: Wages 68207-134, on Feb. 28, 2002.

정해져 있지 않아 소속 기관의 경영실적 평가결과에 따라서는 경영평가성과급을 지급받지 못할 수도 있다. 이처럼 경영평가성과급을 지급받지 못하는 경우가 있다고 하더라도 성과급이 전체 급여에서 차지하는 비중, 그 지급 실태와 평균임금 제도의 취지 등에 비추어 볼 때 근로의 대가로 지급된 임금으로 보아야 한다.

3. 경영성과금이 임금이 아닌 경우

(1) 경영성과를 기초로 지급하는 이익분배금[12]

근로기준법 제2조의 규정에 의거 임금이라 함은 사용자가 [근로의 대상]으로 근로자에게 임금, 봉급 기타 어떠한 명칭으로든지 지급하는 일체의 금품을 말하는 것으로, 성과금이 취업규칙 등에 지급조건·금액·지급시기가 정해져 있거나, 모든 근로자에게 관례적으로 지급하여 사회통념상 근로자가 당연히 지급받을 수 있다는 기대를 갖게 되는 경우라면 임금성을 인정할 수 있다.

그러나 취업규칙에 근로조건을 미리 명시하지 않고 노사합의를 통해 경영목표를 정해놓고, 목표에 도달할 경우 일정액 또는 일정비율의 성과급 또는 일시금 등을 지급하기로 정한 경우라면, 이는 그 지급조건의 충족여부가 경영실적 평가결과에 따라 결정되고, 평가결과에 따라 지급조건과 금액을 달리하게 되거나 또는 지급하지 않을 수도 있게 되는 등 그 지급사유의 발생이 불확정적이고 일시적이므로 이를 기왕의 근로인 - 그 지급이 확정되어 사용자에게 지급의무가 부과되어지는 - 근로기준법에 의한 임금으로 볼 수는 없을 것이다.

취업규칙에 의거 연간 기업업무실적을 참작하여 상여금을 지급할 수 있다고 명시하고, 연간 경영실적, 즉 경영이익이 발생되는 경우에는 내부품의 절차를 거쳐 이를 각 사업부서별로 평가하여 동 금품의 지급기준, 지급금액 등을 확정, 지급하고 있는 것으로 보인다. 따라서 이와 같은 이익분배금은 경영이익의 발생이라는 요건의 충족여부에 따라 비로소 지급기준이나 금액이 확정되는 것이므로 이는 그 지급조건이나 목적 등에 비추어 볼 때 기왕의 근로에 대상으로 지급이 확정되는 근로기준법 제2조의 규정에 의한 임금성격을 가진다고 보기는 어려울 것이다.

---

[12] 행정해석: 임금 68207-134 2002.02.28.

Chapter 1 Understanding Wages

(2) Determination if employee incentives are included as wages[13]

The characteristics of valuables that a company pays to its employees: The Labor Union requested that the Company pay employee incentives, which the Company discussed with the Labor Union, but actual payment and method of payment of the incentives could not be agreed upon. The Company decided to pay an incentive based on business performance and paid an actual incentive on March 4, 1999, December 23, 1999, and December 29, 2000, only to incumbent employees, and with different payment criteria and payment rate per employee.

Ruling: The company regulated the employee incentives and general criteria for payment in the Internal Wage Rules, but there were no other rules related to payment, period, or concrete rate for incentives in the Rules of Employment or Collective Bargaining Agreement. Employee Incentives were paid irregularly, with no fixed rate and at different amounts per employee. The company determined payment and method according to company performance. In consideration of this situation, it is hard to deem that employee incentives were paid continuously and periodically as remuneration for work or that such a customary practice was established. As the employer has no obligation to pay incentives in the Rules of Employment, Collective Bargaining, or Wage Regulations, the employee incentives shall not be interpreted as wages.

(3) Whether profit-sharing bonuses are included as wages.[14]

The characteristics of valuables that a company pays to its employees: There were no regulations for profit-sharing bonuses in the Collective Bargaining Agreement. Since the company exceeded its production target by more than 100% from December 1996 to 2000, it paid 100% profit-sharing bonuses on average.

Ruling: The wages regulated in the company's Collective Bargaining Agreement consist of base pay, bonuses, and allowances, but there are no regulations for employee incentives. According to the Wage CBA concluded every year, profit-sharing bonuses are to be paid according to whether a production target scheduled in a given year was achieved. Therefore, the payment method and amount of profit-sharing bonuses were the same each year and these bonuses were paid

---

[13] Daegu District Court ruling on Feb. 21, 2014, 2013Gahap8360.
[14] Changwon District Court ruling on May 17, 2001, 2000Gu3242.

(2) 특별상여금[13]

원고 회사가 근로자에게 지급된 금품의 성격은 노동조합이 회사에게 특별상여금의 지급을 요구하거나 회사가 노동조합의 시사점을 청취한 적은 있었으나, 회사와 노동조합 사이의 합의에 의하여 특별상여금의 지급여부나 그 방법이 정해진 것은 아니었으며, 회사의 경영성과에 따라 그 경영진의 판단에 의하여 지급여부 및 방법이 결정되어, 특별상여금이란 명목으로 1999년 3월 4일, 1999년 12월 23일, 2000년 12월 29일 재직 중인 근로자들을 대상으로 지급기준, 지급률을 달리하여 지급하였다.

판결 내용은 「원고 회사가 급여규정에 특별상여금의 일반적인 지급기준이 규정되어 있을 뿐, 그 밖에 취업규칙, 단체협약 등에 특별상여금의 지급여부, 지급시기 및 구체적인 지급률 등에 관하여 아무런 규정이 없는 점, 지급시기가 부정기적이고 지급률도 일정하지 아니하였으며, 근로자별로 그 액수를 달리 정해 지급된 점, 노동조합과의 합의 없이 회사의 경영성과에 따라 경영진의 판단에 의해 지급여부 및 방법이 결정된 점 등의 제반 사정을 고려하여 보면, 회사와 소속 근로자들 사이에 특별상여금이 근로의 대상으로서 계속적·정기적으로 지급되고 있다거나 그러한 관례가 성립되었다고 할 수 없을 뿐만 아니라, 특별상여금의 지급에 관한 취업규칙, 단체협약, 급여규정 등에 의하여 지급의무가 있다고 할 수도 없으므로 임금으로 볼 수 없다.」

(3) 성과배분 상여금[14]

관련사례를 살펴보면, 원고에게 지급된 금품의 성격은 성과배분상여금에 대해 단체협약에 별도로 그 지급근거가 명시되어 있지 않고, 1996~2000년까지 매년 12월에 생산목표 달성률이 100%를 초과하여 성과배분상여금으로 그 지급기준금액의 100%를 지급 받았다.

판결 내용은 원고 회사의 단체협약 규정상 근로자의 임금은 기본급, 상여금 및 수당으로 구성되어 있고, 특별상여금에 관하여는 아무런 규정이 없는 점, 또한 매년 체결되는 임금협약서의 규정에 의하더라도 성과배분상여금은 당해 연도 초에 계획한 생산목표의 달성여부에 따라 지급여부가 결정되므로 그 지급이 확정되어 있다고 보기 어렵고, 그 지급방법과 금액이 매년 동일하며 위 성과배분상여금이 계획적·정기적으로 지급되고 그 지급에 관하여 단체협약

---
13) 대구지방법원 2014.02.21 선고 2013가합8360 판결.
14) 창원지방법원 2001.5.17 선고 2000구3242 판결.

irregularly. Accordingly, the Company does not have a legal duty to pay profit-sharing bonuses. This means that these bonuses are not considered wages.[15]

(4) Determination if performance bonuses for each company section are to be included as wages.[16]

The characteristics of remuneration that a company paid to its employees: "The Company stipulates in the Rules of Employment that it can pay employee incentives once a year in consideration of business performance for each company division; the payment, method, criteria, and size of incentive shall be determined according to business performance every year." Since establishment of the employee incentive regulations in 1995, payment rates and payment subjects were applied differently in the second half of 1995, in the first half and second half of 1996, in the first half and second half of 1999, and in the first half and second half of 2000. Bonuses were not paid in 1997 and 1998.

Ruling: "Employee incentives were not fixed amounts each time and the Rules of Employment stipulate that 'the Company can pay incentives once a year in consideration of business performance for each company section; the method, criteria, and size of incentive shall be determined according to annual business performance.' Since the reason for the incentive, the concrete payment criteria, the amount, and the time are unfixed, it is difficult for employee incentives to be definitely determined and paid. In consideration of the fact that employee incentives in 1997 and in 1998 were not paid, the employee incentives shall be included as remuneration granted temporarily and irregularly according to the company's business performance."

(5) Whether variable employee incentives are included as wages.[17]

A company paid variable employee incentives in appreciation of employee efforts in smoothly implementing the core business. There were no regulations for variable incentives in the rules of employment. Even though they have been paid a few times temporarily in 1999 and 2000, these bonuses were not paid uniformly and varied individually in payment.

Ruling: "There are no regulations concretely stipulated in the Rules of Employment related to variable or regular incentives. There is also no agreement for variable incentives in the Collective Bargaining Agreement. These bonuses were only

---

[15] Changwon District Court ruling on May 17, 2001, 2000Gu3242.
[16] MOEL Guidelines 02-03886, on Dec. 14, 2002.
[17] MOEL Guidelines 02-03729, on Nov. 18, 2002.

등에 의하여 회사에게 지급의무가 지워져 있다거나 그러한 관계가 성립되었다고 보기 어렵다 할 것이므로 위 성과배분상여금은 임금이 아니다.[15]

(4) 사업부별 성과급[16]

원고 회사가 근로자에게 지급된 금품의 성격은 회사의 취업규칙에 "회사는 각 사업부별 업적을 참작하여 연 1회 이상 성과급을 지급할 수 있다. 단, 성과급의 지급여부, 지급방법, 지급기준 및 지급액에 대해서는 당해연도의 경영실적에 따라 정한다"라고 되어 있으며, 1995년 성과급 제도가 생긴 이래 1995년 하반기, 1996년 상·하반기, 1999년 상·하반기 및 2000년 상·하반기에 지급시기별로 지급률, 지급대상 등을 조금씩 달리하여 지급하고 1997년과 1998년에는 미지급하였다.

재결 내용은 성과급의 지급액이나 지급대상이 매회 일정하지 아니한 점, 회사의 취업규칙에 의하더라도 "회사는 각 사업부별 업적을 참작하여 연 1회 이상 성과급을 지급할 수 있다. 단, 성과급의 지급여부, 지급방법, 지급기준 및 지급액에 대해서는 당해연도의 경영실적에 따라 정한다"라고 되어 있어 지급사유의 발생 여부, 구체적인 지급기준·금액·시기 등이 불확정적이므로 성과급의 지급이 확정되어 있다고 보기 어렵다 할 것이고 이는 1997년과 1998년에는 성과급이 지급되지 않은 것에 의해서도 확인되는 점 등에 비추어 볼 때 회사가 근로자들에게 지급한 성과급은 회사의 경영실적에 따라 일시적·불확정적으로 지급한 시혜적 성격의 금품이다.

(5) 변동성과급[17]

관련사례를 보면, 핵심사업의 순조로운 진행에 대해 근로자들의 노고를 치하하고자 변동성과급이라는 명목으로 금전이 지급되었고, 취업규칙 등에 그 지급이 명시되어 있지 않았으며, 1999년과 2000년에 한시적으로 몇 차례 지급되었을 뿐 지급액도 일률적이지 않고 액수의 차이도 상당하며, 개인 근로자별 지급액에도 차이가 있다.

재결 내용은 「변동성과급 또는 그 밖의 다른 명목으로 성과급 지급에 관한 사항이 취업규칙 등에 구체적으로 명시되어 있지 아니하며, 단체협약을 통해서도

---

[15] 창원지방법원 2001.5.17 선고 2000구3242 판결.
[16] 행정해석: 국행심 02-03886 2002.02.14
[17] 행정해석: 국행심 02-03729, 2002.11.18.

paid once each year, in 1999 and 2000, so it is difficult to regard the variable incentives as a repeated practice to be paid to all employees uniformly and regularly. In consideration of these facts, variable employee incentives cannot be regarded as wages, but remuneration to be paid to employees under friendly and favorable terms according to each employee's business performance."

IV. Related Labor Cases

⟨Case 1⟩ Whether Retention Bonus (or Signing Bonus) is deemed as Wages[18]

1. Introduction

A company can use several methods to retain highly-skilled workers for a long time, with two representative examples. One is through a non-compete clause[19] in the employment contract or rules of employment, whereby the employer prevents capable workers from transferring to competing companies, and the other is through a signing bonus,[20] where the employer tries to restrict the transfer of workers through financial incentives. A non-compete clause is hard to validate as it restricts the freedom of a worker's occupation. The Supreme Court has argued that "even if there is a non-compete agreement between the employer and the employee, if such an arrangement excessively restricts the constitutionally-guaranteed freedom of occupation, or the right to work or free competition, an action contrary to good social order, such as good customs as set forth in Article 103 of the Civil Act, it is invalid."[21] For this reason, many companies prefer signing bonuses, which directly reduce the turnover of good manpower.

I recently received an inquiry from a company about the effectiveness of a

---

[18] Jung, Bongsoo, "Legal Effect of a Retention bonus", 「Labor Law」, Jungang, May 2018.
[19] A non-compete clause means that the employee promises not to transfer to a competitor company, and if the employee subsequently violates the clause, the company whose non-compete clause they violated may claim compensation from the employee.
[20] A signing bonus is a special bonus where a company pays a lump sum to an employee when signing an employment contract, in an effort to recruit talented people.
[21] Supreme Court ruling on Mar. 11, 2010: case number 2009da82244.

변동성과급의 지급에 관한 합의를 한 사실을 확인할 수 없고, 지급횟수도 1999년과 2000년에 각 1회에 그치고 있어 위 변동성과급이 모든 직원에게 일률적·정기적으로 지급되는 관행이 성립되었다고 보기도 어렵다는 점을 고려하여, 위 변동성과급은 임금이라기보다는 사업주가 경영실태 등을 감안하여 그 직원에게 호의적·은혜적으로 지급한 것」에 불과하다.

Ⅳ. 관련 사례

〈노동사례 1〉 리텐션 보너스와 사이닝 보너스가 임금인지 여부[18]

1. 문제의 소재

회사는 우수한 인력을 장기간 확보하기 위한 방법으로 여러 방법을 사용하고 있다. 그 대표적인 것이 2가지가 있는데, 바로 취업규칙이나 근로계약서에 경업금지조항[19]을 두어 경쟁사로의 전직을 방지하거나 사이닝보너스[20]를 이용하여 금전적으로 근로자를 구속하여 전직을 제한하는 것이다. 경업금지조항은 근로자의 직업선택의 자유를 제한할 수 있기 때문에 그 효력을 인정받기가 쉽지 않다. 대법원은 "사용자와 근로자 사이에 경업금지약정이 존재한다고 하더라도, 그와 같은 약정이 헌법상 보장된 근로자의 직업선택의 자유와 근로권 등을 과도하게 제한하거나 자유로운 경쟁을 지나치게 제한하는 경우에는 민법 제103조에 정한 선량한 풍속 기타 사회질서에 반하는 법률행위로서 무효라고 보아야 한다"[21]고 판시하고 있다. 따라서 기업에서는 우수한 인력에 대해 직접적인 효력이 있는 사이닝보너스를 이용하여 이직을 방지하는 경우가 많다.

최근 리텐션 보너스[22] 조항의 효력에 대해 기업으로부터 문의가 들어왔다.

---

[18] 정봉수, "리텐션 보너스(사이닝 보너스)와 법적효력",「월간 노동법률」, 중앙경제사, 2018년 5월호
[19] 경업금지조항은 근로계약서에 경쟁회사로의 이직을 하지 않겠다고 서약하는 것으로, 차후 이를 위반한 경우에 회사는 근로자에게 손해배상을 청구할 수 있다.
[20] 사이닝보너스는 우수한 인재를 채용하기 위하여 기업이 근로자와 근로계약을 체결함과 동시에 근로자에게 일시불로 지급하는 특별보너스를 말한다.
[21] 대법원 2010. 3. 11. 선고 2009다 82244 판결.

Chapter 1 Understanding Wages

retention bonus clause[22]. For this company, 30% of the annual salary is set as bonus, with 50% paid with the 1st year's salary in January, and the remaining 50% paid in January of the following year. In return, the worker must work for three years. The employer wants to include the following clause: "If the employee resigns prior to the agreed three years, the retention bonus shall be returned." The company asked for a legal review of the validity of this. In this case, I concluded that for the retention bonus to be set for three years would be no problem, considering related matters such as the nature of the related wage, the prohibition of forced labor, the prohibition of predetermination of nonobservance, etc.

The following is a review of (ii) the characteristics of a special bonus and violation of the Labor Standards Act; (iii) the legal effect of a signing bonus; and (iv) the criteria for a signing bonus.

2. Characteristics of a Special Bonus and Determining Whether it Violates the Labor Standards Act

(1) Characteristics of a special bonus

The term "wages", as defined in Article 2 of the Labor Standards Act, refers to "wages, salary and any other money and valuable goods an employer pays to a worker for their work, regardless of how such payments are termed." Regarding the wage status of bonuses, they can be regarded as wage if payment conditions and payment timing are set in a collective agreement or rules of employment, etc. and if the payment of such bonus is customary for all employees. If the above conditions are satisfied, such special bonus can be recognized as having the characteristics of wages. Concerning the legal characteristics of a retention bonus, the Ministry of Employment and Labor judged that this bonus could not be considered as wages under the Labor Standards Act if payment was not stipulated in a collective agreement or rules of employment, etc., and if the employer temporarily or voluntarily paid it on condition of securing longer employment.[23] Therefore, it is not included in the average wage for calculation of severance pay.

(2) Determining whether a special bonus violates the Labor Standards Act

"Prohibition of forced labor" as stipulated in Article 7 of the Labor Standards

---

[22] If an employee fails to work for the mandatory tenure, the employee will return some or all of the amount paid in advance, which is called a signing bonus or a retention bonus.
[23] MOEL Guidelines on Apr. 27, 2010: Labor Standards-883

연봉의 30%를 보너스로 정하고, 첫해의 1월 급여일에 보너스의 50%를 지급하고, 다음 해의 1월에 나머지 보너스 50%를 지급한다. 그 대가로 근로자는 3년 차까지 근무해야 한다. 회사에서는 "리텐션 보너스의 효력기간 중인 근로자가 3년 이내에 퇴직하는 경우에는 수령한 금액 일체를 반납하여야 한다"는 규정을 설정하려고 하였을 때 그러한 보너스 반환 규정의 법적 효력 여부에 대해 검토를 요구하였다. 이에 대해 필자는 관련된 임금의 속성, 강제근로금지, 위약예정의 금지 등 법적 판단 하에 유사한 판례를 비교·검토하여 3년간 리텐션 보너스 설정이 가능하다는 법적 의견을 최종적으로 제시하였다.

위의 사례에 대해 구체적으로 살펴보고 덧붙여 (ii) 특별보너스의 성격과 근로기준법 위반여부, (iii) 사이닝보너스의 법적 효력과 관련된 사례, (iv) 사이닝보너스의 판단기준에 대해서도 검토해보고자 한다.

2. 특별보너스 성격과 근로기준법 위반 여부 판단

(1) 근로기준법상 '임금' 정의 및 고용노동부 판단기준

근로기준법 제2조의 규정에 의한 '임금'이라 함은 "사용자가 근로의 대가로 근로자에게 임금, 봉급 그 밖에 어떠한 명칭으로든지 지급하는 일체의 금품"을 말한다. 상여금의 임금성 여부에 대해서는 그 지급이 단체협약, 취업규칙 등에 지급조건과 지급시기 등이 정해져 있거나 전 근로자에게 관례적으로 지급하면 이를 임금으로 볼 수 있으며, 특별상여금의 경우에도 상기와 같은 요건이 충족될 때에 임금성이 인정될 수 있다. 고용노동부는 '리텐션보너스'의 법적 성질에 대해 그 지급이 단체협약, 취업규칙 등에 전혀 정한 바가 없고, 그 지급사유 등이 연장되는 근무기간에 한해 발생하는 등 사용자가 일시적으로 또는 임의로 지급하는 경우라면 근로기준법상 임금으로 볼 수 없다고 판단하고 있다.[23] 따라서 그러한 보너스는 퇴직금 계산 등을 위한 평균임금에도 포함되지 않는다.

(2) 사이닝보너스 반환약정의 근로기준법의 위반 여부

근로기준법 제7조에서 규정한 '강제근로의 금지'는 "① 사용자는 폭행, 협박,

---

[22] 설정된 의무재직기간을 근무하지 못할 경우 미리 지급된 금액의 일부 또는 전부를 반환하도록 약정하는 보너스를 실무상 사이닝(Signing) 보너스, 리텐션 (Retention) 보너스 등의 명칭으로 사용하고 있다.
[23] 노동부 행정해석: 근로기준과-883, 2010.04.27)

Act means that "No employer shall force a worker to work against his own free will through the use of violence, intimidation, confinement or any other means which unlawfully restricts mental or physical freedom." It is forced labor to cause workers to carry out unwanted work. However, it is not forced labor for an employer to direct, supervise or legally sanction workers to fulfill their obligation to provide work under an employment contract.[24] The penal provisions of Article 7 (Prohibition of Forced Labor) impose a penalty of imprisonment of not more than 5 years or a fine of not more than KRW 30 million, while the penalty for violation of Article 20 (Prohibition of Predetermination of Nonobservance) is a fine of less than KRW 10 million. Therefore, in application of the signing bonus case, Article 20 of the LSA, which includes the voluntary intentions of the employees, is more appropriate than Article 7, which governs only direct physical and mental restraint, such as assault, intimidation and confinement.[25]

The prohibition of predetermination of nonobservance prescribed in Article 20 of the Labor Standards Act stipulates that "No employer shall enter into a contract by which a penalty or indemnity for possible damages incurred from breach of a labor contract is predetermined." This is to prevent an employee from being forced to continue to work against their will by previously agreeing to pay a certain amount of money without determining the type and degree of the actual damage to the employer because of non-fulfillment of the employee's employment contract.[26] In order to guarantee performance in a contractual relationship, the Civil Act may apply penalties or damages for default in advance at the conclusion of a contract (Article 398 of the Civil Code 'Liquidated Damages'). However, while a penalty for non-fulfillment of work is a means of securing long-term employment of good manpower for the employer, it does prohibit employees from resigning, because of the burden of paying the penalty.[27] As concerns provisions for the prohibition of 'liquidated damages', labor contracts in the form of penalties for existing wages are not allowed, but reimbursement of training costs and bonuses with reasonable and valid content is permitted, because it does not unduly limit the freedom of resignation.[28]

3. Legal consideration of a signing bonus

---

[24] Lim Jong-yul, 「Labor Law」, 14th ed., Park-young-sa, Feb. 2016, p. 378.
[25] Kwon Oh-Sung, "A Study on the Effectiveness of Signing Retention Bonus Agreements", 「Sungshin Law」, Sungshin Women's University Law Research Institute, Feb. 2013, p. 136.
[26] Supreme Court ruling on Apr. 28, 2004: 2001da53875.
[27] Lim Jong-yul, 「Labor Law」, 14th ed., Park-young-sa, Feb. 2016, p. 388.
[28] Supreme Court ruling on Oct. 23, 2008: 2006da37274.

감금 그 밖에 정신상 또는 신체상의 자유를 부당하게 구속하는 수단으로써 ② 근로자의 자유의사에 어긋나는 근로를 강요하지 못한다"고 기술하고 있다. 그러나 근로계약에 따른 근로제공 의무를 이행하도록 지시, 감독하거나 적법한 제재를 가하는 것은 강제근로가 아니다.[24] 제7조(강제근로의 금지)의 벌칙 조항은 5년이하의 징역 또는 3천만 원 이하의 벌금에 처한다고 규정하고 있는 반면, 제20조(위약예정의 금지) 위반의 경우에는 벌칙을 500만 원 이하의 벌금으로 하고 있다. 사이닝보너스 반환 약정의 법적 유효성 판단에 있어서는 근로자의 자발적 의사로 그러한 약정이 체결되므로 폭행, 협박, 감금 등의 직접적 신체적 정신적 구속만을 규율 하는 근로기준법 제 7조보다는 '위약 예정 금지'를 규정하고 있는 근로기준법 제 20조의 적용이 타당하다고 본다.[25]

근로기준법 제20조에 규정한 '위약금 예정의 금지' 조항은 "사용자는 ① 근로계약 불이행에 대한 ② 위약금 또는 손해배상액을 예정하는 ③ 계약을 체결하지 못한다."고 명시하고 있다. 이는 근로자의 계약 불이행을 이유로 사용자에게 실제로 발생한 손해의 종류나 정도를 묻지 않고 일정 금액을 배상하도록 미리 약정함으로써 근로자의 의사에 반하여 근로의 계속을 강제 당하는 것을 방지하려는 취지이다.[26] 민법은 계약관계에 있어서 계약이행을 담보하기 위하여 계약체결 당시에 미리 채무불이행에 대하여 위약금 또는 손해배상을 약정할 수 있다(민법 제398조 '배상액의 예정'). 그러나 근로계약 불이행에 대한 위약금을 예정하는 것은 사용자에게는 우수한 인력을 장기간 확보하는 수단이 되지만 근로자에게는 퇴직을 원하더라도 위약금 지급의 부담 때문에 퇴직을 어렵게 하기 때문에 이를 금지하고 있다.[27] 위약예정을 금지하는 조항에 대해 기존의 임금에 대한 위약금 형식으로 배상금을 예정하는 근로계약은 허용되지 않지만, 연수비 상환, 사이닝보너스의 경우에는 의무재직 기간 설정에 있어 합리적이고 타당성이 있는 내용인 경우에는 퇴직의 자유를 부당하게 제한하지 않으므로 허용되고 있다.[28]

3. 사이닝보너스 반환 약정의 유효성에 대한 판례

---

[24] 임종률, 「노동법」, 제20판, 박영사, 2022, 378면.
[25] 권오성, '사이닝보너스 반환약정의 유효성에 관한 연구", 「성신법학」, 성신여자대학교 법학연구소,2013.2. 136면.
[26] 대법원 2004. 4. 28 선고, 2001다53875 판결.
[27] 임종률, 「노동법」, 제14판, 박영사, 2016.2. 388면.
[28] 대법원 2008. 10. 23 선고, 2006다37274 판결.

(1) Situations where the return commitment of a signing bonus is valid

1) Suwon Regional Court ruling on May 13, 2013: 2002gahap12355: An employee agreed that he would receive KRW 150 million as a retention bonus for 3 years' compulsory stay, which he would repay if he left the company before the three year period. After 7 months of service, he moved to a competing company. The court ruled, "The retention bonus does not belong to the wage and can be excluded from application of Article 20 of the LSA (Prohibition of Predetermination of Nonobservance), but the company paid the bonus for the purpose of retaining the employee for 3 years. Therefore, the employee should repay the retention bonus."

2) Seoul Regional Court ruling April 29, 2013: 2013kahap231: An employee received a signing bonus of KRW 50 million, which he agreed to repay if he left the company before two years after receiving the money. He then left the company after 7 months. The court ruled, "This signing bonus to retain the employee for a certain period of service cannot be translated as forced labor, nor does it violate Article 20 of the LSA (Prohibition of Predetermination of Nonobservance)."

3) Changwon District Court ruling on November 17, 2007: 2007na9102: According to an agreement between a company and employee, the company was to pay a special bonus to the employee in accordance with the length of service, ranging from 12 months to 41 months of the normal wage, in return for which the employee would stay for two years from the date on which the employee was hired. The agreement stipulated that in the event that the employee resigned from the company, the special bonus would be returned to the company for a period not exceeding two years. The employee who received the bonus from the company submitted a resignation letter and resigned the day after receipt of that bonus. In this case, returning a bonus that is given with the understanding there will be two years of obligatory work does not restrict the freedom of choice of workplace or freedom to resign. The court upheld the agreement the special bonus shall be returned.

(2) Instances where the return commitment of a signing bonus is invalid

1) Supreme Court ruling on Oct. 23, 2008: 2006da37274: When an employee

(1) 사이닝보너스의 반환약정이 유효한 경우

1) 수원지방법원 2003.5.13. 선고 2002가합12355 판결: 입사 당시 회사로부터 전속계약금 조로 금 1억 5,000만 원을 지급받기로 하고 3년간 회사를 위해 전속적으로 근무하기로 하되, 위 기간 중 회사와 동종의 사업목적을 가진 다른 회사로 전직할 경우에는 전속계약금 전액을 회사에 반환하기로 하는 계약을 체결한 직원이 입사 후 7개월 만에 경쟁업체로 전직한 경우가 있었다. 이 사건에서 법원은 전속계약금은 회사가 직원이 근무하는 동안 지급받게 될 근로계약상의 임금과는 별도로 지급한 금액이라는 이유로 근로기준법 제20조의 적용을 배제하고, 직원은 회사에 전속계약금을 반환해야 한다고 판단하였다.

2) 서울중앙지방법원 2013.4.29. 선고 2013카합231 판결: 근로자는 회사로부터 사이닝보너스 5,000만 원을 지급받고, 수령일로부터 2년 이내 퇴사시 수령한 사이닝보너스를 반환하기로 하는 약정을 체결하고, 7개월 만에 퇴사한 사안이다. 이 사건에서 법원은 회사가 근로자에 대해 별도의 상여금을 지급하면서 일정기간 이내 퇴직하는 경우 이를 반환하기로 하는 약정은 근로자의 의사에 반하는 계속 근로를 부당하게 강제하는 것이라고 보기 어려우므로, 근로기준법 제20조에 위반돼 무효라고 보기 어렵다고 판단했다.

3) 창원지법 2007.11.17. 선고 2007나9102 판결: 회사와 근로자간에 근속연수에 따라 통상임금의 12개월분에서 41개월까지 차등하여 회사가 근로자에게 특별상여금을 지급하기로 하되, 근로자가 이를 지급받은 날로부터 2년 이내에 회사의 의사에 반하여 사직하고자 하는 경우에는 이 특별상여금은 2년을 채우지 못한 기간에 해당하는 비율의 금원을 회사에 반환한다'는 취지의 노사합의서가 체결되었다. 그러나 회사로부터 보상금을 지급받은 근로자가 보상금 수령일 익일에 회사에 사직원을 제출하였다. 이에 법원은 노사간에 2년간 의무근무를 조건으로 보상금을 지급하는 내용이고, 근무시간이 1년에 불과한 근로자가 종전에 수령한 임금을 반환하는 것이 아니고, 직장의 선택의 자유나 퇴직의 자유를 제한하는 규정으로 볼 수 없다고 하여, 회사의 반환청구를 긍정하였다.

(2) 사이닝보너스 반환약정이 무효인 경우

1) 대법원 2008.10.23. 선고 2006다37274 판결: 근로자가 입사하면서 회사로

joined a company, he signed a retention bonus agreement whereby he would receive KRW 500 million and serve the company for 10 years. If he resigned before 10 years, he would repay a penalty of KRW 1 billion. In this case, the court ruled that this retention agreement violated Article 20 of the LSA (Prohibition of Predetermination of Nonobservance) and became null and void.

2) Incheon Regional Court ruling on April 29, 2013: 2013gahap3994: An employee promised to stay with a company for at least 5 years, and received KRW 50 million as a retention bonus. In the agreement, the employee agreed to repay 3 times the value of the retention bonus received if he did not fulfill the agreement. After 5 months of service, the employee resigned. The company claimed KRW 150 million, three times the amount of the retention bonus. In this case, the court rejected the employer's claim.

(3) Supreme Court ruling on signing bonuses[29]

1) Case summary: A company that manufactures robot surgical appliances (ROBODOC) hired an experienced engineer in the field of fuel cells at S Company on January 13, 2009 for a period of four years. The company made a recruitment agreement to pay KRW 100 million as a signing bonus separate from the salary. The recruitment agreement contained a stipulation that the company guaranteed employment for seven years, and the employee would work for the company for seven years. The employee resigned on April 12, 2010 for personal reasons. The company sued for return of the signing bonus, but the district court dismissed the plaintiff's (company's) claim (Dongbu District Court, 2010kahap13266). The company appealed, and the Seoul High Court partially accepted the claim that the employee should pay a prorated amount of the signing bonus, stating that the signing bonus was: 1) a special incentive to join the company, 2) a full down payment for 7 years of future employment, and 3) a special bonus to expect 7 years' service (Seoul High Court 2011na22827).

2) Decision: The Supreme Court dismissed the plaintiff's claim, saying, "As the company concluded labor contracts as a way of hiring experienced professional

---

[29] Supreme Court ruling on Jun. 11, 2015: 2012da55518.

부터 5억원을 지급받되, 영업비밀을 침해하지 않고 약정한 10년 동안 근무하겠다는 등을 약속하면서 만약 이를 이행하지 않을 때에는 10억 원을 지불하기로 하는 약정을 한 사안에서, 대법원은 위 약정은 피고가 약정 근무기간 이전에 퇴직하는 등 위 약속을 위반하기만 하면 그로 인해 사용자에게 어떤 손해가 어느 정도 발행했는지 묻지 않고 바로 미리 정한 10억 원을 사용자에게 손해배상액으로 지급하기로 하는 것이므로 근로기준법 제20조가 금지하는 전형적인 위약금 또는 손해배상액의 예정에 해당해 그 효력을 인정할 수 없다고 보았다.

2) 인천지방법원 부천지원 2009.4.10. 선고 2007가합3994 판결: 근로자는 최소 5년간 근무하는 조건으로 입사하고, 금 5,000만 원을 지급받으면서 계약을 이행하지 못할 경우 계약금 성격의 지급금액에 대한 3배를 배상한다는 취지의 약정을 했으나 입사 후 5개월 만에 퇴사했고, 이에 회사가 1억 5,000만 원을 청구한 사안이다. 위 협약서는 직원이 약정근무기간 이전에 퇴직하기만 하면 사용자의 손해를 묻지 않고 바로 1억5,000만 원을 사용자에게 손해배상액으로 지급해야 하는 약정이므로, 근로기준법 제20조에 위반된다고 법원은 판단했다.

(3) 사이닝보너스 사건에 대법원 입장[29]

1) 사건경위: 로봇닥터(ROBODOC)를 제조하는 원고회사가 2009. 1. 13. 연료전지 분야의 유경험자로 약 4년 여 동안 S사에 재직하고 있던 피고를 스카우트 하면서 연봉과 별도로 1억원을 사이닝보너스로 지급한다는 채용합의서를 작성하였다. 이 채용합의서에는 원고회사가 7년간 피고의 고용을 보장하고, 피고는 원고의 회사에 7년간 근무해야 한다는 내용이 포함되어 있었다. 피고는 2010. 4. 12. 개인사유를 이유로 원고회사에서 사직하였고 회사는 이를 이유로 사이닝 보너스의 반환을 청구하였다. 이에 대해 1심은 원고 회사의 청구를 기각하였다(동부지방법원 2010가합13266판결). 이에 원고회사는 항소하였는데, 2심인 서울고등법원은 원고회사가 피고에게 지급한 사이닝보너스는 ① 이직사례금의 성격 뿐 아니라, ② 7년간 전속하는 데 따른 전속계약금, ③ 임금 선급금으로서의 성격을 전제로 한 것이고, 이러한 '7년 근속약정'을 위반한 피고는 회사에게 사이닝보너스의 일부인 7천만을 지급하라는 취지의 원고 일부 승소판결을 하였다(서울

---
[29] 대법원 2015. 6. 11. 선고 2012다55518 판결

personnel, the so-called "signing bonus", the following points should be taken into consideration: ① Whether or not they have the characteristics of compensation for job turnover or the conclusion of a labor contract; ② Whether to pay for the prohibition of resignation during the compulsory working period; ③ Whether or not there is a written statement concerning returning the bonus upon retirement or turnover in the middle of the period." Based on the aforementioned premises, the signing bonus was judged to have the characteristics of a reward because there was no description of a specific method of payment or any return obligation. In other words, the signing bonus for this case is an instance in which the nature of the reward for employment is judged to be stronger than the nature of the mandatory working period of seven years.

4. Conclusion (Criteria for a Signing Bonus)

The judging criteria for a signing bonus must adhere to the following principles:

(i) If there is disagreement over the interpretation of a contract between the parties: ① The contents of the document, ② the motivation and the manner in which the agreement was made, ③ the purpose of achieving by agreement, and ④ the true intention of the parties should reasonably be interpreted according to logic and empirical rules.[30]

(ii) It is effective for the employer to stipulate a return of the employee's bonus, which is provided separately from the employee's wage, for the special purpose of preventing the employee from transferring to another company. In principle, these return arrangements are required to ① balance the amount of the signing bonus award and duration of the contract of employment, and the degree of the former restriction; ② not infringe on the essential condition of the employee's freedom to change jobs; ③ not give the bonus the characteristics of a wage, and ④ have no reason related to the employer for the employee moving to another company.[31]

---

[30] Supreme Court ruling on May 27, 2005: 2004da60065; Supreme Court ruling on Sep. 20, 2009: 2006da158166.
[31] Seoul District Court ruling on Jan. 25, 2005: 2004kadan128716.

고등법원 2011나22827판결).
2) 대법원의 판결 내용: 그러나 대법원은 원고인 회사의 청구를 기각하면서 "기업이 경력 있는 전문 인력을 채용하기 위한 방법으로 근로계약 등을 체결하면서 ① 일회성의 인센티브 명목으로 지급하는 이른바 사이닝보너스가 이직에 따른 보상이나 근로계약 체결에 대한 대가로서의 성격만 가지는지, ② 더 나아가 의무근무기간 동안의 이직금지 내지 전속근무 약속에 대한 대가 및 임금 선급으로서의 성격도 함께 가지는지는 계약서에 특정 기간 동안의 전속 근무를 조건으로 사이닝보너스를 지급한다거나 그 기간의 중간에 퇴직하거나 이직할 경우 이를 반환한다는 등의 문언이 기재되어 있는지 종합적으로 고려하여 판단하여야 할 것이다"라는 전제로 봤을 때 본 사건에 대해서는 구체적 대가적 지급성격이나 반환의무에 대한 기술이 없기 때문에 본 사건의 사이닝보너스는 사례금 성격으로 판단하였다. 즉, 본 사안에 대한 사이닝보너스는 제반 사정을 고려하였을 때 이직사례금의 성격만을 가지므로, 의무 재직기간 근무 위반을 이유로 그 반환을 청구할 수 없다고 판단한 사례이다.

4. 사이닝보너스에 대한 판단기준

사이닝보너스의 판단기준은 다음의 원칙을 준수해야 한다.
(i) 당사자 사이에 계약의 해석을 둘러싸고 이견이 있어 문제가 되는 경우에는 ① 문언의 내용, ② 그러한 약정이 이루어진 동기와 경위, ③ 약정에 의하여 달성하려는 목적, ④ 당사자의 진정한 의사 등을 종합적으로 고찰하여 논리와 경험칙에 따라 합리적으로 해석하여야 한다.[30]
(ii) 타 업체로의 전직을 막기 위한 특별한 목적으로 전직을 제한하면서 사용자가 근로자에게 임금과는 별도로 제공하는 사이닝보너스에 대해 기간 만료 전의 전직 등 근로자의 특약불이행을 이유로 반환약정을 하는 것은 유효하다. 그러나 이러한 반환약정은 원칙적으로 ① 제공되는 사이닝보너스의 액수와 근로계약기간 및 전직제한의 정도가 적정하게 균형을 이뤄야 하고, ② 근로자의 전직 자유의 본질적인 내용을 침해해서는 아니 되며, ③ 제공된 사이닝보너스가 임금으로서의 성격을 가지고 있어서는 안 되며, ④ 근로자의 전직에 사용자의 귀책사유가 없어야 한다.[31]

---

[30] 대법원 2005.5.27. 선고 2004다60065 판결, 대법원 2007.9.209. 선고 2006다158166 판결.

Chapter 1 Understanding Wages

In other words, it must be clear that the signing bonus is awarded on the condition that it is paid for a period of mandatory service; the duration of such obligatory service should be as short as possible and; the returning amount should be the same or less than the amount that the employee received for the mandatory service period. In addition, a contract for returning the bonus award is valid only if the employee voluntarily resigns.

〈Case 2〉 Labor Inspection over Unpaid Wages for Temporary Workers

1. Introduction

I would like to introduce a recent case regarding claims for unpaid wages against a local council and how it was handled. Since 2016, the local council has been hiring 30 audit assistants for 40 days each year to assist with administrative audits. These assistants worked for KRW 100,000 per day, 5 days a week and 8 hours a day.

An audit assistant sought to claim the weekly holiday allowance and annual paid leave, neither of which had been given, but the local council explained that the assistant would not be regarded as a worker because he was hired for a commissioned position only during the administrative audit period. In response, the audit assistant filed a complaint with the Labor Office on December 9, 2022, stating that the local council owed him unpaid wages. During investigation by the Labor Office on December 28, the local council argued that audit assistants were not workers because they were used for commissioned work only during the administrative audit period in accordance with local ordinances. However, the Labor Office ordered the local council to pay KRW 800,000 in unpaid weekly holiday allowance and unused annual paid leave allowance since the complainant was a worker. The local council paid the amount ordered by the Labor Office. However, the complainant requested criminal punishment whether the delayed wages were paid or not. On February 17, 2023, the labor inspector visited the local council and conducted a labor inspection. The labor inspector pointed out 6 violations of the Labor Standards Act during the inspection, and ordered the payment of unpaid wages amounting to KRW 96 million, by March 7, 2023.

Herein, I would like to review the six violations pointed out by the labor inspectors during the inspection, and look carefully into three major disputed issues that came up: (1) the details on unpaid wages, (2) the retroactive scope of unpaid wages, and (3) criminal penalties against the local council.

다시 말해서, 사이닝보너스가 일정 의무복무기간을 근무할 것을 조건으로 지급되는 것이라는 점을 분명히 하여야 하고, 그러한 의무복무기간이 가급적 단기간이어야 하며, 근로자가 의무복무기간 내에 전직하는 경우 그 배상액이 수령한 금액 내여야 하고, 근로자가 자발적으로 퇴직하는 경우에만 사이닝보너스 반환 약정이 효력을 갖는다고 할 수 있다.

〈노동사례 2〉 지방의회의 일급직 사무보조자(위촉직)의 임금체불

1. 사실관계

최근 모 지방의회에서 발생한 임금체불 사건과 그 처리과정에 대해서 소개하고자 한다. 의회는 행정감사 수행을 위해 2016년부터 매년 30여명 사무보조인을 40여일간 채용하고 있다. 근로조건은 일급 10만 원이고, 주 5일과 하루 8시간 근무하는 조건이었다.

한 사무보조인은 의회에 대하여 '주휴수당' 미지급과 '연차유급휴가' 미지급 부분에 대해 이의를 제기하였으나, 의회는 행정감사 기간 동안만 '위촉직'으로 채용하고 있기 때문에 근로자로 볼 수 없다고 설명하면서 요구한 금품을 지급하지 않았다. 이에 사무보조인은 2022년 12월 9일, 노동청에 의회가 임금체불을 하였다는 내용으로 진정을 제기하였다. 의회 담당자는 12월 28일 노동청 조사 시 지방조례에 따라 행정감사 기간 동안만 업무지원을 받기 위해 사무보조인들을 위촉직으로 채용하였기 때문에 근로자가 아니라고 주장하였다.

그러나 노동청은 진정인이 근로자에 해당되기 때문에 미지급된 주휴수당과 월차수당 80만 원 지급을 지시하였다. 의회는 노동청에서 제시한 금액을 모두 지급하였다. 그러나 진정인은 의회에 대해 임금체불 지급여부와 상관없이 형사처벌을 요구하였다. 이에 근로감독관은 2023년 2월 17일 지방의회를 방문하여 근로감독을 실시하였고 사업장 근로감독을 통해 근로기준법 위반사항 6가지(아래 본문 참조)를 지적하고, 2023년 3월 7일 까지 미지급 수당 9600

---

31) 서울중앙지방법원 2005.1.25. 선고 2004가단128716 판결

2. Details of the Corrective Orders from the Labor Inspection

On February 17, 2023, the labor inspector visited the local council and conducted a labor inspection on the tasks of administrative assistants, and issued corrective orders for six items.

(1) Violation of the Labor Standards Act, Article 17, Paragraph 2 (Duty to Create a Written Employment Contract)

1) Corrective order: Labor contracts shall be issued to workers and include specifications on major working conditions such as wages, contractual working hours, weekly holidays, and annual paid leave. However, since the working conditions of 133 audit assistants, including the complainant, were not specified in writing and issued to the assistants, evidence (copies of employment contracts, etc.) that this has been done must be submitted.

2) Follow-up actions and basis: The local council acknowledged its failure to create and issue appropriate labor contracts and agreed to do so in the future. The assistants were, in fact, temporary workers to assist during specific periods of administrative audit, but, notwithstanding this, the employer shall preserve a register of workers and important documents concerning labor contracts for three years, as prescribed by Presidential Decree. These important documents related to labor contracts are: 1. Labor contracts, 2. Wage ledgers, 3. Documents on wage determination, payment method and basis for wage calculation, 4. Documents on employment, dismissal and termination of employment relations, 6. Documents about leaves, etc. The three-year retention period for these important documents begins with the date of termination of the employment relationship. If the labor contract is not made in writing, the employer is subject to a fine of up to KRW 5 million.[32] In addition, if an employee requests a certificate verifying the period of employment, type of work, position and wages, and other necessary matters even after the worker resigns, the employer shall immediately provide such certificate with the actual facts thereon. Persons who can claim a certificate of employment shall be workers who have continuously worked for 30 days or more. Requests for such certificates can be made by the worker up to 3 years after resignation.[33]

---

[32] Labor Standards Act, Article 42 (Retention of Contract Documents) and the Enforcement Decree, Article 22 (Subsidized Documents, etc.) and Article 114 (Penalty)

[33] Labor Standards Act, Article 39 (Certificate of Use) and the Enforcement Decree, Article 19 (Requests for Certificate of Employment)

만 원의 지급을 명하였다.

이번 호에는 노동청 근로감독관이 근로감독을 통해 지적한 6가지 구체적 내용에 대한 판단과 주요 쟁점이 되었던 (ⅰ) 임금체불에 대한 내용, (ⅱ) 임금체불에 대한 소급 범위, 그리고 (ⅲ) 지방의회에 대한 형사 처벌과 관련된 내용에 대해 구체적으로 살펴보고자 한다.

2. 시정지시 내용과 이해

2023년 2월 17일 근로감독관은 지방의회를 방문하여 행정보조 업무들에 대하여 근로감독을 실시하였고, 다음 6가지에 대해 시정지시를 하였다.

(1) 근로기준법 제17조 제2항 위반 (서면작성의무)
1) 시정지시: 근로계약을 체결할 때에 근로자에게 임금, 소정근로시간, 주휴일, 연차유급휴가 등 주요 근로조건을 명시하여 교부하여야 한다. 그러나 진정인 등 사무보조자 133명의 근로조건을 서면으로 명시하여 교부하지 않았으므로 이를 이행하고 증빙자료 (근로계약서 사본 등)를 제출하여야 한다.
2) 조치내용과 관련 근거: 의회는 근로계약서 미작성을 인정하고 앞으로 시정을 약속하였다. 사실상 한시적으로 의회의 행정감사를 위해 고용된 근로자들이었고, 모두 퇴사하였다. 그럼에도 불구하고 사용자는 근로자 명부와 대통령령으로 정하는 근로계약에 관한 중요한 서류를 3년간 보존해야 한다. 대통령령으로 정하는 근로계약에 관한 중요한 서류는 1. 근로계약서, 2. 임금대장, 3. 임금의 결정, 지급방법과 임금계산의 기초에 관한 서류, 4. 고용, 해고, 퇴직에 관한 서류, 6. 휴가에 관한 서류 등이다. 이러한 근로계약에 관한 중요한 서류보존기간은 근로관계가 끝난 날로부터 기산하여 3년이다. 근로계약서를 미작성한 경우 사용자는 500만 원 이하의 벌금에 처해진다.[32] 그리고 사용자는 근로자가 퇴직한 후라도 사용 기간, 업무 종류, 지위와 임금, 그 밖에 필요한 사항에 관한 증명서를 청구하면 사실대로 적은 증명서를 즉시 내주어야 한다. 사용증명서를 청구할 수 있는 자는 계속하여 30일 이상 근무한 근로자로 하되, 청구할 수 있는 기한은 퇴직 후 3년 이내로 한다.[33]

---

[32] 근로기준법 제42조 (계약 서류의 보존) 와 시행령 제22조(보조 대상 서류 등), 제114조 (벌칙)

Chapter 1 Understanding Wages

(2) Violation of the Labor Standards Act, Article 36 (Settlement of Payment)
1) Corrective order: The employer shall pay all money and valuables including wages within 14 days from the date of the termination of employment relations, unless there is an agreement otherwise between the parties regarding an extension of the payment period. However, the local council failed to pay a total of KRW 96.1 million to its audit assistants: weekly holiday allowances of KRW 82.2 million (132 persons) and annual paid leave allowance of KRW 10.9 million (109 persons). Proof of payment must be submitted to the Labor Office (e.g. receipt of deposit or payment confirmation).
2) Follow-up actions and basis: Considering the statute of limitations for overdue wages, the local council paid weekly holiday allowances and annual paid leave allowances to audit assistants who had worked during the past five years. If a worker dies or employment relations are terminated, the employer shall pay wages, compensation, and all other money and goods within 14 days from the occurrence of the reason for payment. However, it is specified that in special circumstances, the period may be extended by agreement between the parties. If money and other valuables are not paid within 14 days after the termination of employment relations, the employer will be subject to imprisonment for up to 3 years or a fine of up to KRW 30 million.[34]

(3) Violation of the Labor Standards Act, Article 48, Paragraph 2 (Pay Slips)
1) Corrective order: When paying wages, the employer shall issue to the worker a wage statement in writing with matters as prescribed by Presidential Decree, such as the composition of wages, method of calculation, details of deductions, etc. and submit proof (copy of pay slips) to the Labor Office.
2) Follow-up actions and basis: The local council acknowledged that it had failed to issue pay slips and agreed to correct the situation. The employer must issue wage statements to workers when paying them. This regulation applies even to workplaces with fewer than 5 employees, even if only one part-time worker is employed. In addition to a statement of the total amount, information related to the method of calculating wages must be written so that workers can confirm that they have been paid fairly in accordance with the amount of time they worked and the conditions given in the initial contract with the employer. If the employer fails to issue such a wage statement, an administrative fine of up to KRW 5 million won shall be imposed.[35]

---

[34] Labor Standards Act, Article 36 of the (Settlement of Payment) and Article 109 (Punishment)

(2) 근로기준법 제36조 위반 (금품 청산)

1) 시정지시: 사용자는 당사자 사이에 지급기일 연장에 관한 합의가 없는 한 퇴직일로부터 14일 이내에 임금 등 일체의 금품을 지급하여야 하나, 사무보조인에게는 주휴수당 82,200,000원 (132명) 및 연차유급휴가 미사용 수당 10,900,000원 (109명) 총합 96,100,000원을 지급하지 않았으므로 이를 지급하고 증빙자료 (입금증 또는 지급확인서 등)를 제출하여야 한다.

2) 조치내용과 관련 근거: 의회는 임금체불의 공소시효를 고려하여 최근 5년간 활동한 사무보조인에 대한 주휴수당과 연차유급휴가 수당을 지급하였다. 사용자는 근로자가 사망 또는 퇴직한 경우에는 그 지급 사유가 발생한 때부터 14일 이내에 임금, 보상금, 그 밖의 모든 금품을 지급하여야 한다. 다만, 특별한 사정이 있을 경우에는 당사자 사이의 합의에 의하여 기일을 연장할 수 있다고 명시하고 있다. 퇴직 후 14일 이내에 임금 등 금품을 미지급한 경우, 사용자는 3년이하의 징역 또는 3천만 원 이하의 벌금에 처해진다.[34]

(3) 근로기준법 제48조 제2항 위반 (임금명세서)

1) 시정지시: 사용자는 임금을 지급하는 때에는 근로자에게 임금의 구성항목, 계산방법, 공제 내역 등 대통령령으로 정하는 사항을 적은 임금명세서를 서면으로 교부하여야 하나, 임금명세서를 교부하지 않았으므로 이를 시정하고 증빙자료 (임금명세서 사본)를 제출하여야 한다.

2) 조치내용과 관련근거: 의회는 임금명세서 미교부를 인정하고 시정을 약속했다. 사용자는 근로자에게 임금을 지급하는 때에 근로자에게 반드시 임금명세서를 교부하여야 한다. 해당 규정은 5인 미만 사업장의 경우에도 적용되므로 아르바이트 한 명 만을 고용하고 있다 하더라도 임금명세서를 교부하여야 한다. 근로자들이 사용자와 처음에 계약한 대로 일한 만큼 급여가 지급되었는지 확인할 수 있도록 총액 뿐만 아니라 급여의 계산 방식 등과 관련한 정보를 적도록 하고 있다. 사용자가 임금명세서를 교부하지 않은 경우에는 500만 원 이하의 과태료에 처해진다.[35]

---

33) 근로기준법 제39조 (사용증명서)와 시행령 제19조 (사용증명서의 청구)
34) 근로기준법 제36조 (금품청산)와 제109조 (벌칙)
35) 근로기준법 제48조 (임금명세서) 제2항, 제116조 (과태료)

(4) Violation of the Labor Standards Act, Article 60, Paragraph 2 (Annual Paid Leave)

1) Corrective order: The employer did not grant annual paid leave to 109 audit assistants, despite the requirement that it grant one day of paid leave for every one month of work to workers who have worked continuously for less than one year. Verification materials must be submitted to the Labor Office.

2) Follow-up actions and basis: The local council paid annual paid leave allowances to audit assistants who had worked during the past five years in accordance with the statute of limitations for unpaid wages. An employer shall grant one day of paid leave for every month of work to a worker who has worked continuously for less than one year. If such annual paid leave is not granted, the unused leave shall be compensated in money. If the annual paid leave allowance is not paid, the employer shall be subject to imprisonment for up to two years or a fine of up to KRW 20 million.[36]

(5) Violation of the Labor Standards Act, Article 70, Paragraph 1 (Restrictions on Night Work and Holiday Work)

1) Corrective order: When a female worker aged 18 or older is required to work at night or on holidays, worker consent shall be obtained, but this was not done. Evidence needs to be submitted to the Labor Office that such consent was obtained.

2) Follow-up actions and basis: The local council promised to thoroughly implement this requirement with employment of new workers. Female workers aged 18 or older may be allowed to work at night and on holidays with their prior consent. Violation of this is punishable with imprisonment for up to two years or a fine of up to KRW 20 million.[37]

(6) Violation of the Minimum Wage Act, Article 11 (Duty to Inform)

1) Corrective order: The employer shall post the minimum wage in a place where the workers of the business can easily see it, or widely publicize it to workers in other appropriate ways, as prescribed by Presidential Decree. Since the minimum wage notice obligation has been violated, correct the matter and submit verification evidence (posted photos, etc.).

2) Follow-up actions and basis: The local council posted the required information in a notice on its website. Employers have a duty to notify workers of the

---

[35] Labor Standards Act, Article 48, paragraph 2 (Pay Slips) and Article 116 (Administrative Fines)
[36] Labor Standards Act, Article 2 and 5 (Annual Paid Leave) and Article 110 (Punishment)
[37] Labor Standards Act, Article 70 (Restrictions on Night and Holiday Work) and Article 110 (Punishment)

(4) 근로기준법 제60조 제2항 위반 (연차유급휴가)

1) 시정지시: 사용자는 계속하여 근로한 기간이 1년 미만인 근로자에게 1개월 개근 시 1일의 유급휴가를 주어야 함에도 불구하고 사무보조인 109명에게 연차유급휴가를 부여하지 아니하였으므로 이를 시정하고 증빙자료를 제출하기 바란다.

2) 조치내용과 관련근거: 의회는 임금체불의 공소시효에 해당하는 최근 5년 동안 활동한 사무보조인들의 연차유급휴가 수당을 지급하였다. 사용자는 계속하여 근로한 기간이 1년 미만인 근로자에게 1개월 개근 시 1일의 유급휴가를 주어야 한다. 이러한 연차유급휴가를 부여하지 못한 경우에는 그 미사용휴가에 대해 금전으로 보상하여야 한다. 연차유급휴가 수당을 미지급한 경우 사용자는 2년이하의 징역 또는 2천만 이하의 벌금에 처해진다.[36]

(5) 근로기준법 제70조 제1항 위반 (야간근로와 휴일근로의 제한)

1) 시정지시: 18세 이상의 여성을 야간근로 및 휴일근로를 시킬 경우 근로자의 동의를 받아야 하나 이를 이행하지 아니하였으므로, 여성근로자에 대하여 야간근로 및 휴일근로에 대한 동의를 받고, 증빙자료를 제출하기 바란다.

2) 조치내용과 관련근거: 의회는 해당사항에 대해 철저한 이행을 약속하였다. 18세 이상의 여성근로자에 대하여는 그 근로자의 동의를 받아 야간 및 휴일에도 근로하게 할 수 있다. 이를 위반한 경우 2년 이하의 징역 또는 2천만 원 이하의 벌금에 처해진다.[37]

(6) 최저임금법 제11조 위반 (주지 의무)

1) 시정지시: 최저임금의 적용을 받는 사용자는 '대통령'으로 정하는 바에 따라 해당 최저임금을 그 사업의 그 사업의 근로자가 쉽게 볼 수 있는 장소에 게시하거나 그 외의 적당한 방법으로 근로자에게 널리 알려야 함에도 불구하고 최저임금 주지의무를 위반하였으므로 이를 이행하고 증빙자료 (게시 사진 등)를 제출하기 바란다.

2) 조치내용과 관련근거: 의회는 홈페이지 공지사항에 해당사항을 게시하였다.

---

[36] 근로기준법 제60조 (연차 유급휴가) 제2항과 제5항. 제110조 (벌칙)
[37] 근로기준법 제70조 (야간근로와 휴일근로의 제한), 제110조(벌칙)

minimum wage by posting it in a place where workers can easily see it or by other appropriate means. Matters to be posted include (i) the minimum wage of workers subject to application, (ii) wages that are not included in the minimum wage, (iii) scope of workers excluded from application of the minimum wage in the business in accordance with the law, (iv) the effective period of the minimum wage. Violation of this duty to inform is punishable with a fine of not more than KRW 1 million.[38]

3. Major Issues Disputed on during the Labor Inspection

(1) Details on unpaid wages

1) Related details: An audit assistant who worked from October 11, 2022 to December 2 (39 days) submitted a claim to the Labor Office for unpaid weekly holiday allowance and annual paid leave allowance. The local council attended an investigation hearing of the Labor Office on December 28, 2022 and submitted to an investigation, and agreed the day after the investigation to pay KRW 800,000 for weekly holiday and annual paid leave allowances. On February 17, 2023, the labor inspector visited the local council and conducted a labor inspection on the employment relationship with audit assistants. The labor inspector found that the local council had not paid weekly holiday allowance or unused annual paid leave allowance during employment of its audit assistants. The Labor Office directed the local council to retroactively pay unpaid wages to all audit assistants employed during the last five years.

2) Judgment: If a worker hired for hourly or daily wage continues to work, an additional weekly holiday allowance shall be paid. If wages are calculated on a monthly basis, the weekly holiday allowance shall be included in the monthly wage. A related precedent states that the hourly or daily wage system does not include weekly holiday pay, which is a statutory allowance under Article 55 of the Labor Standards Act (LSA), paid even if the employees do not actually work on such paid holidays. Therefore, if a worker on the hourly or daily wage system receives a fixed allowance paid for a certain period of time exceeding one month, he or she can claim the difference between the weekly holiday pay calculated based on the newly calculated hourly wage and the previously paid fixed allowance, and this is not a duplicated pay for the weekly holiday pay."[39]

---

[38] Minimum Wage Act, Article 11 (Duty to Inform) and Article 31 (Administrative Fine)
[39] Supreme Court ruling on Jan. 28, 2010, 2009da74144; see also Supreme Court ruling on Aug. 20, 2014, 2014da6275

사용자는 최저임금에 관한 사항을 근로자가 쉽게 볼 수 있는 장소에 게시하거나, 그 외 적당한 방법으로 알려야 할 주지의무가 있다. 특히, "게시되어야 할 사항"으로 적용을 받는 근로자의 최저임금액, 최저임금에 산입하지 아니하는 임금, 법에 따라 해당 사업에서 최저임금의 적용을 제외할 근로자의 범위, 최저임금의 효력발생 연월일이 있다. 주지의무 위반은 100만 원 이하의 과태료에 처해진다.[38]

3. 근로감독의 내용 중 주요 쟁점

(1) 임금체불에 대한 쟁점 내용

1) 사실관계 : 2022년 10월 11일 - 12월 2일 까지(39일)을 근무한 사무보조자 1명이 의회가 주휴수당과 연차유급휴가 수당을 지급하지 않았다고 하여 노동청에 진정을 제기하였다. 의회는 2022년 12월 28일 노동청에 출석하여 조사를 받았고, 해당 의회는 조사받은 다음날 주휴수당과 연차수당 80만 원을 지급하였다. 노동청의 근로감독관은 2023년 2월 17일 해당 의회를 방문하여 사무보조인 고용관계에 대해 근로감독을 실시하였다. 근로감독관은 의회가 사무보조인들을 사용하면서 주휴수당과 연차유급휴가의 미사용 수당을 지급하지 않았다는 사실을 확인하였다. 노동청은 의회에 대하여 공소시효에 해당되는 지난 5년 동안 고용했던 사무보조원 전체에 대해 소급하여 미지급한 수당을 지급하도록 지시하였다.

2) 관련판례 : 시급, 일급으로 고용된 근로자가 계속해서 근무하는 경우에는 주휴수당을 별도로 추가하여 지급하여야 하고, 월급으로 계산된 임금의 경우에는 주휴수당이 월 급여에 포함되어 있다. 관련 판례는 시급제 또는 일급제는 근로기준법 제55조에 따라 부여되는 유급휴일에 실제로 근무를 하지 않더라도 근무를 한 것으로 간주하여 지급되는 법정수당인 주휴수당이 포함되어 있지 않다. 따라서 시급제 또는 일급제 근로자가 1개월을 초과하는 일정기간마다 지급되는 고정수당을 받았다면 새로이 산정한 시간급 통상임금을 기준으로 계산한 주휴수당액과의 차액을 청구할 수 있고, 이를 주휴수당의 중복 청구라고 할 수 없다. 고 판시하고 있다.[39]

---

[38] 최저임금법 제11조 (주지의무), 제31조(과태료)
[39] 대법원 2010.1.28. 선고 2009다74144 판결, 대법원 2014.8.20. 선고 2014다6275 판결 참조

(2) Retroactive payment of unpaid wages

1) Related details: The labor inspector conducted an on-site audit on February 17, and on February 21, 2023, directed the local council to pay an amount equivalent to KRW 96.1 million, calculated as unpaid weekly holiday allowances of KRW 85.2 million (for 132 persons) and unused annual paid leave allowances of KRW 10.9 million (for 109 persons over the past 5 years between 2018 and 2022.

2) Judgment: Extinctive prescription refers to expiration of the period during which an employee with the right to receive compensation may exercise a claim against the employer in the event of a delay in the payment of wages or severance pay. The extinctive prescription for prosecution refers to expiration of the period when prosecution can occur for violating labor law, such as delaying the payment of wages, and begins either on the date the violation occurred or the date a continuing violation ends.

   The period before the extinctive prescription kicks in for prosecution of violation of labor-related acts in terms of delayed payment of wages was extended from 3 years to 5 years in 2007. The period before the extinctive prescription for prosecution kicks in shall be deemed to have started 14 days from the date the wages should have been paid or the date the violations terminate.[40] According to Article 49 of the LSA, the extinctive prescription for a wage bond kicks in after 3 years. However, since the extinctive prescription for prosecution is now 5 years, prosecution for delayed payment of wages will continue to be possible.[41] Thus, an employee may file a claim for unpaid wages for a period of 5 years.

(3) Criminal punishment for late payment of wages

1) Related content: On December 9, 2022, one audit assistant filed a complaint with the Labor Office that wages were overdue. On December 28, the local council was investigated by the Labor Office, and the next day, it paid KRW 800,000 in unpaid weekly holiday pay and unused annual paid leave. However, the petitioner requested criminal punishment for violation of the LSA, regardless of whether the unpaid wages were paid.

2) Judgment: Late payment of wages is subject to criminal punishment. Workers who have received unpaid wage want their employer to be punished. However, prosecutors did not prosecute the local council as the employer responsible for the late payment of wages. The reason for this is that the local council's violation of the obligation to pay weekly holiday allowance and unused annual

---

[40] Criminal Procedure Act, Article 249, Paragraph 1, Item 5 (Duration of Criminal Prescription) and Article 252 (Starting Time for Statute of Limitations)
[41] MOEL Guide, Guide on Handling Unpaid Wages, 2016, pp. 31-32.

(2) 임금체불에 대한 소급 범위

1) 사실관계: 노동청은 2023년 2월 17일에 현장조사를 실시하였고, 2월 21일 지난 5년간 2018년부터 2022년 사이 미지급한 주휴수당 85,200,000원(132명)과 연차유급휴가 미사용 수당 10,900,000원(109명) 총합 96,100,000원의 지급을 지시하였다.

2) 관련판례: 소멸시효는 돈 받을 권리가 있는 근로자가 사용자를 상대로 임금이나 퇴직금의 체불이 있는 경우에 청구권을 행사할 수 있는 기간을 말한다. 이에 대해 공소시효는 임금체불 등 노동법 위반 사용자를 법 위반행위가 있는 날 또는 법 위반행위가 계속되는 경우 종료일로부터 형벌권을 행사할 수 있는 기간을 말한다.

   임금체불로 인한 노동관계법령 위반 범죄의 공소시효 기간은 2007년에 기존 3년에서 5년으로 연장되었다. 공소시효 기산점은 범죄행위가 종료된 때부터 임금지급일 또는 퇴직일로부터 14일이 경과한 때까지를 말한다.[40] 이에 반해 임금채권의 소멸시효는 3년이다(근기법 제49조). 임금채권의 소멸시효 3년이 완성되었다 하더라도 공소시효가 아직 남아 있기 때문에 임금체불사업주에 대해 형사처벌이 가능하다.[41] 따라서 공소시효를 근거로 하여 근로자는 체불된 임금에 대해 5년간 청구가 가능하다.

(3) 임금체불에 대한 형사처벌

1) 사실관계: 2022년 12월 9일 사무보조인 1인은 임금체불이 되었다고 노동청에 진정을 제기하였다. 12월 28일 의회의 담당자가 노동청의 조사를 받았고, 그 다음날 주휴수당과 연차유급휴가 미사용 수당 80만 원 지급을 완료하였다. 그러나 진정인은 체불임금 수령과는 별개로 근로기준법 위반에 대해 의회의 형사처벌을 요구하였다.

2) 관련판례: 임금체불은 형사처벌의 대상이 된다. 임금체불금을 지급받은 근로자가 사용자의 처벌을 원하고 있다. 그러나 검찰은 임금체불을 한 사용자인 의회에 대해 기소하지 않았다. 그 이유는 피진정인인 의회가 임금체불 위반에 대한 고의성이 없다고 판단하였다. 관련 판례는 임금과 퇴직금 지급의무의 존재에 관하여 다툴 만한 근거가 있는 것이라면 사용자가 그 임금과 퇴직금을 지급하지 아니한 데에는 상당한 이유가 있다고 보아야 할

---
40) 형사소송법 제249조(공소시효의 기간) 제1항 제5호, 제252조(시효의 기산점)
41) 고용노동부 근로기준정책과, 「체불사건 업무처리 요령」, 2016. 31-32면.

leave allowance was not intentional. A related precedent states, If there are grounds to dispute the existence of the obligation to pay wages and severance pay, it should be seen that there is a considerable reason why the employer did not pay the wages and severance pay. It is difficult to reason that the employer intentionally committed the crime of violating Article 36 of the Labor Standards Act (Settlement of Payment). Whether there are grounds for dispute regarding the existence and scope of the obligation to pay wages and severance pay depends on the reason for the employer's refusal to pay and the basis for the payment obligation, and the organization and scale of the company operated by the employer. Also, all matters such as business purpose, and the existence and scope of payment obligations, such as other wages, should be judged in light of the general circumstances at the time of the dispute. Even if the employer's civil liability for payment is recognized retroactively, it should not be immediately concluded that the employer's violation of Article 36 of the Labor Standards Act is recognized intentionally.[42]

4. Conclusion

This case is a good example of the characteristics of labor law. Labor law violations do not end with correction of a single person's violation. Through this example of unpaid wages for daily wage workers, the following characteristics of labor law can be understood.

First, even if an administrative agency temporarily hires a commissioned worker, if that worker provides work under the management supervision of the employer and receives wages, employee status is recognized.

Second, a notice of violation of the LSA is applied to all workers in the same category, and unpaid wages can be claimed retroactively for 5 years, which is the statute of limitations for criminal punishment.

Thirdly, even if a violation regarding wages occurs, if there was no intentional violation of the law and there exists a legitimate reason for not paying the wages in question, criminal punishment may be avoided.

〈Case 3〉 Case related to Hiring Academy Instructors as Freelancers[43]

1. Summary of the case

---

[42] Supreme Court ruling on June 28, 2007, 2007do1539.
[43] Jung, Bongsoo, "Are C Language Institute's Native English Instructors Employees or Freelancers?", 「Labor Law」, Jungang, December 2013.

것이다. 사용자에게 근로기준법 제36조 (금품청산)의 위반죄에 고의가 있었다고 인정하기 어렵고, 임금 및 퇴직금 지급의무의 존부 및 범위에 관하여 다툴 만한 근거 여부는 사용자의 지급거절 이유와 그 지급의무의 근거, 그리고 사용자가 운영하는 회사의 조직과 규모, 사업 목적 등 제반 사항, 기타 임금 등 지급의무의 존부 및 범위에 관한 다툼 당시의 제반 정황에 비추어 판단하여야 한다. 사후적으로 사용자의 민사상 지급책임이 인정된다고 하여 곧바로 사용자에 대한 근로기준법 제36조의 위반에 대해 고의가 인정된다고 단정해서는 안 된다.고 판시하고 있다.[42]

4. 시사점

이번 지방의회의 한시적인 일급 위탁직의 임금체불 사건은 노동법의 특징을 잘 설명해 준 사례다. 노동법 위반은 단 한 사람의 위반에 대한 시정으로 끝나지 않는다. 이번 지방의회의 일급직 근로자의 임금체불 사례를 통해서 다음과 같은 노동법의 특징을 이해할 수 있다.

첫째, 행정기관에서 위촉직으로 일시적으로 채용하였다고 하더라도 사용자의 관리감독 하에서 근로를 제공하고 임금을 받았다고 한다면 근로자 신분이 된다.

둘째, 근로기준법의 위반에 대한 지적은 동종 근로자 전체에 적용되고, 공소시효 기간인 5년 동안 소급하여 미지급된 임금을 청구할 수 있다.

셋째로, 임금체불의 위반행위가 발생하였다고 하더라도 법위반의 고의성이 없었고, 지급하지 않았던 이유가 별도로 있었던 경우에는 형사처벌을 면할 수 있다는 사실이다.

〈노동사례 3〉 원어민 강사를 프리랜서로 고용한 노동사례[43]

1. 사건개요

---

[42] 대법원 2007.6.28 선고 2007도1539 판결
[43] 정봉수, "C 어학원 원어민 강사의 근로자성 인정여부", 「월간 노동법률」, 중앙경제사, 2013년 12월호

Chapter 1 Understanding Wages

The case of unpaid wages for C Language Institute started when 17 instructors submitted a petition to the Gangnam Labor Office for unpaid severance pay, weekly holiday allowance and annual paid leave allowance against C Language Institute on February 22, 2011. The Language Institute claimed that its native instructors were freelancers contracted with its "Agreement for Teaching Services' and were not employees to which the Labor Standards Act applied. Upon receipt of the petition, the Gangnam Labor Office did a thorough investigation of the petition over 18 months, and concluded that the Language Institute's 17 instructors were freelancers, not employees (Labor Improvement Team 4, September 28, 2012). Upon this conclusion, 24 instructors (the original 17 and 7 new applicants), began a civil action. On October 17, 2013, the Seoul Central District Court determined that C Language Institute's native instructors were employees under the Labor Standards Act (2011gahap121413), and ruled that the Language Institute was obligated to pay severance pay, weekly holiday allowance, and annual paid leave allowance. After this, the Language Institute filed an appeal against the District Court's decision.

2. Main dispute

The main point of this case was whether native instructors are employees or freelancers. The courts used the legal criteria for determining whether someone is an employee or not in their judgment. The Defendant claimed that the Plaintiffs 1) signed an 'Agreement for Teaching Services' voluntarily, not an employment agreement, and also paid a business tax; 2) that the Defendant paid remarkably high benefits in consideration of there being no severance pay; and 3) that, as the Plaintiffs agreed that this agreement would not include severance pay, if the Plaintiffs requested additional severance pay, it would be a violation of the good-faith principle.

3. Major Points in the Defendant's View & the Supreme Court's Judgment

On June 11, 2015, the Supreme Court ruled that native English instructors (hereinafter referred to as "the Plaintiff") working for "C" Language Institute (hereinafter referred to as "the Defendant") are employees rather than freelancers, and are entitled to severance pay, annual paid leave allowance, and weekly holiday allowance (Supreme Court ruling 2014da88161).[44]

(1) Type of contract

---

[44] This article discusses the Supreme Court Ruling (2014da88161, June 11, 2015) and the related Seoul High Court ruling (2013na68704, November 24, 2014).

'C어학원 원어민 강사의 근로자성 사건'은 2011년 2월 22일 강사 17명이 어학원을 상대로 퇴직금, 주휴수당, 연차수당을 미지급하였다고 강남노동사무소에 진정을 제기하면서 시작되었다. 어학원은 원어민 강사들이'강의서비스 계약서'를 체결한 프리랜서이고 근로자가 아니기 때문에 근로기준법 적용 대상이 아니라고 주장하였다. 이에 대해 강남노동사무소는 1년 6개월의 조사기간을 통해 어학원 강사 17명은 프리랜서이고 근로자가 아니라는 판단을 하고 사건을 종결하였다(근로개선지도4과, 2012.9.28.). 이에 원어민 강사 17명과 추가된 근로자 7명을 포함하여 24명이 민사소송을 제기하였다. 이에 서울중앙지방법원은 2013년 10월 17일에 C어학원의 원어민 강사들은 근로기준법상 근로자에 해당한다고 판단(2011가합121413)하여, 퇴직금, 주휴수당, 연차휴가 근로수당을 지급해야 한다고 판결하였다. 이에 어학원측은 이 결정에 불복하여 재심을 신청하였다.

2. 주요쟁점

이 사건의 주요 쟁점은 원고의 신분이 근로자인지 프리랜서인지의 여하에 달려있다. 이를 판단하는 방법으로 법원은 근로자성 판례법리를 사용하고 있다. 피고는 원고가 근로계약이 아닌 강의서비스 계약을 체결하였고, 원고의 사업소득세를 납부하였으며, 퇴직금이 없음을 고려하여 현저히 많은 보수를 지급했고, 원고들도 이에 동의하여 (퇴직금이 없다는 것) 계약을 하였기 때문에, 추가적으로 이를 청구하는 것은 신의칙에 반한다고 주장하였다.

3. 법원의 판단

2015년 6월 11일 대법원은 C어학원(이하 "피고"라고 함)의 원어민 강사들(이하 "원고"라고 함)이 프리랜서가 아닌 근로자임을 인정하고, 피고에게 원고의 근로자신분으로 발생하는 퇴직금, 연차휴가수당, 주휴수당에 대해 지급의무가 있다고 판결하였다(대법원 2014다88161).[44]

(1) 계약의 명칭

---

[44] 주요내용은 이 사건의 대법원판례와 관련된 하급심 판례 (서울고법 2014. 11. 24. 선고 2013나68704)을 참고하여 기술하였음.

Chapter 1 Understanding Wages

The Defendant called the contract for native English teachers an "Agreement for Teaching Services" and designated the Plaintiffs as "instructors". In particular, the Defendant claimed, "the plaintiffs, mainly from famous colleges of advanced countries such as the United States, are people who will return to their home countries after working for a short time at a high level of remuneration while experiencing Korean culture and retaining their freedom at the same time as foreigners. Because of these special characteristics, their economic and social conditions are equal or superior in the relationship with the Defendant. In reference to this, the contracts with native English instructors were delegation contracts or lecture service contracts, which are similar to subcontracts."

The court recognized as "employees" those who signed a contract entitled "Service Contract Regarding Instructions at the Institute & Instruction and Management of Students" or "Lesson Service Offer Contract"[45]. In addition, even though some plaintiffs working for the Defendant consider themselves freelancers, not employees, the essence of the relationship between the Plaintiffs and the Defendant does not change. Whether a person is considered an employee under the Labor Standards Act shall be decided by whether that person offers work to the employer as a subordinate of the employer in a business or workplace to earn wages in actual practice, regardless of the type of contract.

(2) Salary including severance pay & agreement excluding severance pay

The Defendant claimed ① "the possibility of recognizing the status of "employee" is slim because the Plaintiffs' monthly salary, which was between 3,469,128 won and 3,979,976 won, is higher than the average Korean teacher's monthly salary, which is 1,030,000 won, the salary of other regular employees of the Defendant, and the monthly salary of native English teaching assistants who work for the Education Office, which pays them 1,800,000 won to 2,700,000 won." ② According to the Agreement for Teaching Services, "The Instructor agrees and understands that they shall not receive any benefits available to full-time employees including but not limited to severance pay, health insurance, and pension payments, all of which are the sole responsibility of the Instructor."

As for this, the Court explained that "① The Defendant's claims lack legal grounds because not only are the duties dissimilar to those of the Korean teachers, regular employees, and native English teaching assistants who work for the Education Office, the amount of salary does not determine whether or not they are employees." ② The Court also stipulated that "Severance pay is the deferred remuneration to be paid in return for continuous employment to an employee who leaves employment after serving a certain period of time. The concrete right to request severance pay occurs on the condition of the fact of termination of

---

[45] Supreme Court ruling 2004da29736 on Dec 7, 2006; SC ruling 2005doo8436 on Jan 25, 2007

피고는 이 사건 원어민강사 계약의 명칭을 강의서비스 계약(Agreement for Teaching Services)으로 하고, 계약서상 원고들의 명칭을 강사(Instructor)로 정하는 등의 계약서를 작성하였다. 특히, 피고는 "원고들이 주로 미국 등 선진국의 명문대 출신의 외국인으로 한국 문화를 체험함과 동시에 자유로운 생활을 영위하면서 단기간 동안 높은 보수를 받고 일하다가 다시 본국으로 귀국하려는 사람들로, 그 특수성으로 인하여 사회·경제적으로 피고와 대등 또는 우월한 지위에 있었으며, 이러한 점에서 이 사건 원어민강사 계약은 위임계약이거나 도급적 성격을 가진 강의서비스계약에 해당된다."고 주장한다.

이에 대해 법원은 계약명칭이 '학원강의 및 수강생 지도·관리에 관한 용역계약' 또는 '강의용역제공계약서'로 되어 있음에도 해당 원고들의 근로자성을 인정한 바 있으며,[45] 설령 피고의 영어학원에서 근무하는 일부 원어민강사들이 피고 주장과 같이 스스로를 근로자가 아니라 프리랜서로 생각하고 있다고 하여, 원고들과 피고 사이의 근로관계의 실질이 달라진다는 것은 아니라고 판단하고 있다. 즉, 법원은 계약의 명칭과 상관없이 그 실질에 있어 근로자가 사업 또는 사업장에 임금을 목적으로 종속적인 관계에서 근로를 제공하는지 여부를 살펴보아야 한다고 판단하였다.

(2) 퇴직금 포함된 임금 및 퇴직금 지급 제외 약정

피고는 "① 원고들이 주당 평균 24시간(월 104시간)만 강의를 하였음에도 불구하고, 한국인 학원강사의 월 평균 소득인 1,030,000원보다 높고, 피고의 정규직 직원들의 보수보다 높으며, 교육청 소속인 원어민 영어보조교사의 급여인 월 1,800,000원에서 2,700,000원보다 높은, 월 3,469,128원에서 3,979,976원에 달하는 보수를 받았기에, 원고들의 근로자성은 희박하다"고 주장하였다. ② 원어민강사 계약에 따르면, "퇴직금, 건강보험 및 연금을 포함하여 정규직 근로자에게 제공되는 여타의 급부금 지급에 해당되지 않음에 동의하고, 이들 사항은 강사의 단독 책임으로 한다."고 규정되어 있다.

이에 대해 법원은 "①에 대해 원고들의 근로의 내용 및 조건을 한국인 일반 학원강사, 피고의 정규직 직원, 교육청 소속의 원어민 영어보조교사의 것과 동일하다고 볼 수 없을 뿐만 아니라, 노무제공자가 지급받는 보수의 액수가 근로자인지 여부를 결정하는 것도 아니라고 판단하였다. ② 에 대해서는 퇴직금은 사용자가 일정기간을 계속 근로하고 퇴직하는 근로자에게 그 계속

---

[45] 대법원 2006. 12. 7. 선고 2004다29736 판결; 대법원 2007. 1. 25. 선고 2005두8436 판결.

continuous employment. It is null and void due to it being a violation of the Labor Standards Act compulsory regulations, if an employee previously signed a special contract that the employee would give up the right to request severance pay at the time of resigning from their job."[46]

(3) Judgment on whether or not the requests are a violation against the principle of good faith

The Defendant claimed that the Plaintiffs' claims were not acceptable because they violated the principle of Good Faith in light of justice and the principle of equity for the following reason: If the Plaintiff's claims were validated, the Defendant would have no choice but to bear additional loss from the burden of paying severance pay, other legal allowances and social security insurance premiums, etc, while the Plaintiffs will enjoy unintended additional benefits. This would result in unexpected, excessive cost to the Defendant, and consequentially, have serious impact on the Defendant's stock price, and seriously threaten the growth of the Defendant as an ongoing business.

As reviewed, the Court ruled that attempting to restrict the basic rights of an employee guaranteed by compulsory provisions such as the right to claim severance payment by applying the principle of good faith is to go against the constitutional value and the nature of compulsory provisions of the Labor Standards Act. Therefore, it is unacceptable, as long as there are no special circumstances that would affect the judgment, to give priority to the wrongful belief of the employer over the legitimate right of the employees by categorizing the Plaintiff's claims as a violation of the principle of Good Faith even though the Labor Standards Act guarantees the employee's definite rights as compulsory provisions. If the Defendant's claims were accepted with only the evidence the Defendant had submitted, it is unlikely that it will lead to severe managerial difficulties for the Defendant or be a menace to the Defendant's existence. In addition, it cannot be recognized that the Plaintiffs' claims for severance payment, etc, is illegitimate and goes against the principle of Good Faith due only to the claims the Defendant has submitted."[47]

---

[46] Supreme Court ruling 97da49732 on March 27, 1998
[47] Supreme Court ruling 2012da89399 on December 18, 2013

근로에 대한 대가로서 지급하는 후불적 임금의 성질을 띤 금원으로서 구체적인 퇴직금 청구권은 계속 근로가 끝나는 퇴직이라는 사실을 요건으로 하여 발생되는 것이고, 최종 퇴직 시 발생하는 퇴직금청구권을 사전에 포기하는 것은 강행법규인 근로기준법에 위반되어 무효가 된다."[46]고 판시하고 있다.

(3) 신의칙 위반 적용여부

피고는 "원고들의 청구가 받아들여지면 피고는 퇴직금은 물론 기타 법정수당 및 4대 보험료 등 부담으로 원어민강사들과 계약조건을 정할 당시 전혀 예정하지 않았던 추가적인 손실을 부담할 수 밖에 없고, 반면 원어민강사들은 자신들이 의도하지도 않은 추가적인 이득을 누리게 된다. 이는 피고에게 예상치 못한 대규모 손실을 초래할 뿐만 아니라, 결과적으로 피고의 주가에도 심각한 영향을 끼쳐 피고의 계속 기업으로서의 성장을 심각하게 위협하게 될 것인데, 이러한 결과는 정의와 형평의 관념에 비추어 신의에 현저히 반하여 용인될 수 없다."고 주장하였다.

이 사안에 대해 법원은 "신의칙의 적용을 통하여 퇴직금청구권과 같은 법률상 강행규정으로 보장된 근로자의 기본적 권리를 제약하려고 시도하는 것은 헌법적 가치나 근로기준법의 강행규정성에 정면으로 반하는 것이어서, 근로기준법이 강행규정으로 근로자에게 일정한 권리를 보장하고 있음에도 사용자가 신의칙을 내세워 사용자의 그릇된 신뢰를 권리자인 근로자의 정당한 권리 찾기에 우선하는 것은 특단의 사정이 없는 이상 허용될 수 없다고 보았다. 이 사건의 청구가 받아들여지면 피고에게 중대한 경영상의 어려움이 초래되거나, 피고의 존립이 위태롭게 될 것임이 인정되지 않을 뿐 아니라, 피고가 들고 있는 위와 같은 이유만으로 원고들이 근로기준법상 강행규정에 기하여 하는 이 사건 퇴직금 등 청구가 신의칙에 반하는 위법한 것이라 볼 수 없다."고 판시하였다.[47]

---

46) 대법원 1998. 3. 27. 선고 97다49732 판결.
47) 대법원 2013. 12. 18. 선고 2012다89399 판결.

Chapter 2 Statutory Wages

I. Ordinary Wages

II. Supreme Court Decision on Ordinary Wage

II-2. Precedents Following the Supreme Court's Unanimous Decision on Ordinary Wages

III. Average Wages

IV. Minimum Wage

V. Shutdown Allowances

IV. Additional Allowances

VII. Related Labor Cases

⟨Case 1⟩ Occupational Accident Compensation

⟨Case 2⟩ Branch Manager's Severance Pay

제2장 법정기준임금

Ⅰ. 통상임금

Ⅱ. 통상임금 관련 대법원 합의체 판결

Ⅱ-2 통상임금 대법원 합의체 판결 이후 판례 경향

Ⅲ. 평균임금

Ⅳ. 최저임금

Ⅴ. 휴업수당

Ⅵ. 가산임금

Ⅶ. 실무사례

〈사례 1〉 **업무상 재해자의 산업재해보상금 계산**

〈사례 2〉 **지사장 퇴직금 진정사건**

Chapter 2 Statutory Wages

Ⅰ. Ordinary Wage

1. Understanding ordinary wage[48]

(1) Concept of Ordinary Wages

Recent judicial rulings concerning rules for calculation and scope of ordinary wages have differed from Ministry of Employment and Labor Guidelines, something which has caused much confusion for corporate management. However, the Supreme Court, with all judges in attendance, offered clarification on December 18, 2013: 'Ordinary wages' means wages which are determined to be paid periodically or in a lump sum to an employee for their prescribed work or whole work. This ordinary wage is used as the standard wage to calculate added allowance for overtime, night and holiday work, annual paid leave allowance, dismissal pay, and for paid leaves that employers have to provide under the Labor Standards Act. If this ordinary wage has not been calculated properly, it is not as simple as re-calculating and paying the correct amount from now on, but the employer shall recalculate all kinds of allowances such as overtime, night and holiday work, and other allowances that were paid over the past three years. Furthermore, the employer shall recalculate the severance pay for resigned or dismissed employees and pay the difference.[49]

The term 'ordinary wages' means hourly wages, daily wages, weekly wages, monthly wages, or subcontract wages determined to be paid in periodic or lump sums to the worker for prescribed or whole labor.[50] That is, 'ordinary wages' means the wages determined to be paid periodically and uniformly within a specific period, regardless of the number of actual work provisions or the amount received as remuneration for quality or quantity of the labor.

(2) Reasons for calculating Ordinary Wages

Ordinary wages apply for ① dismissal allowances replacing advance notices of dismissal, ② wages added for overtime, night, or off-day work, ③ ordinary wages stipulated in the rules of employment to calculate annual paid leave, and ④ in cases where the pay is under 'paid allowance,' not under average wages according to the Labor Standards Act.

---

[48] Jung, Bongsoo, 「Korean Labor Law Bible」 6th Ed., Joongang, 2021, pp. 73-75.
[49] Supreme Court ruling on Dec. 19, 2013: 2012Da89399.
[50] Article 6(1) of the Enforcement Decree to the Labor Standards Act

Ⅰ. 통상임금

1. 통상임금의 이해[48]

(1) 통상임금의 개념

최근 판례가 통상임금의 산정 및 범위와 관련하여 고용노동부의 기존 행정해석과 차이가 있어 기업운영에 많은 혼란을 주어 왔으나, 2013년 12월 18일 대법원 합의체 판결에서 명확한 내용을 제시하였다. 통상임금은 근로자에게 정기적·일률적으로 소정근로 또는 총 근로에 대하여 지급하기로 정해진 금액을 말한다. 이 통상임금은 근로기준법상 사용자에게 부여된 연장·야간·휴일 근로에 대한 가산임금, 연차유급휴가 수당, 해고예고수당, 기타 법령에 유급으로 명시된 기준금액으로 사용된다. 이 통상임금이 잘못 계산 되었다면 앞으로 가산수당 등 임금산정을 제대로 하면 되는 것으로만 끝나는 것이 아니라 지난 3년간에 지급된 연장·야간·휴일근로수당, 기타 각종 유급으로 지급된 수당에 대해 재 정산 되어야 하고, 심지어 퇴직자에 대한 퇴직금 계산도 다시 정산하여 지급해야 한다.[49]

'통상임금'이란 근로자에게 정기적·일률적으로 소정근로 또는 총 근로에 대하여 지급하기로 정해진 시급금액·일급금액·주급금액·월급금액 또는 도급금액을 말한다.[50] 즉, 근로의 질 또는 양의 대가로 실제 근로일수나 수령액에 구애됨이 없이 1임금산정기간 내에서 정기적·일률적으로 지급하기로 정해진 임금을 의미한다.

(2) 통상임금의 산정 사유

통상임금으로 산정해야 하는 경우로는 ① 해고예고에 갈음하는 해고수당, ② 시간외근로, 야간 및 휴일근로에 대한 가산임금, ③ 연차 유급휴가수당의 경우 취업규칙 등의 정함에 따라 통상임금으로 산정하는 경우, ④ 기타 근로기준법에서 '유급'으로 지급하기로 한 임금이다.

---

48) 정봉수, 「한국노동법 영문해설」 제6판, 중앙경제사, 2021, pp. 73-75.
49) 대법원 2013.12.19. 선고 2012다89399판결.
50) 근로기준법시행령 제6조 제1항

Chapter 2 Statutory Wages

(3) Methods of calculating ordinary wages

When calculating ordinary wages, the hourly wage rate is applied in principle. Daily wages, weekly wages, monthly wages, or subcontract wages can be calculated at the hourly wage rate as in the following:

1) Hourly wage rate of daily wages

With respect to wages determined by the daily wage rate, the amount is calculated by dividing the daily wage rate by the contractual working hours per day. Contractual working hours represent those working hours which the workers and employers have agreed upon within the limit of the legal standard working hours (Article 2 (7) of the LSA).

2) Hourly wage rate of weekly wages

With respect to wages determined by the weekly wage rate, the amount is calculated by dividing the weekly wage rate by the contractual working hours per week. Weekly wage refers to ordinary wages that are to be paid on a weekly basis.

3) Hourly wage rate of monthly wages

With respect to wages determined by the monthly wage rate, the amount is calculated by dividing the monthly wage rate by the contractual working hours per month. Monthly wage refers to ordinary wages that are to be paid on a monthly basis.

In cases where legal standard hours are regulated to the same as contractual working hours, the calculation is as follows:

⇒ Where legal standard hours mean 40 hours weekly, excluding rest hours

> Standard hours calculated for monthly ordinary wages
> = (40 hours + 8 hours) x 4.345 weeks ≒ 209 hours

4) Hourly wage rate of subcontract wages

With respect to wages determined by the subcontract wage system, the amount is calculated by dividing the total sum of wages under the subcontract wage system for the period of wage calculation by the whole number of working hours during that period.

<Ministry of Employment and Labor Guidelines>
1) As long as the welfare allowance is paid periodically and uniformly, it shall be included in the realm of ordinary wages.[51]

(3) 통상임금의 산정방법

통상임금은 시간급으로 산정함이 원칙이다. 일급·주급·월급·도급금액을 시간급 통상임금으로 환산하는 방법은 다음과 같다.

1) 일급의 시간급 통상임금

일급금액으로 정해진 임금에 대하여는 그 금액을 1일의 소정근로시간수로 나눈 금액이 시간급 통상임금이 된다. 소정근로시간이란 법정근로시간의 범위 안에서 근로자와 사용자 간에 정한 근로시간으로 정의하고 있다 (근로기준법의 제2조 제7항).

2) 주급의 시간급 통상임금

주급금액으로 정하여진 임금에 대하여는 그 금액을 주의 통상임금 산정 기준시간수로 나눈 금액이 시간급 통상임금이다. 주급 금액이란 1주를 단위로 하여 지급하기로 정해진 통상임금을 말한다.

3) 월급의 시간급 통상임금

월급금액으로 정하여진 임금에 대하여는 그 금액을 월의 통상임금 산정 기준시간수로 나눈 금액이 시간급 통상임금이 된다. 월급 금액이란 1월을 단위로 하여 지급하기로 정하여진 통상임금을 말한다.

법정기준 근로시간을 소정근로시간으로 정한 경우의 계산례는 다음과 같다.
⇒ 주 법정근로시간이 휴게시간을 제외하고 40시간인 경우

월의 통상임금 산정기준 시간수 = (40시간 + 8시간) × 4.345주 ≒ 209시간

4) 도급임금의 시간급 통상임금

도급금액으로 정하여진 임금에 대하여는 그 임금산정기간에 있어서 도급제에 의하여 계산된 임금의 총액을 당해 임금산정기간의 총 근로시간수로 나누어 시간급 통상임금을 산정한다.

<행정해석>
1) 복지수당이 정기적·일률적으로 지급되는 경우 통상임금의 범위에 포함되는 것으로 보아야 한다.[51]

---
[51] 행정해석: 2002.10.04, 임금 68207-730

Chapter 2 Statutory Wages

In cases where the welfare allowance has been paid to all employees periodically and uniformly within a period of wage calculation for the contractual working hours or legal standard working hours for the purpose of supplementing the low wage level of employees working in the social welfare facilities, this allowance shall be included in the realm of ordinary wages. Here, the term "periodic" means that the employer shall pay wages for contractual working hours or legal standard working hours within the period of wage calculation. The term "uniform" means that the employer shall not only pay all employees, but also pay all employees who meet a certain condition or reach a certain level of working conditions. The term "a certain condition" means a fixed condition.

2) Even though the company and the labor union agree in a collective bargaining agreement to include into ordinary wages those wages and valuables which are exclusive in the realm of ordinary wages according to the LSA guidelines, it is not possible to deem that they are converted ordinary wages by the law.[52]

If a company decides by collective bargaining agreement (CBA) and the rules of employment to include into the realm of ordinary wages valuables which are not included in the realm of ordinary wages according to LSA regulation, the company shall follow the promised rules. However, even though the company and the labor union agreed in the CBA and rules of employment to include into ordinary wages those wages and valuables which are exclusive in the realm of ordinary wages according to LSA guidelines, it is not possible to deem that they are converted to ordinary wages according to Article 6 of the Enforcement Decree to the LSA.

2. Substantial criteria for Ordinary Wages

(1) Legal criteria for determining ordinary wages

1) Ordinary wages means wages that an employer pays to an employee as remuneration for their prescribed work or whole work, and those which are paid regularly and uniformly are considered ordinary wages in principle. For legislating the Labor Standards Act and the function and necessity of ordinary wages, what should be included as ordinary wages shall be fixed wages paid regularly and uniformly. This means non-fixed wages are not ordinary wages, as

---

51) MOEL Guidelines: on Oct. 4, 2002, Wage 68207-730
52) MOEL Guidelines: on Oct. 8, 2002, Wage 68207-735

복지수당이 사회복지시설 종사자들의 열악한 임금수준을 보전해주기 위한 목적으로 전 근로자를 대상으로 1임금산정기간내의 소정근로시간 또는 법정근로시간에 대하여 정기적·일률적으로 지급하는 경우라면 이는 통상임금의 범위에 포함되는 것으로 보아야 할 것이다. 여기서 "정기적"이라 함은 1임금산정기간내의 소정근로시간 또는 법정근로시간에 대하여 지급을, "일률적"이라 함은 모든 근로자에게 지급되는 것뿐만 아니라 '일정한 조건 또는 기준에 달한 모든 근로자'에게 지급하는 것도 포함되는 것이며, "일정한 조건"이라 함은 '고정적인 조건'을 의미한다.

2) 근로기준법 규정에 의한 통상임금에서 제외되는 임금 및 금품을 노사관계자간에 통상임금의 범위에 포함하기로 정하였더라도 법 규정에 의한 통상임금으로 전환되었다고 볼 수는 없다.[52]

근로기준법의 규정에 의한 통상임금의 범위에 포함되지 않는 금품을 노사관계자간에 단체협약, 취업규칙 등으로 통상임금의 범위에 포함시켜 제 수당의 지급기준으로 삼기로 정하였다면 그에 따라야 할 것이다. 그러나 근로기준법 규정에 의한 통상임금에서 제외되는 임금 및 금품을 노사관계자간에 단체협약·취업규칙 등으로 통상임금의 범위에 포함하기로 정하였더라도 이를 근로기준법시행령 제6조의 규정에 의한 통상임금으로 전환되었다고 볼 수는 없을 것이다.

2. 통상임금의 구체적 판단기준

(1) 통상임금의 판단법리

1) 소정 근로 또는 총 근로의 대가로 근로자에게 지급되는 금품으로서 그것이 정기적·일률적으로 지급되는 것이면 원칙적으로 모두 통상임금에 속하는 임금이다. 근로기준법의 입법 취지와 통상임금의 기능 및 필요성에 비추어 볼 때 어떤 임금이 통상임금에 해당하려면 그것이 정기적·일률적으로 지급되는 고정적인 임금에 속하여야 한다. 정기적·일률적으로 지급되는 것이 아니거나 실제 근무성적에 따라 지급 여부 및 지급액이 달라지는 것과 같이 고정적인 임금이 아닌 것은 통상임금에 해당하지 않는다. 여기서

---

[52] 행정해석: 2002.10.08, 임금 68207-735

Chapter 2 Statutory Wages

they are not paid regularly and uniformly and may or may not be paid. Here, being paid 'uniformly' not only means that payment is made to all employees, but also to all employees qualified according to certain conditions or criteria. Here, 'certain criteria' refers to 'fixed conditions' in considering the concept of ordinary wage, because the ordinary wage is used to calculate 'fixed and generally accepted ordinary wage.'[53]

2) Even though a particular allowance or bonus, etc., may be paid for a period exceeding one month, if these are paid regularly and uniformly, these components can be included in ordinary wages.[54]

3) Mutual agreements between employer and employees that exclude a particular allowance considered ordinary wages according to the Labor Standards Act are null and void because such an agreement sets conditions lower than that of the Labor Standards Act.[55]

(3) Application of ordinary wage
1) Bonuses

Bonuses are included into the realm of ordinary wages even if they are not paid regularly every month. Rules for calculating ordinary wages explain the bonus as follows[56] (revised after the Supreme Court ruling on December 18, 2013):

① As the regular bonus is paid regularly and uniformly (e.g. 100% paid every even month) as fixed wages for labor service, it shall be considered ordinary wages as stipulated in the Labor Standards Act.[57]

② The bonus in this case is only applicable to employees working for six months or more with a certain amount paid quarterly, and calculated according to the number of years of service. This bonus is paid every quarter, distinguishing it from annual salary divided into monthly payments, but this difference in payment time does not preclude it from being considered as ordinary wage. As the bonus in this case has been previously fixed, it shall be considered ordinary wage as it is a fixed wage paid regularly and uniformly.[58]

---

[53] Supreme Court ruling on Jan. 29, 2010:2009Da74144
[54] Supreme Court ruling on Feb. 9, 1996: 94Da19501; Supreme Court ruling on Jun. 13, 2003: 2002Da74282
[55] Supreme Court ruling on Nov. 29, 2007: 2006Da81523
[56] MOEL Regulation 476, Jan. 22, 2002; Supreme Court ruling
[57] Incheon District Court ruling on Feb. 23, 2012: 2011Gahap6096; Seoul Appellate Court ruling on Oct. 1, 2010: 2010na34618
[58] Supreme Court ruling on Mar. 29, 2012: 2010Da91046

「일률적」으로 지급되는 것이라 함은 「모든 근로자」에게 지급되는 것뿐만 아니라 「일정한 조건 또는 기준에 달한 모든 근로자」에게 지급되는 것도 포함된다. 여기서 말하는 「일정한 조건」이란 「고정적이고 평균적인 임금」을 산출하려는 통상임금의 개념에 비추어 볼 때 「고정적인 조건」이어야 한다.[53]

2) 근로자에 대한 임금이 1개월을 초과하는 기간마다 지급되는 것이라도 그것이 정기적·일률적으로 지급되는 것이면 통상임금에 포함될 수 있다.[54]

3) 성질상 근로기준법에 정한 통상임금에 산입될 수당을 통상임금에서 제외하기로 하는 노사 간 합의는 같은 법이 정한 기준에 미치지 못하는 근로조건을 정한 계약으로서 무효이다.[55]

(3) 통상임금의 적용

1) 상여금

상여금을 매월 정기적으로 지급하는 방식을 취하고 있다면 통상임금의 범위에서 포함된다. 「통상임금 산정지침에 따른 상여금」은 다음과 같다[56]. (2013년 대법원 판례 반영)

① 정기상여금(매월 짝수달 100%지급)은 근로의 대가로서 정기적·일률적으로 지급되는 고정적 임금이라고 봄이 타당하므로 근로기준법상 통상임금에 해당된다.[57]

② 이 사건 상여금은 6개월을 초과하여 계속 근무한 근로자에게 근속연수의 증가에 따라 미리 정해놓은 각 비율을 적용하여 산정한 금액을 분기별로 지급하는 것으로서, 매월 월급형태로 지급되는 근속수당과 달리 분기별로 지급되기는 하지만 그러한 사정만으로 통상임금이 아니라고 단정할 수 없다. 이 사건 상여금은 그 금액이 확정된 것이어서 정기적·일률적으로 지급되는 고정적인 임금인 통상임금에 해당한다.[58]

---

53) 대법원 2010.1.28.선고 2009다74144판결.
54) 대법원 1996.2.9. 선고 94다19501판결; 대법원 2003.6.13. 선고 2002다74282판결.
55) 대법원 2007.11.29. 선고 2006다 81523 판결 등 참조
56) 노동부예규 제476호, 2002.1.22 에 대법원 판결 반영한 내용
57) 인천지방법원 2011가합6096, 2012.02.23; 서울고등법원 2010나34618 2010.10.01
58) 대법원 2012.03.29. 선고 2010다91046 판결.

Chapter 2 Statutory Wages

Name of payment made to employees	Ord. Wage	Avg. Wage	Other Paymt
Bonuses			
A. In cases where payment conditions, amounts, and payment rates are regulated in the rules of employment, or where employees are paid habitually and naturally expect to get paid: regular bonuses, exercise subsidies, etc.	○	○	
B. In cases where payment is not made habitually, but paid temporarily or definitely in accordance with company profits according to the employer's discretion and favor			○

2) **Payments made for an employee's living costs or welfare, regardless of working hours**

① The company has paid all cleaning workers a fixed meal allowance, household subsidy, transportation subsidy, morning meal costs, sanitation allowance, and snack allowances as fixed amounts every month, all of which shall be considered ordinary wages to be paid regularly and uniformly as reward for labor service.[59]

② If a welfare allowance has been paid uniformly, regularly, and at a fixed rate to all employees of the same business according to the collective wage agreement, this is not money paid temporarily and according to favor for welfare, but wages paid as remuneration for labor service according to employment relations. In addition, this is not wages paid individually or at a variable rate, but fixed wages for ordinary working days and working hours, so shall be considered ordinary wage.[60]

③ Even though some employees with lower work attendance rates have been paid transportation and meal allowances differently than other workers, these allowances have been paid to all employees and shall be considered ordinary wages.[61]

④ Even though a company enters into an agreement with employees that it will not calculate into ordinary wage the meal allowances that have been paid at a fixed rate to all employees, this shall be considered an illegal employment contract.[62]

---

[59] Ulsan District Court ruling on Feb. 3, 2006: 2005Gadan8384.
[60] Busan Appellate Court ruling on Sep. 25, 1996: 96Gu2583.
[61] Seoul District Court ruling on May 18, 2006: 2005Gahap57290.
[62] Supreme Court ruling on Feb. 22, 1994: 93Da9620.

근로자에게 지급되는 금품의 명칭	통상임금	평균임금	기타금품
상여금 가. 취업규칙 등에 지급조건, 금액, 지급시기가 정해져 있거나 전 근로자에게 관례적으로 지급하여 사회통념상 근로자가 당연히 지급 받을 수 있다는 기대를 갖게 되는 경우 : 정기상여금, 체력단련비 등	○	○	
나. 관례적으로 지급한 사례가 없고, 기업이윤에 따라 일시적, 불확정적으로 사용자의 재량이나 호의에 의해 지급하는 경우 경영성과배분금, 격려금, 생산장려금, 포상금, 인센티브 등			○

2) **근로시간과 관계없이 근로자의 생활보조적, 복리후생적으로 지급되는 금품**

① 모든 환경미화원들에게 정액급식비, 가계보조비, 교통보조비, 급량비(조식대), 위생비, 간식대로 매월 일정금액을 지급하였으므로, 이는 근로의 대상으로서 정기적·일률적으로 지급되는 고정적인 임금으로 통상임금에 포함된다.[59]

② 복지수당이 임금협약에 따라 동일직종 근로자 모두에게 일률적, 정기적, 고정적으로 지급되는 것이라면, 이는 복지후생을 위한 임의적, 은혜적 금품이 아니라 사용종속관계에서 행하는 근로의 대상으로서 지급되는 금품, 즉 임금에 해당되고, 또 개인적, 비 고정적 임금이 아니라 통상의 근로일, 근로시간에 대한 고정적 임금이어서 통상임금에 속한다고 본다.[60]

③ 모든 근로자에게 지급하되 예외적으로 출근비율이 낮은 근로자에게는 다른 방식으로 지급하겠다는 취지의 교통비 및 중식대도 통상임금에 포함된다.[61]

④ 전 근로자에게 일정액으로 지급하는 식대보조비는 통상임금산정시 포함시키지 않기로 노사 간 합의가 있었어도 이는 위법한 근로계약이다.[62]

---

[59] 울산 지법 2006.02.03. 선고 2005가단8384 판결
[60] 부산고등법원 1996.09.25. 선고 96구2583 판결
[61] 서울지방법원 2006.05.18. 선고 2005가합57290 판결
[62] 대법원 1994.02.22. 선고 93다9620 판결

Chapter 2 Statutory Wages

⑤ Service allowances have accumulated according to the length of service for all cleaning workers employed for at least one year; meal, transportation, sanitation, and hazard allowances have been paid at a fixed rate every month to all cleaning workers. Quarterly, attendance, exercise, and traditional holiday allowances have been paid to all cleaning workers regularly and at a fixed rate if they meet certain criteria. As these allowances are fixed wages paid regularly and uniformly as reward for labor service, they shall be considered ordinary wages."[63]

Name of payment made to employees	Ord. Wage	Avg. Wage	Other Paymt
① Commuting allowances, vehicle maintenance subsidies A. If rendered periodically and uniformly to all employees	○	○	
B. If rendered variably according to the number of days in attendance or to a few employees			○
② Company housing allowances, winter fuel allowances, kimchi allowances A. If rendered periodically and uniformly to all employees	○	○	
B. If rendered temporarily or to a few employees			○
③ Family allowances, education allowances A. If rendered uniformly to all employees regardless of marital status	○	○	
B. If rendered only according to the number of family members or to a few employees (paid as child education allowances, employee training allowances, etc.)			○
④ Meals or meal allowances A. If rendered uniformly to all employees by means of a labor contract, Ministry of Employment and Labor, or etc.	○	○	
B. Actual meals paid in accordance with the number of days in attendance			○

---

[63] Supreme Court ruling on Sep. 8, 2011: 2011Da22061.

⑤ 1년을 초과하여 계속 근무한 환경미화원들에게 근속연수가 증가함에 따라 일정 금액을 가산하여 1년 근속 당 일정금액을 지급한 근속가산금과 모든 환경미화원에게 매월 정액으로 지급한 급량비, 교통보조비, 위생수당, 위험수당 및 모든 환경미화원들에게 일정한 기준에 따라 정기적·고정적으로 지급한 기말수당, 정근수당, 체력단련비, 명절휴가비는 모두 근로의 대가로 정기적·일률적으로 지급되는 고정적인 임금이므로 통상임금에 포함된다.[63]

근로자에게 지급되는 금품의 명칭	통상임금	평균임금	기타금품
① 통근수당, 차량유지비			
가. 전 근로자에게 정기적, 일률적으로 지급하는 경우	○	○	
나. 출근일수에 따라 변동적으로 지급하거나 일부 근로자에게 지급 경우			○
② 사택수당, 월동연료수당, 김장수당			
가. 전 근로자에게 정기적·일률적으로 지급하는 경우	○	○	
나. 일시적으로 지급하거나 일부 근로자에게 지급하는 경우			○
③ 가족수당, 교육수당			
가. 독신자를 포함하여 전 근로자에게 일률적으로 지급하는 경우	○	○	
나. 가족수에 따라 차등 지급되거나 일부 근로자에게만 지급하는 경우(학자보조금, 근로자 교육비 지원 등의 명칭으로 지급)			○
④ 급식 및 급식비			
가. 근로계약, 취업규칙 등에 규정된 급식비로써 근무일 수에 관계없이 전 근로자에게 일률적으로 지급하는 경우	○	○	
나. 출근일수에 따라 차등 지급하는 경우			○

---

[63] 대법원 2011.09.08. 선고 2011다22061 판결.

II. Supreme Court Decision on Ordinary Wage

The recent Supreme Court ruling, in which all justices attended, regarding the ordinary wage case holds significant historical importance in simplifying South Korea's wage system. This Supreme Court ruling consists of two judgments. One deemed annual regular bonuses as part of the ordinary wage. The other deemed various monthly, fixed, and uniform allowances as part of the ordinary wage.

1. First case (Regular bonuses deemed as ordinary wages)[64]

(1) Background:

The defendant company (hereinafter, referred to as "the Company") has paid bonuses on every even month, in accordance with the Company's Bonus Payment Regulation, with the full amount paid to employees with at least two months of service. However, a different amount calculated by application of a pre-determined rate, according to the corresponding period of the bonus payment, is paid to new employees with less than two months of service, those who have just returned after taking at least two months of leave, and those who are on leave. As for those who resigned during the corresponding period of bonus payment, the company pays the pro-rated amount according to the number of days worked. When determining the amount of wages to be included in ordinary wages in the collective agreement concluded on October 8, 2008, the Company and the labor union excluded the bonuses from calculation of ordinary wage, assuming that the bonuses in this case were not included in ordinary wage in the Labor Standards Act.

(2) Legal issues considered
① Whether or not the bonuses in this case are included in ordinary wage;
② Although the Company and the union agreed to exclude the bonuses from calculation of ordinary wages, if an employee applied for additional wage, claiming that the agreement was invalid, whether or not this claim violated the good-faith principle.

(3) Court ruling
① Even though the Company paid the bonus for a period exceeding one month

---
[64] Supreme Court ruling on Dec. 19, 2013: 2012Da89399.

Ⅱ. 통상임금 관련 대법원 합의체 판결

통상임금 사건에 관하여 대법원판사 전원 참석하여 결정한 이번 대법원 판결은 우리나라의 임금체계를 단순화 시킨 역사적인 의미를 가진다. 이 대법원 판결은 2개의 판결로 구성하고 있다. 하나는 연 단위의 정기적 상여금을 통상임금으로 판단한 것이다. 다른 하나는 매월 정기적, 고정적, 일률적으로 지급하는 각종 수당을 통상임금으로 판단하였다는 것이다.

1. 제1판결 임금사건 (정기 상여금을 통상임금으로 판단)[64]

(1) 사실관계:

피고회사는 상여금지급규칙에 따라, 이 사건 상여금을 짝수 달에 지급하였다. 근속기간이 2개월을 초과한 근로자에게는 전액을, 근속기간이 2개월을 초과하지 않는 신규 입사자나 2개월 이상 장기 휴직 후 복직한 자, 휴직자에 대하여는 상여금 지급대상기간 중 해당 구간에 따라 미리 정해 놓은 비율을 적용하여 산정한 금액을 각기 다르게 지급하였다. 상여금 지급대상기간 중에 퇴직한 근로자에 대해서는 근무일수에 따라 일할 계산하여 지급하였다. 피고와 노동조합은 2008년 10월 8일 체결한 단체협약에서 통상임금에 산입될 임금의 범위를 정하면서, 이 사건 상여금이 근로기준법 소정의 통상임금에 해당하지 않는다는 전제하에 이 사건 상여금을 통상임금 산입에서 제외하였다.

(2) 이 사건의 쟁점:
① 피고회사의 상여금이 통상임금에 해당하는지 여부;
② 노사가 상여금을 통상임금 산정에서 제외하기로 합의하였음에도, 근로자인 원고가 그 합의의 무효를 주장하며 추가임금을 청구하는 것이 신의칙에 반하는지 여부

(3) 판결:
① 이 사건 회사의 임금산정기간인 1개월을 초과한 2개월마다 지급되더라도

---
[64] 대법원 2013. 12. 18. 선고 2012다89399 판결.

Chapter 2 Statutory Wages

(every two months during each period of wage payment), this amount has satisfied the requirement of periodic payment, as it was paid periodically. Also, since whether or not the payment was made, and the amount of the payment had already been determined uniformly for all employees, the bonus qualifies as uniform and fixed. As the bonus payment varies according to the particular service period (as of two months), it could be misunderstood that there is no uniformity or it could incorrectly be regarded as money not previously determined. However, in considering it in the situation of overtime work (when the ordinary wage needs to be calculated), whether the employees concerned had served two months or not was already determined. As those who resigned received their bonus in proportion to the number of days they worked, the bonus is recognized as uniform and fixed. As explained above, those on leave were treated differently, due to their extraordinary situations, and so it is not an obstacle to consider that payment ordinary wage. Accordingly, the regular bonus in this case shall be included in ordinary wage.

② A labor contract which establishes working conditions that do not meet the standards provided for in the Labor Standards Act shall be null (Article 15 of the Labor Standards Act). Accordingly, even though the employer and the union agreed to exclude the regular bonus as legally included in ordinary wage, this mutual agreement is invalid as it is in violation of the Labor Standards Act. As the above agreement is invalid, it is a principle that the employer shall recalculate the overtime work allowance, adding the wages included in legal ordinary wage, and that the employee can apply for retroactive payment for the variance from the amount already paid. However, this retroactive claim can be valid only for the amount payable for the past three years.

2. Second case (Various allowances consistently provided are considered part of the ordinary wage)[65]

(1) Background and controversial points: Whether the amount of kimchi bonus should be determined based on whether it is part of ordinary wage; Whether Lunar New Year and Chuseok (Korean Thanksgiving) bonuses, summer leave bonuses, gift allowances, birthday allowances, individual pension premium subsidies, group insurance, etc., which were paid to incumbent employees as of a particular time period, are included in ordinary wage.

(2) Court ruling: Even though there is a possibility that the above bonuses etc., which were paid only to those in active service as of a particular time period,

---

[65] Supreme Court ruling on Dec. 18, 2013: 2012Da94643.

정기적으로 지급되었기 때문에 정기성 요건 충족한다. 또한 그 지급여부 및 지급액이 이미 모든 근로자에게 일률적으로 확정되어 있기 때문에 일률성과 고정성 인정된다. 근속기간에 따라 달리 지급되므로(2개월 기준) 일률성이 없거나 사전에 확정되어 있지 않은 임금으로 오인할 수 있으나, 초과근로를 하는 시점(통상임금 산정이 필요한 시점)에서 볼 때, 해당 근로자가 2개월의 근속기간을 채우고 있는지 여부는 이미 확정되어 있는 사실이고, 중간퇴직자에게도 근무일수에 비례하여 상여금을 지급하므로, 일률성과 고정성이 인정된다. 위에서 설명한 바와 같이, 휴직자에 대한 특별한 취급도 해당 개인의 특수한 사정을 고려한 것에 불과하므로, 통상임금 인정에 장애사유가 되지 않는다. 따라서 이 사건 정기상여금은 통상임금에 해당한다.
② 근로기준법이 정한 기준보다 낮은 임금 등 불리한 근로조건 계약은 무효(근로기준법 제15조 참조)이다. 따라서 법률상 통상임금에 해당하는 정기상여금 등의 임금을 통상임금에서 제외하기로 노사가 합의하였다 하더라도 위 합의는 근로기준법에 위반되어 무효이다. 위와 같은 합의가 무효이므로, 법률상 통상임금에 해당하는 임금을 통상임금 산정에 포함시켜 다시 초과근로수당을 계산한 다음, 소급하여 이미 지급받은 것과의 차액을 추가임금으로 청구할 수 있다. 다만, 사용자가 소멸시효 항변을 할 경우 최종 3년분만 인정 가능하다.

2. 제2판결 임금사건 (고정적 지급하는 각종수당은 통상임금)[65]

(1) 주요 사실관계 및 쟁점: 지급 직전 노사협의를 통해 액수를 정하기로 한 김장보너스의 통상임금 해당 여부. 특정 시점에 재직 중인 근로자에게만 지급하기로 한 것으로 볼 여지가 있는 설·추석 상여금, 하기휴가비, 선물비, 생일자지원금, 개인연금지원금, 단체보험료 등의 통상임금 해당 여부
(2) 판결: 이 사건 회사의 설·추석 상여금, 하기휴가비, 선물비, 생일자지원금, 개인연금지원금, 단체보험료 등은 특정 시점에 재직 중인 근로자에게만 지급하기로 한 것으로 볼 여지가 있음에도 불구하고, 이에 대한

---

[65] 대법원 2013. 12. 18. 선고, 2012다94643 판결.

may be seen as ordinary wage, the subordinate judicial ruling that considers them as ordinary wages is overturned as being incorrect.

3. The Supreme Court's Judgment criteria

(1) The concept of ordinary wage

Ordinary wage is the wage determined to be paid uniformly when contractual labor service is provided. All allowances which legally qualify as ordinary wage shall be included in ordinary wage regardless of the title of the allowance. It is recognized as the basic wage when calculating additional wages for extended work, night-time and holiday work, allowance replacing advance notice of dismissal, and the unused annual leave allowance. Additional wages under the Labor Standards Act shall be 150%, calculated by adding 50% of ordinary wage.

(2) Criteria for inclusion in ordinary wage

① **Requirements of ordinary wage:**

Since ordinary wage becomes the basic wage used to calculate additional wages, it should be considered financial remuneration reflecting the value of labor service provided ordinarily for contractual working hours in accordance with the employment contract (remuneration for labor). Accordingly, the additional wages paid for special work provided, and not for assigned work as per the employment contract, shall not be considered ordinary wage. In addition, this ordinary wage must have been determined before providing actual overtime work. The reason for this is that the previously determined ordinary wage calculation shall be used immediately when the overtime work is actually provided. Requirements of the ordinary wage shall be comprised of all three components: ① periodicity; ② uniformity, and ③ fixedness.

② **Requirement of periodicity:**

> [Regular bonuses] Employees are paid their ordinary wage once a month in return for work, but their regular bonus is paid either every two months, once per quarter, or once a year, depending on the company. These bonuses are regarded as having a character of periodicity if they are paid

추가심리 없이 이를 통상임금으로 인정한 원심은 심리가 미진하므로 파기한다.

3. 대법원 판결의 구체적 설명

(1) 통상임금의 개념
　통상임금이란 근로계약에서 정한 근로를 제공하면 확정적으로 지급되는 임금이다. 명칭과 관계없이 통상임금의 법적인 요건을 갖추면 모두 통상임금에 해당한다. 통상임금은 연장·야간·휴일 근로에 대한 가산임금, 해고예고수당 및 연차휴가수당 등을 산정하는 기준임금이 된다. 근로기준법상 초과근로수당은 통상임금에 50%를 가산한 150%이다.

(2) 통상임금의 요건
① 통상임금의 개념적 징표와 요건
　　　통상임금은 초과근로수당 산정 등을 위한 기초임금이므로, 근로자가 근로계약에 따른 정상적인 근로시간에 통상적으로 제공하는 근로의 가치를 금전적으로 평가한 것이어야 한다(소정근로의 대가). 따라서 근로계약에서 정한 근로가 아닌 특별한 근로를 제공하고 추가로 지급받은 임금은 통상임금 아니다. 또한 근로자가 실제로 초과근로를 제공하기 전에 미리 확정되어 있어야 한다. 그래야만 실제 초과근로가 제공될 때 사전에 확정된 통상임금을 기초로 하여 가산임금을 곧바로 산정할 수 있기 때문이다. 통상임금의 요건 → 근로의 대가로서의 임금이 ① 정기성, ② 일률성, ③ 고정성을 모두 갖추고 있어야 통상임금에 해당한다.
② 정기성 요건:

> [정기상여금의 경우] 보통 근로의 대가를 1개월에 한 번씩 월급으로 받지만, 정기상여금은 월급과 달리 2개월마다 지급하는 회사도 있고, 분기마다 지급하는 회사도 있고, 1년마다 지급하는 회사도 있을 수 있다. 이처럼 상여금이 월급과는 달리 2개월마다, 3개월마다, 6개월마다, 1년마다 등으로 지급이 되더라도 정기적으로만 지급이 되면 정기성을 갖춘

Chapter 2 Statutory Wages

> periodically, despite being paid every two months, every quarter, every half year or each year. Accordingly, the regular bonus normally paid for a period exceeding one month can be included into the ordinary wage.

This is a wage which is paid periodically for a previously-determined period. Even if it is paid for a period exceeding one month, if it is paid periodically for a regular period, it is included in ordinary wage.

③ **Requirement of uniformity:**

It is considered ordinary wage only when it is paid to all employees or all employees meeting identical conditions or criteria. Even though the bonus is not paid to all employees, but only to those who meet the identical conditions or criteria, it is considered to have a characteristic of uniformity. Accordingly, identical condition here means that it is not changeable from time to time, but is fixed. Even though there may be some restrictions concerning payment of a particular wage to an employee on leave, returning from leave, or under disciplinary measures, these restrictions are designed to consider the individual special circumstances, but cannot deny the uniformity of wages to normal employees maintaining a regular employment relationship. Therefore, this wage is included in ordinary wage.

As ordinary wage includes the concept evaluating the value of contractual work, the identical conditions or criteria shall be conditions related to work. Accordingly, the family allowance paid only to those employees with dependent family cannot be considered ordinary wage, as the payment condition is not related to work performed. Provided, that in cases where the company pays a fixed allowance under the description of family allowance to all employees, and then pays an additional amount to employees with a dependent family, the fixed amount that is paid to all employees uniformly as remuneration of work shall be included in ordinary wage, but the additionally-paid family allowance shall not.

④ **Requirement of fixedness:**

When an employee works overtime, whether or not the company has to pay shall be determined in advance, regardless of any achievements, performance or other additional conditions. In this case, such payment is considered as having a characteristic of fixedness. Fixed wage means the least amount to be guaranteed to be paid as remuneration for labor to the employee who provided that labor for

> 것이다. 따라서 1개월을 초과하는 기간마다 지급되는 것이 일반적인 정기상여금도 통상임금이 될 수 있다.

미리 정해진 일정한 기간마다 정기적으로 지급되는 임금이어야 한다. 어떤 임금이 1개월을 초과하는 기간마다 지급이 되더라도, 일정한 기간마다 정기적으로 지급되는 것이면 통상임금에 포함될 수 있다.

③ 일률성 요건:

「모든 근로자」 또는 「일정한 조건이나 기준에 달한 모든 근로자」에게 일률적으로 지급되어야 통상임금이 될 수 있다. 모든 근로자에게 지급되는 것은 아니더라도 일정한 조건이나 기준에 달한 근로자들에게는 모두 지급되는 것이면 일률성이 인정된다. 여기서 「일정한 조건」이란 시시때때로 변동되지 않는 고정적인 조건이어야 한다. 휴직자나 복직자 또는 징계대상자 등에 대하여 특정한 임금의 지급이 제한되어 있더라도, 이는 해당 근로자의 개인적인 특수성을 고려한 것일 뿐이므로, 정상적인 근로관계를 유지하고 있는 근로자에 대하여 그 해당 임금의 일률성이 부정되지는 아니한다. 즉 그 해당 임금도 통상임금이다. 통상임금이 소정근로의 가치를 평가한 개념이므로 일정한 조건 또는 기준은 근로와 관련된 조건이어야 한다. 따라서 부양가족이 있는 근로자에게만 지급되는 가족수당은 그 조건이 근로와 무관하므로 통상임금 아니다. 다만, 모든 근로자에게 기본금액을 가족수당 명목으로 지급하면서, 실제로 부양가족이 있는 근로자에게는 일정액을 추가로 지급하는 경우, 그 기본금액은 모든 근로자에게 일률적으로 지급되는 근로의 대가와 같으므로 통상임금에 해당한다. 그러나 추가 지급되는 가족수당은 통상임금 아니다.

④ 고정성 요건:

초과근로를 제공할 당시에, 그 지급 여부가 업적, 성과 기타 추가적인 조건과 관계없이 사전에 이미 확정되어 있는 것이어야 고정성이 인정된다. 따라서 고정적인 임금이란, 명칭을 묻지 않고, 소정근로시간을 근무한 근로자가 그 다음날 퇴직한다 하더라도 근로의 대가로 당연하고도 확정적으로 지급받게 되는 최소한의 임금을 의미한다. 일반적인 정기상여금의

contractual working hours, even if the employee resigned the next day, and regardless of what that wage may be called. A general regular bonus is considered as fixed as this is determined as regular payment. An allowance that is paid only upon satisfaction of an additional condition or any other allowance that is paid a varying amount according to whether or not it satisfies a certain condition shall not be considered ordinary wage as there is no fixedness. In this instance, an additional condition suggests an unclear condition for its achievement in considering it at the time of performing overtime work. Caution should be taken that the part of wage not affected by the condition shall be the ordinary wage as a fixed wage. The incentive pay conditional upon actual performance results is the most suitable example, and shall not be considered ordinary wage as its payment is not fixed. Even in this instance, as much as the least amount guaranteed for payment regardless of performance is fixed, that portion shall be included in ordinary wage.

(3) Judgment criteria:

In order to become ordinary wage designed to calculate additional wages for night-time, holiday, and extended work, in its evaluation for overtime work, the wage to be paid for the work stipulated in the employment contract shall be paid periodically for a certain time frame (periodicity), be paid uniformly to all employees or all employees corresponding to the identical conditions or criteria related to work (uniformity), and be previously determined to be paid regardless of achievement, performance results, or other additional conditions (fixedness). When the above conditions are satisfied, it is ordinary wage regardless of what it may be called.

4. Substantial applications

(1) Wage changed according to the length of service period (long-service allowance)

Service period is related to the employees' proficiency (long experience) and so corresponds to identical conditions or criteria related to work, and all employees meeting these conditions and criteria shall be paid uniformly. In considering overtime work, the employees' service period is not an unclear condition for either its period or its fulfillment. Therefore, as there is uniformity, this is ordinary wage.

경우 이미 정기적인 지급이 확정되어 있기 때문에 고정성이 인정된다. 근로제공 이외에 추가적인 조건이 충족되어야 지급되는 임금이나, 그 충족 여부에 따라 지급액이 달라지는 임금 부분은 고정성이 없어 통상임금 아니다. 여기서 「추가적인 조건이란」 초과근무를 하는 시점에 성취 여부가 불분명한 조건을 의미한다. 다만, 그 조건에 따라 달라지지 않는 부분만큼은 고정성이 있어 통상임금이 될 수 있음을 유의해야 한다. 실제 근무성적에 따라 지급여부나 지급액이 달라지는 성과급과 같은 임금이 고정성이 없어 통상임금이 될 수 없는 대표적인 경우이다. 다만, 이 경우에도 최소한도로 보장되는 부분만큼은 근무성적과 무관하게 누구나 받을 수 있는 고정적인 것이므로, 통상임금이다.

(3) 판단기준:

야간, 휴일, 연장근무 등 초과근로수당 산정 등의 기준이 되는 통상임금이 되기 위해서는, 초과근무를 하는 시점에서 판단해 보았을 때, 근로계약에서 정한 근로의 대가로 지급될 어떤 항목의 임금이, 일정한 주기에 따라 정기적으로 지급이 되고(정기성), 「모든 근로자」나 「근로와 관련된 일정한 조건 또는 기준에 해당하는 모든 근로자」에게 일률적으로 지급이 되며(일률성), 그 지급 여부가 업적이나 성과 기타 추가적인 조건과 관계없이 「사전에 이미 확정되어 있는 것」 (고정성)이어야 하는데, 이러한 요건을 갖추면 그 명칭과 관계없이 통상임금에 해당한다.

4. 구체적인 적용

(1) 근속기간에 따라 달라지는 임금(근속수당 등)

근속기간은 근로자의 숙련도와 밀접하게 관련되므로 일률성에 있어서 「근로와 관련된 일정한 조건 또는 기준」에 해당하고 그 조건 또는 기준을 충족한 모든 근로자에게 지급되는 임금이므로 일률성이 인정된다. 초과근로를 하는 시점에서 보았을 때, 그 근로자의 근속기간이 얼마나 되는지는 이미 확정되어 있는 사실이지, 성취 여부가 불확실한 조건이 아니다. 따라서 고정성 인정되므로 통상임금이다.

Chapter 2 Statutory Wages

(2) Wage variance based on the number of working days

This wage requires the additional condition of fulfillment of working days in addition to the provision of work, and so, as this wage is not determined at the time of providing overtime work, it cannot be a fixed amount, and therefore is not ordinary wage. That is, as the employee must complete the correct number of working days in order to get paid, the wage corresponding to this cannot be guaranteed to be paid.

(3) Wage to be paid only for incumbent employees during a particular period

This wage, because of its payment to incumbent employees regardless of work performed, is not paid in return for contractual work. In considering it at the time of performing overtime work, whether the employee is working in a particular period or not is not certain, and so there is no fixedness. If an employee resigns before a particular period, that employee cannot receive that particular allowance. Provided, that even if the employee resigned before the particular period, if they receives an amount calculated in proportion to the number of working days, the amount pro-rated for working days is the ordinary wage. Let us assume, for example, that a bonus is paid every even month, and an additional bonus is paid for the Chuseok and Lunar New Year holidays. The bonus paid every second month is paid on a pro-rated basis at the time of resignation, but traditional holiday bonuses are not paid to employees who resign before the particular traditional holiday. In this case, the bonus paid every two months is fixed, and is paid on a pro-rated basis of working days, regardless of a resignation prior to the payment day, and so this bonus is included in ordinary wage. However, as the traditional holiday bonus is not paid in situations where an employee resigns prior to those holidays, it is not included in ordinary wage.

(4) Wage paid according to special skills, experience, etc. (technology, qualifications, license allowances, etc.)

These allowances are paid to employees with special skills and experience related to work, corresponding to the identical conditions or criteria, which satisfies the requirement of uniformity. When considering it while the employee is providing overtime work, as the corresponding technology and particular experience are already determined, this can be considered as fixedness, and so is included in ordinary wage.

(2) 근무일수에 따라 달라지는 임금

근로제공 이외에 일정 근무일수를 채워야 한다는 추가적인 조건 달성이 필요하므로, 초과근로를 제공하는 시점에서 확정할 수 없는 불확실한 조건에 해당하므로 이는 고정성이 없어 통상임금이 아니다. 즉 근로자가 그 근무일수를 다 채워서 지급되기 때문에 그에 해당하는 임금을 받을 수 있을지 여부가 불확실하다.

(3) 특정시점에 재직 중인 근로자에게만 지급되는 임금

근로와 무관하게 재직만이 지급 조건이므로 소정근로의 대가로 보기 어렵다. 초과근로를 제공하는 시점에서 보았을 때, 그 근로자가 그 특정시점에 재직하고 있을지 여부는 불확실하기 때문에 고정성이 없다. 그 특정시점이 도래하기 전에 퇴직하면 당해 임금을 전혀 지급받지 못하기 때문이다. 다만, 근로자가 특정시점 전에 퇴직하더라도 그 근무일수에 비례한 만큼의 임금을 받을 수 있다면, 「근무일수에 비례하여 지급되는 한도에서는」 당연히 통상임금이다. 예컨대, 짝수 달마다 상여금을 지급하고, 이와 별도로 추석과 설날에 명절 상여금을 지급하기로 하였는데, 2달마다 지급되는 상여금은 퇴직 시 일할 계산하여 지급하기로 하였지만, 명절 상여금은 명절이 되기 전 퇴직한 사람에게는 지급하지 않기로 한 경우: 2달마다 지급되는 상여금은 지급여부가 확정되어 있고 상여금 지급시점에 퇴직하더라도 근무일수에 비례하여 근무일수만큼을 지급하기 때문에 통상임금이다. 그러나 명절상여금은 명절 지급일 이전에 퇴직하면 전혀 지급받지 못하기 때문에 통상임금이 아니다.

(4) 특수한 기술, 경력 등을 조건으로 하는 임금 (기술수당, 자격수당, 면허수당 등)

특수한 기술이나 경력이라는 「근로와 관련된 일정한 조건 또는 기준에 해당하는 모든 근로자」에게 일률적으로 지급이 되므로 일률성 요건 충족된다. 근로자가 초과근로를 제공하는 시점에서 보았을 때, 해당 기술의 보유나 특정한 경력의 구비 여부가 이미 확정되어 있기 때문에 고정성이 인정된다. 따라서 통상임금에 해당한다.

Chapter 2 Statutory Wages

(5) Wages depending on performance results

Incentives are the bonuses payable upon favorable evaluation of the performance results for the specific period worked, and by determining whether or not payment is due and the amount to be paid. At the time of providing overtime work, performance evaluation and follow-up incentive, plus the amount of payment, are not yet determined. Accordingly, as this payment has a condition that cannot be determined in advance and thereby not admissible as fixed, it is not ordinary wage. However, even if an employee receives the lowest scores in their work performance evaluation, and if a minimum is still paid, this minimum amount can be determined as the amount to be paid regardless of their lowest scores, and so this amount is included in ordinary wage, as it is fixed. In cases where the incentive is already determined to be paid this year based on the performance results of last year, as the payment and amount are already guaranteed at the time of working overtime, this incentive is fixed and belongs to the ordinary wage. Provided, that if the incentive that should have been paid last year was delayed only in its payment, this is not a fixed amount and is not included in ordinary wage.

[Examples]

(A) Work performance was scored as A, B, or C: those receiving the lowest grade, C, were paid 1 million won, those receiving a B were paid 2 million won, and those receiving an A were paid 3 million won. Therefore, a minimum of 1 million won was guaranteed, and this 1 million won shall be included in ordinary wage. The additional money paid for the higher grades are not ordinary wages.

(B) Work performance was scored as A, B, or C: those receiving the lowest grade, C, were paid nothing, those receiving a B were paid 2 million won, and those receiving an A were paid 3 million won. In this case, as those receiving a C will not be paid at all, the incentive bonuses are not included in ordinary wage.

---

(6) Amount of Kimchi bonus not confirmed

The collective agreement stipulates that 'a kimchi bonus is paid during Kimjang (the kimchi-making period), with the amount determined through labor-management consultation.' The amount was determined in this way just prior to the payment date. In this case, the amount to be paid cannot be confirmed at the time of overtime work performance, and therefore cannot be regarded as a fixed payment or included in ordinary wage.

(5) 근무실적에 좌우되는 임금

성과급은 특정기간 근무실적을 평가하여 이를 토대로 지급여부나 지급액이 결정되는 임금이다. 초과근로를 제공하는 시점에서 근무실적에 대한 평가와 그에 따른 성과급 지급여부 및 지급액이 확정되어 있지 아니하다. 따라서 사전에 확정될 수 없는 사실을 조건으로 하기 때문에 고정성이 인정되지 않아 통상임금이 아니다. 다만, 근무실적에서 최하등급을 받더라도 최소한의 일정액은 보장되는 경우라면, 그 최소한도의 금액만큼은 받는 것이 확정되어 있기 때문에 고정적인 임금으로 통상임금에 해당한다. 전년도 근무실적에 따라 당해 연도에 성과급의 지급 여부나 지급액을 정하는 경우에도, 초과 근무를 제공하는 시점인 당해 연도에 그 성과급의 지급 여부나 지급액수가 확정되어 있으므로 고정성이 있어 통상임금에 해당한다. 단, 전년도에 지급해야 할 것을 그 지급시기만 늦춘 것에 불과한 것일 경우에는 일반적인 성과급과 마찬가지 이므로, 고정성이 없어 통상임금이 아니다.

[구체적인 사례]
(1) 근무실적을 A, B, C로 평가하여 최하 C등급은 100만 원, B등급은 200만 원, A등급은 300만 원의 성과급을 지급하기로 하였다면 최소 100만 원은 보장되므로 100만 원만큼만 통상임금, 나머지는 통상임금이 아니다.
(2) 근무실적을 A, B, C로 평가하여 최하 C등급은 0원, B등급은 200만 원, A등급은 300만 원의 성과급을 지급하기로 하였다면, C등급을 받을 경우 성과급이 없기 때문에 위 회사의 성과급은 전부 통상임금이 아니다.

---

(6) 지급액수가 확정되어 있지 않은 김장보너스

단체협약상 「김장철에 김장보너스를 지급하며, 지급금액은 노사 협의하여 지급한다」라고 되어 있고, 매년 김장보너스 지급 직전에 노사협의를 통해 그 금액이 정해졌는데, 금액이 일정하지 않았던 경우 초과근로를 제공하는 시점에서, 노사협의에 따른 그 지급액수를 확정할 수 없으므로, 사전에 이미 확정되어 있는 임금이 아니다. 따라서 고정성 없으므로, 통상임금이 아니다.

Chapter 2 Statutory Wages

Type of Wage	Characteristics of Wage	Ordinary Wage or Not
Technology Allowance	Allowance paid to employees with technological or other qualifications (qualification, license allowances, etc.)	Ordinary wage
Length of Service Allowance	Wage which varies according to the length of service	Ordinary wage
Family Allowance	Varies by the number of dependents	Non-ordinary wage (not related to work)
Family Allowance	Paid regardless of the number of dependents	Ordinary wage (described as family allowance, but it is paid uniformly)
Incentive Bonus	Both payment and amount are determined by work performance	Non-ordinary wage (Condition is variable; not considered fixed)
Incentive Bonus	Minimum amount guaranteed	The lowest fixed amount is ordinary wage (paid uniformly and in a fixed amount)
Regular Bonus	Bonus (regular bonus) paid periodically	Ordinary wage
Regular Bonus	Temporary and/or irregular bonus paid at the employer's discretion (Incentive/Performance-based incentive)	Non-ordinary wage (not determined in advance or paid in a non-fixed amount)
Allowances paid at a particular period	Allowance paid to incumbent employees at a specific period (holiday bonus or vacation allowance)	Non-ordinary wage (Not remuneration for labor, not fixed)
Allowances paid at a particular period	If resignation takes effect before the payment day, the allowance is paid on a pro-rated basis.	Ordinary wage (pro-rated pay and fixed amount)

5. Claim of additional wage due to inclusion of regular bonus into ordinary wage, and application of good-faith principle

Any labor-management agreement that excludes regular bonus corresponding to the statutory ordinary wage in the calculation of ordinary wage is null and void due to it being a violation of the Labor Standards Act. However, both the company and the labor union have believed for a long time that regular bonuses are not included in

임금명목	임금의 특징	통상임금 해당여부
기술수당	기술이나 자격보유자에게 지급되는 수당(자격수당, 면허수당 등)	통상임금 ○
근속수당	근속기간에 따라 지급여부나 지급액이 달라지는 임금	통상임금 ○
가족수당	부양가족 수에 따라 달라지는 가족수당	통상임금 × (근로와 무관한 조건)
	부양가족 수와 관계없이 모든 근로자에게 지급되는 가족수당 분	통상임금 ○ (명목만 가족수당, 일률성 인정)
성과급	근무실적을 평가하여 지급여부나 지급액이 결정되는 임금	통상임금 × (조건에 좌우됨, 고정성 인정 ×)
	최소한도가 보장되는 성과급	그 최소한도 만큼만 통상임금 ○ (그 만큼은 일률적, 고정적 지급)
상여금	정기적인 지급이 확정되어 있는 상여금(정기상여금)	통상임금 ○
	기업실적에 따라 일시적, 부정기적, 사용자 재량에 따른 상여금 (경영성과분배금, 격려금, 인센티브)	통상임금 × (사전 미확정, 고정성 인정 ×)
특정시점 재직 시에만 지급되는 금품	특정시점에 재직 중인 근로자만 지급받는 금품(명절귀향비나 휴가비의 경우 그러한 경우가 많음)	통상임금 × (근로의 대가 ×, 고정성 ×)
	특정시점 되기 전 퇴직 시에는 근무일수 비례하여 지급되는 금품	통상임금 ○ (근무일수 비례하여 지급되는 한도에서는 고정성 ○)

5. 정기상여금의 통상임금 포함에 따른 추가임금 청구와 신의칙 적용

 법률상 통상임금에 해당하는 정기상여금 등을 통상임금 산정에서 제외하기로 하는 노사합의는 근로기준법에 위반되므로 무효이다. 그러나 '정기상여금'에 있어서, 노사가 그 간의 사회적 인식과 근로관행에 따라 통상임금에 해당하지

ordinary wages, according to social recognition and working practices, and have agreed to exclude them from the calculation of ordinary wages, determining wage increases and other working conditions on the basis of that belief. ① When the company and the labor union agree to wage increases, the increase is generally determined as based on total wage, not the detailed components of the wage, within the company's labor cost limits. ② If the company and the labor union had been aware that the regular bonus was included in ordinary wages, the company may have changed other conditions and striven to adjust the amount to maintain the previously agreed-upon wage level. ③ If the employees are able to apply for additional wages, claiming that the non-inclusion of regular bonus into the ordinary wage is null and void, the fact remains that they have already received all the wage increases in accordance with the collective agreement between the company and the union for those days, and this would allow them to receive additional wages, exceeding the company's labor cost limits as a result. This would result in unexpected, excessive costs to the company, leading to severe managerial difficulties, which cannot be acceptable in light of the notion of justice and equity. In this type of situation, the employees' claim is not granted due to it being a violation of the good-faith principle. That is, in this case, the employees cannot retroactively claim a recalculated overtime work allowance based on regular bonuses being included in ordinary wage.

II-2. Precedents Following the Supreme Court's Unanimous Decision on Ordinary Wages

A. Introduction

Ordinary wages refer to predetermined compensation agreed upon for the hours an employee is contractually obligated to work. It is mandated that the employment contract explicitly specify both ordinary wages and contractual working hours (Article 17 of the Labor Standards Act). Ordinary wages serve as the basis for calculating additional compensation for overtime work, holiday work, night work, and similar categories. To maintain ordinary wages at the lowest possible level, employers have introduced a system of annual regular bonuses. Consequently, the wage structure in our country consisted of 50% ordinary wages and 50% non-ordinary wages. The groundbreaking decision that significantly rectified this distorted wage structure was a unanimous Supreme Court ruling in 2013. The core

않는다고 신뢰하여 이를 통상임금 산정에서 제외하기로 합의하고 이를 토대로 임금총액과 다른 근로조건을 정하였다. ① 임금에 관한 노사 합의 시 기업의 한정된 수익 내에서 세부항목별이 아닌 임금총액을 기준으로 임금 등을 정하는 것이 일반적이고, ② 노사가 정기상여금이 통상임금에 해당함을 알았다면 다른 조건 등을 변경하여 합의된 종전 총액과 실질적인 차이가 없도록 조정하였을 것이며, ③ 만약 정기상여금이 통상임금 산정에서 제외된 부분만을 무효로 주장하면서 근로자가 추가임금을 청구할 수 있다면, 근로자는 임금협상 당시 노사가 서로 합의한 조건에 따른 임금을 모두 지급받으면서, 다른 한편으로는 그 합의된 조건이 무효임을 주장하며 기업의 한정된 수익을 넘는 추가임금을 지급받게 되는 결과가 된다. 이는 근로자의 추가청구로 인해 사용자 측이 예기치 못한 과도한 재정적 지출을 부담하게 됨으로써 기업에 중대한 경영상 어려움을 초래하게 되기 때문에 정의와 형평성 관념에 비추어 용인될 수 없다. 이러한 경우에 한해서는 근로자의 추가임금 청구가 신의성실의 원칙에 위반되어 허용될 수 없다. 이러한 경우 정기상여금을 통상임금 산정에 포함시켜 다시 계산한 통상임금을 기초로, 소급하여 초과근로수당 차액을 청구할 수가 없다.

II-2 통상임금 대법원 합의체 판결 이후 판례 경향

A. 개요

통상임금은 근로자가 소정근로시간에 근무한 대가로 받기로 한 사전적으로 약속된 임금이다. 근로계약 체결 시에도 반드시 통상임금과 소정근로시간을 명시하도록 되어 있다(근로기준법 제17조). 이는, 사전에 지급하기로 정해진 임금뿐만 아니라 연장근로, 휴일근로, 야간근로 등에 대한 가산 임금을 계산하기 위한 기준으로 삼고 있으므로 사용자는 통상임금의 최대한 낮은 수준을 유지하기 위해서 연단위로 지급하는 정기 상여금제도를 도입하였다. 그 결과 우리나라 임금은 50%의 통상임금과 50%의 비통상임금으로 구성되어 있다. 이렇게 왜곡된 임금 구조를 획기적으로 바로잡은 판결이 2013년 대법원

meaning of this decision can be summarized into two key points. Firstly, the decision established that regular bonuses paid at certain intervals exceeding one month as remuneration for work are considered part of ordinary wages. Secondly, any consensus reached among employers and employees to exclude certain wages, falling under ordinary wages according to the Labor Standards Act, from ordinary wages, is invalid.[66]

The Supreme Court's 2013 decision regarding ordinary wages has provided clear guidelines for the components and payment methods of ordinary wages. Nevertheless, disputes have arisen in practical application. Firstly, while it was ruled that regular bonuses paid on specific dates and only to incumbent employees (not those who resigned before those specific payment dates) and not settled on a daily basis upon resignation should not be considered ordinary wages, subsequent judgments contradict this. Secondly, there is ambiguity concerning whether retroactively claiming an allowance calculated as a new ordinary wage when a fixed bonus is included in ordinary wages contradicts the principle of good faith.

In connection with these issues, I would like to examine the criteria for judgments related to ordinary wages only paid to incumbent employees and delve into specific application of the good faith principle concerning retroactive claims for allowances.

B. Criteria for Determining Payment only for Incumbent Employees

The 2013 Supreme Court decision on ordinary wages established that wages designated to be paid only to incumbent employees at specific points in time, regardless of whether they have actually worked their regular hours, become eligibility criteria for receiving wages at those particular points in time. Such wages are generally withheld from individuals who were previously engaged in labor but were not in active service at those specific points in time, while individuals in active service at those specific points in time typically receive them without regard to the nature of their previous work. In cases where wages are paid under such conditions, it is difficult to consider them as compensation for contractual working hours worked. Even if an employee provides labor, if they resign before the arrival of that specific point in time, they will not receive the corresponding wages. Therefore, whether the payment condition will be met at the time when the employee provides labor is uncertain, suggesting little connection to work already provided.

Hence, the courts have determined that such payments only to incumbent employees are not considered ordinary wages. However, it was noted that if bonuses

---

[66] Supreme Court ruling on Dec. 18, 2013, 2012Da89399 En Banc Unanimous Decision.

합의체 판결이다. 이 판결의 핵심은 두 가지이다. 첫째, 근로의 대가로 1개월을 초과하는 일정기간마다 지급하는 정기상여금은 통상임금에 해당된다. 둘째, 근로기준법 상 통상임금에 속하는 임금을 통상임금에서 제외하기로 한 합의는 효력이 없다.[66]

위 판결은 통상임금의 구성항목이나 지급방법에 대해 명확한 기준을 정하여 주었다. 그런데도 현실에서는 서로 다툼이 되는 사례가 간혹 발생하고 있다. 살펴보면, 정기상여금을 퇴직 시 정산하지 않고 재직자에 한해 정기 상여금을 지급하는 경우에는 통상임금으로 볼 수 없다고 판결하였지만, 후속 판결에서 이 기준에 반하는 판결이 다수 나오고 있다. 다음으로, 고정 상여금이 통상임금으로 포함된 경우, 새로운 통상임금으로 계산된 수당을 소급하여 청구하는 것이 신의성실 원칙(신의칙)에 반하는지에 대한 기준이 모호하다는 것이다.

관련한 재직자 기준에 대한 판례를 살펴보고, 소급하여 청구한 수당에 대한 신의칙 효력에 대해 구체적으로 살펴보고자 한다.

B. 재직자 요건 판단기준

2013년 대법원 합의체판결은 근로자가 소정근로를 했는지 여부와는 관계없이 지급일 기타 특정 시점에 재직 중인 근로자에게만 지급하기로 정해져 있는 임금은 그 특정 시점에 재직 중일 것이 임금을 지급받을 수 있는 자격 요건이 된다. 그러한 임금은 기왕에 근로를 제공했던 사람이라도 특정 시점에 재직하지 않는 사람에게는 지급하지 아니하는 반면, 그 특정 시점에 재직하는 사람에게는 기왕의 근로 제공 내용을 묻지 아니하고 모두 이를 지급하는 것이 일반적이다. 그와 같은 조건으로 지급되는 임금이라면, 그 임금은 소정근로에 대한 대가의 성질을 가지는 것이라고 보기 어렵다. 근로자가 임의의 날에 근로를 제공하더라도 그 특정 시점이 도래하기 전에 퇴직하면 당해 임금을 전혀 지급받지 못하여 근로자가 임의의 날에 연장야간휴일 근로를 제공하는 시점에서 그 지급조건이 성취될지 여부는 불확실하므로, 고정성도 결여한 것으로 보아야 한다. 라고 하여 그 재직자에게 지급하는 경우에는 통상임금이 아니라고 판단하였다. 다만, 근로자가 특정 시점 전에 퇴직하더라도 그 근무

---

[66] 대법원 2013. 12. 18. 선고 2012다89399 전원합의체 판결.

are paid in proportion to the number of days worked even if an employee resigns before a specific point in time, there is no substantial difference from wages paid for each day worked. Therefore, in cases where wages are paid proportionally to the number of days worked, the absence of connection to work already provided is not considered a factor.

Normally, regarding regular bonuses, if an employee resigns before the wage payment date, a daily settlement is calculated and paid. However, holiday bonuses or summer vacation allowances, for instance, are often intended to be paid on specific dates, and, therefore, they are not paid if an employee resigns before those dates. Thus, the criteria for payments only to incumbent employees should be limited to such special bonuses.

Nevertheless, precedents have applied the incumbent employee criteria even to regular bonuses and have not recognized them as ordinary wages if the employee is no longer actively employed at the time of payment. Fortunately, recent precedents have ruled that the incumbent employee criteria do not have any bearing on the determination of ordinary wages for regular bonuses. In other words, the argument that regular bonuses, which are regularly, uniformly, and consistently paid as remuneration for labor, should be excluded from ordinary wages solely based on the incumbent employee criterion at the time of resignation is considered erroneous. Several such cases are pending before the Supreme Court's decisions, awaiting a final decision.[67] Consequently, there is an urgent need for clear guidelines at this juncture.

C. Precedents Recognized as Ordinary Wages for Regular Bonuses Despite Payment only to Incumbent Employees

1. Supreme Court Decision dated November 10, 2022, Case No. 2022da252578[68]

In this case, the defendant stipulated in salary regulations that regular bonuses would be paid "only to those who remain employed at the time of payment." Accordingly, they paid regular bonuses to those who were still employed at the time of payment. The regular bonuses, paid regularly and continuously to employees at a rate of 600% annually, can be considered as definitively paid as long as the employees provide regular labor. Hence, it is reasonable to categorize them as ordinary wages, which are fixed, uniform, and consistently paid. Additionally,

---

[67] Seoul High Court Decision 2016na2087702 is awaiting a Supreme Court (2019da244942); Busan High Court Decision 2018na55282 is awaiting a Supreme Court (2019다289525) decision.

[68] Supreme Court Decision on November 10, 2022, Case No. 2022da252578; Court of Original Jurisdiction: Seoul High Court Decision on May 4, 2022, Case No. 2019na2037630. Wage Claim Case by the Financial Supervisory Service.

일수에 비례한 만큼의 임금이 지급되는 경우에는 앞서 본 매 근무일마다 지급되는 임금과 실질적인 차이가 없으므로, 근무일수에 비례하여 지급되는 한도에서는 고정성이 부정되지 않는다.고 하였다.

일반적으로 정기상여금의 경우에도 퇴직하는 시기가 임금 지급일 이전인 경우 일일 정산한다. 그러나 명절상여금이나 여름휴가비 등은 특정한 날에 지급하는 목적성이 있기 때문에 그 해당하는 날 이전에 퇴직하는 경우에는 지급하지 않는 경우가 많다. 따라서 재직일 기준은 이러한 특별 상여금에 한정되어 판단하여야 할 것이다.

그러나 판례는 재직자 기준을 적용하여 지급일 현재 재직하지 않는 경우 정기 상여금에 대해 통상임금으로 인정하지 않고 있다. 다행스럽게도 최신 판례는 정기 상여금의 재직자 요건은 통상임금 판단에 있어 효력이 없다는 판결을 하고 있다. 즉, 정기 상여금이 근로의 대가로 정기적, 일률적, 고정적으로 지급되고 있지만, 퇴직 시 재직자 요건 하나 때문에 통상임금에서 제외된다는 것은 잘못된 판단이라는 지적이다. 이와 관련한 여러 판례들이 대법원으로 넘겨져서 최종판결을 기다리고 있다.[67] 이에 대한 명확한 기준이 필요하다.

C. 퇴직 시 재직자 기준이 있음에도 통상임금으로 인정한 사례

1. 대법원 2022. 11. 10. 선고 2022다252578 판결 (금융감독원)[68]

피고는 급여규정에서 정기상여금은 지급기준일 현재 재직 중에 있는 자에 한하여 지급한다고 규정하고 있다. 이에 따라 지급기준일 현재 재직 중에 있는 자에 한하여 정기상여금을 지급하였다. 연 600%의 지급률에 따라 근로자에게 정기적계속적으로 지급된 정기상여금은 소정근로를 제공하기만 하면 그 지급이 확정된 것이라고 볼 수 있으므로 정기적일률적으로 고정 지급되는 통상임금에 해당한다고 봄이 타당하다. 정기상여금의 금액, 지급방법, 지급실태 등에 전체 임금에서 이 사건 정기상여금이 차지하는 비중이 매우 높은 점을

---

[67] 서울고등법원 2016나2087702 판결은 대법원(2019다244942)에, 부산고등법원 2018 나55282 판결은 대법원 (2019다289525)에서 각각 대법원 판결을 기다리고 있다.
[68] 대법원 2022. 11. 10. 선고 2022다252578 판결: 심리불속행기각, 원심: 서울고등법원 2022. 5. 4. 선고 2019나2037630 판결. 금융감독원 임금청구사건.

Chapter 2 Statutory Wages

considering the significant proportion that these regular bonuses occupy of total wages, including factors such as the amount, payment method, and payment frequency, it becomes evident that these regular bonuses are not merely a form of compound fringe benefits, indemnification, or gratuitous compensation, nor are they remuneration for specific periods of service. Instead, from the employee's perspective, they can be regarded as wages that are expected to be received as a fundamental and definitive compensation, akin to the base salary, as long as the employee provides regular labor.

2. Seoul High Court Decision dated December 2, 2020, Case No. 2016na2032917

In this case, the annual amount of the bonus was determined to be 800% of the monthly base salary, and such an amount was firmly established as remuneration for annual regular labor. Therefore, this bonus can be considered a fixed wage that is granted to employees simply for providing annual regular labor, irrespective of the achievement of additional conditions. Furthermore, the "incumbent employee criterion" in this case, even if it results in unpaid or excess amounts when compared to calculations made for employees who provided regular labor for a full year but resigned prematurely, is merely a matter of calculation for the sake of convenience. It does not negate the nature of this bonus as a fixed wage. In particular, even when assessing connection to labor provided, the exceptional circumstance of "resignation," which occurs only once during the employment period, cannot be used as a basis for negating such connection.

3. Seoul High Court Decision dated December 18, 2018, Case No. 2017na2025282 (Transferred to the Supreme Court's Unanimous Decision Process (2019da204876)) [69]

Withholding payment for labor already provided, even when an employer unilaterally adds an incumbent employee condition to regular bonuses and an employee resigns before the payment date, constitutes a unilateral withholding of accrued wages and cannot be considered valid. Furthermore, even in cases where the incumbent employee condition is stipulated in valid employment rules or individual employment contracts, withholding payment for the portion corresponding to the labor already provided is invalid as it amounts to preemptively waiving the wages that should be received as compensation for labor that has already been provided.

4. Seoul High Court Decision dated May 14, 2019, Case No. 2016na2087702 (Transferred to the Supreme Court Grand Bench (2019da244942)) [70]

---

[69] Seoul High Court Decision on December 18, 2018, Case No. 2017na2025282: Wage Claim Lawsuit by SeAH Besteel

더하여 보면, 본 상여금은 단순히 복리후생적·실비변상적·은혜적 성격 또는 사기진작을 위한 금원이거나 특정 시점의 재직에 대한 대가로 지급되는 금원으로 볼 수는 없고, 기본급과 마찬가지로 소정근로를 제공하기만 하면 그에 대한 기본적이고 확정적인 대가로 당연히 수령을 기대하는 임금에 해당한다고 볼 수 있다.

2. 서울고등법원 2020. 12. 2. 선고 2016나2032917 판결

이 사건 상여금의 연간 지급액이 월 기본급의 800%로 확정되어 있고, 지급률은 연간 소정근로의 대가인바, 본 상여금은 근로자가 연간 소정근로를 제공하기만 하면 추가 조건의 성취 여부와 관계없이 당연히 지급되는 임금으로써 고정적인 임금에 해당한다. 또한, 이 사건 '재직자 요건'으로, 근로자가 1년의 소정근로를 제공하지 못한 채 중도 퇴직하는 경우, 계산상 편의를 위해 미지급 또는 초과지급 금액이 있더라도 추가 정산하지 않기로 한 것에 불과해, 이 사건 상여금이 갖고 있는 고정적인 임금의 성질을 부정할 수 없다. 즉, 근로기간 중 단 한번 발생하는 '퇴직'이라는 예외적인 사정을 근거로 한 고정성을 부정할 수 없다.

3. 서울고등법원 2018. 12. 18. 선고 2017나2025282 판결 (대상판결은 대법원 전원합의체 (2019다204876)에 회부됨) (세아베스틸)[69]

사용자가 정기상여금에 일방적으로 재직자조건을 부가하여 지급일 전에 퇴직하는 근로자에 대하여 이미 제공한 근로에 상응하는 부분까지도 지급하지 아니하는 것은 기발생 한 임금에 대한 일방적인 부지급을 선언하는 것으로써 그 유효성을 인정할 수 없다. 나아가 유효한 취업규칙이나 개별적 근로계약 등에 재직자조건이 규정된 경우에도 이미 제공한 근로에 상응하는 부분을 지급하지 아니하는 범위에서는 근로제공의 대가로 지급받아야 할 임금을 사전에 포기하게 하는 것으로써 이는 무효이다.

4. 서울고등법원 2019. 5. 14. 선고 2016나2087702 판결 (대상판결은 대법원 (2019다244942)에 회부됨) (기술보증기금)[70]

---

[69] 서울고등법원 2018. 12. 18. 선고 2017나2025282 판결. 세아베스틸 임금청구소송

Regular fixed payments of a fixed amount continuously and periodically paid constitute compensation for labor, even if the payment period is on a multi-month basis: it is merely an accumulation of compensation for labor over those months. Even if an employee resigns before the regular fixed payment date, they should naturally be entitled to receive the payment corresponding to the labor they have actually provided. However, not paying basic performance bonuses and evaluation performance bonuses based on the "incumbent employee criterion" is difficult to validate as it unilaterally withholds payment for labor already provided. This practice also makes it difficult to recognize the effectiveness of preemptively waiving accrued wages. In this particular case, given that 1) basic performance bonuses and evaluation performance bonuses were paid alternately on a bi-monthly basis, 2) the amount exceeded 50% of the monthly base salary, and 3) they were paid regardless of evaluation results, from the employee's perspective, these payments were considered as fundamental and definitive compensation, provided they fulfilled their labor obligations.

D. Precedents Where Regular Bonuses Paid only to Incumbent Employees Were Not Recognized as Ordinary Wages

1. Supreme Court Decision dated April 9, 2020, Case No. 2017da4638

The defendant annually paid the plaintiffs an 800% bonus, consisting of 100% of their ordinary wages in even-numbered months and during major holidays such as New Year's and Chuseok. The salary regulations specified that "bonuses shall be paid only to those who remain employed at the time of payment," and in practice, only those employees still employed at the time of payment received bonuses. The defendant calculated ordinary wages based on the collective agreement, employment rules, etc., excluding fixed bonuses, and paid statutory allowances such as overtime pay, holiday pay, special pay for extra hours, and annual leave pay, among others, on the basis of the agreed-upon ordinary wages. The defendant paid fixed bonuses only to employees still employed at the time of wage payment and did not pay bonuses to those who resigned before the payment date. Therefore, since this bonus was paid only to employees still employed at a specific point in time, it cannot be considered fixed.

2. Supreme Court Decision dated September 21, 2017, Case No. 2016da15150 (Hyundai Steel) [71]

---

[70] Seoul High Court Decision on May 14, 2019, Case No. 2016na2087702: Wage Claim Lawsuit by the Korea Technology Finance Corporation (KTFC).

고정적인 금액이 계속적·정기적으로 지급되는 형태의 정기 고정급은 근로의 대가인 임금에 해당하고 그 지급기간이 수개월 단위인 경우에도 이는 근로의 대가를 수개월간 누적해 후불하는 것에 불과하다. 정기 고정급 지급일 이전에 퇴직하는 근로자라고 하더라도 자신이 실제로 제공한 근로에 상응하는 정기 고정급에 대해서는 당연히 그 지급을 구할 수 있어야 한다. 그런데, '재직자 요건'을 이유로 후불적 임금에 해당하는 기본성과급과 평가성과급을 지급하지 않는 것은, 이미 제공한 근로에 대한 대가에 대한 부지급을 일방적으로 선언하는 것으로 그 유효성을 인정하기 어렵고, 이는 기발생된 임금을 사전에 포기하도록 하는 것으로써 그 효력을 인정하기 어렵다. 본 사안에서 ① 기본성과급과 평가성과급이 격월 주기로 교차로 지급되는 점, ② 그 액수가 월 기본급의 50% 이상에 이르는 점, ③ 기본성과급과 평가성과급이 평가결과에 상관없이 지급됐던 이상, 근로자로서는 근로를 제공하기만 하면 그에 대한 기본적이고 확정적인 대가로써 지급하였다.

D. 퇴직 시 재직자 요건 때문에 통상임금을 불인정한 사례

1. 대법원 2020. 4. 9. 선고 2017다4638 판결

피고는 원고들에게 매년 짝수 월과 설, 추석에 각 통상임금의 100%씩 총 800% 상여금을 지급하였다. 급여규정에서 상여금은 지급일 현재 재직 중에 있는 자에 한하여 지급한다고 명시되어 있었고, 실제로 지급일 당시 재직 중인 사람만 상여금을 지급 받았다. 피고는 원고들에게 이 사건 단체협약, 취업규칙 등에서 정한 바에 따라 고정 상여금을 제외한 기본급, 제 수당 만을 반영하여 통상임금을 산정하였고, 약정통상임금을 기초로 시간외근무수당, 휴일근무수당, 특근수당, 연차수당 등의 법정수당을 지급하였다. 피고는 고정 상여금을 임금 지급일 현재 재직하고 있는 자에게만 지급하였고, 임금지급일 이전에 퇴직하는 경우에는 상여금을 지급하지 않았다. 따라서 이 사건 상여금은 특정 시점 재직 자에 한해서 지급되었기 때문에 고정성을 인정할 수 없다.

2. 대법원 2017. 9. 21. 산고 2016다15150 판결 (현대제철)[71]

---

70) 서울고등법원 2019. 5. 14. 선고 2016나2087702 판결, 기술보증기금 임금청구소송

The collective agreement in this case stipulated that "the company shall pay an annual bonus of 750% to all employees still employed at the time the bonus is paid." In practice, bonuses were paid only to employees whose employment relations had not terminated at the time of the bonus payment date, and no bonuses were paid to employees who resigned before that date. Consequently, it can be acknowledged that the defendant was required to pay the bonuses only to employees that were still employed by the bonus payment date, making it uncertain whether the payment condition would be met at the time when the employee provides labor. Therefore, there is no clear connection to labor provided and cannot be considered ordinary wages.

3. Supreme Court Decision dated September 26, 2017, Case No. 2017da232020 (ThyssenKrupp Elevator) [72]

The defendant company had been paying employees an 800% bonus, totaling 100% of their base salary and allowances for even-numbered months, as well as on the Chuseok and New Year holidays, in accordance with a collective agreement. However, when calculating ordinary wages, the defendant excluded this bonus. The defendant company did not pay this bonus to employees who were not employed at the time the bonus was paid, as employees were required to remain employed on the payment date. Since this bonus was conditional on the employee still being employed on the payment date, it cannot be considered part of ordinary wages due to the absence of both compensation for regular labor and connection to labor provided.

E. Recognition and Non-recognition of Retroactive Claims for Allowances

1. Principles for determining good faith

The court's position is that in cases where a good faith agreement between labor and management violates the mandatory provisions of the Labor Standards Act, the agreement is of no effect. In other words, the standards set by the Labor Standards Act are minimum standards, so mandatory provisions should take precedence over good faith agreements. However, exception can be made when a company is facing financial difficulties. In such cases, good faith agreements may be recognized.

(1) Supreme Court Decision dated March 11, 2021, Case No. 2017da259513

When determining whether to apply good faith agreements over mandatory

---

[71] Busan High Court Decision on February 17, 2016, Case No. 2015na3044 (Appeal); Supreme Court Decision on September 21, 2017, Case No. 2016da15150 (Appeal Dismissed) (Hyundai Steel).

[72] Seoul Southern District Court Decision on April 27, 2017, Case No. 2016na60674 (Trial Court); Supreme Court Decision on September 26, 2017, Case No. 2017da232020 (ThyssenKrupp Elevator Korea Wage Claim Case).

이 사건 단체협약은 회사는 상여금 지급일 현재 재직 중인 전 종업원에게 연 750%의 상여금을 지급한다고 정하고 있다. 실제로 상여금 지급기준일에 재직 중인 근로자들에게만 상여금을 지급하고 지급일 이전에 퇴직한 근로자들에게는 해당 월의 상여금을 전혀 지급하지 않은 사실을 인정할 수 있다. 결국 피고의 상여금은 임의의 날에 연장근로를 제공하더라도 상여금 지급일까지 재직하여야 한다는 추가적인 조건이 충족되어야 지급된 것으로 보이므로, 근로자가 근로를 제공하는 시점에서 그 지급조건이 성취될지 여부가 불확실하여 고정성을 결여한 것으로서 통상임금에 해당된다고 볼 수 없다.

3. 대법원 2017. 9. 26. 선고 2017다232020 판결 (티센크루프 엘리베이트)[72]

피고 회사가 단체협약에 따라 근로자들에게 짝수 달과 설, 추석에 기본급과 수당의 100%씩 합계 연 800%의 이 사건 상여금을 지급하여 왔으나, 통상임금의 산정에서는 이 사건 상여금을 제외하여 산정하였다. 피고 회사는 퇴직자가 상여금 지급일에 재직하지 않은 직원들에게는 이 사건 상여금을 지급하지 아니 하였다. 이 사건 상여금은 지급일에 근로자가 재직할 것을 요건으로 하였기 때문에 이 사건 상여금은 소정근로에 대한 대가성과 고정성이 인정되지 않으므로 통상임금에 포함된다고 할 수 없다.

E. 소급 청구한 수당에 대한 신의칙 인정과 불인정 사례

1. 신의측 관련 판단기준

법원은 노사간 합의에 의한 신의칙이 근로기준법의 강행규정을 위반하는 경우에는 효력이 없다는 입장이다. 즉, 근로기준법에서 정한 기준은 최저기준이므로 강행규정이 신의측 보다 우선적으로 적용되어야 한다는 것이다. 다만, 예외적으로 회사의 재정상 어려움 있는 경우에는 신의칙을 인정하고 있다.

(1) 대법원 2021. 3. 11. 선고 2017다259513 판결

근로관계를 규율하는 강행규정보다 신의칙을 우선하여 적용할 것인지를

---

[71] 부산고등법원 2016. 2. 17. 선고 2015나3044 판결 (상고), 대법원 2017. 9. 21. 산고 2016다15150 판결 (상고 기각): 현대제철 임금청구사건
[72] 서울남부지방법원 2017. 4. 27. 선고 2016나60674 판결(원심). 대법원 2017. 9. 26. 선고 2017다232020 판결. 티센크루프엘리베이트 코리아 임금청구사건

provisions that regulate labor relations, it is necessary to consider the legislative intent of the Labor Standards Act, which establish minimum standards for working conditions to ensure and improve the basic livelihood of workers. Moreover, companies are the ones responsible for running businesses, and the business situation can change frequently due to various economic and social factors both inside and outside the company. Rejecting additional statutory allowances claimed by employees based on the recalculation of ordinary wages, on the grounds that it would cause significant operational difficulties for the employer or jeopardize the company's existence, could effectively shift the business risks to employees. Therefore, the question of whether an employee's additional statutory allowance claim would cause significant operational difficulties for the employer or jeopardize the company's existence, in violation of good faith principles, should be assessed with caution and rigor.

(2) **Supreme Court Decision dated December 16, 2021, Case No. 2016da7975**

Whether an employee's additional statutory allowance claim based on the recalculation of ordinary wages causes significant operational difficulties for a company or jeopardizes its existence should be determined by considering multiple factors such as the size of the additional statutory allowance, the real wage increase resulting from payment of the additional statutory allowance, the rate of increase in ordinary wages, the company's net profit and its fluctuation, the available funds, total labor costs, revenue, the company's continuity and profitability, and overall trends in the industry to which the company belongs. Even if a company is temporarily facing operational difficulties, if the employer made reasonable and objective predictions regarding its operations, and there is a possibility of overcoming such operational difficulties in the future, good faith agreements should not be easily rejected to deny employees' claims for additional statutory allowances.

2. Cases recognizing good faith agreements

(1) **Supreme Court Decision dated July 9, 2020, Case No. 2015da71917 (GM Korea)**

In this case, the regular year-end bonus amounted to 700% of the monthly ordinary wages, and considering the overtime work routinely performed by production workers, the statutory allowances that the defendant would have to additionally bear based on the recalculation of wages significantly exceeded the

판단할 때에는 근로조건의 최저기준을 정하여 근로자의 기본적 생활을 보장향상시키고자 하는 근로기준법 등의 입법 취지를 충분히 고려할 필요가 있다. 또한 기업을 경영하는 주체는 사용자이고, 기업의 경영 상황은 기업 내외부의 여러 경제적·사회적 사정에 따라 수시로 변할 수 있으므로, 통상임금 재산정에 따른 근로자의 추가 법정수당 청구를 중대한 경영상의 어려움을 초래하거나 기업 존립을 위태롭게 한다는 이유로 배척한다면, 기업 경영에 따른 위험을 사실상 근로자에게 전가하는 결과가 초래될 수 있다. 따라서 근로자의 추가 법정수당 청구가 사용자에게 중대한 경영상의 어려움을 초래하거나 기업의 존립을 위태롭게 하여 신의칙에 위반되는지는 신중하고 엄격하게 판단하여야 한다.

(2) **대법원 2021. 12. 16. 선고 2016다7975 판결**

통상임금 재산정에 따른 근로자의 추가 법정수당 청구가 기업에 중대한 경영상의 어려움을 초래하거나 기업 존립을 위태롭게 하는지는 추가 법정수당의 규모, 추가 법정수당 지급으로 인한 실질임금 인상률, 통상임금 상승률, 기업의 당기순이익과 그 변동추이, 동원 가능한 자금의 규모, 인건비 총액, 매출액, 기업의 계속성·수익성, 기업이 속한 산업계의 전체적인 동향 등 기업운영을 둘러싼 여러 사정을 종합적으로 고려해서 판단해야 한다. 기업이 일시적으로 경영상의 어려움에 처하더라도 사용자가 합리적이고 객관적으로 경영 예측을 하였다면 그러한 경영상태의 악화를 충분히 예견할 수 있었고 향후 경영상 어려움을 극복할 가능성이 있는 경우에는 신의칙을 들어 근로자의 추가 법정수당 청구를 쉽게 배척해서는 안 된다.

2. 신의칙 인정 사례

(1) **대법원 2020. 7. 9. 선고 2015다71917 판결 (한국지엠)**

이 사건 정기상여금은 월 통상임금의 연 700%에 해당하고, 생산직 근로자들에게 상시적으로 이루어지는 초과근로까지 감안한다면 피고가 추가로 부담하게 될 법정수당은 임금협상 당시 노사가 협상의 자료로 삼은 법정수당의 범위를 현저히 초과한다. ① 피고의 당기순이익 누계액은 2008년부터 2010년까지가 -6,000여 억 원, 2008년부터 2014년까지가 -8,000여 억 원에 이른다. ② 2008년부터 2014년까지 피고의 부채비율은

range of statutory allowances used as reference during wage negotiations. The defendant's accumulated net profit was negative, reaching around minus KRW 6 trillion from 2008 to 2010 and minus KRW 8 trillion from 2008 to 2014. The defendant's debt ratio from 2008 to 2014 was significantly higher than that of similar companies, and the current ratio did not match that of similar companies. Additionally, the amount of borrowed funds exceeded KRW 2 trillion as of the end of 2014. Considering these circumstances, the plaintiff's claim for additional statutory allowances for the regular year-end bonus, calculated by including it as part of ordinary wages, would result in the pursuit of unexpected benefits far exceeding the agreed-upon wage level between labor and management. It would also impose an unforeseen financial burden on the defendant, potentially causing significant operational difficulties or endangering the defendant's existence. Therefore, the plaintiff's claim could not be allowed, as it would violate the principle of good faith.

(2) Supreme Court Decision dated July 9, 2020, Case No. 2017da7170 (SsangYong Motor)

If the year-end bonus were included in ordinary wages, the estimated additional amount that the defendant would have to pay to functional employees each year from 2010 to 2012 would be around KRW 20 billion. The defendant had been incurring significant losses since 2008, and around 2009, the defendant's very existence was threatened. Starting in 2009, labor and management (the defendant) agreed to various cost-cutting measures, such as freezing the basic wages of the defendant's employees, reducing bonuses, and not paying certain welfare benefits, in order to overcome the defendant's crisis. Considering these circumstances, if the plaintiff's claim for statutory allowances related to bonuses and retirement payments were granted, the plaintiffs would gain unexpected benefits that would exceed the originally agreed-upon wage level, while the defendant would face unforeseen financial expenses, potentially leading to significant operational difficulties. Therefore, the plaintiffs' claim was in violation of the principle of good faith.

3. Cases where an agreement was not recognized as being in good faith

(1) Supreme Court Decision dated March 11, 2021, Case No. 2017da259513 (Kumho Tire)

If the bonuses in this case were included in ordinary wages, the ordinary wages

동종업체에 비해 상당히 높고, 유동비율은 동종업체에 미치지 못하며, 차입금 규모도 2014년 연말 기준 2조 원을 초과하고 있다. 매년 지출하는 경상연구개발비가 평균 6,000여 억 원에 이르러 2014년 연말 기준 보유 현금을 이 사건 추가 법정수당 지급에 사용할 경우 부채변제나 연구개발이 중단되거나 심각한 유동성 위기를 겪을 가능성이 높다. 위 같은 사정을 종합하여 보면, 원고들이 이 사건 정기상여금을 통상임금에 포함하여 미지급 법정수당의 추가 지급을 구하는 것은 노사가 합의한 임금수준을 훨씬 초과하는 예상외의 이익을 추구하고 피고에게 예측하지 못한 새로운 재정적 부담을 지워 중대한 경영상의 어려움을 초래하거나 피고의 존립을 위태롭게 하게 될 수 있다. 따라서 원고들의 위 청구는 신의칙에 위배되어 허용될 수 없다.

(2) **대법원 2020. 7. 9. 선고 2017다7170 판결 (쌍용자동차)**

상여금을 통상임금에 포함시킬 경우 피고가 기능직 사원에게 지급해야 할 추가 부담액 추정치는 2010년부터 2012년까지 매년 200여 억 원 남짓한 액수가 된다. 피고는 2008년 이후 2015년까지 계속 큰 폭의 적자를 내었고, 2009년경에는 피고의 존립 자체가 위태롭기도 하였다. 피고 노사는 2009년부터 피고 근로자들의 기본급 동결, 상여금 일부 반납, 복지성 급여 부지급에 합의하는 등 이 사건 청구기간 당시 각종 비용을 절감하여 피고의 위기를 극복하려 하였다. 위와 같은 사정을 종합하여 보면, 피고에게 상여금 관련 법정수당과 퇴직금 지급을 명할 경우 원고들은 당초 합의한 임금수준을 초과하는 예상외의 이익을 얻는 반면 피고는 예측하지 못한 새로운 재정적 지출을 하게 됨으로써 중대한 경영상의 어려움에 빠지게 될 것으로 보이므로, 원고들의 위 청구는 신의칙에 위반된다.

3. 신의칙 불인정 사례

(1) **대법원 2021. 3. 11. 선고 2017다259513 판결 (금호타이어)**

이 사건 상여금이 통상임금에 포함될 경우 피고 소속 근로자의 통상임금이 약정 통상임금보다 상당히 증가하고 그로 인하여 피고가 지급하여야 할 임금 총액도 상당히 증가하여 당초 예측하지 않았던 새로운 재정적 부담이 될 수 있다. 그러나 이 사건에서 인정된 추가 법정수당의 규모를

of the defendant's employees could significantly increase compared to the agreed-upon ordinary wages. Consequently, the total wage amount that the defendant would have to pay would also increase substantially, resulting in a new and unforeseen financial burden. However, when considering the size and trends of the defendant's annual revenue, gross profit, net profit, total debt, and total equity, which far exceed the KRW 2 trillion being maintained for the additional statutory allowances that were recognized in this case, it cannot be considered that these circumstances would directly and substantially cause significant operational difficulties or endanger the existence of the defendant.

(2) Supreme Court Decision dated December 16, 2021, Case No. 2016da7975 (Hyundai Heavy Industries)

The deterioration in the financial situation as described cannot be regarded as a circumstance that the defendant could not have foreseen. Risks and disadvantages due to fluctuations in domestic and international economic conditions are within the range that companies, like the defendant, which have been engaged in large-scale business for a long time, can anticipate or bear. Given the size of the defendant's business, this can be seen as a temporary difficulty that could be overcome.

(3) Supreme Court Decision dated April 23, 2019, Case Nos. 2016da37167 and 37174 (Hanjin Heavy Industries)

Examining the following circumstances in light of legal principles, it cannot be concluded that paying additional statutory allowances by including regular bonuses in ordinary wages would directly and substantially cause significant operational difficulties for the defendant or endanger the existence of its business.

① The additional statutory allowances that the defendant would bear due to the plaintiffs' claims amounted to approximately KRW 500 million. The defendant's annual revenue remained stable at around KRW 5 trillion to KRW 6 trillion without significant fluctuation. The size of these additional statutory allowances accounted for only about 0.1% of the defendant's annual revenue.

② The defendant's cash assets held annually far exceeded the amount required to cover the additional statutory allowances by approximately 160 times.

③ The defendant had no significant difficulties in securing the funds needed to cover the additional statutory allowances, given the smooth cash inflow from its business operations.

안정적으로 유지되고 있는 2조 원을 훨씬 초과하는 연 매출액 및 매출총이익, 당기순이익, 부채총계, 자본총계의 규모와 추이에 비추어 보면, 이러한 사정이 추가 법정수당의 지급으로 인하여 직접적으로 피고에게 중대한 경영상의 어려움을 초래하거나 기업의 존립을 위태롭게 한다고 볼 충분한 근거가 될 수 없다.

(2) 대법원 2021. 12. 16. 선고 2016다7975 판결 (현대중공업)

이러한 경영상태의 악화는 피고가 예견할 수 없었던 사정이라고 보기 어렵다. 국내외 경제상황의 변동에 따른 위험과 불이익은 피고와 같이 오랫동안 대규모 사업을 영위해 온 기업이 예견할 수 있거나 부담해야 할 범위에 있고, 피고의 기업 규모 등에 비추어 극복할 가능성이 있는 일시적 어려움이라고 볼 수 있다.

피고의 매출액, 영업이익, 당기순이익 등 경영 지표는 2013년경까지 전반적으로 양호하였다. 같은 기간 피고의 매출총이익률, 영업이익률, 당기순이익률은 2007년 이후 피고의 주된 제조분야인 선박 가격의 지속적 하락 등의 영향으로 감소 추세를 보였으나, 피고의 경영 상태가 열악한 수준이었다고 보기 어렵다.

(3) 대법원 2019. 4. 23 선고 2016다37167, 37174 판결 (한진중공업)

다음과 같은 사정들을 위 법리에 비추어 살펴보면, 정기상여금을 통상임금에 포함시킴으로써 추가 법정수당을 지급한다고 하여 피고에게 중대한 경영상의 어려움을 초래하거나 그 기업의 존립을 위태롭게 한다고 단정할 수 없으므로, 미지급 법정수당 청구가 신의칙에 위배된다고 볼 수는 없다.

① 원고들의 제소로 인하여 피고가 부담할 추가 법정수당은 약 5억 원 상당으로 보인다. 피고의 매출액이 매년 큰 등락 없이 5조 원 내지 6조 원 상당으로 안정적으로 유지되고 있는 한편, 위 추가 법정수당의 규모는 피고의 연 매출액의 약 0.1%에 불과하다. 또한 이는 피고가 매년 지출하는 인건비 약 1,500억 원의 0.3% 정도이다.

② 피고가 매년 보유하는 현금성자산도 피고가 부담할 위 추가 법정수당의 약 160배에 이른다.

③ 피고의 영업활동으로 인한 현금 유입이 원활하여 피고가 추가 법정수당을 변제할 재원을 마련하는 데 현저한 어려움이 있다고 보기는 어렵다.

F. Conclusion

The Supreme Court's unanimous decision in 2013 regarding ordinary wages can be considered a groundbreaking event in South Korea's wage structure and payment methods. It simplified the components of wages that were previously complex. Through this, it clarified that wages are compensation for labor and played a substantial role in reducing actual working hours. Despite its significant role, some companies continue to maintain the existing fixed bonus system by setting criteria for employee resignation dates, even though fixed bonuses should technically be included as part of the basic salary. This has led to the persistence of distorted wage systems. It is hoped that a prompt and clear judgment from the Supreme Court on the criteria for employees will occur. Additionally, while the application of the principle of good faith to retroactive claims related to the existing method of calculating ordinary wages is recognized as an exception, disputes still arise in practice, indicating the need for clear interpretations through legal precedents.

III. Average Wages

1. Purpose of calculating average wages

The basic principle of average wage is to calculate the ordinary living wage of workers as a matter of fact. Severance pay is based on the average wage for the same reason.[73] According to Article 2 (2) of the Labor Standards Act, if the total wage decreases due to abnormal work, the average wage will be lower than the normal wage, so then the ordinary wage is used.[74] The precedent also stipulates that if the amount calculated as the average wage is lower than the ordinary wage of the worker concerned, the ordinary wage shall be the average wage in Article 2 Paragraph 2 of the Labor Standards Act. The purpose for this is to guarantee the minimum average wage in case the wage is significantly lower than in normal cases

---

[73] Supreme Court ruling on Nov. 12, 1999: 98da49357.
[74] Gwangju Appellate Court ruling on Dec. 22, 2015: 2004nu1062.

F. 의견

2013년 대법원 합의체 판결은 우리나라의 임금의 구성항목과 지급방법에서 큰 변화를 가져온 획기적인 사건이라고 할 수 있다. 이로인해 기존의 복잡한 임금의 구성항목이 단순하게 되었다. 이를 통하여 임금이 근로의 대가성이라는 사실을 명확히 하였고, 근로시간을 실질적으로 줄이는 역할을 하였다. 이러한 중요한 역할을 하였음에도 불구하고, 고정상여금에 대해 퇴직자에 대한 재직자 기준을 설정함으로써 기존의 고정상여금 제도를 계속 유지하는 기업이 발생하고 있다. 사실상 고정적 상여금은 기본급으로 포함하여야 함에도 불구하고, 재직자 요건을 들어 기존의 왜곡된 급여체계를 유지하는 경우가 상존하고 있다. 조속히 대법원의 합의체를 통해서 재직자 요건에 대해 명확한 판단이 이루어 지기를 바란다. 또한 기존의 통상임금 산정방식에 대한 소급청구에 관한 신의칙 적용은 예외적으로 인정되고 있지만, 아직도 현장에서 다툼이 되고 있어, 판례를 통한 명확한 해석이 필요하다고 할 수 있다.

III. 평균임금

1. 평균임금 사용의 취지

평균임금은 근로자의 통상 생활임금을 사실대로 산정하는 것을 기본원리로 하고 있다. 퇴직금도 그러한 이유로 인해 평균임금을 기준으로 산정하고 있다[73]. 근로기준법 제2조 제2항은 비정상적인 근무로 인하여 임금총액이 저하될 경우 평균임금이 통상임금 보다 낮아지는데, 이 경우 근로자 보호를 위하여 사용된다[74]. 판례도 근로기준법 제2조 제2항은 평균임금으로 산출된 금액이 당해 근로자의 통상임금보다 저액일 경우에는 그 통상임금액을 평균임금으로 한다고 규정하고 있다. 그 취지는 평균임금 산정사유가 발생하기 전

---
73) 대법원 1999. 11. 12. 선고 98다49357 판결.
74) 광주고등법원 2015. 12. 22. 선고 2004누1062 판결.

due to reasons attributable to the worker or an inability to work normally due to reasons attributable to the worker during the three months prior to the occurrence of the reason for calculating the average wage.[75] Here, ordinary wages refer to fixed wages in advance that are set to be paid regularly and uniformly regardless of the actual provision of work. For this reason, Article 2 (2) of the Labor Standards Act is used in cases where the average wage falls short of the ordinary wage.[76]

Since the total wage is the average wage, it has always been higher than ordinary wage, which reflects only fixed and regular wages. For this reason, Article 46 of the Labor Standards Act stipulates that 70% of the average wage or 100% of the ordinary wage must be paid as leave of absence allowance for periods attributable to the employer. This is because the use of average wages is the basis for severance pay regulations and accident compensation for workers. However, ordinary wage is calculated for the purpose of calculating hourly wage, and so such ordinary wage is used when calculating paid allowances stipulated in the Labor Standards Act, such as overtime pay and unused annual allowance under the Labor Standards Act. Because ordinary wages refer to fixed and pre-promised wages paid for the contractual working hours when a labor contract is drawn up, while the average wage is paid according to the rate of attendance at work, it does not decrease.

2. Methods for calculating average wages[77]

(1) General Calculation

Average wages mean the actual wages paid for actual work provided and calculated into the daily wage rate. Average wages are the amount calculated by dividing the total amount of wages paid to the relevant worker during three calendar months prior to the date of calculation by the total number of calendar days during those three calendar months.

$$\text{Average Wages} = \frac{\text{Total amount of wages paid for the last three calendar months}}{\text{Total number of calendar days in the last three calendar months(89-92 days)}}$$

---

[75] Seoul Administrative Court ruling on July 1, 1999: 98gu19789.
[76] Supreme Court ruling on June 28, 1991: 90daka14758; Supreme Court ruling on Dec. 26, 1990: 90daka12493.
[77] Jung, Bongsoo, 「Korean Labor Law Bible」 5th Ed., Joongang, 2016, pp. 76-80.

3개월 동안 근로자의 귀책사유로 인하여 휴업하거나 정상적인 근로를 하지 못하여 통상의 경우보다 임금이 현저히 낮아지는 경우에 대비하여 평균임금을 최대한 보장하려는 데 있다고 판시하고 있다[75]. 여기서 통상임금은 실제 근로제공과 상관없이 정기적, 일률적으로 지급하기로 정하여진 사전적 고정급 임금을 의미한다. 이러한 이유로 근로기준법 제2조 제2항은 평균임금이 저하되어 통상임금에 미치지 못하는 경우에 사용된다[76].

임금총액이 평균임금이기 때문에 고정적이고 정기적인 임금만 반영하는 통상임금보다 항상 높게 나온다. 이러한 이유로 근기법 제46조의 사용자의 귀책사유로 휴업한 기간에 대한 휴업수당도 평균임금의 70%나 통상임금의 100%를 지급해야 한다고 규정하고 있다. 이는 평균임금의 사용이 근로자 보호를 위한 퇴직금 규정과 재해보상의 근거가 되기 때문이다. 그러나 통상임금은 시간급 계산을 목적으로 계산되고, 근로기준법상 연장근로 수당, 미사용 연차수당 등 근로기준법에 정한 유급수당을 계산하는 경우에 통상임금을 활용한다. 왜냐하면, 통상임금은 근로계약 작성시 소정근로시간에 지급하는 고정적이고 사전에 약속된 임금을 말하므로, 출근율에 따라 실제로 지급받는 평균임금과 달리 저하되지 않는다.

2. 평균임금 산정방법[77]

(1) 일반적인 계산

평균임금은 실제로 제공된 근로에 대해 실제로 지급받은 임금을 의미하며 일급 개념으로 산출된다. 평균임금 산정은 이를 산정해야 할 사유가 발생한 날 이전 3월간에 그 근로자에게 대하여 지급된 임금의 총액을 그 기간의 총 일수로 나눈 금액을 말한다.

$$평균임금 = \frac{\text{사유가 발생한 날 이전 3월간의 임금총액}}{\text{사유가 발생한 날 이전 3월간의 총 일수}} \\ (89일 \sim 92일)$$

---

[75] 서울행정법원 1999. 7. 1. 선고 98구19789 판결.
[76] 대법원 1991. 6. 28. 선고 90다카14758 판결; 1990.12.26. 선고, 90다카 12493 판결
[77] 정봉수, 「한국노동법 영문해설」 제5판, 중앙경제사, 2016, pp. 76-80.

1) The total amount of wages paid for the last three calendar months

The total amount of wages includes all wages of the Labor Standards Act excluding other forms of payment. In determining whether individual items of pay may be identified as wages reflected into the calculation of average wages, the following criteria shall be considered: 1) the items are paid regularly and periodically; 2) they are mandated by the employer according to collective bargaining, rules of employment, salary regulations, the labor contract, or habitual practice; or 3) employees identified under general conditions are paid uniformly. If individual items of pay meet any of these criteria, the items of pay shall be considered wages regardless of their titles.[78]

In cases where bonuses are paid once per annum and paid for periods exceeding one month, the total monetary value of the bonus paid for a certain month shall not be included into the calculation of average wages. The bonuses shall be calculated by dividing the total monetary value of bonuses paid to a relevant employee (during the twelve calendar months before the day on which cause for calculating their average wages occurs) by the total number of calendar months, which is 3/12 times the total monetary value of bonuses paid per year.[79]

2) Total number of calendar days in the last three calendar months prior to the occurrence date

The date on which the event occurred or the incident which necessitates such calculation means, in the event of resignation, the day in which the employer accepts the letter of resignation submitted by the employee. In the event of an industrial accident, it is the day on which the injury occurred, or the day when the disease is confirmed by diagnosis. However, the periods excluded from calculation are periods of shutdown on account of the employer, periods of maternity leave, periods of suspension from work for medical treatment owing to occupational injury or disease, periods of childcare leave, periods of strike, periods of approved suspension from work, and periods of suspension of service owing to performance of duties.

The period of three months does not signify 90 days, but three (3) calendar months (89~92 days) from the occurrence date. For employment of less than three months, the actual period served is calculated.

---

[78] Seoul Central District Court ruling on Jun. 21, 2007, 2006Na20978.
[79] MOEL Guidelines: on Feb. 24, 2003, Wages 68207-120.

1) 3월간 임금 총액

　　임금 총액에는 기타 금품을 제외한 근로기준법상 임금 모두가 포함된다. 어떤 금품이 평균임금 산정의 기초가 되는 임금에 해당하는지 여부를 가늠할 수 있는 구체적인 사정으로서 ① 근로자에게 계속적·정기적으로 지급되며 그 지급에 관해 단체협약, 취업규칙, 급여규정, 근로계약, ② 노동관행 등에 의해 사용자에게 그 지급의무가 있고, 또한 ③ 일정한 요건에 해당하는 근로자에게 일률적으로 지급하는 것이라면, 그 명칭 여하를 불문하고 임금이라고 볼 수 있다.[78]

　　상여금의 지급률을 연간단위로 설정하여 1개월을 넘는 단위로 지급하고 있는 경우에는 이를 지급 받은 그 월의 임금으로 취급하여 일시에 전액을 평균임금에 산입하는 것이 아니며, 평균임금을 산정하여야 할 사유가 발생한 날 이전 12개월의 기간 동안에 지급 받은 상여금 전액을 그 기간 동안의 근로월수로 분할 계산하여 즉, 3/12을 평균임금산정 기준 임금 총액에 산입한다.[79]

2) 사유발생일 이전 3월간의 총일수 계산

　　사유가 발생한 날과 그 지급사유가 발생한 때라 함은 사직서를 제출한 경우 사용자가 이를 수리한 날을 말한다. 재해보상의 경우에는 사상의 원인이 되는 사고가 발생한 날 또는 진단에 의해 질병이 발생 되었다고 확정된 날을 말한다. 다만, 평균임금 산정대상기간에서 제외되는 기간은 사용자 귀책사유로 인한 휴업기간, 산전·산후 휴가기간, 업무상 질병·부상 기간, 육아휴직기간, 쟁의행위기간, 업무 외 질병 휴직기간, 공의직무 수행 기간 등이다.

　　3월간은 90일을 말하는 것이 아니고 기산일로부터 소급하여 역월 3개월간 포함된 일수(89~92일)를 말한다. 취업 후 3월 미만인 경우에는 그 기간 만을 대상으로 평균임금을 산정한다.

---

[78] 서울지방법원 2007.6.21 선고 2006나20978 판결
[79] 행정해석: 임금 68207-120 2003.02.24

Chapter 2 Statutory Wages

<Example of Average Wage>

①Company Name	KangNam Labor Law Firm	②Employee Name	Bongsoo Jung	③Date of birth		④Position	
⑤Last day of employment	31-Aug-2023			⑥Starting Date	01-Jan-2018	⑦Salary Calculation	2,069 Days
⑧Wage payment method				⑨Employment type			

Calculation Details

⑩Salary Calculation		01-Jun-2023 From 31-May-2023 To	01-Jun-2023 From 30-Jun-2023 To	01-Jul-2023 From 31-Jul-2023 To	01-Aug-2023 From 31-Aug-2023 To	Total
⑪Total No. of Days		0 Days	30 Days	31 Days	31 Days	92 Days
S a l a r y d e t a i l s	⑫Basic Salary	0 KRW	5,000,000 KRW	5,000,000 KRW	5,000,000 KRW	15,000,000 KRW
	⑬Meal Allowance	KRW	KRW	KRW	KRW	- KRW
		KRW	KRW	KRW	KRW	- KRW
		KRW	KRW	KRW	KRW	- KRW
		KRW	KRW	KRW	KRW	- KRW
		KRW	KRW	KRW	KRW	- KRW
	⑭Bonus	10,000,000 KRW	*	3 / 12	=	2,500,000 KRW
	⑮Annual Allowance	2,000,000 KRW	*	3 / 12	=	500,000 KRW
	Total	0 KRW	5,000,000 KRW	5,000,000 KRW	5,000,000 KRW	18,000,000 KRW
⑯Daily average wage		Total salary 18,000,000 KRW / (Total days) 92 Days				195,652.17 KRW

(2) Exceptional case: Calculation of average wages during periods of leave

1) "Average wages" where an employee came to resign after a period of leave from work that the employee took with approval from the employer due to non-occupational injury, illness or other reason shall be calculated as follows: "average wages" to calculate severance pay refer to the amount calculated by dividing the total amount of wages paid to the relevant employee during three calendar months prior to the date of calculation by the total number of calendar days during those three calendar months (Article 2 of the LSA). If the amount calculated by this method is lower than the ordinary wages of the employee concerned, the amount of the ordinary wages shall be deemed as average wages.

2) In cases where the period of calculating average wages includes the period falling under a period of leave from work with approval from the employer caused by nonoccupational injury, illness, or other reason, the period and wages paid for that period shall be deducted respectively from a basis period for the calculation of average wages and the total amount of average wage (Article 2 of the Enforcement Decree to the LSA). Therefore, in cases where an employee took a leave of absence for non-occupational injury, illness or other reason in

<퇴직금 지불을 위한 평균임금 산정 예시>

①사업장명	KangNam Labor Law Firm	②근로자성명	Bongsoo Jung	③생년월일		④직종	
⑤산정사유 발생 년월일	2023-08-31			⑥채용 년월일	2018-01-01	⑦재직기간	2,069 일
⑧임금지급 방법					⑨고용형태별		

산 정 내 역

	⑩임금계산 기간	2023-06-01 부터 2023-05-31 까지	2023-06-01 부터 2023-06-30 까지	2023-07-01 부터 2023-07-31 까지	2023-08-01 부터 2023-08-31 까지	합계
	⑪총 일 수	0일	30일	31일	31일	92일
임금내역	⑫기 본 급	0원	5,000,000 원	5,000,000 원	5,000,000 원	15,000,000 원
	⑬고정수당	원	원	원	원	- 원
		원	원	원	원	- 원
		원	원	원	원	- 원
		원	원	원	원	- 원
		원	원	원	원	- 원
	⑭상 여 금	10,000,000 원	*	3 /	12 =	2,500,000 원
	⑮연차수당	2,000,000 원	*	3 /	12 =	500,000 원
	합 계 액	0원	5,000,000 원	5,000,000 원	5,000,000 원	18,000,000 원
⑯평균임금		총입금액 18,000,000 원 / (총일수) 92 일				195,652.17 원
⑰통상임금		(근로기준법 시행령 제31조) - 원				
⑱퇴 직 금		195,652 원 * 30일 * 2,069 / 365 = 33,271,590 원				

(2) 예외적인 경우: 휴직기간의 평균임금 산정방법

1) 업무 외 부상이나 질병, 그 밖의 사유로 사용자의 승인을 받아 휴업한 후 퇴직하게 된 경우에 평균임금을 다음과 같이 계산한다. 퇴직금 산정을 위한 평균임금은 이를 산정하여야 할 사유가 발생한 날 이전 3개월 동안에 그 근로자에게 지급된 임금의 총액을 그 기간의 총 일수로 나눈 금액을 말하며 (「근로기준법」 제2조), 이러한 방법으로 산출된 평균임금액이 당해 근로자의 통상임금보다 금액이 적을 경우에는 그 통상임금을 평균임금으로 하도록 정하고 있다.

2) 평균임금 산정기간 중에 업무 외 부상 또는 질병으로 사용자의 승인을 받아 휴업한 경우에는 그 기간과 그 기간에 지불된 임금은 평균임금 산정기준이 되는 기간과 임금의 총액에서 각각 공제하도록 규정하고 있다 (근로기준법시행령 제2조). 따라서 근로자가 업무 외 부상이나 질병, 그 밖의 사유로 사용자의 승인을 받아 휴업한 기간일 경우에는

accordance with Article 2 (8) of the Enforcement Decree to the LSA (with approval from the employer), the remaining period and wages excluding the period mentioned above shall be used for the calculation of average wages. If the leave of absence exceeds three months, the first day of the leave of absence shall be the date for calculating average wages based on the previous three months. In any case, if the amount calculated above is lower than the ordinary wages of the employee concerned, the amount of the ordinary wages shall be deemed as average wages.[80]

3) In cases where leave of absence is due to the employee's choice or actions, this period shall be included in the standard period in calculating average wages.[81] In cases where an employee could not provide labor service during the period required for calculating average wages due to the employee's choice or actions, this period shall be included in the standard period in calculating average wages. On the other hand, in cases where an employee took a leave of absence with approval from the employer, caused by non-occupational injury, diseases or other reasons according to Article 2 (8) of the Enforcement Decree to the LSA, the remaining period and wages excluding the period mentioned above shall be used for the calculation of average wages. If the leave of absence exceeded three months, the first day of the leave of absence shall be the date for calculating average wages based on the previous three months. In any case, if the amount calculated above is lower than the ordinary wages of the employee concerned, the amount of the ordinary wages shall be deemed average wages.

3. Adjustment of average wage

(1) Average wage in special cases[82]

1) When the period excluded from the calculation of average wage is 3 months or longer (Article 1)

If the period of time excluded from the calculation of average wage is at least three months (Article 2 (1) of the Enforcement Decree to the LSA), the average wage shall be calculated based on the date on which the cause for calculating average wage occurs. The same shall apply mutatis mutandis to adjustment of average wage (Article 5 of the Enforcement Decree to the LSA). In this case, "the

---

[80] MOEL Guidelines: Retirement Pension Dept-518, Oct. 21, 2008
[81] MOEL Guidelines: Wage 68207-132, Feb. 27, 2003.
[82] Enforcement Decree to the Labor Standards Act, Article 4 (Average Wage in Special Cases) Where it is impossible to calculate an average wage in accordance with Article 2 (1) 6 of the Act and Articles 2 and 3 of this Decree, such an average wage shall be as determined by the Minister of Employment and Labor; [Special Case Notice for Calculation of Average Wages by the Minister of Employment and Labor (No. 2015-77, noticed on October 14, 2015)]

동 기간을 제외한 나머지 일수 및 임금을 대상으로 평균임금으로 산정하여야 한다. 휴직한 기간이 3개월을 초과하여 평균 임금 산정기준기간이 없게 되는 경우에는 휴직한 첫 날을 평균임금산정 사유발생일로 보아 이전 3월간을 대상으로 평균임금을 산정하여야 한다. 아울러, 위와 같은 방법으로 산출된 평균임금액이 당해 근로자의 통상임금보다 저액일 경우에는 그 통상임금액을 평균임금으로 하여야 한다.[80]

3) 휴직기간이 근로자 귀책사유에 해당되는 경우 평균임금산정 기준기간에 포함하여 평균임금을 산정하여야 한다.[81] 만일 평균임금 산정기준이 되는 기간에 근로를 제공하지 못한 사유가 결근 등 근로자 귀책사유에 해당되는 경우에는 동기간도 평균임금산정 기준기간에 포함하여 평균임금을 산정하여야 한다. 반면에 휴직기간이 같은 법 시행령 제2조 제1항 제8호의 규정에 의한 업무 외 부상·질병 기타의 사유로 인하여 사용자의 승인을 얻어 휴업한 기간으로 볼 수 있는 경우에는 동기간을 제외한 나머지 일수 및 임금을 대상으로 평균임금을 산정하여야 한다. 휴직한 기간이 3개월을 초과하여 평균임금 산정기준기간이 없게 되는 경우에는 휴직한 첫 날을 평균임금산정 사유발생일로 보아 이전 3월 간을 대상으로 평균임금을 산정하여야 한다. 아울러 위와 같은 방법으로 산출된 평균임금액이 당해 근로자의 통상임금보다 저액일 경우에는 그 통상임금액을 평균임금으로 하여야 한다.

3. 평균임금 조정

(1) 특별한 경우의 평균임금[82]

1) 평균임금의 계산에서 제외되는 기간이 3개월 이상인 경우(제1조)

평균임금의 계산에서 제외되는 기간이 3개월 이상인 경우(근기법 시행령 제2조 제1항) 제외되는 기간의 최초일을 평균임금의 산정사유가 발생한 날로 보아 평균임금을 산정한다. 평균임금의 조정(근기법 시행령 제5조)의

---

80) 행정해석 : 2008.10.21, 퇴직연금복지과-518
81) 행정해석: 2003.02.27, 임금 68207-132
82) 근로기준법 시행령 제4조(특별한 경우의 평균임금) 법 제2조제1항제6호, 이 영 제2조 및 제3조에 따라 평균임금을 산정할 수 없는 경우에는 고용노동부장관이 정하는 바에 따른다; [고용노동부 평균임금산정 특례 고시(제2015-77호, 2015. 10. 14.)]

month when the injury and illness occurred" shall be deemed to be "the month of the first day of the period excluded from the calculation of average wage".

2) If the reason for calculating the average wage occurred on the first day work is provided (Article 2)

If the reason for calculating the average wage occurs on the first day work is provided, the average wage is calculated from the average daily wage that was supposed to be paid the worker.

3) When wages are paid collectively by two or more workers (Article 3)

In the event wages are paid collectively with two or more workers in one pair, the employee's career, production performance, working days, technical skills, responsibilities, and distribution practices shall be taken into account, unless a pre-determined payment method is provided for individual workers. We estimate the wage per worker and use the amount to estimate the average wage.

4) If part of the total wage is not clear (Article 4)

If the period in which the average wage is included includes payment of an additional portion in the average wage, the average wage shall be deducted from the total amount of wages paid out of the extra period from the total number of days.

5) When the total amount of wages is not clear (Article 5)

If the average wage cannot be calculated in accordance with the provisions of Article 1 through Article 4 of the Special Notice on Calculation of Average Wage, the head of the regional Employment and Labor Office shall consider the average wage of the worker as deemed appropriate in consideration of the following:

① Matters concerning wage level and inflation assessment in the area where the workplace is located;

② Matters concerning the monthly salary, monthly income, and monthly average salary reported under the Income Tax Act, the National Pension Act, the National Health Insurance Act, and the Employment Insurance Act;

③ Matters concerning wages of workers engaged in the same occupation as the worker at workplaces of the same or similar size as the type of business in the area where the workplace is located;

④ Matters concerning documentary evidence, such as records held by the person or his / her family, etc. (in this case, only if the employer approves) of the money received during the period providing work at the workplace;

⑤ Matters concerning employment labor statistics, such as the "Report on Labor Status by Employment Type" and the "Labor Work Survey Report", which are surveyed and published by the Minister of Employment and Labor.

경우에도 이를 준용한다. 이 경우 "부상 또는 질병이 발생한 달"은 "평균임금의 계산에서 제외되는 기간의 최초일이 속한 달"로 본다.

2) **근로제공의 초일에 평균임금 산정사유가 발생한 경우(제2조)**

근로를 제공한 첫 날에 평균임금 산정사유가 발생한 경우에는 그 근로자에게 지급하기로 한 임금의 1일 평균액으로 평균임금을 추산한다.

3) **임금이 근로자 2명 이상 일괄하여 지급되는 경우(제3조)**

근로자 2명 이상을 1개조로 하여 임금을 일괄하여 지급하는 경우 개별 근로자에 대한 배분방법을 미리 정하지 않았다면 근로자의 경력, 생산실적, 실근로일수, 기술·기능, 책임, 배분에 관한 관행 등을 감안하여 근로자 1명당 임금액을 추정하여 그 금액으로 평균임금을 추산한다.

4) **임금총액의 일부가 명확하지 아니한 경우(제4조)**

평균임금의 산정기간 중에 지급된 임금의 일부를 확인할 수 없는 기간이 포함된 경우에는 그 기간을 빼고 남은 기간에 지급된 임금의 총액을 남은 기간의 총 일수로 나눈 금액을 평균임금으로 본다.

5) **임금총액의 전부가 명확하지 아니한 경우 등(제5조)**

평균임금산정 특례고시 제1조부터 제4조까지의 규정에 따라 평균임금을 산정할 수 없는 경우에는 지방고용노동관서장이 다음 각 호의 사항을 감안하여 적정하다고 결정한 금액을 해당 근로자의 평균임금으로 본다.

① 해당 사업장이 있는 지역의 임금수준 및 물가사정에 관한 사항

② 해당 근로자에 대한 「소득세법」 및 관련 법령에 따라 기재된 소득자별 근로소득원천징수부, 「국민연금법」·「국민건강보험법」·「고용보험법」에 따라 신고된 보수월액·소득월액·월평균임금 등에 관한 사항

③ 해당 사업장이 있는 지역의 업종과 규모가 동일하거나 유사한 사업장에서 해당 근로자와 동일한 직종에 종사한 근로자의 임금에 관한 사항

④ 해당 사업장의 근로제공기간 중에 받은 금품에 대하여 본인 또는 그 가족 등이 보유하고 있는 기록(이 경우 사업주가 인정하는 경우에만 한정한다) 등 증빙서류에 관한 사항

⑤ 고용노동부장관이 조사·발간하는 "고용형태별 근로실태 조사보고서" 및 "사업체 노동력 조사보고서" 등 고용노동통계에 관한 사항

(2) Adjustment of average wage in special cases (Article 5 of the Enforcement Decree to the LSA)

1) The average wage applicable to the calculation of compensation, etc. for the employee pursuant to accident compensation under the Labor Standards Act shall, when the average amount of monthly ordinary wage per employee (hereinafter referred to as the "average amount") paid to employees in the same business category in the same business or workplace to which the relevant employee belongs has changed by at least five percent from the average amount paid in the month when an injury or a disease occurs, be such amount increased or decreased at the aforesaid rate of change, but such rate shall apply to the month immediately following the month of occurrence of grounds for change and the months subsequent thereto: Provided, That the second or latter adjustment of average wages shall be calculated based on the average amount of the month in which a cause for immediately preceding change occurred.

2) Where the business or workplace to which the relevant employee belongs is permanently closed down, the adjustment of average wage under paragraph (1) shall be based on a business or workplace with the same business type and scale as at the time when an occupational injury or disease was inflicted on the employee.

3) If there is no employee engaged in the same occupational category as the relevant worker, the adjustment of average wage under paragraph (1) or (2) shall be based on employees engaged in the occupation of similar category.

4) The average wage applicable to computation of retirement benefits under Article 8 of the Act on the Guarantee of Employees' Retirement Benefits, which shall be paid to an employee who suffers from an occupational injury or disease, shall be the average wage adjusted in accordance with paragraphs (1) through (3).

4. Ministry of Employment and Labor Guidelines & judicial rulings

(1) Items to be included in average wages

1) As long as a meal allowance is paid periodically and uniformly, this cannot be pure welfare or a bonus expressing favor, but shall be regarded as money characteristic of wages paid as remuneration for labor service.[83]

2) As the total wages calculated for average wages are any money and valuable goods an employer pays to a worker for their work, what the worker receives continuously and regularly, and what the employer has to pay according to the

---

[83] Supreme Court ruling on May 15, 2001, 2001Do1186.

(2) 특별한 경우의 평균임금이 조정(근기법 시행령 제5조)

1) 근로기준법 재해보상 규정에 따른 보상금 등을 산정할 때 적용할 평균임금은 그 근로자가 소속한 사업 또는 사업장에서 같은 직종의 근로자에게 지급된 통상임금의 1명당 1개월 평균액(이하 "평균액"이라 한다)이 그 부상 또는 질병이 발생한 달에 지급된 평균액보다 100분의 5 이상 변동된 경우에는 그 변동비율에 따라 인상되거나 인하된 금액으로 하되, 그 변동사유가 발생한 달의 다음 달부터 적용한다. 다만, 제2회 이후의 평균임금을 조정하는 때에는 직전 회의 변동 사유가 발생한 달의 평균액을 산정기준으로 한다.
2) 제1항에 따라 평균임금을 조정하는 경우 그 근로자가 소속한 사업 또는 사업장이 폐지된 때에는 그 근로자가 업무상 부상 또는 질병이 발생한 당시에 그 사업 또는 사업장과 같은 종류, 같은 규모의 사업 또는 사업장을 기준으로 한다.
3) 제1항이나 제2항에 따라 평균임금을 조정하는 경우 그 근로자의 직종과 같은 직종의 근로자가 없는 때에는 그 직종과 유사한 직종의 근로자를 기준으로 한다.
4) 업무상 부상을 당하거나 질병에 걸린 근로자에게 지급할 「근로자퇴직급여보장법」 제8조에 따른 퇴직금을 산정할 때 적용할 평균임금은 제1항부터 제3항까지의 규정에 따라 조정된 평균임금으로 한다.

4. 판례 및 행정해석

(1) 평균임금 포함여부

1) 식대가 정기적 일률적으로 지급되는 한, 그것을 근로제공과 무관한 단순한 복지후생이거나 은혜적인 급부라 할 수 없으므로 근로 대가로서의 임금의 성질을 지닌 것으로 보아야 할 것이다.[83]
2) 평균임금의 산정기초인 임금총액에는 사용자가 근로의 대상으로 근로자에게 지급하는 일체의 금품으로서 근로자에게 계속적·정기적으로 지급되고 단체협약, 취업규칙 등에 의하여 사용자에게 그 지급의무가 지워져 있는

---
83) 대법원 2001.5.15. 선고 2001도1186 판결.

collective agreement and rules of employment, regardless of how such payments are termed, a holiday work allowance shall be included [in calculation of severance pay].[84]

3) As overtime allowance is not money paid under friendly and favorable conditions, but rather, is remuneration the employer has to pay for an employee's work, regardless of its label, overtime allowance shall be included into average wages when calculating severance pay.[85]

4) As incentive bonuses, special bonuses, or production incentives have been determined at the discretion of the employer for their payment, payment rate, and payment period, they are not designated average wages[86]. In cases where an incentive bonus satisfies some specific conditions, it can be admitted as wages and shall also be included into the calculation of average wages. Otherwise, it shall be considered as a form of the employer's praise or favorable reward, which then denies it the character of wages and therefore excluded from the calculation of average wages. If the company did not regulate in the CBA or rules of employment any payment of incentive bonuses, special bonuses or production incentives, but determined them at the employer's discretion according to business performance, then, unless the habitual practice for payment was settled, such remuneration shall be denied as having the character of wages.

However, if the incentive bonuses were to be included in the average wages, according to the CBA or rules of employment, in cases where the company calculates average wages for severance pay and an unused annual leave allowance or, despite the absence of specific regulation, if the company has repeatedly included incentive bonuses in the calculation of average wages for severance pay for a long time, this common business practice may be deemed working conditions. In cases where the employer wishes to unfavorably change the working conditions admitted as habitual practice, the company must go through the proper procedure required to unfavorably revise the rules of employment.

(2) Wages paid irregularly for periods exceeding 3 months
1) Bonuses

---

[84] Supreme Court ruling on Apr. 14, 1992, 91Da5587
[85] Seoul District Court ruling on May 26, 2005, 2005Na175.
[86] MOEL Guidelines: Labor Standard 1758, Mar. 25, 2005.

것이면 그 명칭이 어떠하든 모두 포함된다 할 것이므로, 휴일근로수당이 이에 포함됨은 당연하다.[84]

3) 연장근로수당은 임의적·은혜적으로 지급된 급여라 할 수 없고 그 명칭을 불문하고 근로의 대상으로서 사용자에게 지급의무가 발생하는 임금이라고 할 것이므로, 퇴직금산정의 기초인 평균임금에 연장근로수당도 포함된다.[85]

4) 경영성과급, 특별상여금 및 생산장려금 등의 지급여부·지급률·지급시기 등이 대표이사에 의해 임의적으로 결정되어 왔다면 평균임금에 해당되지 않는다.[86] 성과급적 특별상여금의 경우에도 요건이 충족될 때에 임금성이 인정될 수 있으며, 평균임금 산정 시에도 포함되어야 할 것이나, 그렇지 못한 경우에는 이는 사업주의 포상적·은혜적 급부로 보아야 할 것으로 임금성이 부인되므로 평균임금 산정 시 제외될 수 있을 것이다.

회사가 경영성과급, 특별상여금 및 생산장려금 등의 지급에 대하여 단체협약이나 취업규칙 등에 전혀 정한 바가 없고, 지급여부·지급률·지급시기 등이 경영성과에 따라 대표이사에 의해 임의적으로 결정되어 왔으며, 지급관행이 생겼다고 보기도 어려운 경우에는 임금성이 부인될 수 있을 것이다. 그러나 회사의 단체협약 및 취업규칙 등에 퇴직금 및 연차휴가수당 지급을 위한 평균임금 산정 시 이러한 경영성과급 등을 포함하여 산정한다고 규정되어 있거나, 명시적인 규정은 없더라도 경영성과급 등을 포함하여 산정한 퇴직금 등의 지급이 장기간 반복됨으로써 노사당사자간에 관행으로 형성되어 사용자에게 지급의무가 있다고 여겨질 수 있을 경우에는 이러한 관행은 근로조건화 되었다고 할 수 있을 것이며, 관행화 된 근로조건을 불이익하게 변경하고자 할 경우에는 취업규칙 불이익 변경절차를 거쳐야 할 것으로 사료된다.

(2) 3개월의 초과하는 기간에 지급한 임금
1) 상여금

---

[84] 대법원 1992.4.14. 선고 91다 5587 판결
[85] 서울중앙지법 2005.5.26. 선고 2005나175 판결.
[86] 행정해석: 2005.03.25, 근로기준과-1758.

There are no regulations stipulated in labor law about matters concerning payment of bonuses, but bonuses shall be deemed wages as remuneration for work when they are stipulated in the rules of employment for payment conditions, amount, and payment period, or when they have been paid so habitually to all employees that the employee may have natural expectations to receive a bonus as a matter of course. On the other hand, in cases where the payment rate of bonuses was established per year-unit and paid for the period exceeding one month, the total amount of bonus paid for a certain month shall not be included into calculation of average wages. The bonuses shall be calculated by dividing the total amount of bonuses paid to a relevant employee during the twelve calendar months before the day on which a cause for calculating his average wages occurred by the total number of calendar months, which is 3/12 times the total amount of bonuses paid per year.[87]

2) Whether to include annual paid leave allowance into average wages to calculate severance pay

① Unused annual paid leave allowance already occurring before retirement

By the criteria of the attendance rate during the year prior to the retirement year, 3/12 of the unused annual paid leave allowance among annual paid leave occurring the year prior to the retirement year shall be included into "the basic wage items to calculate average wage for severance pay."

② Unused annual paid leave allowance occurring only just because of retirement

The unused annual paid leave allowance that the employee is granted just because of retirement in the retirement year according to the attendance rate of the year before the retirement year shall not be included into "the basic wage items to calculate average wage for severance pay," because the unused annual paid leave allowance is not wages paid during the calculation of average wage.

(3) The period for calculation of average wages

1) Calculation of average wages during periods of leave[88]

Average wages where an employee resigned after a period of leave from work that the employee took with approval from the employer due to non-occupational injury, illness or other reason shall be calculated as follows: average wages to calculate severance pay refer to the amount calculated by dividing the total amount of wages paid to the relevant employee during three calendar months prior to the date of calculation by the total number of calendar days during those three calendar months (Article 2 of the LSA). If the amount calculated by this

---

[87] MOEL Guidelines: Wages 68207-120.
[88] MOEL Guidelines: Retirement Pension Dept-518, on Oct. 21, 2008.

상여금의 지급 등에 대하여는 노동관계법에 별도 규정되어 있지 아니하나, 취업규칙 등에 지급조건, 금액, 지급시기가 정해져 있거나 전 근로자에게 관례적으로 지급하여 사회통념상 근로자가 당연히 지급 받을 수 있다는 기대를 갖게 되는 경우에는 근로의 대상성을 갖는 임금으로 보고 있다. 한편 상여금의 지급률을 연간단위로 설정하여 1개월을 넘는 단위로 지급하고 있는 경우에는 이를 지급 받은 그 월의 임금으로 취급하여 일시에 전액을 평균임금에 산입하는 것이 아니며, 평균임금을 산정하여야 할 사유가 발생한 날 이전 12개월의 기간 동안에 지급 받은 상여금 전액을 그 기간 동안의 근로월수로 분할 계산하여 즉, 3/12을 평균임금산정 기준 임금총액에 산입한다.[87]

2) 연차유급휴가수당의 퇴직금 산정을 위한 평균임금 포함여부

① 퇴직하기 전 이미 발생한 연차유급휴가미사용수당

　퇴직 전전년도 출근율에 의하여 퇴직 전년도에 발생한 연차유급휴가 중 미사용하고 근로한 일수에 대한 연차유급휴가미사용수당액의 3/12을 "퇴직금 산정을 위한 평균임금 산정 기준임금"에 포함한다.

② 퇴직으로 인해 비로소 지급사유가 발생한 연차유급휴가미사용수당

　퇴직전년도 출근율에 의하여 퇴직년도에 발생한 연차유급휴가를 미사용하고 퇴직함으로써 비로소 지급사유가 발생한 연차유급휴가미사용수당은 평균임금의 정의상 산정사유 발생일 이전에 그 근로자에 대하여 지급된 임금이 아니므로 "퇴직금 산정을 위한 평균임금 산정 기준임금"에 포함되지 아니한다.

(3) 평균임금 산정대상기간

1) 휴직기간의 평균임금 산정[88]

　업무 외 부상이나 질병, 그 밖의 사유로 사용자의 승인을 받아 휴업한 후 퇴직하게 된 경우에 평균임금을 다음과 같이 계산한다. 퇴직금산정을 위한 평균임금은 이를 산정하여야 할 사유가 발생한 날 이전 3개월 동안에 그 근로자에게 지급된 임금의 총액을 그 기간의 총 일수로 나눈 금액을

---

[87] 행정해석: 임금 68207-120
[88] 행정해석: 퇴직연금복지과-518, 2008.10.21.

method is lower than the ordinary wages of the employee concerned, the amount of ordinary wages shall be deemed as average wages. In cases where the period of calculating average wages includes the period falling under a period of leave from work with approval from the employer caused by non-occupational injury, illness, or other reason, the period and wages paid for that period shall be deducted respectively from a basis period for the calculation of average wages and the total amount of average wage (Article 2 of the Enforcement Decree to the LSA).

Therefore, in cases where an employee took a leave of absence for non-occupational injury, illness or other reason in accordance with Article 2 (8) of the Enforcement Decree to the LSA (with approval from the employer), the remaining period and wages excluding the leave of absence shall be used for the calculation of average wages. If the leave of absence exceeds three months, the first day of the leave of absence shall be the date for calculating average wages based on the previous three months. In any case, if the amount calculated above is lower than the ordinary wages of the employee concerned, the amount of the ordinary wages shall be deemed as average wages.

2) **The period of suspension from office in calculating average wages**[89]

In this case, the criteria for calculating average wages shall be decided upon whether the suspension from office is justifiable or not. If the suspension from office is justifiable, the suspension period and the wages paid during the suspension period shall be included in the total period and amount of wages respectively in calculating average wages, provided that, when the amount calculated for average wages is lower than the ordinary wages of the employee concerned, the amount of ordinary wages shall be deemed average wages. If the suspension from office is unjustifiable, it is legitimate that the suspension period and the wages paid for the suspension period shall be deducted respectively from a basis period for the calculation of average wages and the total amount of average wages according to Article 2 (8) of the Enforcement Decree to the LSA.

3) **Calculation of average wages for a full-time officer of the labor union.**[90]

In cases where a full-time officer of the labor union, who is engaged exclusively in affairs of the labor union without providing labor service, resigns from the company at the same time as his union service period expires, the initial day (last day of wage payment) of the labor union's full-time officer for calculating average wages shall be considered the "date on which a cause for calculating his average wage occurred," unless there is a special agreement to the contrary.[91]

---

[89] MOEL Guidelines: Wage 68207-562, Jul. 16, 2003
[90] MOEL Guidelines: Wage 68207-317.
[91] MOEL Guidelines: Wage 68207-545.

말하며 (「근로기준법」 제2조), 이러한 방법으로 산출된 평균임금액이 당해 근로자의 통상임금보다 적은 금액일 경우에는 그 통상임금을 평균임금으로 하도록 정하고 있다. 평균임금 산정기간 중에 업무상외 부상 또는 질병으로 사용자의 승인을 받아 휴업한 경우에는 그 기간과 그 기간에 지불된 임금은 평균임금 산정기준이 되는 기간과 임금의 총액에서 각각 공제하도록 규정하고 있다 (근로기준법시행령 제2조).

따라서 근로자가 업무 외 부상이나 질병, 그 밖의 사유로 사용자의 승인을 받아 휴업한 기간일 경우에는 동기간을 제외한 나머지 일수 및 임금을 대상으로 평균임금으로 산정하여야 하며, 휴직한 기간이 3개월을 초과하여 평균임금 산정기준기간이 없게 되는 경우에는 휴직한 첫 날을 평균임금산정 사유발생일로 보아 이전 3월간을 대상으로 평균임금을 산정하여야 한다. 아울러, 위와 같은 방법으로 산출된 평균임금액이 당해 근로자의 통상 임금보다 작은 액수일 경우에는 그 통상임금액을 평균임금으로 하여야 한다.

2) **대기발령기간의 평균임금 산정**[89]

평균임금 산정기준은 대기발령의 정당성 여부에 따라 달리 보아야 한다. 대기발령이 정당한 처분이라면 그 기간과 그 기간 중에 지불된 임금은 평균임금 산정기준이 되는 기간과 임금의 총액에 각각 포함하여 평균임금을 산정하고, 다만, 평균임금이 통상임금보다 저액일 경우에는 그 통상임금액을 평균임금으로 보아야 한다. 부당한 처분이라면 이를 근로기준법 시행령 제2조 제1항 제8호에 준하는 것으로 보아 그 기간과 그 기간 동안에 지급받은 임금을 평균임금 산정기준이 되는 기간과 임금의 총액에서 각각 공제하는 것이 타당하다.

3) **노조전임자의 평균임금 산정**[90]

먼저 사업장에 근로를 제공하지 않고 노동조합업무만을 수행한 노동조합 전임자가 전임기간 만료와 동시에 퇴직하는 경우에 있어서 평균임금은 이에 대한 노사간의 정함이 없는 한 노동조합 전임을 개시한 날(최종 임금지급일)을 "평균임금을 산정하여야 할 사유가 발생한 날"로 본다.[91]

---

[89] 행정해석: 2003.07.16, 임금 68207-562
[90] 행정해석: 2001.05.03, 임금 68207-317.
[91] 행정해석: 1994.9.7, 임금 68207-545.

Chapter 2 Statutory Wages

IV. Minimum Wage

1. Concept[92]

The minimum wage system is the nation intervening in the decision-making process between employer and employee, designed to protect employees earning low wages by stipulating and legally requiring employers to pay minimum wage levels or higher. The minimum wage is determined annually on the 5th of August by the Minimum Wage Council, which is composed of 9 representatives from each of the following groups: labor, management, and government. The minimum wage they determine is effective from January 1 to December 31 of the following year. The minimum wage mainly influences small and medium-sized companies who employ low-income workers such as guards, janitors, migrant workers, etc., and this directly affects the process of making decisions on salary.

<Minimum Wages per Year> (Unit: KRW)

Year / Category	2012 1. 1. ~2021.12.31.	2022. 1. 1. ~2022.12.31.	2023. 1. 1. ~2023.12.31.	2024. 1. 1. ~2024.12.31.
Hourly pay	8,720	9,160	9,620원	9,860원
Day pay (8 hours)	69,760	73,280	76,960	78,880
Monthly work hours (209 hours)	1,822,480	1,914,440	2,010,580	2,067,740
Trainee employees (within 3 months)	7,848 (hour) 1,640,232 (month)	8,244 (hour) 1,722,996 (month)	8,658 (hour) 1,809,522 (month)	8,874 (hour) 1,854,666 (month)

* A 10% reduction is applied to probationary workers for the first three months. (Applicable to workers who have signed a labor contract for a period of one year or more.)
* If working the standard weekly 40 hours (209 hours on a monthly basis, including 8 hours of paid leave per week), the minimum wage will apply.

The increase in minimum wage is the most desirable way to reduce the difference in wages between regular and irregular employees, but a great change is expected for SMEs and small-scale service companies that are unable to pay the minimum wage. According to the current minimum wage system in Korea, one minimum wage is applied at all workplaces, without distinction as to the type of

---

[92] Jung, Bongsoo, "Minimum Wage and the Employer's Obligations", 「Labor Law」, Jungang, December 2013.

Ⅳ. 최저임금

1. 최저임금의 의의[92]

　최저임금제란 국가가 노사 간의 임금결정과정에 개입하여 임금의 최저수준을 정하고, 사용자에게 이 수준 이상의 임금을 지급하도록 법으로 강제하여 저임금 근로자를 보호하는 제도이다. 최저임금은 각 9인의 노·사·공익 대표로 구성(총 27인)된 최저임금위원회에서 매년 8월 5일까지 결정하고, 다음 연도 1월 1일부터 12월 31일까지 적용된다. 최저임금은 주로 저임금 근로자를 사용하는 중소기업 사업장에 많은 영향을 가져오며, 저임금 근로자인 경비원, 청소원, 외국인 노동자 등의 임금결정에 직접적인 결과를 가져온다.

<연도별 최저임금>　　　　　　(단위 : 원)

구분 \ 년	2021. 1. 1. ~2021.12.31.	2022. 1. 1. ~2022.12.31.	2023. 1. 1. ~2023.12.31.	2024. 1. 1. ~2024.12.31.
시간급	8,720원	9,160원	9,620원	9,860원
일급 (8시간기준)	69,760원	73,280원	76,960원	78,880원
월환산액 (209시간기준)	1,822,480원	1,914,440원	2,010,580원	2,060,740원
수습근로자 (3월 이내)	7,848원(시급) 1,640,232원(월)	8,244원(시급) 1,722,996원(월)	8,658원(시급) 1,809,522원(월)	8,874원(시급) 1,854,666원(월)

＊ 3개월 이내의 수습근로자는 10% 감액
　(1년 이상의 기간을 정하여 근로계약을 체결한 근로자에 한함)
＊ 주 소정근로 40시간(월 환산 기준 209시간, 주당 유급휴가 8시간 포함) 근무할 경우

　최저임금의 인상은 정규직과 비정규직의 임금수준 차이를 줄일 수 있는 가장 바람직한 방법이지만, 최저임금을 지급하기 어려운 중소기업이나 소규모 서비스업의 경우에 굉장히 큰 변화가 예상되고 있다. 우리나라의 현행 최저임금제도에 의하면 모든 사업장에서 업종이나 지역의 구분 없이 하나의 최저

---

[92] 정봉수, "최저임금과 사업주의 의무", 「월간 노동법률」, 중앙경제사, 2017년 8월호

industry or region, and all employers are obligated to pay at least the minimum wage.

According to the current minimum wage system in Korea, a single minimum wage is applied at all workplaces, without distinction as to the industry or region, and all employers are obligated to pay at least the minimum wage. Employers can pay more than the minimum wage, and parts of employment contracts that stipulate a wage lower than the minimum wage shall be invalid, with the difference to be paid additionally. Employers shall be punished for violations with imprisonment of up to three years or a fine not exceeding KRW 20 million.[93]

In the following, I will explain the employer's obligations, the criteria for determining violations of minimum wage, calculation of hourly wage for minimum wage, and the practical applications thereof.

(1) Scope of Application
The minimum wage shall apply to all businesses or workplaces.
1) Deduction from application of minimum wage: a 10% deduction is applicable for a person who is still in a probationary employment period and three months have not passed from the beginning of employment.
2) Exclusion from application of minimum wage: ① a person who has remarkably low abilities to work due to a mental or physical handicap and for whom the employer has obtained approval from the Ministry of Labor; ② any business using only relatives living together, ③ those hired for household work, and ④ seamen who are subject to the Seaman Act, or ship owners employing such seamen.

(2) Minimum Wage and Employer Obligations
The minimum wage system guarantees the minimum amount of hourly wage for employees. An employer can pay more than the minimum wage, but the part of an employment contract stipulating a wage which is less than the minimum wage shall be invalid, and any missing amount from the minimum wage must be paid additionally. For violations, the employer shall be punished by imprisonment for up to three years or a fine not exceeding KRW 20 million (Articles 6 and 28 of the Minimum Wage Act). In addition, when a minimum wage is announced, the employer shall inform employees of 1) the new minimum wage rate, 2) the scope of wages excluded from application of minimum wage, and 3) the effective date.

---
[93] The Minimum Wage Act, Article 6 and 28.

임금만 적용되고, 사용자는 최저임금액 이상 지급해야 할 의무를 진다.

우리나라의 현행 최저임금제도에 의하면 모든 사업장에서 업종이나 지역의 구분 없이 하나의 최저임금만 적용되고, 사용자는 최저임금액 이상 지급해야 할 의무를 진다. 최저임금은 근로자에 대하여 임금의 최저수준을 보장하는 제도이므로 사용자는 최저임금액 이상을 지급하여야 하고, 최저임금액에 미달하는 임금을 정한 근로계약은 그 부분에 한하여 무효로 하며, 무효로 된 부분에 있어 최저임금을 지급하여야 한다. 이를 위반한 경우 3년 이하의 징역 또는 2천만 원 이하의 벌금에 처한다.[93]

아래에서는 최저임금의 적용에서 사업주의 의무, 최저임금의 위반여부, 판단기준, 최저임금의 시간급 계산을 살펴보고, 구체적 최저임금 적용 사례를 살펴보고자 한다.

(1) 최저임금 적용범위

근로자를 사용하는 모든 사업 또는 사업장에 적용된다.
1) 감액적용대상은 수습사용 중에 있는 자로서 수습사용 한날부터 3월 이내인 자는 10% 감액 적용이 가능하다.
2) 적용제외 대상은 ① 정신 또는 신체의 장애로 근로능력이 현저히 낮은 자로서 사용자가 고용노동부장관 인가를 받은 자, ② 동거하는 친족만을 사용하는 사업의 종사자, ③ 가사사용인, ④ 선원법의 적용을 받는 선원 및 선원을 사용하는 선박의 소유자

(2) 최저임금과 관련 사업주 의무

최저임금은 근로자에 대하여 임금의 최저수준을 보장하는 제도이므로 사용자는 최저임금액 이상을 지급하여야 하고, 최저임금액에 미달하는 임금을 정한 근로계약은 그 부분에 한하여 무효로 하며, 무효로 된 부분에 있어 최저임금액과의 차액의 임금을 추가적으로 지급하여야 한다. 이를 위반한 경우 3년 이하의 징역 또는 2천만 원 이하의 벌금에 처한다(최저임금법 제6조, 28조). 또한 사용자는 최저임금이 고시되면 최저임금액, 최저임금에 산입하지 않는 임금의 범위, 효력발생일 등에 관하여 근로자들이 쉽게 볼 수 있는 장소에

---
93) 최저임금법 제6조, 28조

Chapter 2 Statutory Wages

This notice must be posted in places where it can be easily seen by all employees, or through other appropriate methods. For violations of this, the employer shall be punished by a fine up to KRW one million (Article 11 and Article 31 of the Act). Exceptions to the application of minimum wage are those to whom any of the following subparagraphs apply and for whom the employer obtains permission from the Minister of Employment and Labor: ① A person who has remarkably low abilities to work due to a mental or physical handicap and ② Other people as deemed inappropriate for application of the minimum wage.[94]

1) **Obligation to give notice**

   When the minimum wage is announced, the employer shall inform employees of ① the minimum wage rate, ② scope of wages excluded from application of minimum wage, and ③ effective date. This notice must be posted in places where it can be easily seen by employees, or through other appropriate methods.

2) **Obligation to pay minimum wage**

   An employer shall pay the minimum wage in full to employees covered by the minimum wage rules. If a labor contract between an employer and employee provides for a wage that is less than the minimum wage rate, such provision shall be null and void and the invalidated provision regarded as stipulating that the same wage as the minimum wage rate shall be paid.

3) **Joint liability for contractor**

   In the event that a project is carried out under contract, if the contractee has paid their employees wages lower than the minimum wage rate for reasons for which the contractor is liable, the contractor, along with the contractee, shall take joint liability. The reasons a contractor will be considered liable are 1) a contractor's act of determining unit labor costs lower than the minimum wage rate at the time of the signing of the contract; and 2) a contractor's act of lowering unit labor costs to below the minimum wage rate in the middle of the contract period.

4) **Supplement allowance due to reduced contractual working hours**

   Even though the contractual working hours are reduced due to the Labor Standards Act (Article 50), the employer cannot lower the previously paid wages subject to the minimum wage without justifiable reason. If the salary paid after reducing contractual working hours is less than the amount paid before working hours were reduced, a supplemental allowance shall be paid.

5) **Penal provisions for violation of the minimum wage level**

   ① Imprisonment of up to three years or a fine not exceeding 20 million won

---

[94] The Minimum Wage Act, Article 7 (Exclusion from Application of Minimum Wage)

게시하거나 그 외의 적당한 방법으로 근로자에게 주지시켜야 한다. 이를 위반한 경우 100만 원 이하의 과태료가 부과된다(동법 제11조, 31조). 최저임금의 적용에 예외는 ① 정신장애나 신체장애로 근로능력이 현저히 낮은 자와 ② 그 밖에 최저임금을 적용하는 것이 적당하지 아니하다고 인정되는 자로 고용노동부장관의 승인을 받은 자이다.[94]

1) 사용자의 주지의무

　　사용자는 최저임금이 고시되면 ① 최저임금액, ② 최저임금에 산입하지 않는 임금의 범위, ③ 효력발생일 등에 관하여 근로자들이 쉽게 볼 수 있는 장소에 게시하거나 그 외의 적당한 방법으로 근로자에게 주지시켜야 한다.

2) 최저임금의 지급의무

　　사용자는 최저임금의 적용을 받는 근로자에 대하여 최저임금액 이상을 지급하여야 한다. 최저임금액에 미달하는 임금을 정한 근로계약은 그 부분에 한하여 이를 무효로 하며, 무효로 된 부분은 최저임금액과 동일한 임금을 지급하기로 한 것으로 간주된다.

3) 도급사업자의 연대책임

　　도급으로 사업을 행하는 경우 수급인이 도급인의 책임 있는 사유로 근로자에게 최저임금액에 미달하는 임금을 지급한 때에는 도급인은 해당 수급인과 연대하여 책임을 진다. 그 책임있는 사유의 범위는 ① 도급인이 도급계약의 체결 당시 인건비 단가를 최저임금액에 미치지 못하는 금액으로 결정하는 행위, ② 도급인이 도급계약 기간 중 인건비 단가를 최저임금액에 미치지 못하는 금액으로 결정하는 행위

4) 근로시간 단축에 따른 임금보전

　　사용자는 강행규정에 의해 근로시간(근로기준법 제50조)의 소정근로시간이 단축되는 경우라도 정당한 사유 없이 최저임금의 적용대상이 되는 임금을 단축 전 금액보다 낮출 수 없다. 이 경우, 단축 전 소정근로시간으로 산정한 최저임금액과 단축 후의 소정근로시간으로 산정한 최저임금액(최저임금액 인상분 포함)을 비교하여 적은 경우에만 임금보전을 한다.

5) 최저임금법 위반의 벌칙

① 3년 이하의 징역 또는 2천만 이하의 벌금

---

[94] 최저임금법 제7조(최저임금의 적용제외)

- paying lower than the minimum wage rate
- lowering the previous wages on grounds of the minimum wage, according to the 'Minimum Wage Act'
- failure to pay the required supplement allowance if reduced contractual working hours result in reduced wages

② Fine not exceeding one million won
- failure to inform employees of the minimum wage announced by decision of the Minister of Employment and Labor

2. Criteria for determining violations of minimum wage

To determine whether the wages paid by a workplace are less than the minimum wage, ① the total wages included in the minimum wage from the wages paid monthly, ② will be divided by the monthly contractual working hours, and then hourly minimum wage calculated, ③ and then the amount will be compared with the current minimum wage.[95]

The scope of wages to be included in calculation of minimum wage according to the Minimum Wage Act includes 1) wages or allowances to be paid according to wage items stipulated in a collective agreement, the rules of employment, and/or an employment contract, or repeated regular payments; and 2) wages or allowances to be paid periodically or in a lump sum once or more every month for contractual labor according to previously agreed-upon payment conditions and payment rate (Article 2 of the Enforcement Decree to the Act (Table 2).

* Wages excluded from minimum wage rules (Table 1 of the Act):

(1) Wages, other than those paid regularly once or more every month

① Diligence allowances paid for superior attendance over periods exceeding one month;
② Length of service allowances paid for continuous work over periods exceeding one month;
③ Incentives, efficiency allowances, or bonuses presented for various reasons over periods exceeding one month; and
④ Other allowances paid temporarily or incidentally, such as marriage

---

[95] Supreme Court ruling on Jun. 29, 2007 2004 da 48836 (Calculation of minimum wage).

- 근로자에 대하여 최저임금액 이상의 임금을 지급하지 아니한 경우
  - '최저임금법'에 의한 최저임금을 이유로 종전의 임금수준을 저하시키는 경우
  - 근로시간 단축에 따른 임금보전을 행하지 않는 경우
② 100만 원 이하의 과태료
  - 노동부장관이 결정 고시한 최저임금액 등을 근로자에게 주지시키지 않은 경우

2. 최저임금의 위반여부 판단기준

사업장에서 지급하는 임금이 최저임금 위반인지 여부를 판단하기 위해서는 ① 월 단위로 지급받는 임금에서 최저임금에 포함되는 임금 총액을, ② 월 소정근로시간으로 나누어 시간당 임금으로 환산해, ③ 고시된 최저임금과 비교하여야 한다.[95]

최저임금 산정 시 포함되는 임금 범위는 ① 단체협약·취업규칙 또는 근로계약에 임금항목으로서 지급근거가 명시되어 있거나 관례에 따라 지급하는 임금 또는 수당 ② 미리 정해진 지급조건과 지급률에 따라 소정근로에 대하여 매월 1회 이상 정기적·일률적으로 지급하는 임금 또는 수당이다(동법 시행규칙 제2조 별표2).

최저임금에 산입되지 않는 임금의 범위(동법 시행규칙 제2조 별표1)는 다음과 같다.

(1) 매월 1회 이상 정기적으로 지급하는 임금 외의 임금:
  ① 1월을 초과하는 기간의 출근성적에 의하여 지급하는 정근수당,
  ② 1월을 초과하는 일정기간의 계속근무에 대하여 지급하는 근속수당,
  ③ 1월을 초과하는 기간에 걸친 사유에 의하여 산정하는 장려수당, 능률수당 또는 상여금,
  ④ 기타 결혼수당, 월동수당, 김장수당, 체력단련비 등 임시 또는 돌발적인 사유에 따라 지급하거나, 지급조건이 사전에 정해진 경우에도 그

---
[95] 대법원 2007. 6. 29. 선고 2004다48836판결 (최저임금 계산)

Chapter 2 Statutory Wages

allowances, winter fuel allowances, kimchi allowances, exercise subsidies, etc., and which have no fixed payment date or are irregularly paid, even though payment conditions were determined in advance.

(2) Wages, other than those paid for contractual working hours or contractual working days

① Annual or monthly paid allowances, work allowance on paid leave, work allowance on paid holidays;

② Wages and additional allowances for extended work or holiday work;

③ Additional allowances for night work;

④ Day & night-duty allowances; and

⑤ Wages not admitted to be paid for a contractual working day, regardless of how such payments are termed.

(3) Other wages deemed inappropriate to be included in the minimum wage:

Actual or similar expenses to support employee welfare such as meals, dormitory accommodation or other housing, company shuttle buses, etc.

3. Hourly wage calculation for the minimum wage

The minimum wage shall be determined in units of hours, days, weeks, or months. When determining the minimum wage in units of days, weeks or months, the hourly wage shall also be indicated. The hourly wage determined for a month shall be the monthly amount divided by the number of contractual working hours in one month. In order to calculate the hourly wage of the monthly wage, the amount of the wage divided by the number of working hours per month becomes the hourly minimum wage (Article 5 of the Act, Article 5 of its Enforcement Decree). The prescribed working time of one month includes paid weekly holiday allowances (Article 55 of the Labor Standards Act) and paid allowances on off-days according to a collective agreement. The related court ruling and administrative interpretations are as follows:

(1) Court ruling

The court ruling for the contractual working hours per month is that "Article 5 of the Enforcement Decree to the Minimum Wage Act stipulates that the wages paid on a weekly or monthly basis shall be wages divided by the number of contractual working hours per week or month. The so-called "weekly holiday

사유 발생일이 확정되지 아니하거나 불규칙적인 임금·수당이 이에 해당된다.

(2) 소정의 근로시간 또는 소정의 근로일에 대하여 지급하는 임금외의 임금:
① 연·월차휴가 근로수당, 유급휴가 근로수당, 유급휴일 근로수당,
② 연장시간 근로, 휴일근로에 대한 임금 및 가산임금,
③ 야간근로에 대한 가산임금,
④ 일·숙직수당,
⑤ 기타 명칭여하에 관계없이 소정근로에 대하여 지급하는 임금이라고 인정할 수 없는 임금이 이에 해당된다.

(3) 기타 최저임금액에 산입하는 것이 적당하지 아니한 임금:
식사, 기숙사, 주택제공, 통근차 운행 등 현물이나 이와 유사한 형태로 지급되는 급여 등 근로자의 복리후생을 위한 성질의 것이 이에 해당된다.

3. 최저임금의 시간급 계산

최저임금액은 시간·일(日)·주(週) 또는 월(月)을 단위로 하여 정한다. 이 경우 일·주 또는 월을 단위로 하여 최저임금액을 정할 때에는 시간급으로도 표시하여야 한다. 월(月) 단위로 정해진 임금은 그 금액을 1개월의 소정근로시간 수로 나눈 금액으로 한다. 월 임금의 최저임금을 계산하기 위해서는 월 단위의 최저임금에 포함되는 임금을 1개월의 소정근로시간 수로 나눈 금액이 시간급 최저임금이 된다(최저임금법 제5조, 시행령 제5조). 1개월의 소정근로시간은 유급주휴수당(근로기준법 제55조)과 단체협약 등에서 유급으로 처리된 유급수당도 포함한다. 관련한 판례와 행정해석은 다음과 같다.

(1) 판례
1개월의 소정근로시간 수에 대해 판례는 "최저임금법 시행령 제5조는 주 단위 또는 월 단위로 지급된 임금에 대하여 '1주 또는 월의 소정근로시간 수'로 나눈 금액을 시간에 대한 임금으로 하도록 규정하고 있다. 주급제 혹은 월급제

allowance", which is a wage for a paid holiday, is regularly paid at least once a month for given work. Therefore, this regularly paid weekly holiday allowance shall be included in the wage calculation."[96] In a sample case of 40 hours per week, there are 209 contractual working hours for the month, including the weekly holiday allowance.

(2) Practical applications of the minimum wage
1) Quarterly incentives, meal charges and vehicle maintenance expenses
① Quarterly incentives shall not be considered part of the minimum wage.

② The "meal charge (food expenses)" is paid regularly and uniformly to all employees on a monthly basis in accordance with the collective agreement and the rules of employment, and so it is decided to include these in the ordinary wages in the rules of employment. Meal charges are included as wages for the application of minimum wage. A "vehicle management fee" is paid to the driving worker at least once a month in accordance with predetermined payment conditions and is understood as a duty or service allowance for the specific worker, and can therefore be included as wages for the application of minimum wage.[97]

2) Bonuses and sales bonuses
① Bonuses calculated on a yearly basis and regular bonuses
In cases where a bonus is paid equally each month, after it is calculated and fixed for the yearly period, this monthly bonus is included in the minimum wage.

② Sales bonus (based on results)
The sales bonus, for which the monthly amount varies according to the sales results of the individual salesperson, is equivalent to a wage, in accordance with the sales incentive bonus set forth in Article 5 (2) of the Enforcement Decree to the Minimum Wage Act. Therefore, Article 5-2 of the Minimum Wage Act stipulates that the sum of the monthly sales bonus divided by the total number of working hours per month and the monthly salary divided by the number of working hours per month shall be included in the minimum wage.[98]

In cases where a fitness trainer carries out individual fitness training for

---

[96] Supreme Court ruling on Jan. 11, 2007, 2006 da 64245 (Case related to minimum wage)
[97] MOEL Guidelines on Dec. 15, 2010 Wage Welfare-2356
[98] MOEL Guidelines on Feb. 14, 2004 Wage Policy-501; Apr. 3, 1990 Wage 32240-4770; Oct. 2, 2005 Wage Policy-801; Jun. 20, 2003 Wage 68200-471

에서 지급되는 유급휴일에 대한 임금인 이른바 주휴수당은 소정의 근로에 대해 매월 1회 이상 정기적으로 지급되는 임금이라 할 것이어서 비교대상 임금을 산정함에 있어 주휴수당을 가산하여야 한다"고 판시하고 있다.[96] 이 경우 주 40시간의 경우 주휴수당을 포함하여 월의 소정근로시간은 209시간이 된다.

(2) 구체적 최저임금 적용 사례
1) 분기성과급, 식대, 차량관리비
① 분기성과급은 최저임금 산입을 위한 임금에 포함되지 않는다.
② "식비(식대)"는 단체협약 및 취업규칙에 따라 전 근로자에게 매월 정기적·일률적으로 지급하면서 취업규칙에서 통상임금으로 포함하기로 정하였다면 최저임금에 산입되는 임금이다. "차량관리비"는 운전근로자에 한하여 미리 정하여진 지급조건에 따라 일률적으로 매월 1회 이상 정기적으로 지급하고 있다면 이는 특정 업무 종사자에 대한 직무수당 또는 운행수당 등의 성격으로 이해되므로 최저임금 산입을 위한 임금에 포함된다.[97]

2) 상여금 및 판매수당(생산고)
① 1년 단위 산정 상여금, 정기상여금
상여금의 산정기간이 연간 단위로 계산하여 월로 분할하여 균등하게 지급되는 경우에는 최저임금에 포함된다.
② 판매수당(실적에 의한 수당)
영업사원의 판매실적에 따라 매월 금액이 달라지는 판매수당은 「최저임금법 시행령」 제5조제2항에서 정하고 있는 생산고에 따른 임금에 해당된다 할 것이므로 「최저임금법」 제5조의2 및 「최저임금법 시행령」 제5조제3항에 의거 당해 월 총 근로시간수로 나눈 금액과 월 기본급을 월 소정근로 시간수로 나눈 금액을 합산한 후 당해 연도 최저임금과 비교하여 위반 여부를 판단해야 한다.[98]

헬스 트레이너가 회원별 개인수업(PT) 업무를 맡아 수행할 경우, 미리 정하여진 지급조건과 지급률에 따라 추가적으로 수업료를 지급받고 있다면

---

[96] 대법원 2007. 1. 11. 선고 2006다64245 판결 (최저임금 관련 사건)
[97] 행정해석 2010. 12. 15. 임금복지과-2356
[98] 행정해석 2004.2.14. 임금정책과-501; 1990.4.3. 임금32240-4770; 2005. 10. 2. 임금정책과-801; 2003. 6. 20, 임금 68200-471

a member, if the trainer receives an additional fee according to a predetermined payment condition and payment rate, such fee can be considered equivalent to a sales bonus and included in the minimum wage. Such sales bonus is calculated into hourly wage after it is divided by monthly contractual working hours; the wage determined in monthly units, such as the basic wage, is also divided by monthly contractual working hours. The sum of both wages should be evaluated to determine whether it exceeds the minimum wage.[99]

3) Welfare benefits

① It is reasonable that a improvement bonus corresponding to money for welfare, such as an allowance which helps to improve the life of an employee is money which does not count in the minimum wage.[100]

② Even if a "welfare allowance" is included in ordinary wages, if it is explicitly stated in the collective agreement as a subsidy for living expenses or a benefit for welfare, according to Table 1 of Article 2 of the Enforcement Decree to the Minimum Wage Act, it shall be seen as a wage not included in application of the minimum wage in terms of welfare benefits.[101]

4. Minimum wages and ordinary wages

(1) Understanding the difference between minimum wage and ordinary wage

Calculation of the minimum wage is based upon the hourly minimum wage just like ordinary wages. The minimum wage includes all items inclusive of ordinary wage and is evaluated according to actual payments, but ordinary wage shall be the amount determined to be paid in the beginning as it is a base from which to calculate the overtime wage rate. This ordinary wage means wages determined to be paid periodically or in lump sums to the employee for contractual or whole labor. For a related example, an incentive wage due to production volume shall be included in minimum wage, but not included in ordinary wage.

(2) Differences from ordinary wages[102]

---

[99] MOEL Guidelines on Oct. 2, 2015 Labor Standards-4782
[100] MOEL Guidelines on Feb. 7, 2014 Labor Improvement-659
[101] MOEL Guidelines on May 17, 1989 Wage 32240-7146
[102] Supreme Court ruling on Jan. 11, 2007: 2006 da 64245; MOEL Guidelines on Jun. 29, 2006 Wage and

이는 최저임금에 산입되는 생산고 임금에 해당된다고 볼 수 있으므로, 수업료는 총 근로시간으로 나눠 시간당 임금으로 환산한 뒤, 기본급 등 월 단위로 정해진 임금을 소정근로시간(유급으로 지급되는 주휴수당 등 포함)으로 나누어 환산한 시간당 임금과 합산하여 시간급 최저임금 미달 여부를 판단하여 한다.[99]

3) 복리후생 수당

① 근로자의 생활을 보조하는 수당 등 복리후생을 위한 금품에 해당하는 처우개선비는 최저임금에 산입하지 않는 임금으로 봄이 타당하다.[100]

② "복지수당"이 비록 통상임금에 포함되어 지급되고 있다 하더라도 단체협약 등에 명백하게 생계비보조 또는 복리후생적인 성격의 수당임을 명시하고 있다고 한다면 이는 최저임금법시행규칙 제2조 별표 1에서 규정하고 있는 복리후생적인 수당으로 보아 최저임금의 적용을 위한 임금에 산입하지 아니하는 임금으로 보아야 한다.[101]

4. 최저임금과 통상임금

(1) 최저임금과 통상임금의 차이 이해

최저임금은 통상임금과 같이 시간급 최저임금을 기준으로 계산된다. 최저임금은 통상임금이 포함되는 모든 항목이 포함되며, 사후적으로 지급하는 임금으로 평가되지만, 통상임금은 연장근로수당 등의 기초가 되므로 사전적으로 지급이 확정된 임금만을 말한다. 이 통상임금은 근로자에게 정기적이고 일률적으로 소정근로 또는 총근로에 대하여 지급하기로 정하여진 금액을 말한다. 관련된 예로, 생산량에 따른 성과 임금은 최저임금의 산입범위에는 포함되나, 통상임금에는 포함되지 않는다.

(2) 통상임금과의 차이[102]

---

99) 행정해석 2015.10.2.). 근로기준정책과-4782)
100) 행정해석, 2014. 2. 7. 근로개선정책과-659
101) 행정해석 1989. 5. 17. 임금 32240-7146
102) 대법원 2007.01.11. 선고 2006다64245 판결; 행정해석 2006. 6. 29, 임금근로시간정책팀-1539; 2006. 12. 20. 임금근로시간정책팀-3848

Chapter 2 Statutory Wages

Item	Ordinary wage	Minimum wage
Definition/ Purpose	Ordinary wage refers to hourly wages, daily wages, weekly wages, monthly wages, or contract wages which are determined to be paid periodically or in lump sum to a worker for their prescribed work or whole work.	The purpose of this Act is to bring stability to workers and improve labor force quality by guaranteeing a minimum level of wages (Article 1 of the Minimum Wage Act).
Calculation method	Calculated into hourly wage rate (Monthly ordinary wage ÷ monthly contractual working hours).	Calculated into hourly wage rate (Monthly minimum wage ÷ monthly contractual working hours).
Legal enforcement	No legal enforcement.	Legal enforcement, with cases of violation rendered invalid.
Usage	Wages determined to be paid in advance; used for paid leave allowances.	Wages actually paid; used for guaranteeing employee livelihood.
(i) Meal	Included in ordinary wage.	Included in minimum wage.
(ii) Performance bonus	1) Fixed bonuses are included in ordinary wages. 2) Performance bonuses are recognized as ordinary wage to the extent that they are guaranteed to a minimum. 3) Sales bonuses are excluded.	1) Annual bonus payments are excluded. 2) Monthly fixed bonuses. 3) Monthly performance bonuses 4) Sales bonuses are included in minimum wage.
(iii) Welfare allowance	Regular, uniform, and fixed welfare allowances are included.	Monthly regular, uniform, and fixed welfare allowances are included.

Working Hours 1539; MOEL Guidelines on Dec. 20, 2006 Wage and Working Hours 3848

구 분	통상임금	최저임금
목 적	근로자에게 정기적이고 일률적으로 소정근로 또는 총 근로에 대하여 지급하기로 정한 시간급 금액, 일급 금액, 주급 금액, 월급 금액 또는 도급 금액을 말한다(근기법 시행령 제6조).	근로자에 대하여 임금의 최저수준을 보장하여 근로자의 생활 안정과 노동력의 질적 향상을 꾀함을 목적으로 한다(최임법 제1조).
계산방법	시간급으로 계산 (월 통상임금 ÷ 월 소정근로시간)	시간급으로 계산 (월 최저임금 ÷ 월 소정근로시간)
법적강제 여 부	법적강제 없음	법적 강제 및 위반시 무효
사 용	사전적 임금으로 유급수당 계산 근거	사후적 임금으로 근로자의 생활 보장
(ⅰ) 식 대	통상임금 포함	최저임금 포함
(ⅱ) 성과급	1) 고정상여금은 통상임금에 포함 2) 성과상여금은 최저한도로 보장되는 한도 내에서 통상임금 인정 3) 판매수당 미포함	1) 연단위 산정하여 매월 지급하는 상여금 제외됨. 2) 매월 산정단위 상여금 최저임금 포함, 3) 매월 단위 성과상여금 최저임금 포함 4) 생산고(판매수당)에 따른 임금 포함
(ⅲ) 복지수당	정기적 일률적 고정적 복지수당 포함	월 단위 정기적 일률적 복지수당 포함

5. Opinion

The 2018 and 2019 minimum wage increase (30%), in addition to the court ruling[103] in December 2013 concerning the enlarged scope of ordinary wage, has had a considerable impact on company wage structures. In particular, production workers in the automobile industry have 243 fixed working hours per month, which was designed to lower the ordinary wage through the bonus system. Such companies have maintained long working hours by lowering the overtime, nighttime and holiday work allowances. However, it will not be possible to maintain this trend with the higher minimum wage.

Three things are expected through the minimum wage increase. First, it will be an opportunity to simplify the current wage structure. There is a high possibility that the wage structure will be restructured with a base salary added to the minimum wage range, performance bonuses, and statutory allowances. Second, the steep increase in wages may lead to a reduction in hours of work and the creation of new employment. Third, it will be an opportunity to overcome polarization in the working conditions for regular and irregular workers. I expect the increase in minimum wage to have a positive effect on SMEs while it may be a burden to management.

V. Shutdown Allowances

1. Legal Standards for shutdown Allowances

(1) Concept

> Article 46 of the LSA (Pay for Suspension of Business)
> ① If a business is suspended for reasons attributable to an employer, the employer shall pay the workers concerned a payment of seventy percent or more of average remuneration during the period of suspension. If the amount equivalent to seventy percent of average remuneration exceeds

---

[103] Supreme Court ruling on Dec. 18, 2013, 2012 da 8389

5. 의견

 2018년과 2019년 최저임금 30% 인상이 2013년 12월에 있었던 통상임금 확대 판례[103]와 아울러 기업체의 임금구조상 상당한 영향을 끼치고 있다. 특히 자동차 산업의 생산직 근로자의 경우 상여금 제도를 통해 기본급을 낮추어 연장, 야간, 휴일근로수당을 낮게 하여 오랜 동안 장시간 근로를 유지하고 있었지만, 통상임금 확대 판례와 이번 최저임금 인상으로 인해 상당한 타격을 입게 되었다.

 그러나, 이번 최저임금 인상을 통해 기대되는 부분도 있다. 첫째, 현행 임금구조를 단순화시키는 계기가 될 것이다. 최저임금 범위에 산입되는 기본급, 성과상여금, 법정수당으로 임금구조가 재편될 가능성이 크다. 둘째, 급격한 임금상승으로 장시간근로가 줄고, 새로운 고용창출로 이어질 수 있다. 셋째, 정규직과 비정규직의 근로조건에 있어 양극화를 극복할 수 있는 계기가 될 것이다. 이번 최저임금의 인상을 통해 중소기업에 있어 경영상 부담감을 주는 것에 못지않게 긍정적 효과도 있기를 기대해 본다.

V. 휴업수당

1. 휴업수당의 법적 기준

(1) 의 의

> 근로기준법 제46조 【휴업수당】
> ① 사용자의 귀책사유로 휴업하는 경우에 사용자는 휴업기간 동안 그 근로자에게 평균임금의 100분의 70 이상의 수당을 지급하여야 한다. 다만, 평균임금의 100분의 70에 해당하는 금액이 통상임금을 초과

---

103) 대법원 2013. 12. 18. 선고, 2012다89399 판결

Chapter 2 Statutory Wages

> normal remuneration, then normal remuneration may be paid.
> ② An employer who cannot continue business operations for unavoidable reasons may, upon approval from the Labor Relations Commission, pay remuneration lower than the standards stipulated in paragraph ① for the suspension of business.
>
> LSA Enforcement Decree, Article 26 (Calculation of Suspension Allowance)
> Where an employee has received a part of wage during a period of suspension due to any reason attributable to the employer, the employer shall, in compliance with the main sentence of Article 46 (1) of the Act, pay him/her an allowance equivalent to at least 70 percent of the difference calculated by subtracting that part of wage already paid to the said employee from the average wage: Provided, That where ordinary wage are paid as suspension allowance in accordance with the proviso to Article 46 (1) of the Act, the difference between the ordinary wage and the part already paid during the period of suspension shall be paid.
>
> LSA, Article 109 (Penal Provisions) Employers shall be punished for violations of the above Article 46 (Pay for Suspension of Business) with imprisonment of not more than 3 years or a fine of not more than KRW 30 million.

According to the Labor Standards Act, when a worker is suspended for reasons attributable to the employer, the employer is required to pay at least 70% of the average wage(or 100% of the ordinary wage)(Article 46(1)). However, if it is impossible to continue the business for unavoidable reasons, an amount that is less than the legal shutdown allowance may be paid if this is approved by the Labor Commission(Article 46(1)). In order to guarantee the effectiveness of the shutdown compensation system, an employer who violates the provisions of shutdown compensation shall be sentenced to imprisonment of not more than three years or fined not more than KRW 30 million(Article 109).

Shutdown allowances are intended to guarantee the right of workers to live by providing certain allowances when they are unable to work for reasons not attributable to them. On the other hand, if an employer is forced, for unavoidable reasons, to pay legal shutdown allowances until the business can no longer continue, this will cause excessive burden on the employer and will severely hinder operations, which may result in insolvency of the company. This is why an exemption for shutdown compensation is stipulated.[104]

---

[104] Lim Jong-Ryul, Labor Law, 20th ed. Park Young-sa, 2022, p. 422; Jung Myung-hyun, Duality of Legal

> 하는 경우에는 통상임금을 휴업수당으로 지급할 수 있다.
> ② 제1항에도 불구하고 부득이한 사유로 사업을 계속하는 것이 불가능하여 노동위원회의 승인을 받은 경우에는 제1항의 기준에 못 미치는 휴업수당을 지급할 수 있다.
>
> 근로기준법 시행령 제26조 【휴업수당의 산출】
> 사용자의 귀책사유로 휴업한 기간 중에 근로자가 임금의 일부를 지급받은 경우에는 사용자는 법 제46조 제1항 본문에 따라 그 근로자에게 평균임금에서 그 지급받은 임금을 뺀 금액을 계산하여 그 금액의 100분의 70 이상에 해당하는 수당을 지급하여야 한다. 다만, 법 제46조 제1항 단서에 따라 통상임금을 휴업수당으로 지급하는 경우에는 통상임금에서 휴업한 기간 중에 지급받은 임금을 뺀 금액을 지급하여야 한다.
>
> 제109조 【벌칙】 휴업수당 규정을 위반한 자(법 제46조)는 3년 이하의 징역 또는 3천만 원 이하의 벌금에 처한다.

근로기준법에서는 사용자의 귀책사유로 휴업하는 경우에는 그 근로자에게 평균임금의 100분의 70% 이상의 수당(또는 통상임금의 100%)을 지급하여야 한다(제46조 제1항). 다만, 부득이한 사유로 사업을 계속하는 것이 불가능하여 노동위원회의 승인을 받은 경우에는 법정휴업수당에 미달하는 수당을 지급할 수 있다고 규정하고 있다(제46조 제1항). 휴업보상제도의 실효성을 보장하기 위하여 휴업보상 지급규정을 위반한 자는 3년 이하의 징역 또는 3천만 원 이하의 벌금에 처한다고 규정하고 있다(제109조).

휴업수당은 근로자의 귀책사유가 아닌 이유로 근로를 할 수 없게 된 경우에 일정한 수당을 근로자에게 지급하여 근로자의 생존권을 보장하는데 그 취지가 있다. 이와 함께 사용자가 부득이한 사유로 사업계속이 불가능한 경우까지 법정휴업수당 지급을 강제한다면 사용자에게 지나친 부담을 주어 기업의 운영에 막대한 지장을 초래하여 기업의 파산을 촉진하는 결과까지 초래할 수 있다는 점을 고려한 휴업보상에의 감면규정을 두고 있다.[104]

---

[104] 임종률, 노동법 제18판, 박영사, 2020, 422면; 정명현, 휴업수당의 법적 성질의 이중성, 저스티스 147, 한국법학원, 2015.4, 253면.

Shutdown refers to a situation in which a worker is unable to provide work against his/her will despite being willing to provide the work under the employment contract.[105] Civil Act provisions relating to the shutdown of a business provide exemption of employer fault in case of a force majeure beyond the employer's responsibility.[106] However, if an employee fails to receive work due to the employer's fault, it is possible to claim the full amount of wage, and not just the shutdown allowance.[107] In cases like this, the Civil Act provisions have difficulty in proving the employer's intention or negligence, so the Labor Standards Act provides a shutdown allowance system to guarantee the minimum life standards of workers without relying on the Civil Act's risk-bearing principle.[108]

(2) Requirements for shutdown allowance

As a requirement for shutdown,

first, there must be fault attributable to the employer. Employer's fault is any reason that may arise within the employer's managerial influence.

Second, the business should not be closed due to force majeure. Force majeure means that the reason for the shutdown of a business should occur from outside and the employer could do nothing to control it. Typical examples would be natural disasters, war, and large regional blackouts.

Third, it is assumed that shutdown(full or partial closure) has taken place.

(3) Amount of suspension allowances

1) Full payment of wage

In case of a shutdown due to an employer's intention or negligence, the full wage shall be paid. This includes suspension without legitimate reason, forced leave, and unfair dismissal. In accordance with Article 538(1) of the Civil Act, the employer shall pay 100% of wage, not shutdown allowances, when workers are

---

Characteristics for shutdown Allowance, Justice Magazine (147), Korea Law Institute, April 2015, p. 253.

[105] Supreme Court ruling on Oct. 11, 2012: 2012da12870.

[106] Civil Act: Article 537 (Obligor's Burden to Bear Risk)
If the performance of an obligation of one of the parties to a bilateral contract becomes impossible by any cause for which neither of the parties is responsible, the obligor may not be entitled to counter-performance.

[107] Article 538 (Impossibility of Performance due to Cause for Which Obligee is Responsible)
(1) If the performance of an obligation of one of the parties to a bilateral contract becomes impossible by any cause for which the obligee is responsible, the obligor may demand counter-performance. The same applies to cases where performance becomes impossible by any cause for which neither of the parties is responsible in the case of mora creditoris. (2) In cases in the preceding paragraph, if the obligor has received any benefit by being relieved of his own obligation, he shall return such benefit to the obligee.

[108] Labor Law Case Study Group, Interpretation of the Labor Standards Act (III), 2nd ed. Parkyoungsa, 2020, p. 121.

'휴업'이란 근로자가 근로계약에 따라 근로를 제공할 의사가 있음에도 불구하고 그 의사에 반하여 근로를 제공하지 못하는 경우를 말한다.[105] 휴업과 관련된 민법 조항은 사용자의 귀책사유가 없는 불가항력적인 사항으로 근로를 수령하지 못한 경우에 책임을 면한다고 규정하고 있다.[106] 그러나 사용자의 책임있는 사유로 근로를 이행하지 못한 경우에는 휴업수당이 아니라 사용자에게 임금 전액을 청구할 수 있다고 규정하고 있다.[107] 이 경우 민법 조항은 사용자의 고의나 과실 등을 증명해야 하는 어려움이 있기 때문에 민법상 위험 부담 법리에 의존하지 않고도 근로기준법은 근로자의 최저 생활을 보장하려는 취지에서 휴업보상제도를 두고 있다.[108]

(2) 휴업수당의 지급요건

휴업의 요건으로

첫째, 사용자의 귀책사유가 있어야 한다. 사용자의 귀책사유는 사용자의 세력권 내에서 발생할 수 있는 모든 사유를 말한다.

둘째, 불가항력으로 인한 휴업이 아니어야 한다. 불가항력이란 휴업의 사유가 외부로부터 발생하여 사용자의 권한 범위 밖에서 발생한 사유를 말한다. 대표적인 사례가 자연재해, 전쟁, 지역의 대규모 정전사태 등이다.

셋째, 휴업을 할 것을 전제로 한다. 휴업은 전면적 휴업도 될 수 있고, 부분적 휴업도 될 수 있다.

(3) 휴업수당의 규모

1) 임금 전액지급

사용자의 자신의 고의나 과실로 인해 휴업하는 경우 임금 전액을 지급해야 한다. 여기에는 정당한 사유없는 대기발령, 강제휴직, 부당해고 등이 해당된다. 이는 민법 제538조 제1항에 의거하여 사용자의 불법행위로

---

105) 대법원 2012.10.11, 2012다12870.
106) 민법 제537조【채무자위험부담주의】쌍무계약의 당사자 일방의 채무가 당사자쌍방의 책임없는 사유로 이행할 수 없게 된 때는 채무자는 상대방의 이행을 청구하지 못한다.
107) 민법 제538조【채권자귀책사유로 인한 이행불능】① 쌍무계약의 당사자일방의 채무가 채권자의 책임있는 사유로 이행할 수 없게 된 때는 채무자는 상대방의 이행을 청구할 수 있다. 채권자의 수령지체 중에 당사자 쌍방의 책임없는 사유로 이행할 수 없게 된 때에도 같다. ② 전항의 경우에 채무자는 자기의 채무를 면함으로써 이익을 얻은 때는 이를 채권자에게 상환하여야 한다.
108) 노동법실무연구회, 근로기준법 주해(Ⅲ), 제2판, 박영사, 2020, 121면.

suspended due to illegal activity by the employer. However, an interim benefit obtained during the same period may be deducted pursuant to paragraph 2 of Article 538 of the Civil Act.[109]

2) Shutdown allowances

In case of shutdown due to an employer's fault, an allowance shall be paid of at least 70% of the average wage.[110] In principle, employer's fault is a management obstacle that occurs within the scope of the employer's power and will include situations such as being closed due to shortage of funds, shortage of raw materials, decrease in order volume, reduction of market and output, shortage of raw materials in subcontracted factories due to the parent company's poor management, or shortage of operations due to insufficient funds.[111] A partial shutdown allowance shall be paid when only part of the workplace is closed or when working hours are reduced.[112]

3) Reduction of shutdown allowances

In order to reduce shutdown allowances, an employer may have urgent cause to not continue business operations for unavoidable reasons, and will need to get approval from the Labor Relations Commission(Article 46(2) of the LSA).[113] This means that if a company expects to go bankrupt, even if the employer is at fault, it may pay less than the legal shutdown allowance if so approved by the Labor Relations Commission.[114]

Conditions for the reduction of shutdown allowance require ① as a substantial requirement, the inability to continue business operations for unavoidable reasons and ② as a procedural requirement, the approval of the Labor Relations

---

[109] Supreme Court ruling on June 28, 1991: 90daka25277 (Damage compensation).

[110] Judgment of reasons attributable to an employer
  (1) Reasons attributable to an employer: ① Closure of business due to economic reasons; ② Shortage of raw material, reduction of orders; ③ Electricity failure, stagnant sale of products, or capital shortage; ④ Plant transfer, destruction by fire, machinery damage, or reduction of work volume; and ⑤ Subsidiary plant's shortage of raw materials and funds owing to the head company's financial difficulties.
  (2) Reasons not attributable to an employer: ① Flooding of the entire plant; ② Closure due to illegal political strike; ③ Legal plant lockout; ④ Incendiary fire by a third party (arson); and ⑤ Plant closure due to natural disasters.

[111] MOEL Guidelines: Gungi 68207-106, Sep. 21, 1999; Wage Policy Team - 711, Mar. 29, 2006

[112] MOEL Guidelines: The shutdown Allowance System, Labor Standards - 387, Feb. 13, 2000.

[113] MOEL Guide: Gungi 68207-598, Feb. 28, 2000.

[114] MOEL Guidelines: Standards of the Shutdown Allowance System, Labor Standards Team - 387, Feb. 13, 2009: Approval Process of Labor Commission Decision on Shutdown Allowance (by Employer) ? Submission of Application for Approval of Reduced Shutdown Allowance (to the Labor Relations Commission) ? Confirmation and Review (by related official) ? Deliberation & Resolution (Judgement Committee, within 30 days) ? Notification.

인하여 근로자가 휴업하는 경우의 휴업수당이 아니라 임금 100%를 지급해야 한다. 다만, 민법 제538조의 제2항에 의거하여 중간이익을 공제할 수 있다.[109]

2) 휴업수당 지급

사용자의 귀책사유로 인하여 휴업하는 경우 평균임금의 70% 이상의 휴업수당을 지급해야 한다.[110] 사용자의 귀책사유란 원칙적으로 사용자의 세력범위 안에서 생긴 경영장애로 자금난, 원자재 부족, 주문량 감소, 시장불황과 생산량 감축, 모회사의 경영난에 따른 하청공장의 자재부족이나 자금난에 의한 조업단축 등으로 인한 휴업을 말한다.[111] 사업장의 일부만 휴업하는 경우나 1일 근로시간 중 일부 근로시간을 단축하는 경우에 부분휴업 수당을 지급한다.[112]

3) 휴업수당의 감액

휴업수당을 감액하여 지급할 수 있는 경우는 사용자의 귀책사유에도 불구하고 부득이한 사유로 사업계속이 불가능하여 노동위원회의 승인을 얻은 경우이다(근기법 제46조 제2항).[113] 이는 기업의 도산이 예상될 정도의 피해가 발생할 경우 사용자의 귀책사유가 있다고 하더라도 노동위원회의 승인을 받은 경우 법정 휴업수당에 못 미치는 휴업수당을 지급할 수 있다.[114]

휴업수당 감액요건에는 ① 실질적 요건으로 부득이한 사유로 사업계속이 불가능할 것을 요하며, ② 절차적 요건으로 노동위원회의 승인으로 요한다. 부득이한 사유로 인해 사업계속이 불가능하다 할지라도, 노동위원회로부터 승인을 받지 못해 절차적 요건을 충족하지 못한다면 휴업수당의 지급을

---

109) 대법원 1991.6.28, 90다카25277(손해배상).
110) 사용자 귀책사유 유무 판단
   (1) 사용자의 귀책사유 인정: ① 불황 등으로 인한 경영상 휴업, ② 원료 부족, 주문 감소 ③ 정전, 제품판매 부진, 자금난, ④ 공장 이전.소실, 기계 파손, 작업량 감소, ⑤ 모회사 경영난에 따른 하청공장의 자재.자금난
   (2) 사용자의 귀책사유 불인정: ① 전체 공장의 침수, ② 불법정치파업으로 휴업, ③ 정당한 직장폐쇄, ④ 제3자의 방화로 인한 화재, ⑤ 천재 기타 자연현상 등에 의한 휴업.
111) 행정해석: 근기 68207-106, 1999.9.21; 임금근로시간정책팀-711, 2006.3.29.
112) 고용노동부 행정해석: 휴업수당제도 기준, 근로기준과-387, 2009.2.13.
113) 행정해석: 근기 68207-598, 2000.2.28.
114) 고용노동부 행정해석: 휴업수당제도 기준, 근로기준과-387, 2009.2.13: 노동위원회의 승인절차 휴업결정(사용자) → 기준미달 휴업수당 지급승인 신청서 제출(관할 지방노동위원회) → 확인.검토(심사담당) → 심의.의결(심판위원회, 30일 이내) → 통보.

Commission. Even if it is impossible to operate the business for unavoidable reasons, it is not possible to avoid or reduce shutdown allowances without obtaining approval from the Labor Commission.[115]

Shutdown allowances can be paid at less than 70% of the average wage, and can even be avoided.[116]

4) Unpaid leave

Employer's fault under Article 46 of the Labor Standards Act refers to managerial obstacles that occur within the scope of the employer's power and includes situations such as financial shortages, shortage of raw materials, and market recession. If it is impossible to continue the business due to force majeure circumstances, such as a natural disaster, this cannot be regarded as the fault of the employer[117] because it is impossible for the employer to manage and control such occurrences. There is no obligation to pay shutdown allowances, regardless of whether the Labor Relations Commission has approved them.[118]

2. Cases of Shutdown Allowances

(1) Full payment

1) If an employee's(unfair) dismissal was invalidated or canceled, the employee's status as a worker would still be in existence, and it would be considered that the worker's failure to provide work was attributable to the employer. Article 538(1) of the Civil Act may request the payment of all wage available for the dismissed period.[119]

2) If suspension of vehicle driving(discontinuance) measures against a worker was found to be unreasonable, in which case the employee was not able to provide work due to the employer's fault, the employer shall pay a shutdown allowance as prescribed by Article 46 of the Labor Standards Act. If, however, the employee is deemed unable to provide work due to intention or negligence of the employer, a claim for the full amount of wage under Article 538(1) of the Civil Act shall also occur.[120]

---

[115] Supreme Court ruling on Sep. 17, 1968: 68nu151.
[116] Supreme Court ruling on Nov. 24, 2000: 99doo4280.
[117] MOEL Guidelines: Labor Standards Team - 802, Feb. 16, 2010
[118] MOEL Guidelines: Gungi 68207-598, Feb. 28, 2000
[119] Supreme Court ruling on Dec. 22, 1981: 81da626.
[120] MOEL Guidelines: Wage/Working Hour Team - 711, Mar. 29, 2006.

면하거나 감액할 수 없다.[115]

　　휴업수당 감액수준은 평균임금의 100분의 70 이하의 휴업수당을 지급할 수 있으며, 전액 감액도 가능하다.[116]

4) 무급휴업

　　근로기준법 제46조에 의한 '사용자의 귀책사유'는 원칙적으로 사용자의 세력범위 안에서 생긴 경영장애로서 자금난, 원자재 부족, 시장불황 등으로 인한 경우를 말하며 천재지변이나 재난과 같이 사용자에게 책임을 물을 수 없는 불가항력적인 사정으로 사업 계속이 불가능하게 된 경우에는 사용자의 귀책사유로 볼 수 없다.[117] 천재지변 등 불가항력적인 사유는 사용자의 지배관리가 불가능하므로 사용자의 귀책사유로 볼 수 없다. 이때 노동위원회의 승인 여부와 관계없이 휴업수당 지급의 의무가 없다.[118]

2. 휴업수당의 적용사례

(1) 임금전액 지급

1) 사용자의 부당한 해고처분이 무효이거나 취소된 때는 그동안 해고당사자의 근로자 지위는 계속되고 있었던 것이 되고, 근로자가 그간 근로 제공을 하지 못한 것은 사용자의 귀책사유로 인한 것이라 할 것이니 근로자는 민법 제538조 제1항에 의하여 계속 근로하였을 경우 받을 수 있는 임금의 전부 지급을 청구할 수 있다.[119]

2) 사용자의 근로자에 대한 차량승무정지(배차중단) 조치가 부당한 것으로 판명된 경우라면 사용자의 귀책사유로 인해 근로를 제공할 수 없게 된 경우 근로기준법 제46조 소정의 휴업수당을 지급하여야 할 것이나, 사용자의 고의나 과실로 인하여 근로를 제공하지 못한 것으로 인정되는 경우에는 민법 제538조 제1항의 규정에 의한 임금전액에 대한 청구권도 동시에 발생한다.[120]

---

115) 대법원 1968.9.17, 68누151.
116) 대법원 200.11.24, 99두4280.
117) 행정해석: 근로기준과-802, 2010.2.16.
118) 행정해석: 근기 68207-598, 2000.2.28.
119) 대법원 1981.12.22, 81다626.

Chapter 2 Statutory Wages

(2) Payment of shutdown allowances

1) If a contractor was given an order to suspend operations by the government, if subcontractors also had to shut down their operations(which cannot be translated as force majeure), the subcontractors should pay shutdown allowances to their workers.[121]

2) If a contractor's removal of hazardous chemicals restricts access to a subcontractor's workers and if they fail to provide work, this is hardly considered to be force majeure beyond the scope of the employer.[122]

(3) Reduction of suspension allowances

1) A Bupyeong plant closed for more than three months due to a sharp drop in sales after an incident with contaminated dumplings, and the inventory increased during this period. As a result, managerial difficulties can be understood as about 80 workers were dismissed for business reasons. Unless consumer confidence was restored in the near future, normal operation would be difficult. Therefore, it is possible to reduce the shutdown allowance if it is impossible to continue the business for unavoidable reasons(Incheon LRC 2004 shutdown 1).

2) Due to bankruptcy, deficits accumulated even after the company liquidation procedure began, and there was no alternative for normalization as attempts to sell the company were unsuccessful. In this case, unavoidable shutdown is a valid reason for the reduction of shutdown allowances(Incheon LRC 2000 shutdown 1).

3) A situation in which a company goes to the brink of bankruptcy due to an unforeseen fire is considered an unavoidable reason for the employer(NLRC 89 Shutdown 1).

(4) Unpaid leave

1) An employer is not obliged to pay any shutdown allowance for a period of suspension due to interruption of work by a third party.[123]

2) Absence or leave of absence due to natural disaster or other similar instances, and disciplinary actions such as suspension from work, temporary suspension of work, illness, etc., shall not be regarded as a case of employer fault and shall

---

[121] Supreme Court ruling Sep. 10, 2019: 2019do9604.
[122] MOEL Guidelines: Labor Standards Team - 3535, May 30, 2018
[123] Guidelines: Labor Standards Team - 2855, June 9, 2004

(2) 휴업수당 지급

1) 원청업체에 대한 작업중지명령으로 인한 하청회사의 휴업은 불가항력이라고 주장할 수 없는 사유로 휴업한 것으로 근로자에게 휴업수당을 지급할 의무가 있다.[121]
2) 원청업체의 유해화학 물질 제거 작업에 따라 하도급업체 소속 근로자의 출입이 제한되어 근로를 제공하지 못한 경우라면, 이는 사용자의 세력 범위를 벗어난 불가항력적인 사유로 보기 어렵다.[122]

(3) 휴업수당의 감액

1) 만두파동 이후 3개월 이상 회사 매출이 제로에 가까운 급감, 재고량 증가로 부평공장을 폐쇄하였다. 이로 인하여 약 80명의 근로자를 정리한 사실 등의 경영상 어려움이 인정된다. 앞으로도 소비자의 신뢰가 회복되지 않는 한 정상조업이 어려운 사업계속이 불가능한 경우에 해당하므로 휴업수당 감액에 해당된다(인천지노위 04휴업1).
2) 부도에 따라 회사정리절차가 개시된 이후에도 적자가 누적되고 있고, 경영정상화를 위한 대안이 존재하지 않아 회사매각을 추진하고 있으나 회사매각도 성과를 거두지 못하고 있다. 이 경우에는 부득이한 휴업상태가 휴업수당의 감액 사유에 해당된다(인천지노위 00휴업1).
3) 원인 미상의 화재발생으로 인한 기업이 부도 직전까지 가는 경영상 긴박한 상태의 도래는 사용자로서도 어쩔 수 없는 불가항력적인 사유로 휴업수당을 감할 수밖에 없는 경우에 해당된다(중노위 89휴업1).

(4) 무급휴업

1) 제3자의 출근방해로 인한 피치 못할 휴업기간에 대하여 사용자가 휴업수당을 지급하여야 할 의무는 없다.[123]
2) 천재지변이나 그밖에 이에 준하는 사유, 징계처분으로서 정직, 출근정지, 질병 등에 따른 결근이나 휴직은 사용자의 귀책사유로 볼 수 없고 이는

---

120) 행정해석: 임금근로시간정책팀-711, 2006.3.29
121) 대법원 2019.9.10, 2019도9604.
122) 행정해석: 근로기준정책과-3535, 2018.5.30.
123) 행정해석: 근로기준과-2855, 2004.6.9

not be reason for payment of a shutdown allowance.[124]

(5) Deduction of interim income

Even if an employee whose employer declared a business suspension found another paying job during the period of business suspension or acquired an interim income, the employer shall provide the employee business suspension pay.[125]

Business suspension pay is intended to provide a minimum living for the employees affected by business discontinuance for a reason attributable to the employer. The notion of business suspension includes cases where an individual employee, although they intend to provide work as specified in the labor contract, finds it impossible to do the work. In short, the provision on business suspension pay applies to the employee in question. Therefore, within the range of 70% of the ordinary wage(that is, the business suspension pay rate), interim wage(earned during the suspended period) may not be deducted from shutdown allowance. In other words, only the amount in excess of the business suspension pay rate may be deducted.

3. Opinion

The leave allowance system guarantees workers' right to life by providing shutdown allowances in cases where the worker does not provide labor due to fault on the employer's part. When a workplace is shut down and closed, it is difficult for the workers to survive, so the Labor Standards Act guarantees a wage of 70% on average as a shut-down allowance in case of closure for reasons attributable to the employer. It is possible to reduce a shut-down allowance if there is a huge disruption to the operation of the business to the point where the employer cannot continue to operate. In addition, the Civil Act states that if a worker is suspended due to the intention or negligence of an employer, the full wage shall be paid (Article 538), but if the business is closed through no fault of the employer, the shut-down allowance shall not be paid (Article 537). Payments can be divided into: (i) 100% pay, (ii) payment of shut-down allowances, (iii) reduction of shut-down allowances, and (iv) unpaid leave.

---

[124] Lim Jong-Ryul, Labor Law, 20th edition, Park Young-sa, 2022, p. 423
[125] Supreme Court ruling on Jun. 28, 1991, 90DaKa25277.

휴업수당 지급사유가 되지 않는다.[124]

(5) 중간수입 공제

휴업기간 중에 근로자가 다른 기업에 취업하여 임금을 받는 등 중간수입이 있는 경우에도 휴업수당을 지급해야 한다.[125] 휴업수당은 근로자의 최저생활을 보장하려는 취지에서 사용자의 귀책사유로 인하여 휴업하는 경우에는 사용자는 휴업기간 중 당해 근로자에게 그 평균임금의 100분의 70이상의 수당을 지급하는 것인바, 여기서의 휴업이란 개개의 근로자가 근로계약에 따라 근로를 제공할 의사가 있음에도 불구하고 그 의사에 반하여 취업이 거부되거나 불가능하게 된 경우도 포함된다고 할 것이므로, 근로자가 지급받을 수 있는 임금액 중 휴업수당(평균임금 70%)의 한도에서는 이를 이익공제의 대상으로 삼을 수 없고, 그 휴업수당을 초과하는 금액에서 중간수입을 공제하여야 한다.

3. 시사점

휴업수당제도는 사용자의 귀책사유로 근로자가 근로제공이 없는 경우에도 일정한 휴업수당을 지급하여 근로자의 생존권의 보장을 확보하기 위한 제도이다. 사업장이 폐쇄되고 공장가동을 중단하게 되면 거기서 근무하는 근로자의 생계가 어려워지기 때문에 근로기준법에서는 사용자의 귀책사유로 휴업하는 경우, 평균임금의 70%를 급여로 보장하고 있다. 또한, 사업주 입장에서도 사업 지속이 불가능할 정도로 기업운영에 막대한 지장이 있는 경우 휴업수당을 감액하는 것도 가능하다. 민법에서는 사용자의 고의 과실로 인하여 근로자가 휴업하는 경우 임금 전액을 지급해야 하고(제538조), 사용자의 귀책사유가 없이 휴업하는 경우에는 휴업수당을 지급하지 않아도 된다고 기술하고 있다(제537조). 즉, (i) 임금 100% 지급, (ii) 휴업수당 지급, (iii) 휴업수당 감액, (iv) 무급 휴업을 하는 경우로 구분해 볼 수 있다.

---

[124] 임종률, 노동법, 제20판, 박영사, 2022, 423면.
[125] 대법원 1991.6.28, 90다카25277.

VI. Additional Allowances

> Labor Standards Act, Article 56 (Extended Work, Night Work and Holiday Work)
> ① Employers shall pay an additional 50 percent or more of the ordinary wages for extended work (work during the hours as extended pursuant to the provisions of Articles 53 and 59, and the proviso of Article 69).
> ② Notwithstanding paragraph (1), with regards to holiday work employers shall pay additionally according to the following subparagraphs:
> 1. Holiday work of 8 hours or less: 50 percent of the ordinary wage
> 2. Holiday work beyond 8 hours: one hundred percent of the ordinary wage
> ③ Employers shall pay an additional 50 percent of the ordinary wage for night work (work between 10 P.M. and 6 A.M.)
> LSA, Article 109 (Penal Provisions) Employers shall be punished for violations of the above Article 56 (additional allowances) with imprisonment of not more than 3 years or a fine of not more than KRW 30 million.

1. Overtime work and additional allowances

Overtime work refers to working hours that exceed the standard working hours specified in the Labor Standards Act. Adult employees may extend working hours up to 12 hours per week through mutual agreement by the parties concerned (with no limit on daily working hours). Employers shall pay an additional 50% of ordinary wages for overtime work, night work, and off-day work. The additional pay shall be made for the employee's overtime work after calculating it into their ordinary wages. In cases where contractual working hours (e.g., 4 hours per day) in the collective agreement or rules of employment are less than the legal standard working hours, an additional allowance needs to be paid for extended working hours exceeding the contractual working hours regardless of whether they exceed the legal standard working hours. In this case, if the part-time employee worked for 8 hours, the employer should pay the basic pay for four hours and the overtime work allowance for 6 hours: for 4 hours extended work and additional 2 hours for overtime work, which will be 10 hours wage in total.[126]

VI. 가산임금

> 근로기준법 제56조(연장·야간 및 휴일 근로)
> ① 사용자는 연장근로(제53조·제59조 및 제69조 단서에 따라 연장된 시간의 근로)에 대하여는 통상임금의 100분의 50을 가산하여 근로자에게 지급하여야 한다.
> ② 제1항에도 불구하고 사용자는 휴일근로에 대하여는 다음 각 호의 기준에 따른 금액 이상을 가산하여 근로자에게 지급하여야 한다.
>   1. 8시간 이내의 휴일근로 : 통상임금의 100분의 50
>   2. 8시간을 초과한 휴일근로 : 통상임금의 100분의 100
> ③ 사용자는 야간근로(오후 10시부터 다음 날 오전 6시 사이의 근로를 말한다)에 대하여는 통상임금의 100분의 50이상을 가산하여 근로자에게 지급하여야 한다.
> 제109조(벌칙) 가산임금 규정을 위반한 자(법 제56조)는 3년 이하의 징역 또는 3천만 원 이하의 벌금에 처한다.

1. 연장근로와 가산임금

연장근로(시간외근로)란 근로기준법에서 정한 기준근로시간을 초과하는 근로를 말한다. 성인근로자의 경우 1주 12시간 한도에서 당사자 간의 합의에 의해 연장근로 할 수 있으나, 1일 연장근로 한도는 없다. 사용자는 연장근로에 대하여는 통상임금의 50% 이상을 가산하여 지급해야 한다. 가산임금은 근로자가 연장근로에 대하여 통상임금에 가산하여 지급한다. 단체협약·취업규칙 등에서 법정근로시간에 미달하는 근로시간을 정하고 있는 경우에 그 소정근로시간(예 : 1일 4시간 근무)을 초과하고 법정근로시간을 초과하지 않는 경우라도 가산임금을 지급해야 한다. 이 경우 하루에 8시간을 일한 경우, 4시간에 대한 임금과 4시간 연장에 근로에 대한 6시간 포함하여 총 10시간의 임금을 주어야 한다.[126]

---

[126] 기간제 및 단시간근로자 보호에 관한 법률, 제6조 [단시간근로자의 초과근로 제한]

2. Night work and additional allowances

Night working hours range from 10 p.m. to 6 a.m. the following day. Employers shall pay an additional 50% of ordinary wages for night work. Regardless of working hours within the contractual working hours, pay for night work shall be paid separately as an additional allowance. In cases where overtime work, off-day work, and night work overlap, an additional allowance shall be paid for each. For employees to whom Article 63 of the Labor Standards Act (exceptions may apply) apply, an additional allowance will not be paid for overtime work and off-day work, but only for night work.

3. Holiday work and additional allowance

Employers shall pay an additional 50% of ordinary wages for holiday work. 150% of the ordinary wage shall be paid for up to 8 hours of holiday work, and 200% shall be paid for hours of holiday work over 8 hours. This means that when overtime work and holiday work overlap, the employer shall pay each additional allowance.

4. Limitations on Application: Employees at Workplaces Ordinarily Employing Fewer than Five People[127]

Some workers have limits to the protection offered. The representative example includes workers at workplaces ordinarily employing fewer than five people. The Labor Standards Act (LSA) stipulates that "The Labor Standards Act shall apply to all businesses or workplaces in which five or more workers are ordinarily employed." (Article 11 of the LSA)

In relation to such limitations on application of the Labor Standards Act, some problems have recently emerged. While labor rights are not completely applicable to people employed by workplaces ordinarily employing fewer than five people, they are now finding themselves eligible for severance pay, which in the past was not the case. This new situation has been at the heart of more labor disputes for those workers looking out for their own labor rights.

---

[126] ACT ON THE PROTECTION, ETC. OF FIXED-TERM AND PART-TIME WORKERS, Article 6 (Restrictions on Overtime Work of Part-Time Workers)
(1) If any employer intends to have a part-time worker provide their services in excess of the working hours prescribed in Article 2 of the Labor Standards Act, they shall obtain the consent of such worker. In such cases, the number of overtime hours shall not exceed 12 hours a week
(3) Employers shall pay 50/100 or more of the average wage for overtime work under paragraph (1) in addition to ordinary wages.

[127] Jung, Bongsoo, "Limitations of on Application", 「Labor Law」, Jungang, March 2013.

2. 야간근로와 가산임금

야간근로란 오후 10시부터 익일 아침 6시까지 사이의 근로를 말한다. 사용자는 야간근로에 대하여는 통상임금의 50% 이상을 가산하여 지급해야 한다. 가산임금은 근로자가 야간근로에 대하여 통상임금에 가산하여 지급한다. 소정근로시간 이내의 근로일지라도 야간근로일 경우에는 가산임금을 지급해야 한다. 연장근로·휴일근로·야간근로가 중복된 경우 각각 가산하여 지급한다. 제63조의 적용제외 근로자(근로시간·휴게·휴일규정 적용 제외)에 대해서는 연장근로·휴일근로에 대한 가산임금의 지급문제는 발생하지 않으나, 야간근로에 대해서는 가산임금을 지급해야 한다.

3. 휴일근로와 가산임금

사용자는 휴일근로에 대하여는 통상임금의 50% 이상을 가산하여 지급해야 한다. 1일 8시간 이내의 휴일근로에 대해서는 통상임금의 50%를 가산하여 지급하고(150%), 1일 8시간을 초과하는 휴일근로에 대해서는 통상임금의 100%를 가산하여 지급한다(200%). 이는 연장근로와 휴일근로가 중복되는 경우 휴일근로 가산수당 할증률 적용하여 연장근로와 휴일근로를 중복해서 지급해야 한다.

4. 적용의 제외: 4인 이하 사업장의 근로자[127]

근로자이지만 노동법의 보호를 제한적으로 받는 근로자들이 있다. 그 대표적 사례가 5인 미만 사업장의 근로자이다. "근로기준법은 상시 5명 이상의 근로자를 사용하는 모든 사업 또는 사업장에 적용한다.(근로기준법 제11조)"라고 명시하고 있다.

---

① 사용자는 단시간근로자에 대하여 「근로기준법」 제2조의 소정근로시간을 초과하여 근로하게 하는 경우에는 당해 근로자의 동의를 얻어야 한다. 이 경우 1주간에 12시간을 초과하여 근로하게 할 수 없다.
③ 사용자는 제1항에 따른 초과근로에 대하여 통상임금의 100분의 50 이상을 가산하여 지급하여야 한다.

[127] 정봉수, "근로기준법의 적용제한", 「월간 노동법률」, 중앙경제사, 2013년 3월호

Chapter 2 Statutory Wages

In December 2012, employees at workplaces employing fewer than five people became eligible for severance pay. This has brought a lot of attention to those workers in inferior situations. Major articles of the LSA that are not applicable to such workers include, among others, 1) restrictions on dismissal, 2) suspension allowances, 3) restrictions on extended work, 4) extended work, night work and holiday work, and 5) annual paid leave. Due to their exclusion from these protections, such employees often work in inferior working environments.

(1) Major articles applicable to workplaces ordinarily employing fewer than five people

Topics related to major articles applicable to workplaces ordinarily employing fewer than five people include, among others, 1) written statement of the employment contract, 2) weekly holidays, 3) recesses, 4) accident compensation, 5) payment of money and valuables, 6) payment of wages, 7) restrictions on dismissal timing, 8) advance notice of dismissal, and 9) maternity leave.

Even though the restrictions on dismissal are not applicable, advance notice of dismissal is required, which means that an employer shall give at least thirty days' advance notice to a worker the employer intends to dismiss. If notice is not given thirty days before the dismissal, ordinary wages of at least thirty days shall be paid to the worker. Most articles regarding wages to be paid for labor service are also applicable. That is, minimum wage applies, payment of wages shall be observed, and penal provisions for delayed payment of wages are applicable. Of particular note, severance pay became mandatory December 1, 2010 for the first time: for the two years until December 1, 2012, the employer shall pay 50% of full severance pay to resigning employees, and shall pay 100% for the period beginning January 2013. Regardless of the length of service, severance pay only starts accruing from December 1, 2010. Also, according to Industrial Accident Compensation Insurance requirements, accident compensation for occupational injury, including medical treatment, suspension compensation, handicap compensation, etc. are applicable in the same way as for regular employees.

(2) Major articles not applicable to workplaces ordinarily employing fewer than five people

As the following LSA provisions do not apply to workers at workplaces ordinarily employing fewer than five people, working conditions for such employees are quite inferior.

근로기준법의 적용제한과 관련하여 다음과 같은 문제가 대두되고 있다. 5인 미만 사업장에 근무하는 근로자에게는 근로기본권이 제대로 보장되지 않았으나 최근에 적용되지 않았던 퇴직금 조항이 적용되면서 5인 미만 사업장 근로자들이 자신들의 권리를 찾는 분쟁이 자주 발생하고 있다는 점이다.

2010년 12월부터 4인 이하 사업장의 근로자들도 퇴직금 규정을 적용받게 됨에 따라 이들 취약 근로자들에 대해 사회적 관심을 쏠리고 있다. 적용되지 않는 주요 규정으로는 1) 해고의 제한; 2) 휴업수당; 3) 법정근로시간의 제한, 4) 연장 / 야간 / 휴일 근로에 가산임금; 5) 연차유급휴가 등이 적용되지 않는다. 이러한 핵심 조항이 적용되지 않으므로 근로기본권의 보호를 받지 못하는 취약한 근로환경에서 근무하는 근로자들이라고 할 수 있다.

(1) 4인 이하 사업장에 적용되는 주요 규정

4인 이하 사업장 적용되는 주요 규정으로는 1) 근로계약의 서면작성, 2) 주휴일, 3) 휴게, 4) 재해보상, 5) 임금청산, 6) 임금지급, 7) 해고시기 제한, 8) 해고예고, 9) 출산휴가 등 관련 조항이 적용된다.

해고의 제한규정이 적용되지 않지만, 근로자를 해고하고자 할 경우에는 적어도 30일전에 해고예고를 하여야 하고 이를 하지 못한 경우 1개월의 해고예고수당을 지급해야 한다. 그리고 근로의 대가인 임금에 대해서는 대부분 적용된다. 즉, 최저임금이 적용되고, 임금지급시기를 준수해야 하고, 임금체불에 대한 벌칙조항이 적용된다. 특히 퇴직금의 경우에는 2010.12.1부터 적용되어 최초 2년이 되는 2012.12.1까지는 법정퇴직금의 50%, 그 이후부터는 100% 지급해야 한다. 근로연수가 많은 경우라도 이 퇴직금규정 시행시기부터 계산하여 지급해야 한다. 뿐만 아니라 업무상 재해를 당한 경우에는 일반근로자와 동일하게 산업재해보상보험법에 따른 요양보상, 휴업보상, 장해보상 등 보상 규정 일체를 적용 받는다.

(2) 4인 이하 사업자에 적용되지 않는 주요 규정

4인 이하의 사업장에 근로하는 근로자에게 아래의 규정이 적용되지 않기 때문에 근로기본권의 보호를 받지 못하고 열악한 근로환경에 처해 있다고 할 수 있다.

1) Restrictions on dismissal, etc., a) Employers can still dismiss or discipline workers without justifiable reason; b) Even though a worker is unfairly dismissed, the worker cannot apply to the Labor Relations Commission for remedy; c) An employer does not have to notify workers in writing of reasons for dismissal; d) As the restrictions on dismissal for managerial reasons do not apply to such workers, an employer can dismiss workers at any time if business conditions deteriorate; e) The two-year limitation on the use of temporary workers such as dispatch employees or short-term contract workers does not apply, and the employer can dismiss such workers at any time.

2) Allowances during suspension of business: When an employer suspends business operations, the workers cannot receive suspension allowances. Even though business operations are suspended for reasons attributable to the employer, the employer does not have to pay allowances to workers during such suspensions.

3) Restrictions on working hours: Workplaces ordinarily employing fewer than five people do not have to follow the 40 hours per week limitation or keep to a 5 day workweek. There are no restrictions on extending the work day beyond 8 hours, or even beyond 12 hours, nor does they have to pay additional allowances (50%) for overtime, night shift (22:00 pm to 06:00 am) or holiday work.

4) Annual paid leave: When a worker at a workplace employing at least five people has worked continuously for one year, 15 days of annual paid leave are granted, but workers at workplaces ordinarily employing fewer than five people are not guaranteed any paid, non-statutory holidays. A worker at such workplaces must get permission to take a day off, and the employer can deduct one day's salary.

VI. Related Labor Cases

〈Case Study 1〉 Occupational Accident Compensations[128]

1. Outline of the case

---

[128] Jung, Bongsoo, "Occupational Fatalities and Follow-up Actions", 「Labor Law」, Jungang, Nov 2013.

1) **해고 등의 제한:** ① 정당한 이유가 없어도 근로자들을 마음대로 해고하거나 징계할 수 있다. ② 근로자가 부당한 해고를 당했어도 노동위원회에 의한 구제를 받을 수 없다. ③ 사용자의 일방적인 해고에 대한 서면통지 의무가 없으며, ④ 경영상 해고제한 규정에도 적용되지 않으므로 회사 사정이 좋지 않을 때에는 언제든지 해고할 수 있다. ⑤ 파견근로나 단기간 근로자를 사용할 경우에 자유롭게 언제든지 해고할 수 있기 때문에 2년의 사용기간 제한 규정 적용 없이 계속 사용할 수 있다.
2) **휴업수당:** 회사가 휴업하면 휴업수당을 받을 수 없다. 따라서 회사가 필요시 임의적으로 휴업을 하더라도 특별히 휴업수당을 지급하지 않기 때문에 사용자의 귀책사유로 휴업을 하여도 근로자들은 그 휴업기간 동안 임금이 지급되지 않는다.
3) **근로시간의 제한:** 4인 이하의 사업장은 주40시간 근로자나 주5일제도 해당이 없고 하루 8시간을 초과해 무제한으로 연장근로를 시킬 수 있다. 연장근로도 주12시간 한도에 대한 제한이 없고, 연장근로나 야간근로(22시~06)에 근무를 하거나 휴일에 근무를 해도 50%의 할증임금을 받지 못한다.
4) **연차유급휴가:** 일반 근로자가 1년에 근무에 15일의 연차휴가를 유급으로 사용할 수 있으나, 4인 이하 사업장 근로자들은 유급휴가가 발생하지 않는다. 따라서 휴가를 사용하고자 할 경우에는 사용자의 승인을 얻어 무급으로 휴가를 사용할 수 있다.

Ⅵ. 관련사례

〈사례 1〉 업무상 재해자의 산업재해보상금 계산[128]

1. 사건개요

---

[128] 정봉수, "산재 사망사건과 후속조치 사례", 「월간 노동법률」, 중앙경제사, 2013년 11월호

Chapter 2 Statutory Wages

At 8:20 in the morning on September 6, 2013, Employee A (hereinafter referred to as "the Employee") was in a warehouse guiding a forklift carrying air conditioning equipment. The air conditioner slipped off the left side of the forks and fell on the Employee, which caused serious injury. He was taken to Aju University Hospital in Suwon, where he died during emergency treatment.

[For reference, the Employee was a senior citizen, 72 years of age, with a monthly average wage of ₩1,719,340, and a daily ordinary wage of ₩56,065].

The following information details the major issues companies who face this tragedy must deal with: methods for calculating those industrial accident compensation benefits.

2. Calculating industrial accident compensation (survivors' pension and funeral expenses)

Surviving family members can request survivors' benefits and compensation for funeral expenses in accordance with the Industrial Accident Compensation Insurance Act, so it is desired for companies to calculate the benefits in advance. Compensation for occupational fatalities includes expenses for medical treatment and funeral services, and survivors' benefits. Lump sum payments for survivor's benefits in this case equaled ₩72,884,500, and for funeral expenses ₩9,300,770, for a total of ₩82,185,270. The details for compensation through Industrial Accident Compensation Insurance are as follows:

○ Survivor's benefits: 1,300 days' average wages; Options for receipt of payment: 1) 100% Pension or 2) half pension and half lump sum. In this case, the total lump sum was calculated as ₩56,065 x 1,300 days = ₩72,884,500.

(1) 100% pension (the Employee's daily average wage was ₩56,065)
  ① Basic pension: ₩56,065 x 365 days x 0.47 = ₩9,617,950 per year
  ② Addition for Basic pension: ₩56,065 x 365 days x 0.05 x 1 = ₩1,023,186(Up to four surviving family members can be added for additional basic pension: The victim's directly dependant family members – spouse, parents aged 60 or older, and children aged 19 or younger) If the 100% pension is chosen, the total sum of ① and ② is ₩10,641,136. As this amount is divided by 12 months, the monthly payment would be ₩886,761.

(2) Half pension and half sump sum payment
  ① Lump sum: ₩72,884,500 x 50% = ₩36,442,250

2013년 9월 6일(금) 오전 8:20분 경, 창고 내에서 지게차로 야외용 에어콘을 유도자(재해자)의 지시에 따라 옮기고 있던 도중 지게차에 실린 에어컨이 좌측으로 기울어지면서 유도자인 재해자를 덮쳤고 재해자는 중상을 입고, 급히 수원에 소재한 아주대병원으로 옮겨 응급조치를 받던 중 사망하였다. [재해자의 연령은 72세의 고령자이었고, 월 평균급여 1,719,340원(일일 평균급여 56,065원임)을 받았다.]

아래는 근로자의 산재 사망 사건의 주요 대응 내용으로서 산재보상금액을 미리 준비하여 대응할 수 있도록 해야 한다.

2. 산재보상금(유족급여 및 장의비) 산정

이 산재 사망사건에 대해 회사의 「산업재해보상보험(이하 "산재법"이라 함)」에 따라 유족급여와 장의비를 청구할 수 있으며, 그에 대한 계산을 미리 해놓아야 한다. 산재보상금액은 병원비, 유족급여, 장의비로 구성되어 있다. 그 금액은 유족보상 일시금 72,884,500과 장의비 9,300,770로 총합계 82,185,270원이다. 그 계산의 세부내역은 다음과 같다.

○ 유족보상: 평균임금의 1,300일분으로 수령방법은 1) 전액 연금 또는 2) 연금50% : 일시금50%이다. 유족보상 일시금은 56,065원 × 1,300일 = 72,884,500원이다.

(1) 전액연금수령시 계산 (근로자 일일 평균급여 56,065원)

① 기본연금: 56,065원 × 365일 × 0.47 = 9,617,950원
② 가산금: 56,065원 × 365일 × 0.05 × 1인원 = 1,023,186원(가산인원은 최대 4명까지: 재해자가 실제 부양했던 배우자, 60세이상 부모, 19세 이하 자녀)

연금 100% 수령시 위의 ①과 ② 의 합계는 연간 10,641,136원이다. 따라서 연간 금액을 1/12로 나눈 금액을 매월 886,761원을 수령한다.

(2) 연금50% 및 일시금 50% 수령시 계산

① 일시금: 72,884,500원 × 50% = 36,442,250원

② 50% pension: ₩886,761 x 50% = ₩443,380
○ Funeral expenses: 120 days' Average wages (Minimum: ₩9,300,770 ~ Maximum ₩13,051,700). The calculation in this case was ₩56,065 x 120 days = ₩6,727,800. As this calculated amount is less than the minimum funeral expenses, the minimum amount, ₩9,300,770, shall be paid.

Should the Employee's surviving wife die while the monthly pension payments made total less than the lump sum payment would have been, the remaining money shall be paid out in a lump sum to the next closest surviving family.

⟨Case 2⟩ Branch Manager's Severance Pay[129]

1. Case Summary

Company B is a Korean branch of a newspaper sector company whose head office is located in a foreign country. The company was divided into four business entities in 2002 for the purpose of efficient accounting management. Each entity operates independently in different locations. The business entities are classified as: 1) Report Team, 2) Digital News, 3) Newspaper Distribution, and 4) Advertisement. The business head of each entity was appointed as that entity's representative director.

The Petitioner (hereinafter referred to as "the Employee") joined Company B as a sales manager in September 2000 and worked as a branch manager of the Advertisement business entity starting 2002 until he quit in July 2007. The Employee was the representative director of the entity which maintained only two other employees, a number that was too small for severance pay under the Labor Standards Act to be applicable. Although the company granted legal severance pay to the Employee in consideration of his contributions during his tenure, the amount did not meet the accumulation rate (1.5 times) of severance pay verbally promised to the Employee at the time of his hiring.

The company also failed to reflect individual sales incentive bonus in its calculation of average wages for severance pay. When the Employee appealed to the company for a re-calculation of his severance pay, the company refused. Hence, the Employee submitted an application for payment of delayed severance pay to the Ministry of Employment and Labor via this labor attorney in August 2007.

---

[129] Jung, Bongsoo, "Branch Manager's Severance Pay", 「Labor Law」, Jungang, March 2008.

② 연금: 50% 할인된 금액 886,761 × 50% = 443,380원
○ 장의비: 평균임금의 120일분 (최저 9,300,770원 ~ 최고 13,051,700원) 계산은 56,065원 × 120일 = 6,727,800원, 최저수준에 미치지 못하므로 장의비는 최저금액을 적용하여 9,300,770원이다.

유족연금을 받던 배우자가 유족연금을 수령하던 중에 유족일시금 100%에 해당되지 못하는 연금을 받고 사망하게 될 경우에는 그 다음 연금수령권자에게 유족일시금과 실제 수령한 차액을 계산하여 일시금이 지급된다.

〈사례 2〉 지사장 퇴직금 진정사건[129]

1. 사건개요

B회사는 외국에 본사를 둔 OOO 신문사로 한국에 지점을 설치두고 있다. B회사는 회계상 목적으로 2002년에 4개의 사업체로 나누었고, 각각 별도의 장소에서 독립 법인으로 운영되고 있다. 분리된 법인은 1) 기자팀 사업부, 2) 디지털 뉴스 사업부, 3) 신문배포 사업부, 4) 광고사업부로, 각 사업부의 부서장을 각 사업부의 대표자로 임명하여 관리하고 있다.

진정인은 2000년 9월에 영업매니저로 입사하여 2002년부터 광고사업 법인의 지사장으로 근무하다가 2007년 7월에 퇴사를 하였다. B회사에서는 진정인이 법인의 대표이고 2인의 사업장이므로 퇴직금이 발생하지 않지만, 그간 회사에 대한 공로 등을 고려하여 법정 퇴직금을 지급하였다.

그러나 진정인은 회사 입사 시 퇴직금 누진율 (1.5배)를 적용한다는 것을 구두로 약속 받았고, 회사측에 진정인의 개인 영업성과급에 대해 퇴직금 계산을 위한 평균임금 계산에 포함하지 않았기 때문에 퇴직금이 잘못 산정되었다고 이의를 제기하였지만, 회사는 이에 대해 수용하지 않았다. 이에 진정인은 2007년 8월 퇴직금이 제대로 지급되지 않았다고 노동부에 진정을 제기하였다.

---
[129] 정봉수, "지사장 퇴직금 진정사건", 「월간 노동법률」, 중앙경제사, 2008년 3월호

Chapter 2 Statutory Wages

2. Company B's Claim

1) Company B (hereinafter referred to as "the Company") is not liable for severance pay
because it employs only two employees and does not submit to any rules or agreement stipulated for the payment of severance pay in the rules of employment, labor contract or verbal contract. As already conveyed to the branch manager (the Employee), the Company intends to pay the amount of severance pay calculated by multiplying the average wages by the number of service years during the time of his resignation. This amount will factor in his contributions made to the company during his tenure. Provided, however, that all legal liability shall expire between the Company and the Employee in accordance with payment of severance pay.

2) The incentive bonus requested by the Employee is not wage to be included in average wages under the Labor Standards Act. Even if the bonus was assumed to be included in average wages, the incentive bonus requested by the Employee was paid in March 2007 in remuneration for labor service in 2006. The requested bonus cannot be included into average wages, because it was not paid in return for labor service for the last three months prior to the Employee's retirement date in July 2007.

3. Employee's Claim

1) The Employee was hired as a sales manager for Company B on September 1, 2000, and had continued to work until he quit on July 31, 2007. The wages are comprised of basic monthly basic pay and the annual incentive bonus. The basic monthly pay was paid once every month, and the incentive bonus of a similar amount was given every March for the last 7 years based on the payment criteria of the incentive bonus contracted previously by sales outcomes. When the Employee resigned from the Company, his severance pay did not include the individual sales incentive bonus into the calculation of average wages and failed to reflect the accumulation rate (1.5) of consecutive service years.

2) There were 16 employees in Company B when the Employee was hired, and the Company has maintained a similar number of employees so far. The Company was divided into four business entities in 2002 for the purpose of better accounting management. Each business was established as an independent entity: 1) Report Team, 2) Digital News, 3) Newspaper Distribution, and 4) Advertisement (2 persons). The business head of each entity was appointed as

2. 사용자 주장

1) 당사의 경우 2인 사업장으로 취업규칙, 근로계약상 내지 구두계약상 퇴직금 지급에 관한 규정 및 합의가 없어 퇴직금 지급의무가 없으나, 이미 지사장에게 알린 바와 같이 그 동안의 회사에 대한 근무 등을 고려하여 퇴직 당시의 평균임금에 근속년수를 곱한 금액을 퇴직금으로 지급할 의사가 있다. 다만 위 금원의 지급에 따라 향후 회사와 지사장 사이에 제반 법률관계가 모두 종료되어야 할 것이다.
2) 진정인이 주장하는 인센티브의 경우 근로기준법상 평균임금에 포함되는 임금이 아닐 뿐만 아니라 설사 평균임금의 계산시 포함된다고 가정하더라도 진정인이 주장하는 2007년 3월에 지급된 인센티브는 2006년도 근로의 대가로 지급된 것으로 지사장이 퇴직하는 2007년 7월을 기준으로 퇴직 전 3개월의 근로의 대가로 지급된 것이 아니어서 평균임금에 포함될 수 있는 임금이 아니다.

3. 근로자 주장

1) 근로자는 B회사에 2000년 9월1일에 영업매니저로 입사하여 계속 근무를 하다가 2007월 7월 31일 퇴사를 하였다. 임금은 월 기본급과 연 1회의 성과상여금을 받는 조건이었다. 월 기본급은 매월 일정하게 받았고, 성과상여금은 지난 7년 동안 매년 3월에 영업실적에 따라 사전에 계약한 성과상여금 지급기준에 따라 고정적으로 비슷한 금액을 받았다. 근로자가 회사를 그만두고 퇴직금을 수령하고 보니, 퇴직금에 매년 정기적으로 지급 받았던 개인 영업업적 상여금이 평균임금에 포함되어 있지 않고, 또한 누진율(1.5)를 반영하지 않았다.
2) B회사의 직원은 입사 당시 16명이었으며, 현재까지 비슷한 인원을 유지하고 있다. 회사는 회계상 목적으로 2002년에 4개의 사업으로 나뉘어졌다. 기자팀 사업부, 디지털뉴스 사업부, 신문배포 사업부, 광고사업부(2명)로 별도 법인으로 설립하였고, 각 사업부의 매니저를 대표자로 등록시켰다. 그러나 실제로 위의 신문배포와 광고사업부가 최근까지 하나의 건물에서

the representative director of each entity. However, in practical terms, the Newspaper Distribution business and Advertisement business had been operating in the same building until recently and all four entities have been managed by a single accounting team. The president of the foreign head office has directly overseen, ordered and supervised all four business entities, while Human Resources management has been under an Asia regional head office in 000 country. Even though the president of the company worked in the workplace with fewer than 5 employees, he fell under the definition of an employee under the Labor Standards Act.

3) During the hiring stage, Company B verbally promised Employee a 1.5 times accumulation rate for severance pay. Two former employees were granted such an adjusted severance pay upon retirement. Without the employees' consent, however, the Company decided to abolish this accumulated rate. This new adjustment should be declared null and the Company pay the Employee his severance pay at the accumulated rate.

4) The Employee received an additional 120 million won as incentive bonus in March 2007 due to good sales performance the previous year. The Company did not reflect the individual sales incentive bonus in the calculation of average wages for his severance pay, insisting that the incentive bonus did not apply. However, as the incentive bonus reflects individual sales performance, not corporate business performance, the Employee's individual sales incentive bonus shall also be included in the calculation of his average wages.

4. Related Administrative Interpretations and Judicial Ruling

1) **In cases where there are different entities per business under one company** (Administrative interpretation: Retirement Benefit Team 4126, Oct. 11, 2007):
In cases where an identical employer operates more than one business or workplace at different locations, if the branch offices, sales offices and unit plants are operated under an identical organization and management without independent operations, the related entities are regarded as one business or one workplace. This means that the total number of employees at all entities shall be counted together in pursuant to labor law. However, if each entity maintains different structures and operates independently in terms of business location, accounting and human resource management, each entity shall be considerpay is applicable or not shall be considered according to the specifics. ed an independent business or workplace. Accordingly, whether severance

2) **In cases where the Company unilaterally revises accumulated rate of severance**

영업을 하였고, 현재 위의 4개 사업부의 모든 자금을 하나의 경리부에서 관리하고 있다. 외국본사에서 사장이 4개의 사업부에 직접 지시명령 및 감독을 하고 있고, 인사관리는 B회사의 아시아지역본부인 ○○○국가에서 관할하고 있다. 따라서 당해 근로자는 비록 5인 미만의 사업장에서 근로를 하였고 사업의 대표이사였지만, 실질적으로 근로기준법상 근로자이다.
3) 근로자는 B회사 입사 시 퇴직금 누진율 (1.5배)를 적용한다는 것을 구두로 약속 받았고, 2명의 직원이 퇴사 시 퇴직금에 대해 1.5배의 누진율을 받고 퇴사를 하였다. 그러나 회사에서는 2004년부터 갑자기 근로자들의 동의가 없는 상태에서 퇴직금 누진제를 폐지하여 단수제로 적용하고 있다. 따라서 이는 무효이므로 퇴직금 누진제에 대한 퇴직금을 지급해야 한다.
4) 근로자는 성과상여금으로 작년에 실적이 좋아 2007년 3월에 1억2천만 원을 받았다. 회사에서는 성과상여금이 임금이 아니므로 평균임금에 포함되지 않는다고 퇴직금 계산을 위한 평균임금에서 포함시키지 않고 퇴직금을 계산하였다. 그러나 당해 성과상여금은 기업의 성과가 아닌 개인의 영업성과에 따라 지급된 개인 영업성과급이므로 회사에서는 영업성과급을 평균임금에 삽입하여 계산하여야 한다.

4. 관련행정해석 및 판례

1) **하나의 회사이지만 사업부별로 사업자 등록이 되어 있는 경우** (행정해석: 퇴직급여보장팀 4126, 2007.10.11.)
   동일 사용자가 2개 이상의 사업 또는 사업장을 경영하는 경우 장소적으로 분리되어 있을지라도 지점, 영업소 또는 분공장 등이 동일한 조직과 경영체제 하에 사업의 독립성이 없을 경우에는 하나의 사업 또는 사업장으로 취급되어 이에 근무하는 총 근로자수를 적용대상으로 보아야 할 것이며, 근로의 형태가 각기 다르고 사업장소, 회계, 인사 등이 독립되어 별도로 운영되고 있을 경우에는 이를 각각 독립된 사업 또는 사업장 단위로 취급하여야 하므로 귀 질의상 퇴직금 발생여부에 대해서는 구체적인 사실관계에 따라 판단하여야 한다.
2) **퇴직금 누진제를 회사가 일방적으로 단수제로 변경한 경우**(행정해석:

pay to non-accumulated rate (Administrative interpretation: same as above):

Even though there had been no mention of severance pay stipulated in the contents of the labor contract (and no rules of employment), the Company had promised the Employee severance pay at an accumulated rate according to service years and had applied the system for a considerable period to its former employees. In this case, the Company shall take measures to receive employee consent if it wishes to revise the content, especially in the case of unfavorable revision for its employees.

3) **Administrative guidance and judicial rulings in relation to sales incentive bonus**
   ① Bonuses in the Rules for Calculation of Ordinary Wages (Article 476 of MOEL Regulations, Jan. 22, 2002)
   (i) Cases where bonuses are wages

   In cases where payment conditions, amounts, and payment rate are regulated in the rules of employment, or where employees are paid routinely and expect to get paid: regular bonuses, exercise support fees, etc.

   (ii) Case where bonuses are not wages

   In cases where payment is not paid routinely, but paid temporarily or conditionally in accordance with the company's profit by means of the employer's discretion and favor: Business incentive bonuses, special incentive bonuses, production incentive bonuses, rewards, and incentives

   ② Individual sales incentive bonuses that have been paid regularly and periodically shall be included in average wages. (Seoul District Court, Jun. 21, 2007, 2006 na 20978)
   (i) The Company's salary system consists of basic annual salary and annual incentive salary. The basic annual salary is paid monthly, and the incentive annual salary is paid in January as a lump sum based on the valuation of sales target and outcomes for the corresponding year. The Company pays severance pay that reflects basic annual salary without including annual incentive salary. Insisting that the Company should include incentive annual salary into calculation of average wages because annual incentive salary belongs to wages, the Employee has requested that the Company re-calculate his severance pay. When his application was rejected, he filed a suit against the Company.
   (ii) Whether the items of pay may be identified as wages reflected into the

위와 동일)

근로계약서 (취업규칙 없음)에 퇴직금에 관한 내용이 명시되지는 않았지만 입사시 퇴직금 누진제를 구두로 약속받았고, 타 직원 퇴사 시 퇴직금 누진제를 적용하는 등 상당기간에 걸쳐 퇴직금 누진제를 적용한 것이 인정될 경우 이를 변경하기 위하여는 근로자의 동의 (근로자에게 불리한 변경)를 얻어 근로계약 변경절차를 밟아야 한다.

3) 영업성과급과 관련된 행정지침 및 판례

① 임금산정지침(노동부 예규 제476호, 2002.1.22)에 따라 상여금의 임금 여부

(i) 상여금이 임금인 경우

취업규칙 등에 지급조건, 금액, 지급시기가 정해져 있거나 전 근로자에게 관례적으로 지급하여 사회통념상 근로자가 당연히 지급 받을 수 있다는 기대를 갖게 되는 경우 : 정기상여금, 체력단련비 등

(ii) 상여금이 임금이 아닌 경우

관례적으로 지급한 사례가 없고, 기업이윤에 따라 일시적, 불확정적으로 사용자의 재량이나 호의에 의해 지급하는 경우 경영성과배분금, 격려금, 생산장려금, 포상금, 인센티브 등

② 근로 대가로 계속 정기적으로 지급된 개인영업 성과연봉은 평균임금에 포함 된다 (서울지법 2007.6.21, 2006나 20978)

(i) 회사의 임금체계는 기본연봉과 성과연봉으로 구성되어 있고, 기본연봉은 매월 기본급으로, 성과연봉은 해당 연도 영업목표 및 경영성과를 평가해 익년 1월에 일괄해 지급했다. 회사는 갑에게 퇴직금을 지급하면서 위 성과연봉을 포함시키지 않고 기본연봉을 기초로 평균임금을 산정해 퇴직금을 지급했으나, 갑은 위 성과연봉이 임금이기 때문에 평균임금 산정 시 포함해야 한다면서 퇴직금 재산정을 요구했고 회사가 이를 받아들이지 않자 소송을 제기했다."

(ii) 어떤 금품이 평균임금 산정의 기초가 되는 임금에 해당하는지 여부를 가늠할 수 있는 구체적인 사정으로서 근로자에게 계속적·정기적으로 지급되며 그 지급에 관해 단체협약, 취업규칙, 급여규정, 근로계약, 노동관행 등에 의해 사용자에게 그 지급의무가 지워져 있고, 또한

Chapter 2 Statutory Wages

calculation of average wages shall consider the following criteria: 1) They shall be paid regularly and periodically; 2) They are mandated by the employer according to collective bargaining, rules of employment, salary regulations, labor contract, or habitual practice; or 3) Employees identified under general conditions shall be paid uniformly. In these cases, these items of pay shall be considered as wages regardless of their titles. The annual incentive salary was ruled as wages.

4) **How to include bonuses paid through one year into the amount subject to calculation of average wages** (Feb. 24, 2003, Wages 68207-120)

In cases where a payment rate of bonuses is established per annum and paid for a period exceeding one month, the total bonus paid for a certain month shall not be included into the calculation of average wages. The bonuses shall be calculated by dividing the total amount of bonuses paid to a relevant employee—during the twelve calendar months before the day on which a cause for calculating his average wages occurs— by the total number of calendar months, which is 3/12 times the total amount of bonuses paid per year.

5. Opinion

The Company and the Employee were interviewed by the Labor Supervisor since the Employee's application for payment of delayed severance pay was filed with the Labor Office in August 2007. The Employee has also submitted a Q&A reference (see the above administrative interpretation): Company B's four independent entities are identified as one company, and that the abolition of an accumulated rate of service years in severance pay shall be made null because the Company did not receive employee consent. During this process, the Company proposed that although it will not admit the total amount of incentive bonus received in return for work in 2007, it will accept in the average wages a 5/12 portion of incentive bonus related to that which the Employee received in March 2007 in return for labor service the previous year. The Employee accepted the Company's proposal and received an additional amount (60 million won in addition to statutory severance pay) calculated based upon new average wages. After this settlement, the Employee rescinded his application for payment of delayed severance pay with the Labor Office.

일정한 요건에 해당하는 근로자에게 일률적으로 지급하는 것이라면, 그 명칭 여하를 불문하고 임금이라고 볼 수 있을 것이라면서 영업성과연봉을 임금으로 판단했다.

4) 1년간 지급받은 상여금을 평균임금 대상금품에 산입하는 방법 (2003. 02. 24, 임금 68207-120)

상여금의 지급률을 연간단위로 설정하여 1개월을 넘는 단위로 지급하고 있는 경우에는 이를 지급 받은 그 월의 임금으로 취급하여 일시에 전액을 평균임금에 산입하는 것이 아니며, 평균임금을 산정하여야 할 사유가 발생한 날 이전 12개월의 기간 동안에 지급 받은 상여금 전액을 그 기간 동안의 근로월수로 분할 계산하여 즉, 3/12를 평균임금산정 기준 임금 총액에 산입함.

5. 시사점

2007년 8월에 진정을 제기한 이후, 회사와 근로자는 근로감독관으로부터 당사자 조사를 받았다. 진정인은 노동부로부터 질의회신(위의 행정해석 참조) 내용을 추가로 제출하였는데, 그 내용은 B 회사는 4개의 독립된 법인이지만 사실상 하나의 회사로 볼 수 있다는 내용이었고, 퇴직금 누진제 폐지에 대해 근로자의 동의를 받지 않았기 때문에 위법성이 있다는 내용이었다. 이에 회사는 합의를 요청하면서 성과상여금에 대해 2007년을 대상으로 받은 금액 전체를 인정할 수 없고, 퇴사일 기준 2007년 성과상여금의 5/12에 해당되는 금액을 평균임금에 포함하는 것을 제안하였다. 이에 근로자는 회사의 제안을 받아들여 새로이 계산된 금액인 법정 퇴직금 외 6천 만 원을 추가로 합의하였고, 근로자는 노동부 진정을 취하하였다.

Chapter 3 **Payment of Wages**

Ⅰ. How to Pay Wages
Ⅱ. The Principle of Complete Payment of Wages & Exceptions
Ⅲ. Procedures for Wage Adjustments (Increases, Reductions, Freezes, Returns) and Related Cases
Ⅳ. Annual Salary Systems
Ⅴ. Inclusive Wage System

제3장 임금지급

Ⅰ. 임금 지급 원칙

Ⅱ. 임금 전액지급의 원칙과 예외

Ⅲ. 임금조정 (인상, 삭감, 동결, 반납) 절차와 관련사례

Ⅳ. 연봉제

Ⅴ. 포괄임금제

Chapter 3 Payment of Wages

I. How to Pay Wages[130]

> Article 43 of the LSA. Payment of Wages
> ① Payment of wages shall be directly made in full sum to the worker in cash; however, if otherwise stipulated in special provisions of laws or decrees or in Collective Agreement, wages may be partially deducted or paid in other forms.
> ② Wages shall be paid more than once a month on a fixed day; however, this shall not apply to extraordinary wages, allowances, or any other similar payments, nor to those wages provided for by Presidential Decree.
> LSA Enforcement Decree,
> Article 23 (Exception to Wages to be Paid at Least Once Monthly)
> The term "extraordinary wages, allowances, or other similar payments, or the wages prescribed by Presidential Decree" in the proviso to Article 43 (2) of the Act means those falling under the following subparagraphs:
> 1. Allowance for good attendance payable on the basis of the attendance record for a period exceeding one month;
> 2. Seniority allowance payable for consecutive service for a fixed period exceeding one month;
> 3. Incentive, proficiency allowance, or bonus calculated on a ground sustaining for a period exceeding one month;
> 4. Other various allowances paid on an irregular basis.
> LSA, Article 109 (Penal Provisions)Employers shall be punished for violations of the above Article 43 (Payment of Wages) with imprisonment of not more than 3 years or a fine of not more than KRW 30 million.

The Labor Standards Act states that payment of wages shall be directly made in full sum to the worker in cash and paid more than once per month on a fixed day, thereby including the principles of cash payment, direct payment, total payment, and fixed-day payment.

1. The principle of cash payment

Wages shall be paid in cash, not in kind. Accordingly, wages shall be paid in convertible cash (i.e. bank notes or coins) except for special cases prescribed in law

---

[130] Jung, Bongsoo, 「Korean Labor Law Bible」 5th Ed., Joongang, 2016, pp. 81-83.

I. 임금 지급원칙[130]

> 근로기준법 제43조 【임금지불】
> ① 임금은 통화로 직접 근로자에게 그 전액을 지급하여야 한다. 다만, 법령 또는 단체협약에 특별한 규정이 있는 경우에는 임금의 일부를 공제하거나 통화 이외의 것으로 지급할 수 있다.
> ② 임금은 매월 1회 이상 일정한 기일을 정하여 지급하여야 한다. 다만, 임시로 지급하는 임금, 수당 기타 이에 준하는 것 또는 대통령령이 정하는 임금에 대하여는 그러하지 아니하다.
> 근로기준법 시행령 제23조(매월 1회 이상 지급하여야 할 임금의 예외) 법 제43조 제2항 단서에서 "임시로 지급하는 임금, 수당, 그 밖에 이에 준하는 것 또는 대통령령으로 정하는 임금"이란 다음 각 호의 것을 말한다.
>   1. 1개월을 초과하는 기간의 출근 성적에 따라 지급하는 정근수당
>   2. 1개월을 초과하는 일정 기간을 계속하여 근무한 경우에 지급되는 근속수당
>   3. 1개월을 초과하는 기간에 걸친 사유에 따라 산정되는 장려금, 능률수당 또는 상여금
>   4. 그 밖에 부정기적으로 지급되는 모든 수당
> 제109조(벌칙) 임금지불 규정을 위반한 자(법 제43조)는 3년 이하의 징역 또는 3천만 원 이하의 벌금에 처한다.

근로기준법은 임금의 지급에 관하여 임금은 통화로 직접 근로자에게 그 전액을 지불하여야 하며 매월 1회 이상 일정한 기일을 정하여 지급하여야 한다고 규정하여 통화불, 직접불, 전액불, 정기불의 원칙을 정하고 있다.

1. 통화지급

사용자는 근로자에게 통화로서 임금을 지급하여야 하며, 근로자에게 불리한 현물급여는 금지된다. 따라서 법령이나 단체협약에 의한 예외를 제외하고는

---
[130] 정봉수, 「한국노동법 영문해설」 제6판, 중앙경제사, 2021, pp. 81-83.

Chapter 3 Payment of Wages

or collective agreement. A cashier's check issued by the bank, however, does not violate the principle of cash payment, though bill payment is treated as an agreed extended payment.
1) Legal cases: ① Payment by certified check; ② Payment by shares for incentive pays
2) Illegal cases: ① Payment of a check not guaranteed by the bank; ② Company shares, bills, or goods

2. The principle of direct payment

Wages shall be paid directly to the employees. This rule does not allow exceptions by law or collective agreement, and also does not permit any delegation or proxy. However, the principle is not violated if a family member serves as a messenger in case of any illness affecting the recipient. The family member can collect the payment or it can be transferred into a designated bank account upon the employee's request. However, this excludes seamen, who are exempt from direct payments due to the different working conditions at sea.
1) Legal cases: ① Payment to the wife for inevitable cases; ② Payment to seamen's family; ③ Deduction in cases of seizure for wage credit; ④ Unclear address of the employee
2) Illegal cases: ① Payment to the labor union; ② Payment to parental authority or proxy; ③ Payment to the grantee for wage credit

3. The principle of total payment

Wages shall be paid in total amounts to all employees after applicable deductions according to the law or collective agreement. Legal deductions include income tax, resident tax, medical insurance, national pension, etc. Collective agreement deductions include union membership fees (check-off system).
1) Legal cases: ① Deductions for advance payment; ② Replacement of the taxi driver's insufficient daily deposit by wage; ③ Deductions due to disciplinary action; ④ No wage for no work during strikes
2) Illegal cases: ① Prohibition of pre-determination of non-observance, offsetting wages against advances, and compulsory saving; ② Replacement of compensation for damage due to illegal acts or default

임금은 강제 통용력이 있는 화폐(은행권과 주화)로 지급되어야 한다. 다만, 은행에서 발행하는 자기앞수표는 통화지급의 원칙에 위배되지 않으며 어음으로 지급한 것은 당사자 간의 기일연장 합의에 불과한 것으로 본다.
1) 합법사례 : ① 보증수표의 지불 ② 성과급으로 주식의 지급
2) 불법사례 : ① 은행의 지급 보증이 없는 당좌 수표 지불 ② 회사 주식이나 어음 또는 현물 지급

2. 직접지급

임금은 직접 근로자 본인에게 지급되어야 한다. 이에는 법령이나 단체협약에 의한 예외가 인정되지 않으며, 위임이나 대리에 의한 임금 수령도 인정되지 않는다. 그러나 근로자가 질병 등으로 인해 그 가족이 사자(심부름꾼)로서 임금을 수령하거나 근로자의 희망에 의해 지정된 은행 계좌에 이체하는 경우는 직접불의 원칙에 위배되지 않는다. 다만, 선원인 근로자는 해상근로의 특성으로 직접지급의 예외가 허용된다.
1) 합법사례 : ① 불가피한 경우 부인에게 지급 ② 선원의 가족에게 지급 ③ 임금 채권의 압류 시 사용자가 이를 공제하여 납부 ④ 근로자의 주거불명인 경우
2) 불법사례 : ① 노동조합에 지급 ② 친권자 또는 대리인에 지급 ③ 임금 채권을 양수인에게 지급

3. 전액지급

법령 또는 단체협약에 의해 임금의 공제가 인정되는 경우를 제외하고는 임금은 그 전액을 근로자에게 지불하여야 한다. 법령에 의해 공제가 인정되는 것은 갑종근로소득세, 주민세, 건강보험료, 국민연금 등이 있으며, 단체협약에 의하여 인정되는 경우는 조합비 일괄공제(check-off system)가 있다.
1) 합법사례 : ① 가불임금의 공제 ② 택시기사의 사납금부족액과 임금상계 ③ 징계로 인한 감봉 ④ 쟁의기간 중의 무노동 무임금
2) 불법사례 : ① 위약금 예약, 전차금, 강제저축 ② 불법행위, 채무불이행으로 인한 손해배상과 임금의 상계

Chapter 3 Payment of Wages

4. The principle of fixed-day payment

Wages shall be paid on a fixed day, one or more times in a month, to promote stability for employees. Wages or allowances paid temporarily to be admitted as exceptions shall include: ① Diligence allowances paid for superior attendance during the period exceeding one month; ② Service allowances paid for continuous work during the period exceeding one month; ③ Incentives, efficiency allowances or bonuses presented for various reasons during the period exceeding one month; and ④ Other allowances paid irregularly.

1) Legal cases: Change of payment date
2) Illegal cases: Delayed payment of wages

☞ Ministry of Employment and Labor Guidelines ☜

1. Unless there is a special agreement, an employee who quits their job before the selected day of wage increase may not receive the increased wage.[131]
2. Upon indictment of unfair labor practice by the Labor Relations Commission, the employer shall pay entire wages during the period of dismissal.[132]
3. An employee who terminates employment for personal reasons shall be paid all severance pay and wages owed him or her.[133]
4. If bonus pay is guaranteed every year, an employee resigning before the bonus pay day will be able to receive it in an amount pro-rated to their service days.[134]
5. Although Chuseok bonus is fixed yearly, the amount shall be paid to those who resign before the payment day.[135]
6. If the employer tries their best to pay wages on time but fails to do so due to financial difficulties from stagnant business, then the employer shall not be punished for delayed payment.[136]

---

[131] MOEL Guidelines: Kungi 680207-1877
[132] MOEL Guidelines: Nojunggun 1455.9-2721
[133] MOEL Guidelines: Kungi 1455-8121, 1982.3.24
[134] MOEL Guidelines: Bubmoo 811-9256
[135] MOEL Guidelines: Bubmoo 811-18993, 1978.9.1
[136] Supreme Court ruling on May 10, 1985, 87Do2098

4. 정기지급

근로자의 생활안정을 위하여 임금은 매월 일정한 날에 1회 이상 지급하여야 한다. 매월 1회 이상이라 함은 매월 1일부터 말일까지 적어도 1회 이상 지급하여야 한다는 의미이다. 다만, 임시로 지급되는 다음의 임금·수당은 예외가 인정된다. ① 1월을 초과하는 기간의 출근 성적에 의하여 지급하는 정근수당; ② 1월을 초과하는 일정 기간의 계속 근무에 대하여 지급되는 근속수당; ③ 1월을 초과하는 기간에 걸친 사유에 의하여 산정되는 장려금·능률수당 또는 상여금; ④ 기타 부정기적으로 지급되는 제 수당

(1) 합법사례: 임금 지급기일의 변경
(2) 불법사례: 체불임금

☞ 행정해석 ☜

1. 특약이 없는 한 임금인상 결정 이전 퇴직자에게 임금인상분이 소급 지급되지 않는다.[131]
2. 노동위원회로부터 부당노동행위 판정을 받았다면 해고기간 중 임금 전액을 지급해야 한다.[132]
3. 근로자의 귀책 사유에 의한 징계퇴직자라 하더라도 퇴직금과 임금은 전액 직접 지급해야 한다.[133]
4. 상여금의 지급기일 이전에 퇴직한 근로자에게도 1년간의 보장된 상여금은 월할계산하여 해당분 만큼을 지급하여야 한다.[134]
5. 매년 일정률의 중추절 상여금을 지급한 관례가 있다면 지급일 이전에 퇴직자에게도 지급하여야 한다.[135]
6. 사용자가 임금지급을 위하여 최선의 노력을 다하였으나 경영부진으로 인한 자금사정 악화로 도저히 임금지급기일을 지킬 수 없었던 경우라면 임금 체불의 죄책을 물을 수 없다.[136]

---

[131] 행정해석: 1995.11.21, 근기 680207-1877
[132] 행정해석: 1965.7.5., 노정근 1455.9-2721
[133] 행정해석: 1982.3.24, 근기 1455-8121
[134] 행정해석: 1978.5.4, 법무 811-9256
[135] 행정해석: 1978.9.1, 법무 811-18993
[136] 대법원 1985.5.10. 선고 87도2098 판결

Chapter 3 Payment of Wages

7. An employee dismissed as disciplinary punishment shall be paid severance pay and wages covering service days.[137]
8. Whether an industrial trainee causes actual damage intentionally or by mistake, it is a violation of the Labor Standards Act if the employer deducts their wages for the loss.[138]
9. If a subcontractor fails to pay wages to employees without contributory cause by the immediate preceding contractor, the immediate preceding contractor shall not bear the burden with the subcontractor concerned.[139]

II. The Principle of Complete Payment of Wages & Exceptions[140]

Company A gives a 20 percent discount to its employees when they buy company products, up to a maximum of KRW 2 million per year. Only employees and their direct family members living together may receive this discount when they purchase products. However, it was confirmed that one employee violated this company regulation, so the company issued a written warning and deducted, with the employee's agreement, KRW 500,000 from his salary: the amount involved in the violation. This type of situation has occurred frequently in business, and deals directly with whether a company can recover claimed damages by deducting employee wages.

As the wages paid in return for work provided directly support the employee's ability to sustain him or herself, deducting wages to pay for claims is strictly regulated. Article 43 (Payment of Wages) of the Labor Standards Act stipulates, "(1) Payment of wages shall be made in full to workers; however, if otherwise stipulated by special provisions of laws or decrees or a collective agreement, wages may be partially deducted or may be paid by other means than cash." Other provisions that deal with this subject include Article 20 (Prohibition of Predetermination of Nonobservance)[141], Article 21 (Prohibition of Offsetting Wages against Advances)[142], Article 22 (Prohibition of Compulsory Saving)[143], and Article

---

[137] MOEL Guidelines: Kungi 1455-3680, 1981.5.2
[138] MOEL Guidelines: Kungi 68207-2907, 2000.9.28
[139] MOEL Guidelines: Haeji 125-12829, 1983.8.26
[140] Jung, Bongsoo, "The Principle of Complete Payment of Wages", 「Labor Law」, Jungang, Aug 2016.
[141] Article 20 (Prohibition of Predetermination of Nonobservance): No employer shall enter into a contract by which a penalty or indemnity for possible damages incurred from breach of a labor contract is predetermined.
[142] Article 21 (Prohibition of Offsetting Wages against Advances): No employer shall offset wages against an advance or other credits given in advance on the condition of worker's labor.
[143] Article 22 (Prohibition of Compulsory Saving): (1) No employer shall enter into a contract with a worker, in addition to a labor contract, which stipulates compulsory savings or the management of

7. 업무상 과실로 징계해고된 자에게도 퇴직금과 해당 근로기간에 대한 임금은 지급하여야 한다.[137]
8. 산업연수생의 고의 또는 과실로 인하여 현실적으로 손해가 발생한 경우 그 손해액을 당해 근로자의 임금에서 공제하는 것은 근로기준법 위반이다.[138]
9. 직상수급자의 귀책사유 없이 하수급인이 임금을 체불하였을 시는 직상수급자는 임금지불에 대한 연대책임은 없다.[139]

II. 임금 전액 지급의 원칙과 예외[140]

A 회사는 자사제품에 대해 직원에게 연간 200만 원 한도 내에서 20%를 할인해주고 있다. 그 수혜대상은 직원 본인과 동거 직계가족에 한한다. 한 직원이 이 규정을 위반하여 회사의 물품을 구입한 것이 확인되어 회사는 해당 근로자에게 서면 경고를 하면서, 본인의 동의를 얻어 급여에서 부당이익금 50만 원을 공제하였다. 이와 같은 사례는 일반적으로 많이 발생하는 사례로서 임금채권과 손해배상 채권을 상계할 수 있는 지 여부에 대한 문제와 밀접한 관련이 있다.

근로의 대가로 받는 임금은 근로자의 생존권 보장에 직결되기 때문에 임금에서 채권의 공제를 엄격히 제한하고 있다. 근로기준법 제43조 제1항에서 "임금은 전액을 지급하여야 하며, 임금의 일부 공제는 법령 또는 단체협약에 특별한 규정이 있는 경우에 한한다"고 명시하고 있다. 그 밖에도 '위약 예정의 금지',[141] '전차금 상계의 금지',[142] '강제저축의 금지',[143] '제재 규정(감급)의 제한'[144] 등의 명시적 규정이 있다. 또한 임금 전액지급을 원칙으로 하면서

---

[137] 행정해석: 1981.5.2, 근기 1455-3680
[138] 행정해석: 2000.9.28, 근기 68207-2907
[139] 행정해석: 1983.8.26, 해지 125-12829
[140] 정봉수, "임금 전액지급의 원칙과 예외",「월간 노동법률」, 중앙경제사, 2016년 8월호
[141] 제20조 (위약 예정의 금지) 사용자는 근로계약 불이행에 대한 위약금 또는 손해배상액을 예정하는 계약을 체결하지 못한다.
[142] 제21조 (전차금 상계의 금지) 사용자는 전차금이나 그 밖에 근로할 것을 조건으로 하는 전대(前貸) 채권과 임금을 상계하지 못한다.
[143] 제22조 (강제 저금의 금지) ① 사용자는 근로계약에 덧붙여 강제 저축 또는 저축금의 관리를 규정하는 계약을 체결하지 못한다.

95 (Limitation on Punitive Provisions)[144]. Despite the principle of complete payment, there are a few exceptions. Some legitimate reasons for deductions include: ① deductions allowed by law or decrees (court rulings); ② deductions allowed by the collective agreement; ③ deductions made to correct miscalculation of wages.[145] Also, even though an exception for wage claims has the employee's consent, this needs to be handled in a strictly regulated manner. Here I would like to take a substantial look into exceptions to complete payment of wages.

1. The Principle of Complete Payment & Exceptions

(1) The principle of complete payment

The purpose of complete payment of wages is designed to protect employees and provide stability in their earning of a living by means of prohibiting employers from unilaterally deducting wages and requiring the complete payment of wages. Some exceptions exist, but these are strictly regulated in special provisions of laws or decrees or in collective agreements.[146] The courts have ruled, "In cases where an employer reduces personnel and at the same time unilaterally cuts bonuses, if the employees continue to work without any particular claims, this deduction of wages still amounts to a unilateral decision by the employer and the employees' rights to claim these unilaterally-reduced bonuses shall not be considered waived."[147]

(2) Exceptions
1) Deductions allowed by law and decree

Laws and decrees which allow deductions are limited to income tax law, social security insurance laws, and other stipulated laws. In addition, a court decision to allow seizure of wages can be implemented by seizing one-half of wages exceeding the minimum cost of living (KRW 1.5 million).[148]

---

savings.

[144] Article 95 (Limitation on Punitive Provisions): If a punitive reduction in wages for a worker is stipulated in the rules of employment, the amount of reduction for each infraction shall not exceed half of one day's average wages, and the total amount of reduction shall not exceed one-tenth of the total amount of wages during each period of wage payment.

[145] Lim, Jongyul, 『Labor Law』, 20th Ed., 2022, Park-young-sa, p. 417.

[146] Article 109 (Penal Provisions): (1) Persons who violate the provisions of Article 43 shall be punished by imprisonment of up to three years or by a fine not exceeding twenty million won.

[147] Supreme Court on Jun. 11, 1999, 98 Da 22185

[148] Supreme Court on Mar. 16, 1994, 94 Ma 1882; Civil Execution Act: Article 246 (Claims Subject to Prohibition of Seizure) (1) None of the following claims shall be seized: 4. Amount equivalent to 1/2 of wages, pension, salary, bonus, retirement pension, or other wage claims of similar nature: Provided, that where the amount falls short of the amount prescribed by Presidential Decree in consideration of the minimum cost of living under the National Basic Living Security Act or exceeds the amount prescribed by Presidential Decree in consideration of the cost of living for a standard family, such amount (1.85 million won) prescribed by Presidential Decree shall apply respectively (As of March

최소한의 예외를 두고 있다. 임금 공제가 합법적으로 가능한 것으로는 ① 법령 (법원의 판결문), ② 단체협약, ③ 임금착오 지급에 의한 공제가 있다.[145] 다만, 임금채권에 대해 근로자의 동의를 전제로 전액 지급의 예외, 즉 상계에 대한 예외를 인정하지만 엄격히 규제하고 있다. 이러한 전액 지급의 예외에 대해 살펴보고자 한다.

1. 전액 지급 원칙과 예외

(1) 전액 지급의 원칙

임금 전액지급의 취지는 사용자가 일방적으로 임금을 공제하는 것을 금지하여 근로자에게 임금 전액을 확실하게 지급받게 함으로써 근로자의 경제생활을 위협하는 일이 없도록 그 보호를 도모하려는 데 있다. 임금의 전액 지불에 대한 예외는 법령이나 단체협약으로 가능하다고 명시하여 엄격하게 제한하고 있다.[146] 법원은 "경영위기로 인하여 인원을 감축하면서 상여금을 일방적으로 삭감하고 이에 대해 근로자들이 별다른 이의 없이 근무하고 있는 경우에도 이는 사용자의 일방적인 임금삭감으로 근로자가 상여금 청구권을 포기하였다고 볼 수 없다."고 판시하고 있다.[147]

(2) 전액 지급원칙의 예외

1) 법령에 의한 예외

법령에 의해 공제가 인정되는 경우는 소득세법, 4대보험징수법 등으로 명시된 경우에 한해서 가능하다. 또한 채권자가 법원에서 임금채권에 대한 압류 판결을 받은 경우에는 월 지급되는 임금에 한해서 최저생계비 185만 원을 초과하는 임금의 2분의 1 상당액을 압류할 수 있다.[148]

---

144) 제95조 (제재 규정의 제한) 취업규칙에서 근로자에 대하여 감급(減給)의 제재를 정할 경우에 그 감액은 1회의 금액이 평균임금의 1일분의 2분의1을, 총액이 1임금지급기의 임금 총액의 10분의 1을 초과하지 못한다.
145) 김형배, 『노동법』제27판, 박영사, 2022년, 364면; 임종률, 『노동법』, 제20판, 박영사, 2022, 417면.
146) 제109조 (벌칙) (1) 43조를 위반한 자는 3년 이하의 징역 또는 2천만 원 이하의 벌금에 처한다.
147) 대법원 1999. 06. 11. 선고 98다 22185 판결
148) 대법원 1994. 3. 16. 선고 94마1822판결; 민사집행법 제246조(압류금지채권) 제1항 제4호에서 급료·연금·봉급·상여금·퇴직연금, 그 밖에 이와 비슷한 성질을 가진 급여채권의 2분의 1에 해당하는 금액. 다만 단서에서 근로자의 급여 중 최저생계비(4인 가족 기준 185만 원)에 해당하는 금액의 압류금지 (2021년 3월 기준).

A particularly remarkable judicial ruling was recently made which ruled that deductions can be made from monthly wages, but not from severance pay or retirement pension. "Since Article 7 (Protection of Right to Receive Benefits) of the Employee Retirement Benefit Security Act (ERBSA) stipulates that the right to receive benefits under a retirement pension plan shall neither be transferred to others nor offered as collateral, such provision prohibiting transferring the retirement benefits as collateral is part of statutory law. Accordingly, a court ruling to allow seizure of benefits under a retirement pension plan is null and void, and a third-party debtor can refuse the payment, by quoting the above, from an employee's benefits, even if ordered by a court. On the other hand, Article 246 (Claims Subject to Prohibition of Seizure) of the Civil Execution Act (CEA) regulates that an amount equivalent to a maximum of 1/2 of wages, retirement pension or other wage claims of similar nature can be deducted. Since Article 7 (Protection of Right to Receive Benefits) of the ERBSA and Article 246 (Claims Subject to Prohibition of Seizure) of the CEA are affected by the relationship between general law and special law, it is translated that all benefits under retirement pensions shall not be transferred as collateral."[149] This means that because the ERBSA is a special law, it takes precedence over the CEA, which is a general law.

2) Deductions allowed by a collective agreement

Deductions of union dues (or dues checkoff) are typical deductions allowed by a collective agreement. In cases where the labor union requests that the company deduct 10 times the usual monthly union dues (such as KRW 500,000 from each union member towards preparations for a strike), the company will need to decide whether to cooperate or not. For its part, the Ministry of Employment and Labor (MOEL) expressed its official opinion that if the labor union decides to raise funds to prepare for a strike by means of a legitimate decision-making process such as by resolution at a general meeting of all union members (or union representatives), the company shall cooperate by deducting the special union fees from employee monthly wages even though there is no individual consent to do so.[150] This means that, according to MOEL, it would be considered unfair labor practice for an employer to refuse to deduct the amount requested by the labor union to prepare for a strike.

3) Deductions to correct miscalculation of wages

In cases where an employer overpaid an employee by mistake, equivalent deductions from wages would be to correct the miscalculation, making it possible to adjust wages or severance pay, regardless of the principle of complete payment of wages. Provided, even in this case, the courts have ruled that the amount of retirement

---

2021);
[149] Supreme Court ruling on Jan. 23, 2014, 2013 Da 71180
[150] MOEL Guideline: Jun. 6, 2004, Labor Union – 1501

특히 주목해야 할 최근 판례는 임금채권 압류는 월 임금에서는 가능하지만, 퇴직금이나 퇴직연금에 대해서는 압류할 수 없다고 명확히 판결하고 있다. "근로자퇴직급여보장법 제7조에서 퇴직연금제도의 급여를 받을 권리에 대하여 양도를 금지하고 있으므로 위 양도금지 규정은 강행법규에 해당한다고 볼 것이다. 따라서 퇴직연금제도의 급여를 받을 권리에 대한 압류명령은 실체법상 무효이고, 제3채무자는 그 압류채권의 추심금 청구에 대하여 위 무효를 들어 지급을 거절할 수 있다. 한편 민사집행법은 제246조 제1항 제4호에서 퇴직연금 그 밖에 이와 비슷한 성질을 가진 급여채권은 그 1/2에 해당하는 금액만 압류하지 못하는 것으로 규정하고 있으나, 이는 위 퇴직급여법상의 양도금지 규정과의 사이에서 일반법과 특별법의 관계에 있으므로, 퇴직급여법상의 퇴직연금채권은 그 전액에 관하여 압류가 금지된다고 보아야 한다."[149]

2) 단체협약에 의한 공제

단체협약에 의한 공제는 조합비 공제(check-off)가 대표적인 내용이다. 이와 관련하여 노동조합에서 매월 공제되는 조합원 조합비의 10배에 상당하는 조합원 1인당 50만 원의 쟁의기금의 공제를 요구하는 경우에 회사는 이에 대해 협조해야 하는 문제가 있다. 이에 대해 고용노동부는 개인의 동의가 없더라도 노동조합의 적법한 결의 절차[조합원의 총회(대의원)의 의결이나 노조 규약상 관련이 있는 경우]를 통해 결정한 쟁의기금에 대해서도 조합비 공제로서 공제해주어야 하며, 이 경우에 조합원 개별 동의가 필요하지 않다는 입장이다.[150] 즉, 사용자가 노동조합이 회사를 상대로 투쟁하기 위한 조합비 특별공제를 거부하는 경우에는 부당노동행위에 해당된다고 볼 수 있다.

3) 임금계산 착오 지급에 의한 공제

사용자가 임금계산의 착오 등으로 인하여 임금이 초과로 지급된 경우에는 급여계산상의 문제이므로 임금 전액지급 원칙과 상관없이 급여나 퇴직금에서 정산이 가능하다. 다만, 이 경우에도 법원은 사용자가 근로자에게 부당이득반환채권을 자동채권으로 하여 근로자의 퇴직금 채권을

---

[149] 대법원 2014. 1. 23. 선고 2013다71180 판결
[150] 고용노동부 행정해석: 2004. 6. 5. 노동조합과-1501

benefits deducted to retrieve overpaid wages shall be a maximum of 1/2 of the retirement benefits.[151]

2. Criteria for Judgment & Related Cases Regarding Other Deductions

(1) Criteria for judgment

The principle of complete payment of wages strictly regulates, in accordance with Article 43 of the Labor Standards Act, related judicial rulings and MOEL Guidelines, an employer from deducting an employee's wages to cover damage claims against the employee.[152] This is because such a deduction is determined unilaterally by the employer.

Regarding the justification for this, judicial ruling has stipulated the following criteria for judgment: "It is prohibited for an employer to unilaterally deduct an employee's wages to cover claims against the employee by the employer, but in cases where the employer deducts or replaces the employee's wages after obtaining the employee's consent, as this consent can be regarded as the employee voluntarily agreeing to this deduction, this would not be a violation of Article 43 of the Labor Standards Act. Provided, in view of considering the purpose of the principle of complete payment of wages, determination of whether the employee actually voluntarily agreed to this deduction shall be strictly and carefully made."[153]

(2) Related cases
1) Reimbursement of training expenses

In cases where an employer assigns an employee overseas and subsidizes all training expenses for the employee to attend a training program, and that employee does not serve the compulsory employment period after completing the training, the employer can legitimately require the employee to reimburse part or all of the training expenses covered by the company. Accordingly, a training regulation that exempts an employee from the duty of reimbursement if that employee serves the compulsory employment period after completing the commissioned overseas training is not equivalent to a contract by which a penalty or indemnity is predetermined for

---

[151] Supreme Court ruling on May 20, 2010, 2007 Da 90760
[152] Supreme Court ruling on Sep. 28, 1976, 73 Da 1768
[153] Supreme Court ruling on Oct. 23, 2001, 2001 Da 25184

상계하는 것은 퇴직금 채권의 2분의 1을 초과하는 부분에 해당하는 금액에 관하여만 허용된다고 보고 있다.[151]

2. 기타 공제(상계)의 가능 여부에 대한 판단기준 및 관련 사례

(1) 판단기준

근로자의 임금이 사용자가 가지는 근로자의 불법행위를 원인으로 하는 채권과 상계(공제)가 가능한지에 대해 근로기준법 제43조 제1항의 임금의 전액지급 원칙과 판례와 행정해석에서도 이를 금지하고 있다.[152] 이것은 상계(공제)라는 것이 사용자의 일방적인 의사표시에 의해서 행해지기 때문이다.

이에 대해 상계의 가능 여부에 대한 판단기준을 판례[153]는 다음과 같이 판시하고 있다. "사용자가 근로자에 대하여 가지는 채권을 가지고 일방적으로 근로자의 임금채권을 상계(공제)하는 것은 금지된다고 할 것이지만, 사용자가 근로자의 동의를 얻어 근로자의 임금채권에 대하여 공제(상계)하는 경우에 그 동의가 근로자의 자유로운 의사에 터 잡아 이루어진 것이라고 인정할 만한 합리적인 이유가 객관적으로 존재하는 때에는 근로기준법 제43조 제1항 본문에 위반하지 아니한다고 보아야 할 것이다. 다만 임금 전액지급의 원칙의 취지에 비추어 볼 때 그 동의가 근로자의 자유로운 의사에 기한 것이라는 판단은 엄격하고 신중하게 이루어져야 한다."라고 판시하고 있다.

(2) 관련사례
1) 연수비 상환의 경우

기업체에서 비용을 부담 지출하여 직원을 해외에 파견하여 위탁 교육을 시키고 이를 이수한 직원이 교육 수료 일자로부터 일정한 의무재직기간 이상 근무하지 아니할 때에는 「기업체가 부담한 해당 교육비용의 전부 또는 일부를 상환하도록 할 수 있다. 따라서 해외 위탁교육을 받은 후 의무재직기간 동안 근무하는 경우에는 이를 면제하기로 한 기업체의 교육훈련규정」은 근로기준법 제20조에서 금지된 위약금 또는 손해배상

---
[151] 대법원 2010.5.20. 선고 2007다90760 전원합의체 판결
[152] 대법원 1976. 9. 28. 선고 75다1768 판결
[153] 대법원 2001. 10. 23. 선고 2001다25184 판결

damages incurred from a breach of the labor contract. Neither does such a training regulation violate Article 7 of the LSA (Prohibition of Forced Labor: No employer shall force a worker to work against his own free will through any means which unlawfully restrict mental or physical freedom) nor Article 21 (Prohibition of Offsetting Wages against Advances: No employer shall offset wages against an advance or other credits given in advance on the condition of a worker's labor).[154]

2) Deductions from bonuses

Sometimes an employer reduces or does not pay bonuses, with the labor union consent, in the process of coping with the company's business difficulties. The MOEL has released guidelines for two different cases: bonuses already incurred and bonuses expected to be incurred. In cases where the employer intends to deduct from bonuses already incurred, which were paid in return for employee labor service, this is null and void even with the labor union agreement or revision of company rules. In such cases, individual employee consent must be received. However, the employer reducing or deducting from bonuses expected in the near future is possible through revision of the collective agreement with the labor union consent, or revision of the company rules after obtaining the consent from the labor union or the majority of employees. In such cases, receiving individual employee consent is not necessary.[155]

The courts have made rulings that align with this guideline. The wages (including bonuses) or severance benefits already incurred are considered the employee's private property, so unless the labor union receives an individual employee agreement, it is not possible to deduct or delay those payments through a collective agreement. Accordingly, a collective agreement cannot require employees to reimburse payments already received, unless there is agreement from each individual employee.[156]

3) Housing loans from the company

In cases where an employee resigns before they has reimbursed the company for a housing loan received from the company, or if the employer deducts all unpaid debt in a lump sum from the severance benefits, this may be considered a violation of the principle of complete payment of wages. However, the courts have ruled in favor of lump sum deductions from severance benefits for the following reason: "Since the

---

[154] Supreme Court ruling on Feb. 25, 1992, 91 Da 26232 (Korean Air)
[155] MOEL Guidelines: Apr. 15, 1999, LSA 68207-587
[156] Supreme Court ruling on Jan. 28, 2010, 2009 Da 76317

예정의 약정은 아니다. 근로기준법 제7조가 금지하는 사용자가 정신 또는 신체상의 자유를 부당하게 구속하는 수단으로써 근로자의 자유의사에 반하는 근로를 강요하는 것이거나 같은 법 제21조가 금지하는 전차금 기타 근로할 것을 조건으로 하는 전대채권과 임금을 상계하기로 하는 내용의 것이 아니라고 볼 수 있다.[154]

2) 상여금의 삭감

기업의 경영상 어려움을 타개하기 위해서 노동조합과 합의를 통해서 상여금을 삭감하거나 반납하는 경우가 있다. 이에 대해 고용노동부는 이미 발생한 근로에 대한 상여금과 앞으로 발생할 상여금을 구분하여 판단하고 있다. 이미 발생한 근로의 대가로서의 상여금을 삭감(반납)하는 경우에는 노동조합과의 합의 또는 회사규정의 개정만으로는 무효이고, 개별 근로자들의 동의가 있어야 한다. 그러나 앞으로의 근로조건으로서의 상여금을 삭감(하향조정)하는 경우에는 노동조합과의 합의를 거쳐 단체협약을 개정하거나 회사규정을 노조 또는 근로자 과반수의 동의를 얻어 변경하는 것으로 가능하며, 개별근로자들의 동의는 필요하지 않다.[155]

법원에서도 동일하게 판단하고 있다. 이미 지급 청구권이 발생한 임금(상여금 포함)이나 퇴직금은 근로자의 사적 재산영역으로 옮겨져 근로자의 처분에 맡겨진 것이어서, 노동조합이 근로자들로부터 개별적인 동의를 받지 않는 이상 사용자와 사이의 단체협약만으로 이에 대한 포기나 지급유예와 같은 처분행위를 할 수 없으므로, 단체협약으로 근로자에게 이미 지급한 임금을 반환하도록 하는 것은 그에 관하여 근로자들의 개별적인 동의가 없는 한 효력이 없다.[156]

3) 주택자금 등 대출금의 경우

회사가 주택자금을 근로자에게 대여해주고, 일정액을 급여에서 상환하다가 중도에 퇴직하는 경우에는 사용자가 퇴직금에서 주택자금이미 상환된 전체금액에 대해 공제하는 경우에 전액지급의 원칙에 위배되는지에 대한 문제가 있을 수 있다. 이에 대해 판례는 "단체협약은 노동조합이 사용자 또는 사용자 단체와 근로조건 기타 노사관계에서 발생하는

---
[154] 대법원 1992. 2. 25. 선고 91다26232 판결(대한항공)
[155] 고용노동부 행정해석: 1999. 4. 15. 근기 68207-587
[156] 대법원 2010. 1. 28. 선고 2009다76317 판결

collective agreement is the agreement to determine items occurring in labor and management relations, it can be a real expression of the intentions of both parties. It can also be admitted that the individual employee's voluntary decision and agreement make it possible to deduct wages instead of entering a formal claim for repayment of debts owed to the company by that employee. In view of these points, if the collective agreement was made justifiably and contains items permitting the requirement to reimburse unpaid loans, such a collective agreement does not violate the principle of complete payment of wages."[157]

3. Opinion

As in the cases given above, companies frequently deduct or require reimbursement for claims of illegal acts or other damages. Strictly speaking, this is a violation of the principle of complete payment of wages, which by law prevents the reduction of wages for general claims (debts) that an employee owes to his or her employer. Accordingly, if an employer deducts wages unilaterally to cover these claims, this deduction is invalid and makes the employer subject to punishment for violating the Labor Standards Act.

III. Procedures for Wage Adjustments (Increases, Reductions, Freezes, Returns) and Related Cases

1. Introduction

Labor and management together can freely determine and adjust wages through labor contracts, employment rules, and collective agreements. So far, wage adjustment has been used to mean wage increase as wages have been increased every year due to inflation. However, as the coronavirus epidemic over the past year has caused enormous damage to all industries, many companies have overcome

---

[157] Supreme Court ruling on Jun. 27, 2003, 2003 Da 7623

사항에 관하여 체결하는 협정으로 체결과정에서도 그 진정성과 명확성이 담보되어 있다는 점과, 개별 근로자의 자유로운 의사에 터 잡아 이루어진 동의가 있는 경우 사용자는 근로자에 대한 자동채권과 근로자의 임금채권을 상계할 수 있다는 점 등에 비추어 볼 때, 적법하게 체결된 단체협약이 사용자의 근로자에 대한 대출 원리금 등 채권 등을 공제할 수 있도록 규정하고 있도록 한 단체협약이 임금 전액지급의 원칙에 위배되어 무효라고 볼 수 없다."라고 판시하면서 퇴직금에서 주택자금 대출금 공제를 인정하고 있다.[157]

3. 시사점

앞에서 인용한 사례와 같이 일상적으로 근로자의 불법행위에 대한 배상채권이나 기타 손해배상 채권 등에 대한 공제(변제)가 빈번하게 일어나고 있다. 하지만 이는 임금의 전액지급 원칙을 위반하는 것이다. 임금 전액지급 원칙은 사용자가 근로자에게 가지는 일반채권을 일방적으로 임금채권에서 공제(상계)하는 것을 방지하기 위한 강행규정이기 때문이다. 따라서 사용자가 근로자에게 가지는 채권을 일방적으로 급여에서 공제하는 경우에 그 행위는 무효이고 근로기준법 위반으로 처벌 대상이 될 수 있다는 점을 명심하여야 할 것이다.

Ⅲ. 임금조정 (인상, 삭감, 동결, 반납) 절차와 관련사례

1. 문제의 소재

임금은 노사가 근로계약, 취업규칙, 단체협약을 통해 자유로운 의사로 결정하고, 조정할 수 있다. 지금까지 임금조정을 임금인상이라는 용어로 사용한 것은 물가인상으로 매년 임금이 인상되어 왔기 때문일 것이다. 그러나 지난 1년 동안 코로나 바이러스의 유행으로 전 산업에 막대한 피해를 줌으로써

---

[157] 대법원 2003. 6. 27. 선고 2003다7623 판결

Chapter 3 Payment of Wages

difficulties through other forms of wage adjustment, such as wage cuts, freezes, and returns. An employer unilaterally cutting wages has no effect. Reductions, freezes, or wage returns are unfavorable changes to working conditions, so legal procedures must be adhered to by the labor and management before taking such steps.

Wage cuts refer to reducing wages lower than existing levels for the same job and require collective consent of the affected workers. Wage freezes have the same effect as wage reductions when annual wage increases or service allowances are currently in place, and therefore require collective consent. However, deciding to keep the same wage as before without increasing wages does not require collective consent. Regarding wage returns, since wages are accrued in return for work already performed, those wages belong to individual workers, so the employer must obtain the consent of that individual worker. If the company deducts wages based only on collective consent, not individual consent, those deducted wages will be considered unpaid wages. The table below provides a brief summary of wage reductions, freezes and returns. In the next sections, I will review the related principles and related labor cases in detail.[158]

<Comparison of Wage Reductions, Freezes and Returns>

	Wage Reductions/Freezes	Wage returns
Target wage	Future wage	Wages already accrued
Method of implementation	Collective consent	Individual worker consent
Scope of effectiveness	All workers in same category	Individual workers with consent
Base wages for calculation of average wages	Wages paid after reduction or freeze	Wages paid before return

2. Wage Increases and Wage Reductions

Wage increases are decided through collective bargaining if there is a labor union. Wages have generally been raised every year through collective bargaining between labor and management, and if negotiations do not result in wage increases, the labor

---

[158] Ha, Gap-Rae, 「Labor Law」, 33rd ed., Joongang Economy, 2020, pp. 311-316; Labor Ministry Guidelines: Labor Standards Division-797, Mar. 26, 2009.

많은 회사들이 임금 삭감, 동결, 반납과 같은 임금조정을 통해 노사가 어려움을 다같이 이겨내고 있다. 근로조건의 핵심인 임금은 노사가 협의하여 자유로이 결정하는 것으로 회사가 일방적으로 삭감하면 이는 무효가 된다. 임금인상이 아닌 임금의 삭감, 동결, 반납은 근로자에게 불리한 변경조건 이기에 노사의 적법한 절차를 거쳐야 한다.

임금삭감은 동일한 업무에 대해 기존 임금을 낮추는 것으로 대상 근로자의 집단 동의를 필요로 한다. 임금동결은 매년 호봉승급이나 근속수당의 임금 인상요인이 있는 경우에는 임금 삭감과 같은 효력이 있으므로 집단 동의를 필요로 한다. 그러나 호봉승급 없이 기존 임금과 동일하게 지급하는 경우에는 집단 동의가 필요 없다. 임금반납의 경우에는 기왕의 근로에 대한 대가로 발생한 임금이므로 이는 개별근로자에게 귀속되어 있기 때문에 개별 근로자들의 동의를 받아야 한다.

개별동의가 아닌 집단 동의만 받고 임금을 공제하면 임금체불이 된다. 관련 내용은 아래 표와 같이 정리될 수 있으며, 실제 사례에 적용되는 원칙과 그 사례에 대해 구체적으로 살펴보고자 한다.[158]

<임금 삭감/동결과 반납 비교>

구 분	임금삭감/동결	임금반납
임금조정대상	장래의 임금	이미 발생한 임금
시행 방법	집단적 동의	개별 근로자 동의
효력 범위	동종 전체 근로자	동의한 개별 근로자
평균임금 기준	삭감/동결된 임금	반납하기 전 임금

2. 임금인상 및 임금삭감

임금인상은 노동조합이 있는 경우 집단적 교섭을 통해 이루어진다. 노사 협상을 통해 매년 임금을 인상해왔고, 원만하게 인상되지 않는 경우 노동 조합은 파업을 통해 협상력을 높여 임금인상을 한다. 사용자는 노동조합의

---

[158] 하갑례, 「노동법」, 33판, 중앙경제, 2020, 311-316면. 행정해석: 근로기준과-797, 2009.3.26 참조

union increases the pressure through strikes. Employers generally increase their workers' wages to the minimum extent acceptable to the labor union. Wages can also be reduced through collective bargaining if the economy is bad or the company is in trouble. In this case, if the union consists of a majority of the workers concerned, non-union members are also affected by the wage adjustment concluded by the labor union due to the general binding force of the workplace (Article 35 of the Labor Union Act). In workplaces without a labor union, wage increases are determined unilaterally by the company within an appropriate range through changes to the employment rules or labor contract. However, since wage reductions are regarded as an unfavorable change working conditions, an agreement between labor and management is necessary.

Wage reductions refer to a lower wage than before being paid at a certain point in the future. The total wages paid is lowered by reducing or abolishing the basic wage and/or various allowances, with the process carried out in a manner decided in collective decision-making. If there is a majority union, this is done through a collective agreement, but if there is no majority union, it is necessary to go through the procedures required to make unfavorable changes to the employment rules. Even if labor and management have agreed, wages cannot be reduced below the minimum wage level, and additional rates or legal allowances (such as overtime/night/holiday work allowances, weekly holiday allowance, annual paid allowance, etc.) are not subject to reductions, in accordance with the Labor Standards Act.[159] Also, the reduced wage is not included in the calculation of average wage. Wage reductions are judged differently for each case. Here are some of these individual cases.

(1) Even if individual workers agree on a wage reduction, this cannot replace collective consent. Wage reductions involve paying less in the future for the same work that is currently provided, which makes them an unfavorable change to working conditions. In order for consent to a reduction in wages obtained from individual workers to be considered valid, the collective agreement must be changed according to required procedures.[160]

(2) In order to overcome a management crisis, a company significantly reduced its workforce and unilaterally stopped paying bonuses to workers who were retained. The fact that workers who were retained have continued to work without objection to the unilateral cessation of bonuses, does not mean that

---

[159] Ministry Guidelines: Labor Standards Team-797, Mar. 26, 2009.
[160] Incheon District Court ruling on June 25, 2010: 2009 gahop 14735.

임금인상 요구에 수용가능한 만큼 임금인상을 하게 된다. 노동조합과 교섭을 통해 경기가 좋지 않거나 회사가 어려움에 처한 경우에는 임금삭감도 가능하다. 노동조합이 당해 사업장의 과반수로 구성되어 있는 경우에는 비조합원도 사업장 단위의 일반적 구속력(노동조합법 제35조)에 의해 임금인상이나 삭감도 당해 노동조합이 체결한 임금조정안을 적용 받는다. 노동조합이 없는 사업장의 경우에는 임금인상은 취업규칙이나 근로계약을 변경하는 방법으로 회사가 적정한 범위에서 일방적으로 결정한다. 다만, 임금삭감은 불이익한 근로조건으로의 변경이므로 노사간 협상을 통한 합의가 필요하다.

임금삭감은 종전보다 장래 일정시점 이후로 임금을 낮추어 지급하는 것이다. 기본급이나 각종 수당을 축소 또는 폐지하면서 임금지급 총액을 낮추게 된다. 임금삭감 절차는 집단적 의사결정 방식에 의해 이루어진다. 과반수의 노동조합이 있는 경우에는 단체협약을 통해서 이루어지지만, 과반수 노동조합이 없는 경우에는 취업규칙 불이익 변경절차를 거쳐야 한다. 노사가 합의하였다고 하더라도 최저임금 수준 이하로 삭감할 수 없고, 근로기준법에서 정한 할증률이나 지급의무를 규정하고 있는 법정수당(연장/야간/휴일근로수당, 주휴수당, 연차수당 등)은 감액대상으로 할 수 없다.[159] 또한 삭감된 임금은 평균임금 산정시 포함되지 않는다. 임금삭감과 관련된 사례는 사안별로 달리 판단되며, 개별 사례는 다음과 같다.

(1) 임금삭감에 개별 근로자들이 동의하였다고 하더라도 이를 집단적 동의로 대체할 수 없다. 임금삭감은 장래 일정시점 이후부터 현재와 동일한 내용의 근로제공에 대하여 종전보다 임금을 낮추어서 지급하는 것으로, 이는 근로조건의 불이익변경에 해당한다. 단체협약에서 정한 임금의 삭감에 대한 근로자들의 동의가 유효하기 위하여는 단체협약 변경 절차를 거쳐야 한다.[160]

(2) 회사가 경영 위기 상황을 극복하기 위하여 직원을 대폭 감축하면서 회사에 잔류한 직원들에 대하여 일방적으로 상여금 지급을 중지하였고, 회사에 잔류한 근로자들이 그와 같은 조치에 관하여 별다른 이의 없이 근무하여 왔다는 사정만으로는 근로자들이 장래에 발생할 상여금청구권을 포기

---

[159] 행정해석: 근로기준과-797, 2009.3.26
[160] 인천지방법원 2010.6.25. 선고 2009가합14735 판결.

those workers have given up their right to claim future bonuses.[161]

(3) In accordance with the general binding force of Article 35 of the Labor Union Act, the effect of an agreement on wage reductions with a majority labor union also extends to non-union workers in the same kind of job in a workplace. However, if a separate contract for wages is signed for each worker, such as an annual salary contract, the individual worker's consent for a wage reduction is also required.[162] On the other hand, if the number of workers who were in the labor union at the time of the labor-management agreement on wage reduction did not reach a majority of the workers, the general binding force of Article 35 of the Labor Union Act cannot be granted.[163]

(4) In changing the shift work system, reducing the shift from 4 groups/3 shifts to 3 groups/3 shifts is an unfavorable change for workers. Conversely, if the increase is from 3 groups/3 shifts to 4 groups/3 shifts, unless the contractual working hours are shortened or wages are reduced, it is not regarded as a disadvantageous change to working conditions, even though related wages or allowances are reduced due to the reduction in overtime work.[164]

(5) A change in the pay system can also lead to a reduction in wages. In cases where the amount of wages decreases from a reduction in the proportion of basic salary and an increase in the proportion of performance salary, the court considers it as a disadvantageous change in working conditions even though only some employees' wages decrease while the wages of most employees increase.[165]

(6) If the wage peak system is introduced within the statutory retirement age, it is a disadvantageous change in working conditions because it results in a reduction in wages for workers at that time.[166] In this case, if there is a labor union organized by a majority of workers, the consent of that labor union is required. Here, a union organized by a majority of workers refers to a union organized by a majority of all workers who are subject to the existing employment rules, regardless of the scope of union membership.[167]

---

[161] Supreme Court ruling on June 11, 1999: 98da22185.
[162] Labor Ministry Guidelines: Industrial Relations Team-1112, Nov. 18, 2008.
[163] Supreme Court ruling on May 12, 2005: 2003da 52456.
[164] Labor Ministry Guidelines: Labor Standards Team 68207-1732, Nov. 4, 1994.
[165] Supreme Court ruling on June 28, 2912: 2010da 17468.
[166] Suwon District Court ruling on June 23, 2017: 2016gadan 115485.
[167] Supreme Court ruling on February 29, 2008: 2007da 85997.

하였다고 볼 수 없다.[161]

(3) 단체협약은 노동조합법 제35조의 일반적 구속력에 따라 과반수로 구성된 노동조합과의 임금 삭감에 대한 합의의 효력은 동종의 비조합원 근로자에게도 미친다. 다만 연봉계약과 같이 근로자 개인별로 임금에 관한 별도의 계약을 체결했다면 임금삭감에 대한 개별 근로자의 동의도 필요하다.[162] 한편, 임금삭감에 대한 노사합의 당시 노동조합에 가입한 근로자 수가 근로자의 과반수에 이르지 못하였던 경우에는 노동조합법 제35조의 일반적 구속력을 부여할 수 없으므로 노동조합원이 아닌 근로자에게는 단체협약 변경의 효력이 미치지 않는다.[163]

(4) 교대제를 변경함에 있어, 4조3교대를 3조3교대조로 근무조를 줄이는 것은 근로자에게 불리한 조건으로의 변경이다. 반대로 3조3교대에서 4조3교대로 근무조를 늘린다면, 소정근로시간이 단축되어 임금이 삭감되지 않는 한 연장근로 시간이 줄어들게 되므로 관련 임금이나 수당이 줄더라도 이를 불이익변경으로 보지 않는다.[164]

(5) 급여체계의 변경도 임금 삭감이 될 수 있다. 기본연봉의 비중을 줄이고 성과연봉의 비중을 높여 확정적으로 확보되었던 임금액수가 줄어드는 경우, 법원은 대다수 직원들의 임금이 증가하더라도 일부 직원들의 임금만이 감소하는 경우 불이익 변경으로 보고 있다.[165]

(6) 법정정년 이내에서 임금피크제를 도입하는 경우 해당 시점의 근로자들의 임금삭감을 가져오기 때문에 근로조건의 불이익 변경에 해당된다.[166] 만일 근로자의 과반수로 조직된 노동조합이 있는 경우에는 노동조합의 동의를 필요로 한다. 여기서 과반수로 조직된 노동조합이란 기존의 취업규칙의 적용을 받고 있던 근로자 중 조합원 자격 유무를 불문한 전체 근로자의 과반수로 조직된 노동조합을 의미한다.[167]

---

161) 대법원 1999. 6. 11. 선고 98다22185 판결.
162) 노사관계법제과-1112, 2008.11.18
163) 대법원 2005.5.12. 선고 2003다52456 판결.
164) 행정해석: 근로기준과 68207-1732, 1994.11.4.
165) 대법원 2012.6.28. 선고 2010다17468 판결.
166) 수원지방법원 안양지원 2017.6.23. 선고 2016가단115485 판결.
167) 대법원 2008.2.29. 선고 2007다85997 판결.

3. Wage Freezes

Freezing wages refers to keeping wages the same for future work as was paid for past work of the same type. In cases where a company regularly increases regular wage, ceasing or additionally restricting this regular increase in wage is an unfavorable change to working conditions. The company can freeze wages through amendment of the collective agreement or following the procedures for changing the employment rules disadvantageously. However, it is not a disadvantageous change to working conditions if wages are frozen when there is no regular salary increase.

(1) If the personnel regulations stipulate that regular increases occur on January 1st and July 1st of each year, and if the annual increase in salary has been carried out regularly and uniformly, this is considered to be a habitual wage practice. In this case, if the employer unilaterally freezes the regular increase without engaging with workers in the collective decision-making method, is the courts have deemed that the amount of regular increase that remains unpaid by the regular payment date each month as unpaid wages.[168]

(2) A certain school had financial difficulties, and the principal explained the situation to teachers at a school affairs meeting, suggested that the basic salary increase for general school teachers be frozen that year. The teachers present did not object at the time to this. However, this lack of objection at the meeting with the teachers cannot be considered the same as obtaining collective consent.[169]

4. Wage Returns

Wage returns refer to the return of wage bonds (wages, bonuses, etc.) already incurred for previous work based on the free-will consent of the individual worker. Due to the waiver of the right to claim wages that occurred legally, wages can only be returned through due process. Since a unilaterally-determined wage deduction by the employer violates the principle of paying full wages, individual workers' written consent is required.[170] However, even in this case, any waiver of

---

[168] Labor Ministry Guideline: Wage 68200-649, December 5, 2000
[169] Supreme Court ruling on June 9, 2005: 2005do 1089.
[170] Article 43 of the Labor Standards Act (Wage Payment) and Supreme Court ruling June 11, 1996: 98da22185 Waiver of wage claims is recognized as a clear expression of the employee's intention.

3. 임금동결

임금동결은 동일한 내용의 근로제공에 대해 종전과 같은 임금을 지급하는 것을 말한다. 임금인상을 하지 않더라도 정기호봉승급이 있는 회사에서 승급을 제한하는 경우에는 근로조건의 불이익 변경으로 단체협약의 수정이나 취업규칙의 불이익 변경을 통해서 임금동결을 할 수 있다. 그러나 정기호봉승급이 없는 경우 임금을 동결하더라도 이는 근로조건의 불이익한 변경이 아니다.

(1) 인사규정에서 정기승급을 매년 1월 1일과 7월 1일에 실시하고 정기·일률적으로 호봉승급을 하여 왔다면 이는 임금지급과 관련하여 관행이 성립된 것으로 본다. 이 경우 근로자 집단적 의사결정방식에 의한 적법 절차를 거치지 아니하고 사용자가 일방적으로 정기승급을 동결하였다면 각 근로자별 정기승급이 이루어지는 달의 임금 정기지급일에 정기승급으로 인하여 가산되는 임금이 전액 지급되지 아니한 것으로 본다.[168]

(2) 학교가 재정적 어려움에 시달리던 중 피고인은 신학기 교무회의에서 교사들에게 사정을 설명하고 올해에는 호봉인상은 하되 일반학교 교사들의 본봉을 기준으로 하는 기본급(본봉) 인상은 동결하자고 제의하였고, 그 자리에 참석한 교사들은 이에 대하여 아무런 이의를 제기하지 아니하였다. 이와 같이 사용자인 피고인이 참석한 상태에서 기본급의 동결을 제의하여 이에 대한 교사들의 의견을 묻는 방식으로 회의가 진행되었고 이에 대해 교사들이 이의를 제기하지 아니하였다고 하여 근로자들의 동의가 있었다고 볼 수는 없다.[169]

4. 임금반납

임금반납은 기왕의 근로에 의해 이미 발생된 임금채권(임금, 상여금 등)을 개별근로자의 자유의사에 따른 동의를 바탕으로 반납하는 것을 말한다. 적법하게 발생한 임금청구권의 포기로써 적법 절차를 통해서만 임금반납은 가능하다. 사용자의 일방적 임금공제는 임금의 전액 부지급원칙을 위반하기 때문에

---

[168] 행정해석, 임금 68200-649, 2000.12.5
[169] 대법원 2005.6.9. 선고 2005도1089 판결.

the right to claim severance pay is invalid because it violates the Labor Standards Act.[171]

For procedures to be deemed reasonable, individual workers' consent is required. Since the return of wages is effective only if it is the individual workers' voluntary decision, individual workers must recognize the purpose of wage returns and sign a return consent form in their own name.[172] While the court holds that it is desirable to obtain consent for each individual worker when returning wages, it is also possible to obtain individual consent by having workers sign a name list of workers if the company has sufficiently explained the difficult situation to the workers.[173] An agreement to return wages in the collective agreement has no effect. This is because the return of wages involves wages that already belong to individual workers, and the union cannot be forced to abandon individual member property rights. Wages returned by workers come from the workers' income and are returned voluntarily, and the employer is not obligated to return them again to the worker.[174] Returned wages are included in the calculation of average wages as they are wage bonds that were given to the employee and then returned to the employer by the employee.[175] Examples of cases where a return of wages was not recognized:

(1) To waive unpaid wages for which individual workers have the right to claim payment due to the arrival of the payment period, a collective agreement with the labor union is not enough for the workers to be deemed to have agreed to waive the unpaid wages. It can only be done to the extent that the company has received individual and explicit consent from the workers in advance to waive their right to the unpaid wages. Even if a labor union agrees to give up some worker wages in the collective agreement or through labor-management consultations, this has no effect on labor union members who have not individually consented.[176]

(2) Even if wages and bonuses are returned in accordance with a revised collective agreement, if a worker does not individually consent to the return of wages and bonuses incurred by his/her previous work, that worker shall not have their wages returned. If the workers who did not agree to the return of wages and

---

171) Supreme Court ruling July 26, 2002: 2000da27671.
172) Labor Ministry Guidelines: Labor Standards Team 68207-843, Dec. 13, 1999.
173) Supreme Court ruling on Sep. 29, 2000: 99da67536.
174) Seoul District Court ruling on Apr. 16, 2003: 2002na 20291.
175) Supreme Court ruling on Apr. 10, 2001: 99da39531.
176) Jeonju District Court ruling on Apr. 26, 2000: 99na5708.

개별 근로자의 서면동의가 필요하다.[170] 특히, 퇴직금 청구권의 포기는 근로기준법 위반이 되어 무효이다.[171]

   합당한 절차를 밟기 위해서는 개별 근로자의 동의서가 필요하다. 임금반납은 개별 근로자의 자유의사에 기초할 때만 유효하므로 반드시 개별 근로자들이 임금 반납의 취지를 인식하고 반납동의서를 개별 명의로 작성해야 한다.[172] 다만, 법원은 임금반납 시 개별 근로자 각각의 동의서를 받는 것이 바람직하나 회사가 어려운 사정을 근로자에게 충분히 설명했다면 회람 형식으로 동의 여부를 표시하도록 하는 방식을 취하는 것도 가능하다는 입장이다.[173] 단체협약에 의한 임금반납 합의는 효력이 없다. 임금반납은 이미 조합원 개인에게 귀속된 임금에 대한 것이므로 노동조합이 조합원 개인 재산권을 포기하도록 할 수 없기 때문이다. 근로자가 반납한 임금은 근로자의 소득으로 귀속되었다가 자진 반납한 것으로써 사용자는 반환할 의무가 없다.[174] 다만, 반납된 임금도 평균임금 산정에 포함된다. 반납된 임금은 일단 근로자의 소득으로 귀속되었다가 반납한 임금채권이기에 평균임금 산정에 포함해야 한다.[175] 임금반납으로 효력을 인정받지 못하는 사례는 다음과 같다.

(1) 지급시기가 도래하여 개개의 근로자에게 지급청구권이 발생한 체불임금의 포기에 대해서는 회사가 노동조합과의 단체협약으로 체불임금 포기를 수용한 것만으로는 부족하고 각 근로자로부터 사전에 개별적이고 명시적인 포기권한을 받은 한도에서만 할 수 있다고 할 것이다. 이러한 포기권한 없이 노동조합이 단체협약이나 노사협의 등 집단합의 방식에 따라 근로자의 임금을 사전 또는 사후에 포기하더라도 조합원인 근로자에게는 아무런 효력이 미치지 않는다.[176]

(2) 개정된 단체협약에 의하여 임금과 상여금을 반납하였다고 하더라도 기왕의 근로에 의하여 발생한 임금과 상여금 반납에 대해 당해 근로자가 개별적으로 동의하지 않은 경우 당해 근로자에 대해서는 적용할 수 없다. 이직한

---

170) 근로기준법 제43조(임금지급 원칙)과 대법원 1996.6.11. 선고 98다22185 판결: 근로자의 명백한 의사표시로서 임금채권포기는 인정된다.
171) 대법원 2002.7.26 선고 2000다27671 판결.
172) 행정해석, 근기68207-843, 1999.12.13.
173) 대법원 2000.9.29. 선고 99다67536 판결.
174) 서울지방법원 2003.4.16. 선고 2002나20291 판결.
175) 대법원 2001.4.10. 선고 99다39531 판결.
176) 전주지방법원 2000.4.26. 선고 99나5708 판결.

bonuses later resigned after those wages/bonuses were deducted without their individual consent, those returned wages will be considered unpaid wages.[177]

(3) Daegu 00 Company gave a donation to help Daegu citizens suffering from the corona pandemic in April 2020 by resolution of its labor-management council. It then informed the employees of the council's decision, and deducted KRW 10,000 from each individual. In response, the new labor union filed a complaint with the Daegu Labor Office for violation of Article 43 (Wage Payment) of the Labor Standards Act as these wages were deducted without the individual consent of the workers. The company then requested individual consent from all the workers, but only 50% agreed, so the deducted wages had to be returned to those workers who did not submit individual consent forms.[178]

(4) If each worker agrees to return the allowance for unused annual leave that has occurred, it cannot be considered a violation of the law if the employer does not pay an allowance within the agreed range for unused annual leave. However, if the return of unused annual leave allowance agreed upon by the worker also applies to leave that will occur in the future, procedures must be followed that allow a collective agreement or the employment rules to be changed disadvantageously.[179]

5. Conclusion

To overcome difficulties due to the COVID-19 pandemic, company management is increasingly working with labor to have wages returned or have them reduced or frozen. In such cases, it is necessary to understand and prepare in advance because the legal outcomes vary. The return of bonuses or other allowances is to return the wages vested to the worker for previous work and requires written consent from the individual worker. If the company handles a wage return through the labor union, the problem of delayed payment of wages arises. Wage reductions mean less in wages in the future, so even if management comes to an agreement with individual workers, wage cuts are invalid unless procedures are followed to make a disadvantageous change to the employment rules or collective agreement. Therefore, for wages to be reduced, employment rules and collective agreements must be

---

[177] Labor Ministry Guidelines: Unemployment 68430-84, Oct. 21, 1999.
[178] Daegu Labor Office decided this deduction was illegal. Related Labor Ministry Guidelines: Labor Standards-68207-843, Dec. 13, 1999.
[179] Labor Ministry Guidelines: Labor Standards 684207-871, Mar. 23, 2000.

근로자들이 임금과 상여금 반납에 동의하지 않았다면, 기왕의 근로에 의하여 발생한 임금이 체불된 것으로 볼 수 있다.[177]

(3) 대구○○회사는 2020년 4월 코로나 역병으로 인해 고통받는 대구시민 돕기 성금을 납부하기로 노사협의회에서 결정하고, 직원들에게 통보한 후 개인별로 10,000원을 공제하여 기부하였다. 이에 대해 최근에 생긴 신설노동조합은 근로자들의 개별동의 없이 임금을 공제하였기 때문에 이는 근로기준법 제43조(임금지급원칙)을 위반하였다고 회사를 대구노동청에 고소하였다. 회사는 이에 대해 개별근로자들의 동의를 요청하였으나 50% 정도 밖에 동의하지 않아 개별동의서를 제출하지 않은 근로자들에게는 공제된 임금을 반환하여야만 했다.[178]

(4) 근로자 각자가 기발생한 미사용 연차휴가에 대한 수당을 반납하는데 동의하였다면 당해 근로자에게 동의한 범위내에서 미사용 연차휴가에 대한 수당을 지급하지 않더라도 이를 법 위반이라 볼 수는 없다. 그러나 근로자가 동의한 미사용연차휴가 반납이 향후 발생할 휴가에도 해당될 경우에는 단체협약이나 취업규칙의 불이익 변경 절차를 거쳐야 한다.[179]

5. 시사점

코로나 대유행으로 회사의 어려움을 노사가 함께 타계하기 위하여 회사에서는 임금을 반납하거나 삭감하거나 동결하는 일이 많아지고 있다. 이 경우 사안별로 법률적인 판단이 달라지기 때문에 이에 대한 사전 이해와 준비가 필요하다. 상여금이나 기타수당의 반납은 기왕의 근로에 대해 근로자에게 귀속된 임금을 반환하는 것으로 개별근로자의 서면동의를 필요로 한다. 집단적 동의로 진행하게 되면 임금체불의 문제가 발생한다. 임금삭감은 미래에 발생할 임금을 삭감하는 것이므로 개별근로자와 동의하더라도 취업규칙의 불이익 변경이나 단체협약을 변경하지 않으면 임금삭감의 효력을 가질 수 없다. 따라서 임금삭감을 할 경우에는 반드시 개별근로자들의 동의가 아니라 집단적 동의를 통해 취업규칙과 단체협약을 모두 변경해야 한다. 특히 유리한

---

177) 행정해석: 실업 68430-84, 1999.10.21.
178) 대구노동청은 행정해석 (근기68207-843, 1999.12.13.)과 같이 위법한 임금반납으로 판단함.
179) 행정해석: 근기 684207-871, 2000.3.23.

changed through collective consent rather than individual worker consent. And in particular, according to the principle of favorable conditions, unexpected problems may arise, so it is necessary to change both the labor contract and the employment rules to prevent future disputes.

IV. Annual Salary Systems

The annual salary system is a structure that determines wages according to the criteria of ability and performance during one year of employment.

1. Types

(1) Division according to constituent items of annual salary

The annual salary system is not a legal concept, thus each company can use it differently. The annual salary consists of ① a complete annual salary system including all types of wages, ② a partial annual salary system including parts of legal allowances, and ③ a performance-based annual salary system including allowances and bonuses but excluding legal allowances.

(2) Division according to the level of annual salary adjustment

The annual salary system is divided into two systems. One is the cumulative annual salary system which is distinguished by individuals and usually exceeds the previous year's amount without reduction. The other is the reduction-type annual salary system that deducts from the previous year's amount.

(3) Division according to the range of annual salary adjustment

The annual salary system is divided into two systems in the range of annual salary adjustment. One is the simple annual salary system that includes several items in wages and adjusts the total amount in the annual salary. The other is the mixed annual salary system that is mixed with seniority-type base pay, annual level-up portion, and adjustable components.

조건우선의 원칙에 따라 예상하지 못한 문제가 발생할 수 있으므로 근로계약과 취업규칙을 모두 변경해야 차후 발생할 수 있는 분쟁을 사전에 예방할 수 있다.

Ⅳ. 연봉제

연봉제란 통상 1년을 단위로 하여 능력과 실적을 기준으로 임금을 결정하는 형태를 말한다.

1. 유 형

(1) 구성항목에 따른 구분
연봉제는 법적인 개념이 아니다. 따라서 기업에 따라 운용하는 제도의 내용이 다를 수 있다. 연봉에 어떠한 임금이 포함되느냐에 따라 ① 모든 급여항목을 연봉에 포함하는 완전 연봉제, ② 법정수당 일부를 연봉에 포함하는 부분 연봉제, ③ 법정수당은 제외하고 법정외수당과 상여금을 포함시키는 성과급적 연봉제로 나눌 수 있다.

(2) 연봉조정 정도에 따른 구분
연봉제는 제도 도입 후 매년 연봉을 조정하는 과정에서 삭감 없이 전년도 연봉액 이상으로 정하면서 개인별로 차등을 두는 증액형 연봉제와 전년도보다 삭감될 수도 있는 삭감형 연봉제로 구분될 수 있다.

(3) 연봉조정 범위에 따른 구분
연봉제는 연봉조정의 범위에 따라 임금 중 여러 가지 항목을 연봉제화한 후 전체를 대상으로 연봉을 조정하는 순수 연봉제와 연공서열적 기본급 또는 호봉 승급제 부분과 연봉조정 대상 부분이 섞여 있는 혼합형 연봉제로 나눌 수 있다.

2. Application

The annual salary system is generally applied to directors, managers, or general managers who are working in specific positions such as managerial or supervisory, researching, professional, and sales positions. The company accepts the annual salary system exclusively for these particular areas because it is difficult to apply it to all employees due to restrictive factors such as payment for legal allowances, working hours, etc. of the Labor Standards Act. Even if the annual salary system is applied to a limited number of employees, it does not violate Article 6 of the Labor Standards Act, which prohibits discrimination by nationality, religion, gender, and social status.

3. Application of Legal Working Conditions

(1) Labor Contract

All constituent items of wage and methods of calculation and payment shall be specified in the labor contract according to the Labor Standards Act. Accordingly, a contract in the annual salary system shall also specify personnel data; individual annual salary; methods of calculating and payment of annual salary; duration of annual salary; matters on payment and promotion; legal allowances excluding annual salary; various allowance calculations and payment methods; matters on severance pay; bonus and minimum annual salary; matters on the process of making a protest, etc.

In particular, it is desirable that mutual parties specify legal allowances and calculation of severance pay in a written labor contract in order to prevent any possible conflict between the employee and the employer, provided that, if the annual salary system is applied, the items applied to all employees in general shall be acceptable to regulate the rules of employment.

(2) Rules of employment and collective agreement

In order to introduce the annual salary system, an employer shall specify certain rules in the rules of employment and collective agreement, as well as in a labor contract to the related employee. It is desirable that the rules of employment shall regulate items commonly applied to the employees, as the labor contract shall include individual items.

2. 적용대상

연봉제는 임원, 과장 또는 부장급 이상의 관리·감독직, 연구직, 특수직, 영업직 등 특정 분야를 대상으로 하는 것이 일반적이다. 기업들이 연봉제를 특정 분야에 한정하여 도입하고 있는 이유는 근로기준법상 법정수당 지급, 근로시간 제한 등의 제약 요인으로 모든 근로자에게 연봉제를 적용하는 것이 어렵기 때문이다. 연봉제를 일부 근로자에 대해서만 실시하더라도 국적, 신앙, 성별, 사회적 신분에 의한 차별이 아니므로 근로기준법 제6조 위반으로 볼 수는 없다.

3. 법정 근로조건의 적용

(1) 근로계약

근로기준법은 임금의 구성항목, 계산방법 및 지불방법을 근로계약에 명시토록 규정하고 있으므로 연봉제 계약의 경우에도 인적사항, 개인의 연봉액, 연봉의 결정·계산·지급방법, 연봉의 산정기간, 지급시기 및 승급에 관한 사항, 연봉 외 법정수당과 각종 수당의 계산·지급방법, 퇴직금의 처리, 상여 및 최저 연봉액, 연봉계약의 이의제기 절차 등에 관한 사항 등을 근로계약에 명시하여야 한다.

특히, 연봉제의 경우에는 법정수당 및 퇴직금의 산정과 관련하여 노·사간 다툼의 소지가 많으므로 근로계약을 서면으로 작성하는 것이 바람직하다. 다만, 연봉제를 적용하더라도 근로자에게 공동으로 적용되는 사항에 대해서는 취업규칙에 규정하고 근로계약에는 그러한 사항에 대하여 취업규칙을 따른다고 규정할 수 있다.

(2) 취업규칙과 단체협약

연봉제를 도입하기 위해서는 해당 근로자와 근로계약을 체결하는 것 외에 취업규칙과 단체협약에 근거를 설정하여야 한다. 취업규칙에는 근로자에게 공동으로 적용되는 사항을 규정하고 개별적인 사항은 근로계약에 위임하는 것이 바람직하다.

Chapter 3 Payment of Wages

If the concept of the annual salary system is deemed disadvantageous to certain employees, while revising the rules of employment, an employer shall obtain the collective consent of the majority of employees according to Article 94 of the Labor Standards Act. In this case, obtaining such agreement is necessary only from the employees to whom the annual salary system will apply, and it is enough to collect opinions from other employees.

If the annual salary system is enforced without specific regulations in the collective agreement, the agreed wage increase rate after conclusion of a collective agreement will apply to the annual salary.

(3) Working hours and legal allowances for off-days and leave

Although the annual salary system is applied, working hours and articles concerning off-days and leave shall continue to be applicable.

(4) Severance pay

Severance pay in the annual salary system shall be paid according to the Labor Standards Act. Even if the company pays, as part of the employment contract, severance pay in advance with annual salary, such payment does not have the same effect as lawful severance pay.

(5) Principle of fixed-day payment

The Labor Standards Act stipulates that wages shall be paid once or more per month on a fixed day. Accordingly, the previously decided annual salary shall be paid regularly once or more per month.

(6) Calculation of ordinary wage and average wage

Annual salary is the fixed wage to be rendered during the one-year period of wage calculation, so it includes ordinary wage as well as average wage. In such a case where legal standard working hours are measured as contractual working hours, the yearly ordinary working hours computed as hourly ordinary wage are as follows:

Yearly ordinary working hours: (40 hours + 8 hours)×52 weeks[180] = 2,508 (= monthly contractual working hours×12 months=209×12 = 2,508)

---

[180] 52 weeks: 52.14 = 365 days/7 days

연봉제 도입으로 불이익을 받는 근로자가 있을 때에는 취업규칙을 변경함에 있어 근로기준법 제94조에 따라 집단적인 방식에 의해 근로자 과반수의 동의를 받아야 한다. 이 경우 동의를 받아야 할 대상은 연봉제 적용 대상 근로자들이며 전체근로자에 대해서는 의견 청취로 충분하다.

단체협약에 특별히 규정치 않고 연봉제를 시행하면 연봉액의 인상도 단체협약 결과 합의된 임금인상률의 적용을 받게 된다.

(3) 근로시간, 휴일·휴가 관련 법정수당

연봉제를 도입하더라도 근로기준법상 근로시간, 휴일·휴가 관련 조항은 적용된다.

(4) 퇴직금

연봉제에 있어서도 퇴직금은 근로기준법에 따라 지급된다. 근로계약에서 퇴직금을 미리 연봉 속에 포함시켜 지급하였다 하더라도 이는 법정 퇴직금 지급으로서의 효력이 없다.

(5) 임금 정기지급 원칙

근로기준법은 '임금은 매월 1회 이상 일정한 기일을 정하여 지급해야 한다.'라고 규정하고 있다. 따라서 연봉제를 도입하더라도 이미 결정된 연봉을 분할하여 매월 1회 이상 정기적으로 지급하여야 한다.

(6) 통상임금 및 평균임금의 산정

연봉은 임금산정기간 즉 1년 동안에 지급하기로 정해진 고정급 임금이므로 평균임금은 물론이고 통상임금에도 포함된다고 본다. 법정기준 근로시간을 소정근로시간으로 정한 경우 시간급 통상임금 산정을 위한 연의 통상임금 산정기준시간수는 다음과 같다.

연의 통상임금 산정기준시간 수 = (40시간+8시간) × 52주[180] = 2,508시간(= 월 소정근로시간 × 12개월 = 209 × 12 = 2,508)

---

[180] 52주: 52.14 = 365일/7일

(7) Dismissal

An employer cannot terminate a labor contract merely because the contract date expires. When introducing an annual salary system to which the collective agreement, rules of employment, or labor contract legally and properly apply, an employer has to evaluate work performance based on the job plans submitted during the annual contract period and determine the annual salary for the ensuing period. In this case, an employer who terminates the labor contract because of the employee's refusal to accept the proposal may be liable for unfair dismissal.

V. Inclusive Wage System[181]

The inclusive wage system where an employer pays a fixed monthly salary is convenient for management, but can only be applied in some situations, as it can easily violate the Labor Standards Act. The inclusive wage system is a salary payment system where the employer determines the total wages, which include statutory allowances such as overtime, night, and holiday work allowances in consideration of job characteristics and convenience in calculating wages, and then pays a fixed wage every month. This system is often designed for use at workplaces where it is hard to measure working hours due to the job characteristics or for the convenience of calculating working hours even though those working hours are measurable. However, this inclusive wage system is also commonly used to avoid paying various allowances required under the Labor Standards Act. Originally, statutory allowances under the Labor Standards Act were meant to be paid for actual work provided. If an employer pays wages that include statutory allowances in advance, this could violate the Labor Standards Act, but is allowed, albeit with strict limitations as determined in judicial rulings and administrative guidelines.

When the Labor Standards Act (LSA) is revised, related rulings also change. A representative example is the change of the Supreme Court ruling in relation to the inclusive wage system as contractual working hours are introduced as mandatory items in employment contracts. Prior to July 1, 2007, the LSA stipulated wages, working hours and other working conditions acceptable for employment contracts,

---

[181] Jung, Bongsoo, "Inclusive Wage System", 「Labor Law」, Jungang, May 2019.

(7) 해고

연봉계약 기간이 종료되었다고 하여 근로계약을 종료(해고)할 수 없다. 단체협약, 취업규칙, 근로계약 등에 근거를 두어 적법·타당하게 연봉제를 도입하여 실제로 연봉계약기간 동안의 업무계획을 제출하여 이를 평가받은 후, 그 계획을 토대로 하여 실적을 평가받은 후 그 결과에 따라 다음 연봉계약기간의 연봉액을 결정한 후, 근로자가 이를 받아들이지 않아서 사용자가 근로계약을 종료시키면 부당해고 문제가 생길 수 있다.

V. 포괄임금제[181]

매월 고정적인 임금을 지급하는 포괄임금제는 관리의 편리성이 있지만, 근로기준법에 저촉될 수 있기 때문에 예외적인 경우에만 허용된다. 포괄임금제는 업무의 특수성 또는 계산의 편의를 고려하여 연장·야간·휴일근로 수당 등 법정 수당을 포함하여 임금총액을 결정하고 이에 따라 매월 고정적 급여를 지급하는 제도를 말한다. 이 제도는 업무의 성격 또는 근로형태의 특수성으로 인하여 근로시간 산정이 어려운 경우나 근로시간 산정이 가능하더라도 실무상 계산의 편의를 위해 사용되고 있다. 그런데 근로기준법상 발생하는 각종 법정수당을 지급하지 않기 위해 포괄임금제를 악용하는 경우도 많이 있다. 근로기준법상 법정수당은 원래 실제근로제공을 통해서 발생하는 수당인데, 포괄임금제는 미리 법정 수당을 모두 포함하고 지급하는 것이어서 근로기준법 위반의 소지가 크므로 이에 대해 판례나 행정해석에서는 엄격한 제한을 두고 허용하고 있다.

근로기준법이 변경되면 관련 판례도 변경된다. 대표적인 것이 근로계약에 소정근로시간이 필수 기재사항으로 반영됨에 따라, 포괄임금제에 관한 대법원 판례가 변경된 점이다. 2007년 7월 1일 이전에는 근로기준법상 근로계약 체결 시 임금, 근로시간, 기타의 근로조건을 명시했지만, 그 이후에는 임금, 소정근로시간, 법정휴일, 법정휴가와 기타 근로조건만을 명시하였다. 이는

---

[181] 정봉수, "소정근로시간과 포괄임금제", 「월간 노동법률」, 중앙경제사, 2019년 5월호

but since that date, it now stipulates wages, contractual working hours, statutory holidays, statutory leave and other working conditions. This means that a previous employment contract that specifies only "working hours" remains unclear in content, but the revised law stipulates that it should include "contractual working hours". Contractual working hours refer to the time set by the employer that the employee is to work, within the allowable total working time (40 hours per week, 8 hours per day) (Article 2, paragraph 8 of the LSA). Therefore, since the revision, the wage in accordance with the contractual working hours has to be specified, which in effect limits the inclusive wage system.[182]

In order to understand the content of such changes, it is necessary to examine specifically the meaning of the contractual working hours introduced with revision of the Labor Standards Act in 2007. In this regard, The following will discuss the judicial precedents introduced due to the revised law, and then look into the types of suitable employment contract where an inclusive wage system is justifiable.

Before revision (prior to July 1, 2007)	After revision: Amended and Implemented July 1, 2007 [Law No. 8293]
Article 24 (Stipulation of Working Conditions) The employer shall specify the wages, working hours and other working conditions for workers at the time the employment contract is concluded.	Article 24 (Stipulation of Working Conditions) The employer shall notify the employee of the wages, the contractual working hours in accordance with Article 20, holidays in accordance with the provisions of Article 54, annual paid vacation in accordance with the provisions of Article 59, and other working conditions to be determined.

1. Contractual Working Hours

(1) Regulations on contractual working hours

The contractual working hours shall be determined between the worker and employer in the range of working hours pursuant to Article 50 (Legal Working Hours) of the Labor Standards Act, Article 69 (Working Hours for Minors) or Article 46 (Hazardous and Dangerous Work) of the Industrial Safety and Health Act. This means that the contractual working hours must be set within the statutory

---

[182] Lim, Jongyul, 「Labor Law」 17th Ed., Park-young-sa, 2019, p. 470.

기존의 근로계약은 '근로시간'이라 기재하여 그 내용이 명확하지 않았지만, 개정법은 '소정근로시간'이라 명시하도록 규정하고 있다. 즉, 소정근로시간은 법정근로시간 (1주40시간, 1일 8시간) 내에서 근로자와 사용자가 일하기로 정한 시간을 말한다(근기법 제2조 제8항). 이는 1주 근로시간인 40시간, 1일 8시간 내에서 근로자와 사용자가 근로시간을 정하여야 한다는 것이다. 따라서 개정법 이후에는 소정근로시간에 따른 임금을 명시하도록 되어 있어 사실상 포괄임금제를 제한하고 있다.[182]

이러한 변화의 내용을 제대로 알기 위해서는 2007년의 근로기준법 변경과 함께 도입된 소정근로시간의 의미는 어떤 것인지에 대해 구체적으로 살펴볼 필요가 있으며, 이와 관련하여 판례의 변경된 내용이 어떤 것이고, 앞으로 변경된 포괄임금제를 타당성 있게 도입하기 위한 근로계약 체결방식에 대해 구체적으로 살펴보고자 한다.

변경 전 (2007.7.1. 이전)	변경 후: [개정/시행2007.7.1]
제24조(근로조건의 명시) 사용자는 근로계약 체결시에 근로자에 대하여 임금, 근로시간, 기타의 근로조건을 명시하여야 한다.	제24조(근로조건의 명시) 사용자는 근로계약 체결시에 근로자에 대하여 임금, 제20조의 규정에 따른 소정근로시간, 제54조의 규정에 따른 휴일, 제59조의 규정에 따른 연차유급휴가 그 밖에 대통령령이 정하는 근로조건을 명시하여야 한다.

1. 소정근로시간

(1) 소정근로시간에 관한 법규정

소정근로시간은 근로기준법 제50조(법정근로시간), 제69조(연소자의 근로시간) 또는 「산업안전보건법」 제46조(유해 위험한 작업)에 따른 근로시간의 범위에서 근로자와 사용자 사이에 정한 근로시간을 말한다. 이는 법정 근로시간 내에서 소정근로시간을 정해야 하는 것을 말한다. 근로기준법 제17조는 근로계약 체결 시 임금과 소정근로시간, 기타의 근로조건을 명시하도록 하고

---

[182] 임종률, 「노동법」 제20판, 박영사, 2022, 470면.

working hours. Article 17 of the Labor Standards Act requires wages, contractual working hours and other working conditions to be specified in the process of making an employment contract. Therefore, wages defined in the employment contract are limited to 40 hours a week, and in principle, inclusive wages are a violation of the Labor Standards Act. Article 58 of that Act stipulates that if a worker fails to calculate working time by working all or part of the working hours outside the workplace due to business trips or other reasons, they shall be deemed to have worked the contractual working hours. Even for part-time workers, "the employer shall obtain the consent of the employee concerned if they have a part-time worker work beyond the contractual working hours prescribed in Article 2 of the Labor Standards Act. In this case, they cannot work more than an additional 12 hours a week. The employer shall pay the part-time worker an additional 50% or more of the ordinary wage for the overtime exceeding the contractual working hours" (Article 6 of the Fixed and Part-time Employment Act). In the past, overtime pay was introduced only for working hours exceeding legal standard working hours. However, for part-time workers, the overtime pay shall be paid if working hours exceed contractual working hours (introduced on March 18, 2014). This means that if the part-time worker has 20 contractual working hours per week, an additional wage shall be paid for the hours exceeding those 20 contractual working hours.

(2) Reasons for limiting work hours

Contractual working hours refer to the time that the worker has to work within the legal standard working hours. Here, legal standard working hours generally refer to 40 hours per week and 8 hours per day. The limitation on extended work is up to 12 hours in excess of statutory working hours (Article 53 of the LSA). Overtime work for part-time workers is also recognized within a limit of 12 hours by adding to the weekly contractual working hours of part-time workers. That is, extended hours for part-time workers are judged based on contractual working hours rather than legal standard working hours (Article 6 of the Fixed-Term and Part-time Employment Act). In Article 17 of the LSA, stipulating the contractual working hours in the employment contract is mandatory, and then based upon this, wages and contractual working hours are determined. This limits the maximum working hours and ensures the right of employees to protect their health and pursue happiness.

The inclusive wage system refers to a wage system that does not calculate basic

있다. 따라서 근로계약에서 정하는 임금은 1주 40시간 내에서 정하도록 하고 있으므로, 원칙상 포괄임금은 근로기준법 위반이 된다. 근로기준법 제58조는 근로자가 출장이나 그 밖의 사유로 근로시간의 전부 또는 일부를 사업장 밖에서 근로하여 근로시간을 산정하기 어려운 경우에는 소정근로시간을 근로한 것으로 본다고 규정하고 있다.

단시간 근로자의 경우에도 "사용자는 단시간근로자에 대하여 근로기준법 제2조의 소정근로시간을 초과하여 근로하게 하는 경우에는 당해 근로자의 동의를 얻어야 한다. 이 경우, 1주간 12시간을 초과하여 근로하게 할 수 없다. 사용자가 단시간 근로자의 소정근로시간을 초과하는 연장근로에 대하여 통상임금의 100분의 50 이상을 가산하여 지급하여야 한다"고 규정하고 있다(기간제법 제6조). 기존에는 법정근로시간을 초과하는 근로시간만 연장근로에 따른 연장근로가산수당을 지급하도록 하였으나, 단시간근로자의 경우에는 법정근로시간에 미치지 못하더라도 소정근로시간을 초과하는 경우 연장근로가산수당을 지급하도록 하고 있다(2014. 3. 18 도입). 이는 단시간 근로자의 소정근로시간이 주 20 시간인 경우 이를 초과했을 때 연장근로에 대한 가산임금을 지급해야 한다는 것이다.

(2) 소정근로시간으로 제한하는 이유

소정근로시간은 법정근로시간 내에서 근로자와 사용자가 일하기로 정한 시간을 말한다. 여기서 법정근로시간이라고 하면 일반적으로 1주 40시간, 1일 8시간을 말한다. 연장근로는 법정근로시간을 초과하여 최대 1주 12시간까지로 제한하고 있다(근기법 제53조). 단시간근로자의 연장근로도 단시간근로자의 1주 소정근로시간에 가산하여 12시간 한도 내에서 인정된다. 즉, 단시간근로자의 연장근로는 법정근로시간이 아닌 소정근로시간을 기준으로 판단한다(기간제법 제6조). 근로기준법 제17조에서는 근로계약서의 소정근로시간을 필수 기재사항으로 하여, 임금과 소정근로시간을 정하도록 하고 있으며, 이는 근로시간을 제한하여 근로자의 건강과 행복추구권을 보장하고 사용자의 권리남용을 방지하기 위한 것이다.

포괄임금제는 소정근로시간에 대한 기본임금을 미리 산정하지 않고, 법정근로시간과 추가 연장근로시간에 대한 제수당을 합한 금액을 월급여액이나

Chapter 3 Payment of Wages

wages in advance for a given working time, but rather stipulates that daily or monthly wages shall include the total amount of statutory working hours plus additional working hours.[183] Since the LSA stipulates that basic wages and contractual working hours shall be defined in the employment contract, the inclusive wage system is in effect in violation of that Act.

2. Changes in Court Rulings Regarding the Inclusive Wage System

(1) Court rulings - details of changes

Amendment of the Labor Standards Act resulted in the following changes in rulings on inclusive wages.

Before revision (prior to July 1, 2007)	After revision: The Labor Standards Act [Enforcement 2007.7.1]
The Supreme Court concluded that if an employer receives the consent of the employee as a means of encouraging the convenience of calculating working hours and promoting employee willingness, and it is not disadvantageous to the employee in light of collective agreements and rules of employment, the inclusive wage agreement in a collective wage system is valid.[184]	In 2010, the Supreme Court distinguished between cases where it was difficult to calculate working time and cases where it was not. ① In cases where it is deemed difficult to calculate working hours such as surveillance work, even if a so-called inclusive wage contract is concluded, it is valid if it is not disadvantageous to the employee and is recognized as justified in light of various circumstances. (2) If there is little difficulty in calculating working hours, the principle of wage payment according to working hours in the Labor Standards Act shall apply unless there are special circumstances in which it is impossible to apply the provisions of the Labor Standards Act.[185]

---

[183] Lee, Seunggil, "A Study on Judicial Principles and Benefits of the Inclusive Wage System", 「Labor Law Studies Collection」 29th Ed., Korean Comparative Labor Law Study Association, December 2012, p. 575.

[184] Supreme Court ruling on Oct. 25, 1993, 83do1050; Supreme Court ruling on Apr. 25, 1997, 95da4056; Supreme Court ruling on Mar. 24, 2019, 96da24699; Supreme Court ruling on May 28, 1999, 99da2881; Supreme Court ruling on Jun. 11, 1999, 98da26385.

[185] Supreme Court ruling on May 13, 2010, 2008da6052 (Cares regarding Navy Welfare Corporation)

일당임금으로 정해 근로자에게 지급하기로 하는 임금제도를 말한다.[183] 근로기준법상 근로계약 작성시 필수 기재사항인 기본임금과 소정근로시간을 정하도록 명시되어 있는 점을 볼 때, 포괄임금제는 사실상 근로기준법을 위반하는 임금지급제도라고 할 수 있다.

2. 포괄임금제에 대한 판례 변경

(1) 판례의 변경내용
근로기준법의 개정안으로 인해 포괄임금의 판례 변화는 다음과 같다.

변경 전 (2007.7.1.이전)	변경 후: 근로기준법 [시행2007.7.1]
대법원은 "근로시간, 근무형태와 업무의 성질 등을 참작하여 계산의 편의와 직원의 근무의욕을 고취하는 뜻으로 근로자의 승낙을 받고, 그것이 단체협약이나 취업규칙에 비추어 근로자에게 불이익이 없으며 여러 사정에 비추어 정당하다고 인정되면 포괄임금제의 임금약정은 유효하다"고 판시하여 왔다.[184]	2010년 대법원은 근로시간 산정이 어려운 경우와 그렇지 않은 경우로 구분하였다. ① "감시단속적 근로 등과 같이 근로시간의 산정이 어려운 것으로 인정되는 경우에는 이른바 포괄임금에 의한 임금지급계약을 체결하더라도 그것이 달리 근로자에게 불이익이 없고 여러 사정에 비추어 정당하다고 인정될 때에는 유효하다." 그러나 ② "근로시간의 산정이 어려운 경우가 아니라면 달리 근로기준법상의 근로시간에 관한 규정을 그대로 적용할 수 없다고 볼 만한 특별한 사정이 없는 한, 근로기준법상의 근로시간에 따른 임금지급의 원칙이 적용된다"고 한다.[185]

---

183) 이승길, "포괄임금제의 법리와 효용성에 관한 연구", 「노동법논총」 제29호, 한국비교노동법학회, 2013.12. 575면.
184) 대법원 1993.10.25. 선고 83도1050, 대법원 1997.4.25. 선고 95다4056 판결, 대법원 1998.3.24. 선고 96다24699, 대법원 1999.5.28. 선고 99다2881 판결, 대법원 1999.6.11 선고 98다26385 판결 등 다수.
185) 대법원 2010.5.13. 선고 2008다6052 (해군복지근무지원단 사건)

Related rulings can be divided into those before and those after July 2007. Before July 2007, the courts did not specifically determine contractual working hours because employment contracts were not required to stipulate wage, working time or other conditions. In other words, even if the basic wage was not calculated in advance, but the inclusive wage equaled the sum of applicable allowances plus the monthly wage in a way that was not disadvantageous to the employee, it was considered valid. As a result, it was possible to accept the inclusive wage system for both jobs where the working hours were difficult to calculate, and jobs where the working hours were not difficult to calculate, but the system was conducive to convenient management.

In 2010, however, the Supreme Court ruled that the difficulty of calculating working hours would determine whether an inclusive wage system was justified and that such a system was not acceptable if the working hours could be calculated.[186] This case is considered to set a related precedent because the employment contract specifies contractual working hours in accordance with Article 17 of the LSA. In other words, the basic wage shall be determined on the basis of the contractual working hours when concluding an employment contract, and in principle, an inclusive wage system cannot be introduced when working time can be calculated. Thus, an inclusive wage system is acceptable for workers with supervisory and intermittent duties that make it difficult to calculate working time, but not very suitable for workers whose working time can be calculated.

(2) Trends in rulings on the current inclusive wage system

Since July 2007, consistent judicial precedents have been set, denying the existing inclusive wage system. A Supreme Court ruling in 2014 provides a clear explanation (Supreme Court Decision 2016.66, Decision 12114, 2011). "In cases where an inclusive wage system can be deemed justifiable, it is necessary to consider the type and nature of the work (such as whether it involves surveillance and intermittent work), and the difficulty of calculating the working hours when considering the working time. The amount of allowance included in the statutory allowance is set as a monthly benefit or daily wage, or the basic wage calculated in advance, but if the statutory allowance is not classified and a fixed amount is set as the statutory benefit allowance, it is valid when a wage contract under the

---

[186] Lim, Dongchae, Cho, Younggil, Kim, Junkeun, "A Study on the Court Ruling of the Navy Welfare Corporation regarding the Effect of the Inclusive Wage System", 「Kangwon Law Study」 25th Ed., February 2019, Gangwon University Comparative Law Study Center, p. 453.

기존의 판례는 2007년 7월 이전의 것으로 근로계약을 체결할 경우 임금, 근로시간 등 기타의 조건을 명시하여야 한다는 내용에 따라 소정근로시간에 대한 부분을 구체적으로 판단하지 않았다. 즉, 기본임금을 미리 산정하지 않은 채 제 수당을 합한 금액을 월 급여액으로 지급하는 포괄임금이 근로자에게 불이익이 없다면 유효한 것으로 인정하였다. 이에 따라 근로시간 산정이 어려운 특수한 형태의 근로뿐만 아니라, 근로시간 계산이 가능하지만 편의를 위해 고정연장근로수당을 신설하여 포괄임금제로 하는 경우도 허용하였다.

그러나 2010년 대법원은 포괄임금제의 유효성을 판단하는 요건으로 '근로시간의 산정이 어려운지의 여부'를 제시하고 근로시간의 산정이 가능한 경우에는 포괄임금제가 허용되지 않는다는 취지의 판결을 내렸다.[186] 이 판례는 근로기준법 제17조 근로계약의 내용에 따라 소정근로시간을 필수기재 사항으로 명시하고 있기 때문에 나온 판례라고 본다. 즉, 근로계약 체결 시 기본임금은 소정근로시간을 기준으로 정하여야 하고, 근로시간 산정이 가능한 경우에는 원칙적으로 포괄임금제를 도입할 수 없다. 따라서 포괄임금제는 근로시간 계산이 어려운 감시단속적 근로자 등에 대하여는 적용되지만, 근로시간 산정이 가능한 근로자에 대해서는 포괄임금제로 인정받기가 쉽지 않다.

(2) 현행 포괄임금제에 대한 판례의 경향

2007년 7월 이후, 포괄임금제에 대한 일관성 있는 판례가 제시되면서 기존의 포괄임금제를 부정하고 있다. 2014년 대법원 판례는 이와 관련하여 명확한 설명을 하고 있다(대법원 2014.6.26. 선고 2011도12114 판결). 포괄임금제를 인정할 수 있는 경우로, "감시 단속적 근로 등과 같이 근로시간, 근로 형태와 업무의 성질을 고려할 때 근로시간의 산정이 어려운 것으로 판단되는 경우에는 사용자와 근로자 사이에 기본임금을 미리 산정하지 아니한 채 법정수당까지 포함된 금액을 월급여액이나 일당 임금으로 정하거나 기본임금을 미리 산정하면서도 법정 제 수당을 구분하지 아니한 채 일정액을 법정 제 수당으로 정하여 이를 근로시간에 상관없이 지급하기로 약정하는 내용의 이른바 포괄임금제에 의한 임금 지급계약으로 체결하더라도 그것이 달리 근로자에게 불이익이 없고 여러 사정에 비추어 정당하다고 인정될 때에는 유효하다."고

---

[186] 임동채, 조영길, 김준근, "포괄임금제 효력에 관한 '해군복지근무지원단 판결'의 타당성 고찰", 「강원법학」 제56호, 2019.2. 강원대학교 비교법학연구소, 453면.

inclusive wage system is concluded. However, it should not be disadvantageous to the workers. Therefore, it is justified in light of the various circumstances mentioned above."

In addition, the rulings also reject the inclusive wage system if calculation of the working hours is not difficult, unless there is a special situation where the working hours regulation in the Labor Standards Act cannot be applied. In this case, if a contract is concluded in advance under the inclusive wage system, it is judged whether the inclusive wage contract is legal or not after reviewing if the statutory allowance included in the inclusive wage is correct. If the wages paid under the inclusive wage system fall short of the statutory allowance calculated according to the standards established by the LSA, and if it will be disadvantageous to the employees, it will be null and void. In such a case, the company shall compensate the employee(s) equal to the amount to be paid in legal standard allowances.

(3) When it is difficult to calculate working hours

If the calculation of working hours is difficult, an inclusive wage system can be introduced. The following types of work to which this system is applicable are presented in the Labor Standards Act.

1) Supervisory/intermittent work: The working hours, rest and holiday regulations in the Labor Standards Act shall not apply to workers engaged in supervisory/intermittent work once the employer has received approval from the Minister of Employment and Labor (Article 63 (3) of the LSA).

2) Work outside the workplace: If a worker is unable to calculate working time due to working all or part of the working time outside the workplace (or other reasons), they shall be deemed to have worked the contractual working hours (Article 58 (1)).

3) Discretionary work: The discretionary work in Article 58 (3) of the Labor Standards Act refers to tasks where it is difficult to calculate working time because of the characteristics or performance rather than the amount of work. Written consent is required from the employee representative in order to qualify the work as within the contractual working hours. Specific tasks include designing and analyzing research and development and information processing systems, organizing articles for newspapers and broadcasts, designing and designing-related job, and producing and supervising broadcasting and film production (Article 58, Clause 3).

판시하고 있다.

또한 판례는 포괄임금제를 부정하는 경우로, "그러나 위와 같이 근로시간의 산정이 어려운 경우가 아니라면 근로기준법상의 근로시간에 관한 규정을 그대로 적용할 수 없다고 볼 만한 특별한 사정이 없는 한 근로기준법상의 근로시간에 따른 임금지급의 원칙이 적용되어야 하므로, 이러한 경우에 앞서 본 포괄임금제 방식의 임금 지급계약을 체결한 때에는 그것이 근로기준법이 정한 근로계약에 관한 규제를 위반하는지를 따져 포괄임금에 포함된 법정수당이 근로기준법이 정한 기준에 따라 산정된 법정수당에 미달한다면 그에 해당하는 포괄임금제에 의한 임금 지급계약 부분은 근로자에게 불이익하여 무효라 할 것이고 사용자는 근로기준법의 강행성과 보충성 원칙에 의하여 근로자에게 그 미달하는 법정수당을 지급할 의무가 있다."고 판시하고 있다.

(3) 근로시간 산정이 어려운 경우

근로시간의 산정이 어려운 경우에 대해서는 포괄임금제를 도입할 수 있으며, 이러한 업무는 근로기준법상 제시된 다음과 같은 업무라고 볼 수 있다.

1) 감시 단속적 근로: 감시 단속적 근로자로서 사용자가 고용노동부장관의 적용제외 인가를 받은 경우 근로기준법의 근로시간, 휴게, 휴일 규정을 적용하지 아니한다. 이는 고용노동부장관의 승인을 전제로 근로시간의 적용이 제외된다(근기법 제63조 제3항).

2) 사업장 밖 근로: 근로자가 출장 및 기타 사유로 근로시간의 전부 또는 일부를 사업장 밖에서 근로하여 근로시간을 산정하기 어려운 경우, 소정 근로시간을 근로한 것으로 본다(제58조 제1항).

3) 재량근로: 근로기준법 제58조 제3항의 재량근로업무는 전문적 업무로 근로의 양보다는 질이나 성과가 중시되어 근로시간 산정이 어려운 업무를 말한다. 해당 업무를 소정근로시간으로 인정받기 위해서는 근로자대표와의 서면합의가 필요하다. 구체적 업무로는 연구개발이나 정보처리시스템의 설계나 분석업무, 신문이나 방송 등 기사의 취재 편성 업무, 디자인이나 고안업무, 방송이나 영화 제작의 프로듀서나 감독 업무 등이 있다(제58조 제3항).

3. Case Studies on Introducing an Inclusive Wage System

(1) Inclusive wage agreement for workers in a restaurant business

1) Inclusive wage system: Workers work for 6 days from Monday to Saturday, and 8 hours a day over the hours from 11 am to 10 pm (resting between 2 pm and 5 pm), and earn a monthly salary of 3 million won, including pay for overtime.

   If the employment contract is written as above, 3 million won will be the basic wage, with an extra wage of 753,588 won per month for an additional 8 hours per week (35 hours per month) paid additionally.

2) Suggestions for correction: There are 40 contractual working hours per week and 8 hours per day. The monthly base rate for this is 2,401,560 won, with overtime of 598,437 won for 8 additional working hours per week. Therefore, the monthly total amount is 3 million won. This amount should be divided into two parts: 80 percent as basic pay and 20 percent for overtime pay. To be recognized as a justifiable inclusive wage contract, the monthly wage for the contractual working hours should be clarified, and the additional working hours and wages stipulated and paid.

(2) Inclusive salary for white-collar workers

1) Issue: For some white-collar workers, the monthly wage is set at 76% basic wage and 24% fixed overtime allowance. Under this standard, the inclusive wage-based employment contract includes 40 hours of work per week plus an additional 10 hours per week. The company pays inclusive wages every month to the workers regardless of whether they worked overtime or not. Therefore, it is not necessary for the company to pay an additional overtime allowance for up to 10 hours of extended work. Is this inclusive wage system for these white-collar workers possible under current law?

2) Judging whether the inclusive wage system violates the LSA: There have been two judicial precedents for determining whether an inclusive wage system is possible for white-collar workers. The first involved a white-collar worker employed by a foreign life insurance company. In this case, the court deemed it

3. 포괄임금제 도입에 대한 실무사례

(1) 식당 업무의 포괄임금 계약서

1) 포괄임금제: 1주 6일 근무, 1일 근로시간 8시간으로 오전 11시부터 오후 10시까지 (휴게시간 14:00-17:00 3시간 포함), 급여는 300만 원으로 연장근로 수당을 포함한다.

   위와 같이 포괄임금제 근로계약서를 작성한 경우에는 300만 원이 기본급이 되므로 매월 추가로 1주 8시간(1월 35시간)에 대한 연장가산임금 753,588원을 지급해야 한다.

2) 개선방향: 소정근로시간은 1주 40시간, 1일 8시간을 근무한다. 이에 대한 월 기본급은 2,401,560원이다. 1주에 1일을 추가로 근무하므로 연장근로 수당 598,437원을 추가 지급한다. 따라서 월 수령액은 300만 원으로 한다. 월 임금에 기본급 80%, 고정연장수당 20%를 설정함으로써 1주 8시간, 1월 35시간에 대한 고정연장수당을 포함한다. 포괄임금으로 인정받기 위해서는 소정근로시간에 대한 월지급 임금을 명확히 하여야 하고, 추가로 발생하는 연장근로에 대한 근무시간과 임금을 추가 계산하여 지급하면 합법적인 포괄임금 계약서로 인정된다.

(2) 사무직 근로자의 포괄임금

1) 예상문제: 사무직 근로자의 경우, 월 임금을 76%를 기본임금으로 24%를 고정 연장수당으로 설정하였다. 이 기준을 가지고 1주 40시간 근무에 추가로 1주 10시간의 연장근로를 포함하고 있다는 포괄임금제 근로계약서를 작성하였다. 회사는 근로자에게 연장근로 유무와 상관없이 일정액의 월 임금을 지급하였고, 이 때문에 연장근로 10시간까지는 고정연장수당을 지급하지 않아도 된다. 이러한 사무직 근로자의 포괄임금제는 현행법상 가능한가?

2) 포괄임금제의 위반 여부 판단: 위의 사무직 근로자에 대한 포괄임금제가 가능한지 여부에 대해 판례는 2가지의 기준을 가지고 있다. 첫 번째는 외국계 생명보험회사의 사무직 근로자로 월 20시간의 연장근로에 대한 고정연장수당을 정하여 급여 지급이 이루어졌다. 이 경우 법원은 회사업무 특성상 과업 중심의 업무 문화가 일상화되어 생산직 근로자와 달리 근로

difficult to calculate working hours, unlike production workers, because the business culture common to this company centered on performance tasks due to the nature of the company's insurance sales work. In such cases, the inclusive wage system is recognized.[187] The second involved white-collar workers who concluded an inclusive wage contract by signing a collective agreement offering a fixed overtime allowance of 10 hours per week for 40 hours of work per week. Workers did not receive any extended allowance for up to 10 hours a week even if overtime was performed that week. The Supreme Court concluded that such a wage system cannot be regarded as monthly remuneration based on an hourly wage or as a legitimate inclusive wage system in light of the fact that workers can calculate their hours easily.[188]

Judging from the principle in rulings on the inclusive wage system and the above two examples, the criteria for determining the justification for an inclusive wage system is whether the working hours of workers can be calculated or not.

4. Opinion

The inclusive wage system is applicable to such employees as cargo truck drivers, guards, shift workers, daily workers, etc., where it is difficult to measure working hours due to the job characteristics. Applying this inclusive wage system to these types of jobs can provide reasonable and suitable wages, motivate employees, and make calculation of wages simpler. In cases where working hours are measurable, some companies have introduced inclusive wage systems that include all statutory allowances, as well as annual and monthly leave allowances and severance pay. This creates a high risk that the Labor Standards Act will be violated and can lead to labor disputes with the related employees. Therefore, employers need to well understand the inclusive wage system and its purposes, and need to refrain from abusing it, ensuring their employees receive appropriate wages that include statutory allowances, so as to avoid discouraging them.

---

[187] Seoul Central District Court ruling on Feb. 13, 2018
[188] Supreme Court ruling on Dec. 10, 2009

시간 산정이 어렵다고 판단하였다. 이와 같은 경우에는 포괄임금제를 인정하고 있다.[187] 두 번째는 사무직 근로자의 경우로 1주 40시간 근무에 대해 주당 10시간의 고정연장근로수당을 정한 단체협약을 체결하여 포괄임금제를 실시하였다. 근로자가 1주에 연장근로가 이루어지더라도 주 10시간 까지는 연장근로수당을 지급하지 않았다. 이에 대해 대법원은 임금체계를 월별 보수액을 기준으로 한 시간급 금액이 산정되었다고 볼 수 없고, 근로시간 산정이 가능한 근로자에 대한 포괄임금제 제한법리에 비추어 볼 때, 정당한 포괄임금제로 볼 수 없다고 판단하였다.[188]

본 사안을 포괄임금제 판례법리와 위의 2가지 사례를 가지고 판단해 볼 때, 사무직 근로자의 임금체계에서 고정연장수당을 통한 포괄임금제에 대한 판단기준은 해당 직종에 대한 근로자의 업무가 근로시간 산정이 가능한 업종인지 여부에 따라 포괄임금제의 정당성 여부를 판단할 수 있을 것이다.

4. 의견

포괄임금제는 업무의 특성에 따라 근로시간 산정이 어려운 화물운송기사, 경비원, 격일제근로자, 일용직 근로자 등에 적용되고 있다. 이러한 분야에 포괄임금제를 적용하여 합리적이고 타당한 임금을 적용할 수 있으며, 이에 따른 근로의욕 고취와 더불어 임금계산의 편의를 가져올 수 있다. 그러나 근로시간 계산이 명확한 업무의 경우에도 포괄임금제를 도입하여 법정 가산임금 일체를 포함하여 지급하거나 심지어 연월차수당, 퇴직금까지 포함하여 지급하는 경우를 볼 수 있다. 이는 명백한 근로기준법의 위반 여지가 있으며, 근로자와의 분쟁으로도 응당 이어질 수 있다. 따라서 포괄임금제에 대한 정확한 이해를 통해 포괄임금제를 남용하는 일이 없어야 할 것이며, 해당 분야의 근로자에 대해서는 법정수당을 고려한 임금을 책정하여 근로의욕을 저하시키지 않도록 하여야 할 것이다.

---

[187] 서울중앙지법 2018.2.13. 선고 2017가단5061696 판결.
[188] 대법원 2009.12.10. 선고 2008다57852 판결.

Chapter 4 **The Protection of Wages**

I. Preventive Measures for Delayed Payment of Wages
II. Alternative Payment System
    for Resolving Unpaid Wages
III. Small-Scale Alternative Payment System
    for Resolving Unpaid Wages
IV. Statue of Limitations
V. Related Labor Cases
   〈Case 1〉 A Claim for Insolvency Payment
   〈Case 2〉 Petition for Unpaid Weekly Holiday Allowance
   〈Case 3〉 Whether Compensation Should be Given
            for Unused Annual Leave

제4장 임금채권 보호

Ⅰ. 임금체불 예방조치
Ⅱ. 체불임금 해결을 위한 대지급금 제도
Ⅲ. 소액대지급금제도
Ⅳ. 소멸시효제도
Ⅴ. 실무사례
   〈사례 1〉 대지급금사건
   〈사례 2〉 주휴수당 미지급사건
   〈사례 3〉 미사용 연차휴가수당 미지급사건

Chapter 4 The Protection of Wages

I. Preventive Measures for Delayed Payment of Wages[189]

Providing work not meant to be on a voluntary basis and not receiving wages is slave labor. Thus, delaying payment of wages is a serious offense and subject to imprisonment for up to three years or a fine of up to 30 million won.[190] Delayed payment of wages is punishable for each violation towards individual workers, so if the employer delays payment of wages to a large number of workers, that employer will face heavy penalties. Despite these strong penalties, it is not easy to settle problems related to unpaid wages. Even if a worker who was not paid complains to the local Employment Labor Office (hereinafter referred to as "Labor Office"), and the Labor Office confirms that the wages remain unpaid and the employer is punished, the worker still has to take separate legal action to receive the unpaid wages. If the employer does not have any property, the employer can receive a certain amount of money for the most preferential wages from the Wage Bond Guarantee Fund. Receiving unpaid wages through civil litigation and the Insolvency Payment Claim System is a complex process and takes a long time, which is not helpful in practical terms.

1. High interest levied

In order to prevent delayed payment of wages and early liquidation of unpaid wages, the Labor Standards Act was amended in 2005 to create a "Late Payment Interest System for Unpaid Wages." If an employer fails to pay all or part of wages and retirement benefits owed within 14 days of the required date of payment, the employer shall pay the late payment interest rate prescribed by Presidential Decree (currently 20% per year) for the number of days payment was delayed, starting from the day following the required date of payment. This high interest rate helps to prevent an employer from intentionally paying back wages only when they is forced to, and without consequences. If an employer delays payment of wages due to a natural disaster, armed conflict or other reasons such as legal or actual

---

[189] Jung, Bongsoo, "Preventive Measures for Delayed Wage 「Labor Law」, Jungang, October 2019.
[190] The Labor Standards Act (LSA): Article 109 (paragraph 1).

Ⅰ. 임금체불 예방조치[189]

　근로를 제공하고 임금을 받지 못하는 것은 노예노동에 해당된다. 따라서 임금체불은 중대범죄에 해당하므로 3년 이하의 징역 또는 3천만 이하의 벌금을 처벌받는다.[190] 이 벌칙과 벌금은 체불된 근로자 개인에 해당되므로 다수의 근로자에게 임금을 체불하게 되면 가중처벌을 받는다. 이러한 강력한 처벌조항에도 불구하고 임금체불을 해결하는 방법은 쉽지가 않다. 체불된 근로자가 지방고용노동관서(이하'노동청')에 진정하여 임금체불확인을 받고 사용자를 형사처벌하더라도 사용자가 임금을 지급하지 않는 경우에는 근로자는 별도의 민사소송을 통해서만 체불된 임금을 받을 수 있다. 사업주가 재산이 없는 경우 임금채권보장기금의 대지급금제도를 통해서 최우선변제 임금을 일정한 한도 내에서 지급받을 수 있다. 이러한 민사소송과 대지급금제도를 통해 체불임금을 받는 것은 복잡한 과정과 오랜 시간이 소요되므로 실질적인 도움은 되지 않는다.

1. 지연이자제도

　임금체불의 예방 및 체불임금의 조기청산을 유도하기 위하여 2005년 근로기준법 개정을 통해 '미지급임금에 대한 지연이자 지급제도'가 마련되었다. 사용자는 임금 및 퇴직급여의 전부 또는 일부를 그 지급사유가 발생한 날로부터 14일 이내에 지급하지 아니하는 경우 그 다음날부터 지급하는 날까지의 지연 일수에 대하여 대통령령이 정하는 이율(현행 연20%)에 따른 지연이자를 지급하여야 한다. 지연이자제도는 사용자가 불가피한 사정없이 의도적으로 임금을 체불하는 것을 막기 위해 고율의 이자를 부가하는 제도로 사용자가 천재지변, 법률상 또는 사실상 도산 등으로 임금을 지급할 수 없는 경우에는 적용이 면제된다.

　지연이자제도는 체불사업주로 하여금 법정이자(상법 연6%)보다 높은 연 20%의 이율을 부담하게 하여 신속한 체불청산을 유도하기 위하여 도입되었으나,

---

[189] 정봉수, "임금체불예방제도", 「월간 노동법률」, 중앙경제사, 2019년 10월호
[190] 근로기준법 제109조 제1항.

bankruptcy, this provision shall not apply to the period during which such reasons continue to exist.

> The Labor Standards Act: Article 37 (Late Payment Interest on Unpaid Wages)
> (1) An employer who fails to pay all or part of the wages or benefits (only those paid in a lump sum) pursuant to Article 36 or subparagraph 5 of Article 2 of the Employee Retirement Benefit Security Act, respectively, within fourteen days from the day when the cause for payment occurs, shall pay late payment interest for the number of days from the date following expiry of the fourteen day period until the payment is made, at a rate up to 40/100 and as prescribed by Presidential Decree in consideration of financial conditions, including the late payment interest rate applicable among banks under the Banking Act.
> (2) If an employer delays payment of wages due to a natural disaster, armed conflicts or other reasons prescribed by Presidential Decree, the provisions of paragraph (1) shall not apply to the period during which such reasons continue to exist.

The late payment interest system levies a much higher rate of interest (20% annually) than the statutory interest of 6% a year, as a way to induce quick payment. However, if the employers do not have any money or assets to effect payment, there is no way to protect the affected workers' rights, no matter how high the interest rate.[191] The reasons why 20% annual interest payment is not used well on unpaid wages is as follows. First, there is no penalty for failing to pay the late payment interest, unless the worker takes the employer to civil court.[192] Second, workers tend to agree to withdraw their complaints if they simply receive their unpaid wages. Third, the Labor Inspector only considers whether the unpaid wages have been paid when determining punishment, and not the interest for delaying payment, since there are no items related to delayed payment interest in the "Official Document on Details of Unpaid Wages". Delayed payment interest is only considered in civil lawsuits for unpaid wages, meaning there is very limited effectiveness in preventing wage payment delays.

---

[191] Park, Keun-hoo et al., Ministry of Employment and Labor, "A Study on Expansion of the Wage Bond Guarantee System", Dec. 23, 2016, p. 17.
[192] Ha, Kap-rae, 「The Labor Standards Act」 35th Ed., 2022, p. 296.

체불사업주가 사실상 무자력자가 되어 근로자가 임금채권 자체를 지급받지 못할 경우에는 임금에 대하여 아무리 높은 이율의 이자가 붙더라도 근로자의 권리보장에 실질적인 기여를 하지 못한다는 근본적인 한계점이 있다.[191]

근로기준법 제37조(미지급 임금에 대한 지연이자)

① 사용자는 제36조에 따라 지급하여야 하는 임금 및 「근로자퇴직급여 보장법」 제2조 제5호에 따른 급여(일시금만 해당된다)의 전부 또는 일부를 그 지급 사유가 발생한 날부터 14일 이내에 지급하지 아니한 경우 그 다음 날부터 지급하는 날까지의 지연 일수에 대하여 연 100분의 40 이내의 범위에서 「은행법」에 따른 은행이 적용하는 연체금리 등 경제 여건을 고려하여 대통령령으로 정하는 이율(연 20%)에 따른 지연이자를 지급하여야 한다.

② 제1항은 사용자가 천재·사변, 그 밖에 대통령령으로 정하는 사유에 따라 임금 지급을 지연하는 경우 그 사유가 존속하는 기간에 대하여는 적용하지 아니한다.

체불임금에 대한 연 20%의 지연이자 지급이 현실적으로 강제되지 않고 있는 이유는 첫째, 지연이자를 지급하지 않은데 대한 벌칙규정이 없고, 근로자의 민사상 청구권만 인정되기 때문이다.[192] 둘째, 근로자들이 체불임금만 받으면 진정 또는 고소사건 취하해주려는 경향이 있기 때문이다. 셋째, 노동청이 사법처리 단계에서도 처벌수위 결정시 체불임금 원금 지급여부만 고려될 뿐 지연이자 지급 여부까지는 고려되지 않는다는 점이 작용하고 있기 때문이다. 특히, 체불금품확인원에 기재되는 '체불임금 등 내역'에도 따로 지연이자에 관한 항목이 마련되어 있지 않아 현재 체불 진정사건 조사과정에서 체불금액에 대한 지연이자 조사가 별도로 이루어지기 어려운 상황이다. 따라서 지연이자 적용은 임금체불 민사소송에서만 활용되고 있으므로 사실상 임금체불을 예방하는데 한계가 있다.

---

191) 박근후 외 4명, 고용노동부 용역자료, "임금채권보장제도 확대방안 연구", 2016.12.23. 17면.
192) 하갑례, 「근로기준법」 제35판, 2022, 296면.

Chapter 4 The Protection of Wages

2. Punishment and No-punishment for offenses against one's intention

> The Labor Standards Act: Article 109 (Penal Provisions)
> (1) Any person who violates the provisions of Article 36, 43 (Payment of Wages), 44 (Payment of Wages in Subcontract Businesses), 44-2 (Joint Responsibility for Paying Wages in the Construction Industry), 46 (Allowances during Business Suspension), or 56 (Extended Work, Night Work and Holiday Work) shall be punished by imprisonment of up to three years or by a fine not exceeding 30 million won.
> (2) Prosecution against a person who violates the provisions of Article 36, 43, 44, 44-2, 46 or 56 shall not take place against the clearly expressed wishes of the victim.

No-punishment offenses against one's intention is a system where imprisonment of up to three years or a fine of up to 30 million won is imposed on employers who have delayed payment of wages in principle, but the Ministry of Employment and Labor (MOEL) does not prosecute if it is against the clearly expressed wishes of the related worker(s). Employers were forced to solve voluntary liquidation of unpaid wages through agreement with workers by paying unpaid wages instead of suffering criminal penalties. However, if there is a large number of workers whose wages remain unpaid, the employer shall be deemed to have committed the same offense against each unpaid worker.[193] Accordingly, in order to avoid penalties according to the no-punishment offenses system, written consent from all unpaid workers must be obtained.[194]

II. Alternative Payment System for Resolving Unpaid Wages[195]

The wage claim of an employee can be repaid with priority over other claims. Because wages are the essential means of livelihood for workers, the Labor

---

[193] Supreme Court ruling on Apr. 14, 94da1724.
[194] Labor Inspector's Practical Guide, Ministry of Employment and Labor, "Handling of Unpaid Wages", 2016, p. 33.
[195] Jung, Bongsoo, 『The Korean Labor Law Bible』, 6th ed., 2022. Jungang, pp. 121-124.

2. 처벌과 반의사불벌죄 제도

> 근로기준법 제109조(벌칙)
> ① 제36조(퇴직후 14일 이내 임금지급), 제43조(임금지급의 원칙), 제44조(도급사업의 임금지급), 제44조의2(건설업의 임금지급 연대책임), 제46조(휴업수당) 또는 제56조(가산임금)를 위반한 자는 3년 이하의 징역 또는 3천만 원 이하의 벌금에 처한다.
> ② 제36조, 제43조, 제44조, 제44조의2, 제46조 또는 제56조를 위반한 자에 대하여는 피해자의 명시적인 의사와 다르게 공소를 제기할 수 없다.

반의사불벌죄는 임금지급을 지체한 사용자에 대하여 원칙적으로 3년 이하의 징역 또는 3000만 원 이하의 벌금을 처하도록 하되, 해당 근로자가 처벌을 원하지 않는 경우에는 공소를 제기할 수 없도록 하는 제도이다. 사용자가 형사처벌을 받지 않는 대신에 체불된 임금을 지급함으로써 근로자와의 합의를 통한 자율적인 임금체불청산을 강제하기 위하여 도입되었다. 다만, 임금체불이 다수인 경우 그 범죄가 단일한 것이라고 인정하기 어려울 때에는 지급을 받을 수 없었던 근로자 각자에 대하여 같은 범죄가 있다고 인정하여야 한다.[193] 따라서 반의사불벌죄에 의거하여 처벌을 면하려면 체불된 개별 근로자들의 전원 서면 동의를 얻어야 한다.[194]

II. 체불임금 해결을 위한 대지급금제도[195]

근로자의 임금채권은 다른 채권보다 우선해서 변제받을 수 있다. 근로의 대가인 임금은 절실한 생계수단이기 때문에 근로기준법에서는 임금을 보호하기

---

[193] 대법원 1995.4.14. 선고 94도1724 판결
[194] 고용노동부 근로감독관 실무지침서, "체불사건 업무처리요령", 2016, 33면.
[195] 정봉수, 「한국노동법 영문해설」 제6판, 중앙경제사, 2021, pp. 121-124.

Standards Act has many regulations to protect them. Wages must be paid in cash, and employers can be punished for wage arrears if they pay only a portion of the wages or pay late. In addition, when a worker resigns, the employer must settle any financial relationships with the previous company within 14 days.

Furthermore, in situations where an employer has limited assets or substantial debts and there is a risk that wages will not be paid, there is a provision for "priority repayment of wage claims" so that the unpaid wages of workers can be repaid first. In terms of the priority of claims, wage claims are divided into "first-priority repayment wage claims," which are first priority, and "general wage claims," which are other than first-priority claims. The final three months' wages, shutdown allowances, the last three years of retirement benefits, and accident compensation are included in the first-priority repayment wage claims.

"Judicial bankruptcy" refers to a court's declaration of bankruptcy or commencement of a rehabilitation procedure against a company. This is usually done for large companies with serious debt problems, to resolve complicated debt relationships through court management. If the company one works for is declared judicially bankrupt, it takes a long time to receive unpaid wages. Also, if the business owner of a small or medium-sized enterprise closes the business due to financial difficulties while employee wages are still pending, workers cannot receive unpaid wages, as there may be no remaining property left by the business owner or any remaining property may be under seizure. In such cases, there is a system called the "wage guarantee system," where the government pays unpaid wages on behalf of the employer. The law on wage claims guarantees separate provisions related to the payment of wage guarantees. Employers eligible for wage claim guarantees must operate their business for more than six months and are subject to mandatory industrial accident insurance.

Meanwhile, when a company where a worker was employed goes bankrupt and the employer has no repayment capability, the worker may not receive the wages or retirement benefits they are entitled to. If the employer has repayment capability, there is a system in place where workers can receive unpaid wages and retirement benefits as a top priority through lawsuits and auction procedures in the future, but since this process takes a considerable amount of time and money, there is a need for society to protect the livelihoods of workers and their families during this period. The "Wage Protection System" refers to a system that aims to ensure the basic livelihood stability of workers by providing a certain amount of unpaid wages and retirement benefits on behalf of the employer by the government in case a

위해 많은 규정을 두고 있다. 임금은 반드시 현금으로 지급해야 하며, 임금을 일부만 주거나 늦게 주면 임금체불로 사업주를 처벌할 수 있다. 또한 근로자가 퇴사했을 때 이전 회사와의 금전관계가 정리되도록 14일 이내에 금품을 청산하도록 하고 있다.

아울러 사업주의 재산이 적거나 채무가 많아 임금을 지급받지 못할 우려가 있는 상황에서 근로자의 체불임금이 먼저 지급될 수 있도록 '임금채권 우선변제'라는 조항을 두고 있다. 채권의 배당 순위에서 임금채권은 1순위인 '최우선변제 임금채권'과 1순위 채권외의 나머지인 '일반 임금채권'으로 구분된다. 퇴사 직전 최종 3개월분의 임금과 휴업수당, 최종 3년간의 퇴직금, 그리고 재해보상금이 최우선변제 임금채권에 속한다.

'재판상 도산'이란 법원에서 회사에 대해 파산선고나 회생절차 개시결정을 내리는 것을 말한다. 이는 보통 규모가 큰 기업에서 채무 문제가 심각할 때 법원의 관리를 통해 복잡한 채무관계를 정리하기 위한 목적으로 이뤄지는데, 다니던 회사가 재판상 도산이 되면 체불임금을 받기까지 많은 시간이 소요된다. 또한 중소규모 기업이라면 근로자들의 임금이 밀려 있는 상태에서 사업주가 경영난으로 폐업하는 경우, 사업주에게 남아 있는 재산이 없거나 있더라도 압류가 걸려 있으면 근로자는 밀린 임금을 받을 수 없어 생계에 막대한 지장을 받게 된다. 이런 경우 국가에서 사업주를 대신해 체불임금을 지급해주는 제도로서 '대지급금제도'가 있다. 국가가 사업주를 대신해 우선 지급해주는 체불임금을 '대지급금'이라고 하는데, 대지급금의 지급과 관련된 사항을 임금채권보장법이라는 개별 법률에서 따로 정하고 있다. 임금채권 보장을 받을 수 있는 사업주는 산재보험 당연 적용 사업장으로 6개월 이상 사업을 운영해야 한다.

한편, 근로자가 취업했던 기업이 도산했을 때, 사업주의 변제능력이 없는 경우에는 근로자가 받아야 할 임금이나 퇴직금을 받을 수 없게 된다. 사업주가 변제능력이 있는 경우 향후 소송과 경매절차 등을 통해 근로자들이 지급받지 못한 임금과 퇴직금을 최우선변제 받을 수 있는 제도적 장치가 있지만, 이 같은 절차는 상당한 시간과 비용이 들기 때문에 그 기간 동안 근로자들과 그들 가족을 위한 생계를 사회가 보호해 줄 필요가 있다. '임금채권보장제도'란 기업의 도산으로 인하여 퇴직한 근로자가 임금 및 퇴직금을 지급받지 못하는

retired worker is unable to receive their wages and retirement benefits due to a company's bankruptcy.

1. Reasons for General Alternative Payment

Severance pay refers to the amount that the government pays on behalf of the employer when a retired worker is unable to receive wages due to reasons such as the employer's bankruptcy. The government later recovers this amount from the employer. Bankruptcy rulings and commencement of rehabilitation proceedings under the Corporate Restructuring and Bankruptcy Act are determined by court rulings as bankruptcy.

Next, the fact of bankruptcy by the Minister of Employment and Labor pursuant to the Enforcement Decree of the Wage Claims Guarantee Act (Article 5) is determined by the head of the local labor office to be declared bankrupt at the request of retired workers when the business owner is in fact in a state of bankruptcy due to business deterioration, etc. Admit it. In this case, ① the business owner must virtually cease business activities, ② there must be no prospect of resuming the business, and ③ all requirements must be satisfied, such as being recognized as bankrupt due to inability to pay wages and retirement benefits. Since the majority of bankruptcies that occur in small and medium-sized businesses occur in the form of de facto bankruptcy that does not go through legal procedures, the recognition of facts such as bankruptcy is recognized as a reason for payment of subrogated money. Accordingly, it is stipulated that for companies of a certain size with 300 or less full-time workers who are difficult to be recognized for bankruptcy in court, the head of the local labor office can in fact admit bankruptcy.

2. General Requirements for Alternative Payment

○ First: Employer Requirements

To become an employer eligible for wage guarantee protection, the following requirements must be met: ① The employer must be a business subject to mandatory occupational accident insurance (employing at least one permanent employee). ② The employer must have engaged in the relevant business for a period of at least six months after becoming subject to the applicable laws. ③ The employer must have been declared bankrupt or have had a recognized fact of insolvency.

경우 정부가 사업주를 대신하여 일정 범위의 체불임금과 퇴직금을 지급해 줌으로써 근로자의 기본적인 생활안정을 도모하고자 하는 제도를 말한다.

1. 일반 대지급금 지급사유

대지급금은 사업주의 파산 등 사유로 인하여 퇴직한 근로자가 임금 등을 지급받지 못할 경우 정부가 나중에 사업주로부터 변제받기로 하고 사업주를 대신하여 지급하는 금액을 말한다. 우선 「채무자 회생 및 파산에 관한 법률」에 의한 파산 선고 및 회생절차 개시 결정은 재판상 도산으로 법원의 재판으로 결정된다.

다음으로 임금채권보장법 시행령(제5조)에 의한 고용노동부장관의 도산 등 사실 인정은 사업주가 경영악화 등으로 인해 사실상 도산 상태에 빠져 있는 경우에 퇴직근로자의 청구에 의해 지방노동관서의 장이 도산으로 인정한다. 이 경우 ① 사업주가 사실상 사업활동을 중단하여야 하며, ② 사업을 재개할 전망이 없어야 하며, ③ 임금 및 퇴직금을 지급할 수 없어 사실상 도산 인정을 받는 등 모든 요건을 충족해야 한다. 중소규모에서 발생하는 도산의 다수가 법률상의 절차를 거치지 않는 사실상 도산의 형태로 일어나고 있기 때문에 도산 등 사실인정을 대지급금의 지급사유로 인정하고 있다. 이에 따라 재판상 도산을 인정받기 어려운 상시근로자 300인 이하의 일정규모 기업은 지방노동관서의 장이 사실상 도산을 인정할 수 있도록 규정하고 있다.

2. 일반 대지급금 청구요건

○ 첫째, 사업주 요건

사업주가 임금채권 보장의 대상이 되는 사업주가 되기 위해서는 다음과 같은 요건을 모두 갖추어야 한다. ① 산재보험 당연적용사업(상시근로자 1인 이상 사업)에 해당하는 사업주이어야 한다. ② 법의 적용대상 사업주가 된 후 6개월 이상의 기간 동안 당해 사업을 행한 사업주이어야 한다. ③ 대지급금 지급사유인 파산선고 등을 받았거나 도산 등 사실인정을 받아야 한다.

Chapter 4 The Protection of Wages

○ **Second: Employee Requirements**

The conditions for an employee to receive wage guarantees are as follows: ①The employer at the time of retirement must meet the above employer requirements. ② The employee must retire from the relevant business within three years after the date on which the employer applied for recognition of bankruptcy or insolvency, which must be at least one year after the date of application.

○ **Third: Payment of Wage Guarantees**

The range of unpaid wages guaranteed by wage guarantees is the final three months' wages and the final three years' retirement pay. The wage guarantee system is intended to contribute to the minimum living standard of workers who have retired from bankrupt companies, so the level of wages paid by the government is not the full amount of unpaid wages, but a certain upper limit. Even with regard to wages that are guaranteed to be paid, individual workers' wage levels are not guaranteed to be fully protected, and there is a limit to the upper limit based on age.

For example, if an employee who was receiving a monthly salary of 4 million won retires at the age of 45 and the final five months' wages and the recent five years' retirement pay are unpaid, how much will the general wage guarantee be? The range of unpaid wages guaranteed by wage guarantees is the final three months' wages and the final three years' retirement pay. The final three months' wages are 900 million won (the average monthly wage in January was 4 million won, but the monthly limit based on age is 3 million won), and the final three years' retirement pay is 9 million won (3 million won x 3 years), so the wage guarantee is 18 million won.

<Alternative Payment limits based on age>   Unit: Kwon

Category	Under 30	Age 30 ~ 40	Age 40 ~ 50	Age 50 ~ 60	Over 60
Wages and retirement benefits	2.2 mil.	3.1 mil.	3.5 mil.	3.3 mil.	2.3 mil.
Shutdown allowance	1.54 mil.	2.17 mil.	2.45 mil.	2.31 mil.	1.61 mil.

(Applied from October 14, 2021)

○ 둘째, 근로자 요건

근로자가 대지급금을 지급받을 수 있는 요건은 다음과 같다. ① 퇴직 당시의 사업주가 상기의 사업주 요건을 갖추고 있어야 한다. ② 이러한 요건을 갖추고 있는 사업주가 파산선고나 도산 등 사실인정을 신청한 날로부터 1년 전이 되는 날 이후부터 3년 이내에 당해 사업에서 퇴직해야 한다.

○ 셋째, 대지급금 지급액

대지급금으로 지급이 보장되는 체불임금의 범위는 최종 3월분의 임금과 최종 3년간의 퇴직금이다. 임금채권보장제도는 도산기업에서 퇴직한 근로자들의 최소한의 생활안정에 기여하고자 하는 것이므로, 국가에 의해 대신 지급되는 임금의 수준은 미지급된 임금 등의 전액이 아니라 일정한 상한액의 범위내의 금액이다. 지급이 보장되는 임금채권에 있어서도 개별근로자의 임금수준을 모두 보장해 주는 것이 아니라, 연령에 따른 상한액을 두고 있다.

예를 들면 월 400만 원을 받던 근로자의 퇴직 당시 연령이 45세이고 최종 5월분의 임금과 최근 5년간의 퇴직금이 체불되었다면 일반 대지급금은 얼마일까? 대지급금으로 지급이 보장되는 체불임금의 범위는 최종 3월분의 임금과 최종 3년간의 퇴직금이다. 최종 3월분의 임금은 330만 원 (1월의 평균임금은 400만 원이나 연령에 따른 월정 상한액은 350만 원임) × 3개월 = 1,050만 원이고, 최종 3년간의 퇴직금은 350만 원 × 3년 = 1,050만 원으로 대지급금은 2,100만 원이다.

< 연령에 따른 일반 대지급금 상한액 >

구분	30세 미만	30세 이상 ~ 40세미만	40세 이상 ~ 50세미만	50세 이상 ~ 60세미만	60세 이상
임금 및 퇴직금	220만 원	310만 원	350만 원	330만 원	230만 원
휴업수당	154만 원	217만 원	245만 원	231만 원	161만 원

(2021. 10. 14.부터 적용)

Chapter 4 The Protection of Wages

III. Small-Scale Alternative Payment System for Resolving Unpaid Wages

To resolve unpaid wages, new solutions are being presented in conjunction with legal preventive measures. As a preventive measure, there is a delayed interest rate system of 20% per year to encourage the payment of unpaid wages, and there is a non-indictment crime that allows employers to avoid criminal punishment if they pay the unpaid wages. In addition, if an unpaid worker goes through the Labor Ministry and receives a confirmed court decision for unpaid wages from the Legal Aid Corporation, regardless of the employer's ability to pay, they can receive unpaid wages up to a limit of KRW 10 million from the Wage Credit Fund. This is called the small-scale allowance system, and the limit was expanded from KRW 400 million to KRW 10 million from July 1, 2019, which will be a groundbreaking help in resolving unpaid wages. We will examine in detail the preventive system for unpaid wages and the small-scale allowance system related to this matter.

The term "wage arrears payment" refers to the payment made by the government on behalf of the employer to employees who leave the company without receiving their wages (including shutdown allowances) and retirement benefits due to company bankruptcy or other reasons. There are two types of wage arrears payments: general and small-scale. The general wage arrears payment system is designed to guarantee minimum wages and retirement benefits for employees of bankrupt or insolvent companies. However, even if a company does not go bankrupt, many employees suffer from wage arrears, and the small-scale wage arrears payment system has been introduced as a temporary measure to help them. Previously, even if wage arrears workers who did not receive their wages on time for reasons unrelated to bankruptcy or insolvency won their case in court, they would not receive wage arrears payments if the employer did not pay or could not find property to enforce the judgment. The Ministry of Employment and Labor has introduced a small-scale payment system for wagee arrears that allows the government to pay up to KRW 10 million (KRW 7 million for the final three months of unpaid wages, including shutdown allowances, and KRW 3 million for the final three years of retirement benefits) to workers who have received a final court judgment for wage arrears, regardless of whether the employer has gone bankrupt.

The system allows workers to apply to the Korea Workers' Welfare & Safety Corporation within one year of receiving a court judgment after submitting a wage arrears certification form to the Ministry of Employment and Labor and obtaining a wage arrears confirmation statement from the company's labor standards supervision agency in charge of the area where the company is located, as well as applying for

Ⅲ. 소액대지급금제도

 체불임금을 해결하기 위해 법적인 예방조치와 함께 새로운 체불임금 해결책이 제시되고 있다. 그 예방책으로 체불임금의 지급을 촉진하기 위해 연 20%의 고율의 지연이자제도와 사업주가 체불된 임금을 지급하면 형사처벌을 면해주는 반의사불벌죄가 있다. 이와 함께, 체불근로자는 사용자의 임금지급 능력과 상관없이 노동청을 거쳐 법률구조공단의 지원을 받아 법원에서 체불임금 확정판결문을 받으면, 1000만 원 한도내에서 체불 임금을 임금채권기금에서 수령할 수 있다. 이를 소액 대지급금제도라 하며 기존의 400만 원 한도에서 2019년 7월 1일부터 1000만 원으로 한도가 확대되어 임금체불 해결에 획기적으로 도움이 될 것이다. 이에 관련된 체불임금 예방제도와 소액 대지급금 제도에 대해 구체적으로 살펴보기로 한다.
 대지급금이란 회사의 도산 등으로 인하여 임금(휴업수당 포함) 및 퇴직금을 지급받지 못하고 퇴사하는 근로자에게 국가가 사업주를 대신하여 지급하는 체불임금을 말한다. 대지급금은 일반 대지급금과 소액 대지급금이 있다. 일반 대지급금제도는 도산 및 파산한 기업의 근로자들에게 최소한의 임금과 퇴직금을 보장해주기 위해 마련된 제도를 말한다. 하지만 기업이 파산하지 않아도 체불임금에 시달리는 근로자가 많아졌고 이들을 일시적으로 구제할 수 있는 방안으로 소액 대지급금제도가 도입되었다. 이전에는 도산 및 파산과 무관한 이유로 임금을 제때 받지 못한 체불근로자가 소송에서 승소하더라도 사업주가 체불임금을 주지 않거나 강제집행할 재산을 찾아내지 못하면 체불임금을 받지 못했다. 고용노동부는 이와 같은 문제점을 해결하기 위해 도산여부와 관계없이 체불임금에 대한 확정판결 등을 받은 경우 체불된 최종 3개월분의 임금(휴업수당 포함)과 최종 3년분의 퇴직금 중 미지급 금액을 각각 700만 원(도합 1,000만 원) 한도 내에서 국가가 미리 근로자에게 지급하고 체불사업주에게 구상권을 청구하는 체불임금 소액 대지급금 제도를 시행하고 있다.
 소액 대지급금은 체불근로자가 사업장이 소재하는 고용노동부 관할지청에 체불임금 진정서를 제출한 후 체불금품확인서를 발급받은 다음 거주지 관할 법률구조공단에 무료 법률구조를 신청한 후 관할법원에 소송을 제기하여 확정판결을 받으면 1년 이내에 근로복지공단에 신청하면 받을 수 있다. 참고로

Chapter 4 The Protection of Wages

free legal aid from the Korea Legal Aid Corporation in charge of the area where the worker lives and filing a lawsuit in the court with jurisdiction. Foreign workers can also be covered by the same four types of insurance (workers' compensation insurance, national health insurance, employment insurance, and national pension) as Korean workers. Therefore, if wages are not paid by the company, wages can generally be paid under the Wage Claims Guarantee Act. In addition, for companies or workplaces with less than 300 regular employees that are not covered by the Wage Claims Guarantee Act, or for which the Act does not apply, they are required to take out guarantee insurance or join the Overseas Employment Insurance Program to pay retirement benefits in anticipation of wage arrears.

1. Requirements for Small-scale Alternative Payment

The requirements for alternative payment stipulated by the Wage Guarantee Act are as follows:

① Based on the employer: The employer must have employed one or more permanent employees for six months or more at the workplace where the unpaid worker was employed on the retirement date.[196]
② Eligible employees for payment: The employee who is owed unpaid wages must have filed a lawsuit or applied for a payment order within two years of the day after the unpaid worker retired.[197]
③ Enforcement power secured: The employee must have obtained enforcement power through a court decision or a separate civil suit such as a judgment, payment order, or compliance recommendation from the Legal Aid Corporation.

An unpaid worker who meets these three requirements can receive an alternative payment for the unpaid amount of the last three months' wages (including shutdown allowances) and the unpaid amount of retirement benefits for the last three years, up to a maximum of 10 million won.

2. Procedure for Small-scale Alternative Payment for Unpaid Wages

○ Report Unpaid Wages to the Ministry of Labor
When unpaid wages occur, workers can file a report with the Ministry of Labor to initiate an investigation into the case. Labor inspectors confirm the

---

[196] Article 8(2) of the Enforcement Decree of the Wage Guarantee Act
[197] Article 7(2) of the Enforcement Decree of the Wage Guarantee Act

외국인근로자도 내국인근로자와 동일하게 4대보험(산재보험, 국민건강보험, 고용보험, 국민연금)의 적용을 받을 수 있다. 따라서 사업장에서 임금 등을 지급받지 못한 경우에는 일반적으로 임금채권보장법에 따라 임금을 지급 받을 수 있다. 또한 '임금채권보장법'이 적용되지 않는 사업 또는 사업장이나 상시 300명 미만의 근로자를 사용하는 사업 또는 사업장의 경우에는 임금체불에 대비하여 보증보험에 가입하거나 퇴직금 지급을 위하여 출국만기보험에 가입하도록 되어 있으므로 이 보험에 따라 해결하면 된다.

1. 소액 대지급금 지급요건

임금채권보장법이 규정하고 있는 소액 대지급금의 지급요건은 아래와 같다.
① 사업주 기준: 체불근로자가 재직하던 사업장이 퇴직일 당시 상시 근로자 수 1명 이상을 고용하여 6개월 이상 가동되었을 것[196]
② 지급대상 근로자: 체불근로자가 퇴직한 다음 날부터 2년 이내에 미지급 임금에 관하여 법원에 소제기, 지급명령신청 등을 하였을 것[197]
③ 집행권원 확보: 근로자가 법률구조공단이나 별도의 민사소송을 통해 승소판결, 지급명령, 이행권고결정 등을 받아 집행권원을 확보하였을 것.

위의 3가지 요건을 갖춘 체불근로자가 최종 3개월분의 임금(휴업수당 포함), 최종 3년간의 퇴직금 중 미지급액을 최대 1000만 원까지 소액 대지급금으로 지급받을 수 있다.

2. 체불임금 소액 대지급금 처리절차

○ 노동청에 체불임금 진정
체불임금이 발생하여 근로자가 노동청에 진정을 접수하면 체불임금 사건이 진행된다. 근로감독관은 관계자 출석요구 등으로 사실관계를 확인한 후, 그 과정에서 당사자 사이에 합의가 되거나 체불임금이

---
196) 임금채권보장법 시행령 제8조 제2항
197) 임금채권보장법 시행령 제7조 제2항

Chapter 4 The Protection of Wages

> facts by demanding attendance from the relevant parties. If an agreement is reached or unpaid wages are paid during the process, the case is closed. However, if unpaid wages are not settled despite corrective orders from labor inspectors, criminal proceedings will be initiated. In addition to this process, workers can obtain an "Unpaid Wages Confirmation Certificate" and file a civil lawsuit to secure the right to execute on unpaid wages.
>
> ○ Free Legal Aid from the Legal Aid Corporation
> Workers who want to receive a small amount of unpaid wages can obtain an "Unpaid Wages Confirmation Certificate" from the Ministry of Labor and receive free legal aid from the Legal Aid Corporation in their jurisdiction to secure the right to execute on unpaid wages. Workers who do not qualify for free legal aid (those whose average wage for the last three months is less than 4 million won) must personally file a civil lawsuit with the court to secure the right to execute on unpaid wages and then apply for a small amount of unpaid wages. Workers must submit a claim for a small amount of unpaid wages to the Korea Workers' Welfare Service within one year of securing the right to execute.
>
> ○ Apply for Small-scale Alternative Payment to Workers' Welfare Service
> Welfare Service When a worker submits a claim for a small amount of unpaid wages with an "Unpaid Wages Confirmation Certificate", a right to execute on unpaid wages, and a certificate of finality, the Korea Workers' Welfare Service decides whether to pay the small amount of unpaid wages within 14 days of receiving the claim. If the claim is approved, the Korea Workers' Welfare Service pays the small amount of unpaid wages to the claimant.

3. Differences with the Alternative Payment System

(1) Reason for Payment

The alternative payment system allows payment of unpaid wage only when the company has been declared bankrupt, has started the rehabilitation process, and has received de facto insolvency recognition from the labor department due to its failure to reach bankruptcy or rehabilitation under the law. On the other hand, under the Small-scale Alternative Payment System, unpaid wage is paid regardless of whether the company has gone bankrupt or not.

However, in order to receive a small-scale alternative payment, retired workers must first secure enforcement power from the court for unpaid wages against the employer.

지급되면 종결처리가 이루어진다. 다만, 근로감독관의 시정지시에도 불구하고, 체불임금 청산이 이루어지지 않으면 형사처벌 절차가 진행되고, 이러한 절차와 별도로 근로자는'체불금품확인원'을 발급받은 후 민사소송을 제기하여 체불임금에 관한 집행권원을 확보하게 된다.

○ 법률구조공단에 무료 법률구조지원
소액 대지급금을 지급받고자 하는 체불근로자는 노동청에서 체불금품확인원을 발급받은 후 거주지 관할 법률구조공단에서 무료 법률구조지원을 받아 집행권원을 확보하게 된다. 무료 법률구조지원 대상(최종 3개월의 평균임금이 400만 원 미만자)이 아닌 근로자는 개인적으로 법원에 민사소송을 제기하여 체불임금에 관한 집행권원을 확보한 후 소액 대지급금을 신청하여야 한다. 근로자는 집행권원을 확보한 날로부터 1년 내에 근로복지공단에 소액 대지급금 지급청구서를 제출하여야 한다.

○ 근로복지공단에 소액 대지급금 지급 신청
체불근로자가 체불금품확인원, 집행권원, 확정증명원이 첨부된 소액 대지급금 지급청구서를 제출하면 근로복지공단은 청구서를 받은 날부터 14일 이내에 소액 대지급금 지급여부를 결정하고, 결정되면 청구인에게 소액 대지급금을 지급하게 된다.

3. 일반 대지급금제도와의 차이점

(1) 지급사유

일반 대지급금제도는 사업장에 대해 파산선고 결정 또는 회생절차 개시 결정이 있었거나, 법률상 파산 또는 회생에 이르지 못한 경우 노동청으로부터 사실상 도산인정을 받아야만 대지급금 지급이 가능하나, 이와 달리 소액 대지급금제도는 사업장의 도산여부에 상관없이 대지급금 지급이 이루어진다.

소액 대지급금은 해당 사업장이 사실상 또는 법률상 도산에 이르는 것을 요하지 않는 대신, 퇴직근로자가 먼저 사업주를 상대로 미지급임금에 대해 법원으로부터 집행권원을 확보하여야 한다.

(2) Eligible Workers for Payment

The alternative payment is paid to workers who retired within 3 years from the date of bankruptcy or rehabilitation application, based on the retirement date one year prior to the application. In contrast, the small-scale alternative payment is paid to retired workers who file a lawsuit within 2 years from the day after their retirement.

(3) Employer Criteria

Under the Alternative Payment System, the employer must have operated the business for six months prior to the employee's retirement and then have gone bankrupt or become practically insolvent. Under the Small-scale Alternative payment System, the employer only needs to have operated the business for six months prior to the employee's retirement.

(4) Claim Period

Under the Alternative Payment System, the retirement benefits must be claimed within two years from the bankruptcy or insolvency recognition date. Under the Small-scale Alternative Payment System, the unpaid wage must be claimed within one year from the date of the final judgment.

(5) Payment Amount Range

Both the Alternative Payment System and the Small-scale Alternative Payment System pay the final three months' salary (including shutdown allowance) and the final three years' retirement benefits on behalf of the employer. However, the Alternative Payment System pays a different amount depending on the employee's age, ranging from KRW 2.2 million to KRW 3.5 million per month (up to KRW 21 million in total). The Small-scale Alternative Payment System has a maximum payment amount of KRW 10 million, with a cap of KRW 7 million for wages (including shutdown allowance) and KRW 7 million for retirement benefits, based on the payment standards.

4. Summary

In the case of the general wage payment system, one must be recognized as bankrupt or legally recognized as bankrupt in order to receive wage payments, but the small-scale alternative payment system has a high potential for system utilization as it allows for wage payments even if these conditions are not met. The key

(2) 지급대상 근로자

일반 대지급금 지급대상 근로자는 파산 또는 회생 신청일 기준 1년 전부터 3년 이내 퇴직한 근로자이나, 소액 대지급금 지급대상 근로자는 퇴직일 다음 날부터 2년 이내에 소송을 제기한 퇴직근로자이다.

(3) 사업주 기준

일반 대지급금은 근로자가 퇴직하기 전에 사업주가 해당 사업을 6개월 동안 가동하다가 사실상 또는 법률상 도산에 이르러야 하나, 소액 대지급금은 근로자가 퇴직하기 전에 사업주가 6개월 동안 해당 사업을 가동하기만 하면 된다.

(4) 청구기간

일반 대지급금은 파산선고일 또는 도산인정일로부터 2년 이내에 청구하여야 하며, 소액 대지급금은 확정된 종국판결 등을 확보한 날로부터 1년 이내에 청구하여야 한다.

(5) 지급액 범위

일반 대지급금과 소액 대지급금 모두 최종 3개월치 임금(휴업수당 포함)과 최종 3년치 퇴직금을 사업주 대신 지급하는 것으로 그 지급액 내역은 동일하다. 그러나 일반 대지급금은 연령에 따라 월 220만 원에서 350만 원까지(최대 2,100만 원) 차등 지급한다. 소액 대지급금은 지급기준에 따라, 최대 1000만 원으로 하고 임금(휴업수당 포함)과 퇴직급여를 구분하여 그 상한액을 각각 700만 원으로 한다.

4. 시사점

일반 대지급금제도의 경우 '도산 등 사실인정'을 받거나 법률상 도산을 인정 받아야 하는데, 소액 대지급금제도는 위 요건을 갖추지 않더라도 대지급금을 받을 수 있다는 점에서 제도 활용 가능성이 높다고 볼 수 있다.

소액 대지급금 지급의 핵심적인 요건은 체불금품에 관한 집행권을 받았는지

requirement for small-scale alternative payment is whether the execution right for unpaid wages has been granted or not, so the administrative procedure for wage payment is easier compared to the general alternative payment system. However, the fact that workers still have to go through several administrative agencies and prepare various documents to receive small-scale alternative payments serves as a hindrance to the utilization of the system. To overcome these obstacles, there is a need for the Ministry of Labor, the Labor Relations Commission, and the Employment Welfare Fund to establish a systematic one-stop service for small-scale alternative payments through collaborative work.[198]

There are two systems that can be utilized within legal boundaries to solve the problem of unpaid wages for workers: the delayed interest system and the criminal offense system for intentional non-payment of wages. To improve these systems, the Ministry of Labor must include a delayed interest rate of 20% when calculating unpaid wages at the stage of issuing a certificate of unpaid wages. Furthermore, criminal punishment for intentional non-payment of wages is mostly imposed in the form of fines, with fines also being imposed within 20% of the unpaid wages. In Korea, like in the United States, punitive fines should be imposed that exceed several times the actual unpaid wages to spread the perception that non-payment of wages is a form of slave labor. Additionally, the expanded small-scale alternative payment system is a ground breaking measure as it guarantees workers' wage rights even for general unpaid wages from employers. This system should be actively utilized as a quick and convenient solution for resolving unpaid wages for workers.

IV. Statue of Limitations

1. The purpose of the statue of limitations

Wage claims have the statue of limitations of 3 years. The term 'wage' refers to payment that includes bonuses, overtime work pay, monthly/annual leave pay, and severance pay, as defined in the Labor Standards Act. When an employer fails to pay wage or severance pay to an employee whose employment relationship is discontinued by reason of retirement, etc., the employer shall pay deferral interest at a rate of 20% per year in addition to the unpaid wage or severance pay. However, the deferral interest will not apply to periods during which there exist certain

---

[198] Park Geun-hoo and 4 others, Ministry of Employment and Labor service data, page 131.

여부에 달려있으므로 대지급금 지급에 관한 행정절차가 일반 대지급금제도에 비해 용이하다. 그럼에도 불구하고 실제 소액 대지급금을 지급받기까지 근로자가 몇 군데의 행정기관을 거쳐야 하고, 각각의 서류를 구비해야 한다는 점은 소액 대지급금 제도의 활용성을 떨어지게 하는 장애요인으로 작용한다. 이러한 장애를 극복하기 위해서는 노동청, 법률구조공단, 근로복지공단이 체계적인 업무연계를 통해 소액 대지급금 one-stop 서비스를 마련할 필요가 있다.[198]

근로자의 체불임금 문제를 해결하기 위한 방법으로 법적 테두리 내에서 활용할 수 있는 제도로는 지연이자제도와 반의사불벌죄 제도가 있다. 이를 개선하기 위해서는 노동청의 체불임금확인서 발행단계에서 지연이자 연 20%를 반드시 포함하여 체불임금액을 산정하여야 할 것이다. 또한 반의사불벌죄의 형사처벌도 대부분 벌금형을 부과하는 방식으로 하고 있고, 벌금도 체불금의 20% 이내에서 부과하고 있다. 우리나라도 미국과 같이 징벌적 벌금을 과하여 실제 체불된 임금보다 몇 배의 벌금을 과하도록 하여 체불임금이 노예노동이라는 인식을 확산시켜야 할 것이다. 아울러 이번에 확대된 소액 대지급금 제도는 사업주의 일반적인 체불임금에 대해서까지 근로자의 임금채권을 보장한다는 면에서 획기적인 조치라고 할 수 있다. 이 제도가 근로자에게 신속하고 편리한 체불임금 해소방안으로 적극 활용되어야 할 것이다.

Ⅳ. 소멸시효제도

1. 소멸시효 목적

임금채권의 소멸시효 기간은 3년이다. 여기서 '임금'은 근로기준법상의 임금으로 상여금, 시간외근로수당, 연·월차유급휴가수당, 퇴직금 등이 모두 포함된다. 사용자가 퇴직 등으로 근로관계가 종료된 근로자에게 임금·퇴직금을 체불했을 경우 연 20%의 지연이자 지급의무가 부과된다(근로기준법 제37조).

---

[198] 박근후 외 4명, 고용노동부 용역자료, 131면.

reasons specified in the relevant legislation, such as natural disaster, war, or legal or de facto bankruptcy.

① The right to request payment for unused annual leave is given a three-year statue of limitations. The date of calculation starts on the day after the leave expires, provided that it has not been redeemed for the past one-year period after being granted.[199]

② A labor contract which establishes working conditions that do not meet the standards provided for in the Labor Standards Act shall be null (Article 15 of the Labor Standards Act). Accordingly, even though the employer and the union agreed to exclude the regular bonus as legally included in ordinary wage, this mutual agreement is invalidated as being in violation of the Labor Standards Act. As the above agreement was invalid, it is a principle that the employer should recalculate the overtime work allowance, adding the wages included in legal ordinary wage, and that the employee can apply for retroactive payment for the variance from the amount already paid. However, this retroactive claim can be valid only for the amount payable for the past three years.[200]

The statue of limitations system recognizes the status of rights or claims that have not been exercised for a certain period of time, even if that status does not conform to a true rights relationship.[201] In other words, if people do not exercise specific rights for a certain period of time, they can no longer exercise those rights due to statue of limitations. The reason for this is to limit rights that have not been exercised, and to promote the establishment of legal security and expedite claims or the use of rights. The Labor Standards Act (LSA) also attaches statue of limitations to non-performance of rights to promote their exercise and thereby protect workers.

Since the statue of limitations for deferred wages kicks in after only three years, the amount of claimable wages is gradually reduced as the period before statue of limitations passes. In particular, at the stage of petitions and accusations filed with the Ministry of Employment and Labor, suspensions of the statue of limitations on deferred wages are not allowed, and so action in a civil court is required. In other words, as labor inspectors handle investigations of complaints regarding deferred wages, and determine the facts behind the delay by examining the workers affected and their employers, these legal actions have no effect on the statue of limitations. On the other hand, claims for compensation for occupational accidents are recognized as filing for work compensation with the court. The statue of limitations is suspended and claims for industrial accident compensation can be extended to 5 years.

Since they are both special laws designed to protect workers, the LSA and the

---

[199] Supreme Court ruling on Jun. 30, 1995, 94Da47155.
[200] Supreme Court ruling on Dec.18, 2013, 2012Da89399.
[201] Oh, Young-hwan, Lee, Ro-moon, 「General Provisions of the Civil Code」, 2009, MJ Media, p. 350.

단, 천재·사변, 법률상·사실상 도산 등 법령에 규정된 사유가 존속하는 기간에는 지연이자율의 적용이 제외된다.

① 연차휴가근로수당의 지급청구권은 3년의 소멸시효가 적용되고, 그 기산점은 취득한 날부터 1년의 경과로 휴가 불실시가 확정된 다음 날이 된다.[199]
② 근로기준법이 정한 기준보다 낮은 임금 등 불리한 근로조건 계약은 무효(근로기준법 제15조 참조)이다. 따라서 법률상 통상임금에 해당하는 정기상여금 등의 임금을 통상임금에서 제외하기로 노사가 합의하였다 하더라도 위 합의는 근로기준법에 위반되어 무효이다. 위와 같은 합의가 무효이므로, 법률상 통상임금에 해당하는 임금을 통상임금 산정에 포함시켜 다시 초과근로수당을 계산한 다음, 소급하여 이미 지급받은 것과의 차액을 추가임금으로 청구할 수 있다. 다만, 사용자가 소멸시효 항변을 할 경우 최종 3년치만 인정 가능하다.[200]

소멸시효란 일정한 기간 동안 권리를 행사하지 않는 사실상태가 계속되는 경우에 그 상태가 진실한 권리관계에 합치되지 않더라도 그 사실상태를 인정하려는 제도이다.[201] 즉, 일정한 기간 동안 권리행사를 하지 않는 경우에 시효의 완료로 인하여 더 이상 권리행사를 할 수 없는 것이다. 이러한 소멸시효를 두는 이유는 행사하지 않는 권리를 제한하여 법적 안정을 꾀하고 신속한 권리관계 설정을 촉진하기 위함이다. 근로기준법도 근로자 보호를 위하여 권리행사 불이행에 대한 소멸시효제도를 두고 있다.

임금채권 소멸시효는 3년으로 짧기 때문에 소멸시효 만료로 인해 청구 가능한 임금 체불금이 점점 줄어든다. 특히, 고용노동부의 진정 및 고소 단계에서는 임금체불에 대한 시효의 중단이 인정되지 않기 때문에 이를 해결하는데 있어 민사적 절차인 재판상 청구를 하여야 한다. 다시 말해, 근로감독관이 임금이 체불된 근로자와 해당 사용자를 확정하는 노동청의 진정 또는 고소 단계에서는 소멸시효에 전혀 영향을 주지 않는다. 이에 반해 산재보상의 청구는 업무상 재해 보상에 있어 재판상 청구로 인정받기 때문에 소멸시효가 중단되고, 이에 따른 청구권의 소멸시효도 5년으로 연장된다.

근로자보호를 위한 동일한 특별법임에도 불구하고 근로기준법과 산업재해

---

[199] 대법원 1995.6.30. 선고 94다47155 판결.
[200] 대법원 2013. 12. 18. 선고, 2012다89399 판결.
[201] 오영환, 이로문, 「민법총칙」, 2009, MJ미디어, 350면.

Chapter 4 The Protection of Wages

Industrial Accident Compensation Insurance Act (IACI) differ from other laws in terms of suspensions and duration before the statue of limitations kicks in. I will look into the overall statue of limitations in the LSA.

2. Statue of limitations[202]

(1) Concept

'statue of limitations' refers to expiration of a right that has not been exercised. The principle is that the law does not protect those who 'sleep' on it. This means that if people have a right they can exercise but do not for a certain period of time, they will not be able to exercise it, so that the state of legal tranquility already established will be maintained. Most statue of limitationss in labor law start at three years. A concept similar to the statue of limitations under the LSA is 'exclusive period.' After expiration of an exclusive period, no further legal appeal can be made. Since it aims at the rapid establishment of legal relations, exclusive period differs from statue of limitations.[203]

(2) Details of statue of limitations
1) Wage bonds under the Labor Standards Act

Wage bonds will expire unless the claims for deferred wages are exercised within three years (Article 49 of the LSA). Wage bonds can be categorized as monthly salary, retirement allowance, unused annual allowance and so on. Monthly wages (base salary, overtime allowance, holiday work allowance, etc.) are paid on the salary payment date and rights can be exercised from the time when they are not paid, so salary calculation will begin from the regular payment date. Bonuses shall be calculated when the right to receive the bonus is incurred, while severance pay shall be calculated from the date of retirement due to the obligation to pay the employee on that day.

Annual paid leave is calculated from the date of conversion to a wage claim after using one year for granted annual leave.[204] In other words, if annual paid leave is managed on a yearly basis, if an employee enters 2018, his annual paid leave from

---
[202] Jung, Bongsoo, "Statue of Limitations", 「Labor Law」, Jungang, April 2013.
[203] Supreme Court ruling on Sep. 20, 1996 96da25371
[204] Supreme Court ruling on Sep. 14, 1992 92da17754

보상법은 소멸시효의 중단과 기간에 차이를 두고 있다. 이와 관련된 근로기준법상의 전반적인 시효에 대해 구체적으로 살펴보고자 한다.

2. 소멸시효[202]

(1) 소멸시효 개념

소멸시효는 권리행사를 할 수 있음에도 해당기간 동안 그 권리를 행사하지 않아 시효가 경과하여 더 이상 권리행사를 할 수 없는 상태를 말한다. 법은 권리 위에 잠자는 자를 보호하지 않는다는 원칙이 적용된다. 이는 행사할 수 있는 권리는 있지만, 일정 기간 동안 권리행사를 하지 않는 경우 이를 못하게 함으로써 이미 형성된 법적 평온 상태를 유지하게 한다는 것이다. 노동법상 대부분 소멸시효는 3년을 기준으로 한다. 근로기준법상 소멸시효와 유사한 개념이 제척기간이다. 제척기간이 지나면 더 이상 법적 이의를 제기할 수 없다. 제척기간은 법률관계의 신속한 확정을 목적으로 하므로 소멸시효와 그 기간에 있어 차이가 있다.[203]

(2) 소멸시효 내용

1) 근로기준법상 임금채권

임금채권은 3년간 행사하지 않으면 시효로 소멸한다(근기법 제49조). 임금채권은 월 급여, 퇴직금, 미사용 연차수당 등으로 분류할 수 있으며 유형별 소멸시효 기산점이 다르다. 매월 지급되는 월 임금(기본급, 연장근로수당, 휴일근로수당 등)은 임금 지급일에 지급의무가 발생하고 이때부터 권리를 행사할 수 있으므로 기산점은 정기지급일부터 진행된다. 상여금은 상여금에 관한 권리가 발생한 때 지급의무가 발생하며, 퇴직금은 근로자가 퇴직한 날 다음날에 지급의무가 발생하므로 퇴직일 다음날부터 기산한다. 연차유급휴가는 휴가 사용기간인 1년 완료후 15일이 임금청구권으로 전환되는 시점부터 기산된다.[204] 즉, 연도별 관리로 판단할 경우 2018년 입사자의 경우, 2019년 1월 1일 부터 2019년 12월 31일까지

---

[202] 정봉수, "근로기준법상 소멸시효제도", 「월간 노동법률」, 중앙경제사, 2019년 4월호
[203] 대법원 1996.9.20. 선고 96다25371 판결
[204] 대법원 1992.9.14. 선고 92다17754 판결.

January 1, 2019 to December 31, 2019 will be granted on the first day of 2020 15 days' annual leave if he works at 80 percent or more for the period. During 2020, annual leave shall be used. The starting point for a claim for unused annual leave shall be 2021, and this right shall exist for three years (Article 36, Article 60 of the LSA).

2) Benefits under the Industrial Accident Compensation Insurance Act (IACI Act)

Rights protected by the IACI Act shall extinguish unless they are exercised within 3 years of when the right to claim compensation for a work injury or disease begins. However, the right to receive disability benefits, survivor benefits, funeral expenses benefit, compensation pensions for pneumoconiosis, and survivor's pensions for pneumoconiosis will expire within five years if not exercised (enacted Dec. 13, 2018, Law No. 15665). The insurance benefits of the IACI Act can be divided into the following three categories: ① Claims for continuous insurance benefits, ② Claims for lump sum insurance benefits, and ③ Claims for pension benefits. Each type of pension insurance benefit has a different point when the statue of limitations kicks in.

(i) Claims of continuous insurance benefits include claims to medical care benefits and work suspension benefits. Medical care benefits are paid when a worker is injured or becomes sick in relation to work, and in principle is paid as reimbursement of actual medical expenses (Article 40 of the Act). That is, the period before the statue of limitations for the right to claim this insurance benefit kicks in begins the day after the cost of medical treatment is paid, not when a worker's occupational injury or illness first occurs.[205] Since the work suspension benefit is paid for a period that a worker who has been injured or sick cannot work, the statue of limitations begins the day after the worker first becomes unable to work so they can receive medical treatment (Article 52 of the Act).

(ii) Claims for lump-sum insurance benefits include claims to lump sum payments of disability compensation, survivor compensation, or an allowance of some sort. A lump sum disability compensation payment shall be paid to a worker who has been injured on the job or suffered from a work-related illness, and whose disability continues after recovery. A disability benefit is provided when a worker has completed their treatment and the disability is fixed (Article 57 of the Act). Survivors' compensation is paid in the form of a pension in principle, but if there is no legal beneficiary, a lump sum compensation is possible. The period before the statue of limitations kicks in begins on the day after the relevant worker has died (Article 62 of the Act). Funeral expenses are only paid when they have actually occurred (Article 71).

---

[205] Hwang, Won-hee, "Calculating when the statue of limitations occurs for work-related accident benefits", Labor Law Review, 27, Apr. 2013, Korean Comparative Labor Law Association, p. 382; Supreme Court ruling on Dec. 17, 2008, 2006da35865

80퍼센트 이상 출근한 경우에 한해 15일의 연차휴가가 발생한다. 다음 연도인 2020년 1년동안 연차휴가를 사용하여야 한다. 2021년 1월 1일부터 미사용 연차휴가에 대한 임금청구권의 기산점이 되며, 이는 3년간 청구가 가능하다(근기법 제36조, 제60조).

2) 산재법상 보상급여

산재법은 업무상 부상 또는 질병에 대해 권리를 3년간 행사하지 아니하면 시효로 말미암아 소멸한다. 다만, 장해급여, 유족급여, 장의비, 진폐보상연금 및 진폐유족연금을 받을 권리는 5년간 행사하지 아니하면 시효의 완성으로 보아 소멸한다(시행 2018.12.13, 법률 제15665호, 2018.6.12, 일부개정). 산재법의 보험급여는 다음의 세 가지로 나누어 볼 수 있다. ① 계속적 보험급여의 청구, ② 일시금 보험급여의 청구, 그리고 ③ 연금보험급여 이렇게 세 가지의 형태로 청구하며 각각 소멸시효의 기산점이 다르다.

(ⅰ) 계속적 보험급여의 청구에는 요양급여, 휴업급여 등이 있다. 요양급여는 근로자가 업무상의 사유로 부상을 당하거나 질병에 걸린 경우 지급하며 현물급여가 원칙이다(산재법 제40조). 즉 보험금을 받을 권리의 소멸시효 기산일은 근로자가 업무상 부상 또는 질병에 걸린 날이 아니라 요양에 필요한 비용이 발생한 다음날이 된다.[205] 휴업급여는 업무상 사유로 부상을 당하거나 질병에 걸린 근로자에게 요양으로 인해 취업하지 못한 기간에 대해 지급하므로, 취업하지 못한 다음 날부터 소멸시효 기산일이 시작된다(산재법 제52조).

(ⅱ) 일시금 보험급여의 청구에는 장해보상일시금, 유족보상일시금, 장의비 등이 있다. 장해보상일시금은 근로자가 업무상 부상을 당하거나 질병에 걸려 완치 후에도 장해가 남은 근로자에게 지급한다. 장해급여는 재해근로자가 치료가 종결되어 장해가 고정된 시점에서 진행된다 (산재법 제57조). 유족보상일시금은 연금수급권자가 없는 경우에 한해 지급하며, 소멸시효 기산일은 재해근로자가 사망한 다음날이 된다 (산재법 제62조). 장의비는 실제로 장제를 지낸 경우에 한해 지급한다 (산재법 제71조).

---

[205] 황운희, "산재보험급여의 소멸시효 기산일", 「노동법논총」 제27집, 한국비교노동법학회, 2013.4, 382면; 대법원 2008.4.17 선고 2006다35865 전원합의체 판결.

(iii) Pension insurance benefits include pensions for disabilities and survivors, with payment beginning the first month after the month in which the reason for payment occurred.

In the case of noise-induced hearing loss, the Labor Welfare Corporation's Guidelines for Work Disabilities previously claimed that the 3 years' limitation begins "when leaving the noisy workplace," but the court ruled that it could be considered to have begun at the time of "healing" instead.[206] As a result, in 2016, the Ministry of Employment and Labor changed the statue of limitations for noise-induced hearing loss so that the calculation date begins from diagnosis. Therefore, in recent cases, the court has ruled that "the statue of limitations for a person diagnosed with noise-induced hearing loss after a long absence from the noisy workplace cannot be considered to have come into effect even if they has applied for a disability benefit after three years have passed from the time of diagnosis." [207]

(3) The statue of limitations for wage bonds and the statue of limitations for prosecution

statue of limitations refers to expiration of the period during which an employee who has the right to receive compensation may exercise a claim against the employer in the event of a delay in the payment of wages or severance pay. The statue of limitations for prosecution refers to expiration of the period when prosecution can occur for violating labor law, such as delaying the payment of wages, and begins either on the date the violation occurred or the date a continuing violation ends.

The period before the statue of limitations kicks in for prosecution of violation of labor-related Acts in terms of delayed payment of wages was extended from 3 years to 5 years in 2007 (Article 249, Paragraph 1, Item 5 of the Criminal Procedure Act). The period before the statue of limitations for prosecution kicks in shall be deemed to have started 14 days from the date the wages should have been paid or the date the violations terminate (Article 252 of the Criminal Procedure Act). According to Article 49 of the LSA, the statue of limitations for a wage bond kicks in after three years. However, since the statue of limitations for prosecution is now 5 years, prosecution for delayed payment of wages will continue to be possible.[208] Thus, an employee may file a claim for unpaid wages for a period of five years.

---

[206] Supreme Court ruling Sep. 4, 2014: 2014doo7374; Park, Jong-Tae, "Review of Standards for Recognition of Occupational Hearing Impairment," Monthly Labor Law, May 2017.
[207] Seoul Administrative Court ruling on Apr. 20, 2017: 2017goodan 50655.
[208] MOEL Guide, 「Guide on Handling Unpaid Wages」, 2016, pp. 31-32.

(ⅲ) 연금보험급여에는 장해보상연금, 유족보상연금 등이 있으며, 지급 시기는 그 사유가 발생한 달의 다음 달 초일부터 시작된다.

특히, 소음성 난청의 경우 종전의 근로복지공단 업무지침에는 장해급여청구권에서 '소음작업장을 떠났을 때'를 기준으로 3년의 소멸시효가 완성된다고 판단하였으나, 대법원은 소음성 난청과 관련하여 장해보상청구권은 '치유' 시점으로 본다고 판결하였다.[206] 이에 따라 2016년 고용노동부는 소음성 난청 소멸시효를 '진단일로부터 기산한다'는 내용으로 변경하였다. 이로 인하여 최근 판례에서는 "소음작업장에서 퇴사한 지 한참 후에 소음성 난청 진단을 받은 사람이 - 그 진단을 받은 때로부터 청구기간이 3년이 경과한 때 - 장해급여를 신청하였어도 소멸시효가 완성되었다고 볼 수 없다."[207]고 판시하고 있다.

(3) 임금채권 소멸시효와 공소시효

소멸시효는 돈 받을 권리가 있는 근로자가 사용자를 상대로 임금이나 퇴직금의 체불이 있는 경우에 청구권을 행사할 수 있는 기간을 말한다. 이에 대해 공소시효는 임금체불 등 노동법 위반 사용자를 법 위반행위가 있는 날 또는 법 위반행위가 계속되는 경우 종료일로부터 형벌권을 행사할 수 있는 기간을 말한다.

임금체불로 인한 노동관계법령 위반 범죄의 공소시효 기간은 2007년에 기존 3년에서 5년으로 연장되었다(형사소송법 제249조 제1항 제5호). 공소시효 기산점은 "범죄행위가 종료된 때부터(형소법 제252조) 임금지급일 또는 퇴직일로부터 14일이 경과한 때"까지를 말한다. 이에 반해 임금채권의 소멸시효는 3년이다(근기법 제49조). 임금채권의 소멸시효 3년이 완성되었다 하더라도 공소시효가 아직 남아 있으므로 임금체불사업주에 대한 형사처벌이 가능하다.[208] 따라서 공소시효를 근거로 하여 근로자는 체불된 임금에 대해 5년간 청구가 가능하다.

---

[206] 대법원 2014.9.4 선고 2014두7374 판결. 박종태, "소음성 난청의 업무상 재해 인정기준 검토, 「월간 노동법률」, 중앙경제사, 2017년 5월호
[207] 서울행정법원 2017.4.20 선고 2017구단50655 판결.
[208] 고용노동부 근로기준정책과, 「체불사건 업무처리 요령」, 2016. 31-32면.

3. Suspension of a Statue of Limitations

(1) Concept

Termination of a statue of limitations is the occurrence of the factual condition on which the statue of limitations is based. The reasons for termination of the statue of limitations are: (i) A request for trial (Article 170 of the Civil Act); ② Participation in bankruptcy proceedings (Article 171); ③ Issuance of a payment order from the court (Article 172); ④ A summons for reconciliation (Article 173); ⑤ Unilateral attendance at the court (Article 173); ⑥ Notification by registered mail (Article 174): claim for money in the case of monetary bonds, if the request is made based upon the registered mail, it is only valid for 6 months if a court filing or application for bankruptcy was not made; ⑦ Foreclosures, provisional attachment, provisional dispositions (Article 176) ⑧ Approval (Article 177): meaning that the debtor has confirmed a debt to the creditor.

(2) Details

1) Details of reasons for suspension

Since wage bonds have a 3-year statue of limitations, if an employee has not filed a claim during the 3-year period leading up to statue of limitations, the claim can no longer be made. However, in the event of a trial claim, seizure of the wage bond, or provisional attachment, if the employer agrees to the wage bond, statue of limitations shall not occur. If the employer writes a memorandum on the unpaid wages and pays part of those unpaid wages, statue of limitations shall be suspended.[209]

If the worker informs their employer of the unpaid wages by means of registered mail, this shall be the reason for a six-month suspension of statue of limitations (Article 174 of the Civil Act). However, the notification letter shall have the effect of ceasing the statue of limitations for six months, unless the worker requests a trial, participates in bankruptcy proceedings, responses to reconciliation, has seizure or accepts a provisional disposition.[210]

2) Relationship to delayed payment of wages

(i) Whether an employee's claim for unpaid wages can be a reason for suspending the statue of limitations: A criminal or civil complaint filed

---

[209] Supreme Court ruling on Jun. 10, 2010: 2010da8266.
[210] Ha, Kap-rae, 「Labor Standards Act」, 35th Ed., 2022, Jongang Kyungjaesa, p. 315.

3. 소멸시효 중단

(1) 소멸시효 중단의 개념

소멸시효의 중단은 시효의 기초가 되는 사실상태를 발생하는 것으로 시효가 중단하게 되는 내용이다. 소멸시효의 중단사유는 ① 재판상 청구(민법 제170조): 소의 각하 또는 취하가 있으면 시효중단 효력이 없음; ② 파산절차 참가(제171조); ③ 지급명령(제172조): 법원에 지급명령을 신청한 경우; ④ 화해를 위한 소환(제173조); ⑤ 임의출석(제173조); ⑥ 최고(제174조): 금전채권의 경우 금전청구, 다만 최고를 한 경우 6월 내에 재판상 청구, 파산절차 참가 등을 하지 않는 경우 시효중단 효력 없음; ⑦ 압류, 가압류, 가처분 (제176조) ⑧ 승인(제177조): 채무자가 채권자에게 채무가 있음을 인정한다는 의미이고 보편적으로 지불각서 등이 해당된다.

(2) 소멸시효 중단 내용
1) 중단사유

임금채권은 3년간의 소멸시효를 가지므로, 이를 근로자가 3년 동안 청구하지 않았을 때는 소멸시효의 만료로 인해 더 이상 다툴 수 없다. 다만, 재판상 청구, 임금채권에 대한 압류 또는 가압류를 한 경우, 사용자가 임금채무에 대해 동의한 경우 소멸시효는 중단이 된다. 사용자가 임금체불에 대해 각서를 써주고 체불금의 일부를 변제한 경우에도 소멸시효는 중단이 된다.[209]

임금채권에 있어 미지급한 부분에 대해 사용자에게 내용증명으로 최고를 할 경우에는 6개월간 소멸시효의 중단 사유가 된다(민법 제174조). 다만, 최고는 시효 중단의 효과가 있으나 6개월내에 재판상의 청구, 파산절차참가, 화해를 위한 위한 소환, 압류 또는 가처분을 하지 않으면 소급하여 시효 중단의 효력이 없어진다.[210]

2) 임금체불과의 관계

(ⅰ) 근로자가 체불 임금 진정 제기가 시효 중단 사유가 되는지 여부:

---
[209] 대법원 2010.6.10 선고 2010다8266 판결.
[210] 하갑래, 「근로기준법」, 제35판, 2022년, 중앙경제사, 315면.

against a judicial authority, such as a labor inspector, is not accepted as a trial claim.[211] However, in the event of unfair dismissal, when the related workers are involved in the administrative court's proceedings as auxiliary participants while the National Labor Relations Commission is working as the defendant, the statue of limitations is suspended.[212]

(ii) Whether issuance of a labor supervisor's confirmation of unpaid wages can be termination of the statue of limitations: In cases where a worker who has taken a petition for unpaid wages to the Ministry of Employment and Labor, if the employer simply confirms the amount of unpaid wages, this will not be regarded as statue of limitations. However, if the employer has made a written confirmation of payment of the delayed wages, this can be regarded as a suspension of the statue of limitations.[213]

3) Relationship to the IACI Act

In accordance with the IACI Act, a worker's filing of a claim that they has an occupational injury or illness can terminate the statue of limitations, which will affect all claims related to Industrial Accident Compensation Insurance benefits (Article 113 of the IACI Act). In general, submitting a complaint to the Ministry of Employment and Labor regarding unpaid wages will not be considered a trial claim. However, if an industrial accident application is filed with the Labor Welfare Corporation, it shall be regarded as a trial claim which can terminate statue of limitations. As a precedent, a worker filed an application for occupational accident compensation benefits, but was rejected. Then after he did not apply for review within 90 days after the rejection, the corporation dismissed his late claims due to statue of limitations. However, the Supreme Court recognized that the claim for insurance benefits pursuant to Article 36 (1) of the IACI Act as a reason for termination of statue of limitations, separate from the reason for the statue of limitations under the Civil Act.[214]

4. Conclusion

---

[211] Supreme Court ruling on Mar. 12, 1999: 98da 18214, Kumho construction company
[212] Supreme Court ruling on Feb. 9, 2012: 2011da20034
[213] Kang, Ji-hyeon, "Issues Regarding statue of limitations on Wage Bonds", 「Attorneys」 Vol. 49, 2016, p. 216; Seoul District Court ruling on Jan. 21, 2016: 2015na42147
[214] Supreme Court ruling on Jun. 15, 2018: 2017da9119

근로감독관 등 사법당국에 형사고발이나 고소를 하는 경우에는 재판상 청구로 인정되지 않아 시효중단효력이 없다.[211] 다만, 부당해고 사건에 있어 중앙노동위원회를 피고로 하고 근로자를 보조참가인으로 하여 진행된 행정소송에서는 임금채권에 대한 시효의 중단을 인정하였다.[212]

(ii) 근로감독관의 임금체불확인서 발급이 시효의 중단에 해당하는지 여부: 임금체불이 된 근로자가 회사를 상대로 고용노동부에 진정하여 임금체불을 확정하는 과정에서 사용자의 임금체불에 대해 확인하는 경우에는 소멸시효의 중단으로 볼 수 없으나, 사용자가 임금체불에 대해 변제하겠다는 확인서를 작성해 준 경우에는 소멸시효의 중단으로 볼 수 있다.[213]

3) 산재법과의 관계

산재법상 업무상 부상 또는 질병에 대한 산재보험 청구는 소멸시효를 중단시키고, 산재보험 급여 관련 모든 청구권에도 소멸시효의 중단을 가져온다(산재법 제113조). 일반적으로 임금채권에 대해서 고용노동부에 진정, 고소 등을 제기하는 것을 재판상 청구로 볼 수 없지만, 산재업무의 특성에 따라 근로복지공단에 산재신청을 하는 경우 재판상 청구로 보아 소멸시효의 중단사유가 된다. 이와 관련된 판례로 산재보험급여 수급권자가 보험급여를 신청하였으나, 불승인을 받아 90일 이내에 소를 제가하여야 한다는 처분을 받았음에도 소를 제기하지 않고 있다가 3년 내 다시 보험급여를 청구한 사안에 대해 근로복지공단은 소멸시효가 완성되었다고 부지급 처분을 내렸다. 이에 대해 대법원은 산재보험법 제36조제1항에 따른 보험급여 청구는 이를 민법상의 시효 중단 사유와는 별도의 고유한 시효 중단 사유로 인정하여 소멸시효의 중단 사유로 인정하였다.[214]

4. 시사점

---

[211] 대법원 1999.3.12 선고 98다18214 금호건설사건
[212] 대법원 2012.2.9. 선고 2011다20034 판결
[213] 강지현, "임금채권의 소멸시효 관련 실무상 쟁점",「변호사」제49집, 2016. 216면. 서울중앙지법 2016.1.21. 선고 2015나42147 판결.
[214] 대법원 2018.6.15 선고 대법 2017다9119 판결.

The statue of limitations system promotes legal stability and quick remedy for violation of rights. In industrial accident compensation, it is moving toward better protection of workers by extending the period prior to statue of limitations or terminating it. However, for claim for deferred wages, a lawsuit should be filed with a civil court because the payment of those wages or the filing of a complaint with the Labor Office will not be regarded as a suspension of statue of limitations. In other words, unpaid wages would be reduced gradually due to the completion of statue of limitations as the time would pass by while complaining to the labor office for unpaid wages. Therefore, it is necessary to improve the statue of limitations system against delayed payment of wages. First of all, it is necessary to suspend the statue of limitations just like the claims to the court when a worker takes a petition or complaint to the labor office over unpaid wages. Secondly, the statue of limitations for prosecution was extended from three years to five years in 2007, which has caused some confusion in applications for remedy against late payment of wages. Therefore, in terms of protecting workers, the statue of limitations for wage bonds should be extended from 3 years to 5 years as well.

V. Related Labor Cases

⟨Case 1⟩ A Claim for Insolvency Payment[215]

'Hanguk Ness,' a company located in Namyangju, Gyeonggi Province and established on October 26, 1995, had hired 34 employees and been engaged in the molding business to manufacture window frames. Since the beginning of 2010, the company's sales began to gradually decrease, resulting in accumulated deficits and the closure of its business on November 2, 2010. At the time of closure, the company owed its 34 employees overdue wages and severance pay in the amount of 400 million won. Besides these overdue wages, the company had various debts amounting to 1.2 billion won, which precluded operation of business and the payment of its employees. This firm (KangNam Labor Law Firm) was commissioned to represent the employees and petitioned the Labor Office towards receiving their overdue wages and severance pay. We received confirmation from the Labor Office that the company was bankrupt in actuality, after verifying that company debt was much more than the employer could afford to pay, and that it had been impossible for the company to pay wages for three months. Employees would not be able to receive any wages directly from the employer. Instead, their overdue wages of three months and three years' severance pay came through the insolvency payment system.

---

[215] Jung, Bongsoo, "A Claim for Insolvency Payment", 「Labor Law」, Jungang, April 2011.

소멸시효의 제도는 법적 안정성과 신속한 권리구제를 촉진하기 위한 제도이다. 산재보상시 소멸시효를 연장하거나 소멸시효를 중지하게 하여 근로자 보호를 위한 방향으로 나가고 있다. 그러나 임금체불의 경우에는 임금체불 진정이나 고소사건의 제기가 소멸시효의 중단으로 인정받을 수 없으므로 반드시 민사로 재판청구를 하여야 한다. 즉, 소멸시효로 더 이상의 권리구제를 받지 못하거나 임금 청구에서도 보호되는 임금이 기간의 지남에 따라 작아지게 된다. 따라서 임금체불에 대한 소멸시효제도는 개선이 필요하다. 첫째, 임금체불 진정이나 고소에 대해 재판상 청구로 봐서 소멸시효의 중단될 필요가 있다. 둘째, 공소시효가 2007년 이후 3년에서 5년으로 연장되어 근로자의 보호입장에서 임금채권의 소멸시효도 3년에서 5년으로 연장할 필요가 있다.

V. 실무사례

〈사례 1〉 대지급금사건[215]

경기도 남양주시에 위치해 있는 한국네스(주)는 1995년 10월 26일에 설립되어 34명을 고용하여 창틀제조에 사용되는 금형제작 사업을 영위해 오다가 2010년 이래 매출액 감소로 인한 누적 적자로 인하여 2010년 11월 2일에 폐업을 하게 되었다. 폐업 당시 근로자 34명에게 체불된 임금과 퇴직금이 약 4억에 달했고, 체불임금 외에도 각종 부채가 12억 여 원에 달하여 더 이상 사업운영이 불가능한 상태였으며, 근로자들에게 임금을 지급할 능력이 없었다. 근로자들의 임금체불사건을 맡게 된 본 노무법인은 노동사무소를 통해 당해 근로자의 임금체불 사실을 확인하였으며, 사업장의 부채가 과다하여 3개월 이내에 임금지급이 불가능하다는 사실을 증명한 후, '사실상 도산인정서'를 발급받을 수 있었다. 근로자들은 사업주로부터는 체불된 임금 및 퇴직금을 전혀 받을 수 없었지만, 대지급금제도를 통해 체불된 임금 중 최종 3개월의 임금과 최종 3년간의 퇴직금을 수령할 수 있었다.

---
[215] 정봉수, "대지급금 사건", 「월간 노동법률」, 중앙경제사, 2011년 4월호

⟨Case 2⟩ Petition for Unpaid Weekly Holiday Allowance[216]

1. Summary

On Sep. 21, 2009, a Korean cook (hereinafter referred to as "the Employee") who worked at a US Army restaurant (hereinafter, "the Employer") based in Korea applied to the Seoul Regional Labor Office for his unpaid weekly holiday allowance. The employee claimed that his monthly salary was calculated by multiplying his actual working hours by an hourly wage rate and then allowances, like bonuses, were included, but he did not receive anything called a weekly holiday allowance. He therefore asked that the Employer pay him the unpaid weekly holiday allowance from the previous three years until the present time. The Labor Inspector investigated the claims of both parties related to the case and concluded on Jan. 12, 2010, that the Employer had not violated any related laws.

2. The Employee's claim

According to his employment contract, the Employee received an hourly wage, paid every month, in the amount calculated by multiplying the actual working hours by the hourly wage rate, plus an amount reflecting the Welfare Benefit allowance & PIK allowance, as well as a monthly bonus calculated by dividing 700% of the annual bonus by 12. The Employee has not received anything called a weekly holiday allowance in his salary. Monthly wages were always variable according to the hours worked each month because the wage structure was not a monthly wage system but an hourly wage system. Accordingly, as the Employer did not pay a fixed monthly wage, but paid different wages every month according to the number of hours worked, the Employer should also pay a weekly holiday allowance.

3. The Employer's claim

When paying wages in an hourly wage system, the Employer calculated the wages as (working hours × hourly wage rate) and, instead of adding a weekly holiday allowance, included a fixed monthly 'benefit allowance' and 'PIK'

---

[216] Jung, Bongsoo, "Unpaid Weekly Holiday Allowance", 「Labor Law」, Jungang, May 2013.

〈사례 2〉 주휴수당미지급 진정사건[216]

1. 사건 개요

주한미군 식당에서 근무한 한국인 요리사(이하'근로자'라 함)는 2009년 9월 21일 회사를 상대로 주휴수당을 받지 못하였다고 주장하면서 서울지방노동청에 진정을 제기하였다. 근로자는 자신이 받는 월급이 실제로 일한 시간에 시간급 임금을 곱한 후 보너스 등 수당을 지급받았으며, 주휴수당 명목으로 받은 것이 없으므로 미지급된 주휴수당에 대해 청구 가능한 3년치 수당을 소급하여 추가 지급해야 한다고 주장하였다. 관할 노동사무소에서는 사건을 조사한 후 2010년 1월 12일 회사가 법 위반사항이 없다는 결론을 내리면서 사건을 종결하였다.

2. 근로자측 주장

식당 근무자의 근로계약은 개인별로 시급이 있으므로 실제로 근로한 시간에 시급을 곱한 금액에, 복지수당과 현물수당(PIK)을 더한 후에 상여금 700%를 12분의 1로 나눈 금액을 매월 지급받았다. 급여구성항목에 어디에도 주휴수당의 명칭을 가지고 지급된 사실이 없다는 것이다. 임금체계가 월급제가 아니라 시급제로 운영되었기 때문에 월급은 매월 일한 시간에 따라 변동되는 임금을 지급받았다. 따라서 회사가 매월 일정한 월급제로 급여를 지급한 것이 아니라 시급제를 기준으로 매월 변동되는 급여를 지급하면서 주휴수당을 지급하지 않았기 때문에 회사는 이를 추가로 지급해야 한다.

3. 사용자측 주장

회사는 근로자에게 시급으로 지급할 때, 일한 「시간 × 시급」으로 계산하면서 일주일 만근 한 것에 대한 주휴유급수당이 별도로 계산되어야 하지만, 월 단위 일정액의 복지수당과 현물수당(PIK)을 고정적으로 지급하여 왔고

---

[216] 정봉수, "주휴수당 미지급 진정사건", 「월간 노동법률」, 중앙경제사, 2010년 5월호

allowance, which was an amount exceeding the weekly holiday allowance. Given that this is the case, how would it be possible for the Employer to pay 700% of the annual bonus (divided into 12 months), as well as subsidize middle and high school students' tuition while neglecting to pay the statutory weekly holiday allowance? As the Employer paid an amount equivalent to the weekly holiday allowance each month, even though the Employer did not call it a weekly holiday allowance, this amount can replace the weekly holiday allowance.

4. Related administrative guidelines

1) Inclusion or non-inclusion of paid weekly holiday (Jul. 8, 2008; kunrokijun-2455)
   If an employer pays employees according to a monthly wage system, the monthly wage shall be considered to include a paid weekly allowance, if there are no exceptional situations (Supreme Court ruling 93 da 32514). If the employee receives fixed allowances along with basic hourly wages every month in a monthly wage system, such fixed allowances shall be interpreted to have similar characteristics as wages for paid weekly holiday allowance (Supreme Court ruling 97 da 28421).
2) The weekly holiday does not normally apply to daily workers, but if a daily worker works for six consecutive days, a paid weekly holiday shall be provided. (Apr. 2, 1997, Gungi 68207-424)

    Weekly holiday allowance under the Labor Standards Act shall be given to a worker who fulfills their weekly contractual working hours. However, in principle, the weekly holiday shall not be given to daily workers because it is not possible to calculate weekly contractual working hours for daily workers, as they engage in daily employment contracts.

    The purpose for providing a weekly holiday is to reduce the accumulated fatigue on workers after one week's work, thereby helping to protect their health, and to provide time to participate in social and cultural activities. If a daily worker works for 6 consecutive days per week without absence, actual working days, and not contractual working days, shall be applied and weekly holiday shall be granted. The employer shall pay weekly holiday allowance separately from wages for daily workers, unless the affected worker agrees to receive the weekly holiday allowance in advance, with their daily wages.

이 금액이 주휴수당에 해당되는 금액을 초과하고 있다. 어떤 회사가 법정 주휴수당도 지급하지 않으면서 기본급에 대하여 상여금을 연간 700% 지급하고 있으며, 중 고등학교 자녀에 대하여 학자금까지 지급하겠는가? 회사는 비록 명칭은 주휴수당으로 지급하지 않았지만, 월 단위 주휴수당에 상당하는 금액만큼을 지급하였으므로 이는 주휴수당으로 갈음할 수 있다고 할 수 있다.

4. 관련 행정해석 자료

1) 유급 주휴수당 산정 여부 (2008.07.08, 근로조건지도과-2455)
   근로자에 대한 임금을 월급으로 지급할 경우 특별한 사정이 없는 한 월급은 유급 휴일에 대한 임금도 포함된 것으로 볼 수 있으며(대법 93다32514), 시급제 사원이 기본 시급과 함께 매월 고정 수당을 월급의 형태로 지급받는 경우, 그 고정 수당 중에는 유급 휴일에 대한 임금의 성격을 갖는 부분도 포함 된 것으로 보는 것(대법 97다28421)이 판례의 입장이다.
2) 일용근로자의 경우 주휴일이 적용되지 않지만, 계속해서 1주일에 6일을 근무한 경우 일용근로자에게는 임금과 별도로 주휴일을 유급으로 부여하여야 한다. (1997.04.02, 근기 68207-424)
   근로기준법상의 주휴일은 1주간의 소정근로일수를 개근한 자에게 주도록 되어 있으므로 근로계약이 1일 단위로 체결되어 1주간의 소정근로일수를 산정할 수가 없는 일용근로자에게는 원칙적으로 주휴일을 부여할 수 없다.
   그러나 주휴일의 부여 목적이 1주간의 근로로 인하여 축적된 근로자의 피로를 풀어주고 건강을 확보하게 하며, 여가를 이용할 수 있게 하여 사회적·문화적 생활을 할 수 있도록 하는데 있으므로 일용근로자가 계속해서 근로를 한다면 이때에는 소정근로일수 대신 실근로일수를 기준으로 하여 1주일에 6일을 개근하였으면 주휴일을 부여하여야 한다. 한편, 일용근로자의 경우 주휴수당을 포함하여 임금을 지급받기로 사전에 약정하지 않은 한 주휴수당은 임금과는 별도로 지급되는 것이므로 주휴일이 부여된 일용근로자에게는 임금과는 별도로 주휴수당을 지급하여야 한다.

Chapter 4 The Protection of Wages

5. Judgment on the case

The labor inspector in charge of this case concluded that the Employer had paid a weekly holiday allowance to the Employee as the Employer had paid monthly wages based on the hourly wage system and added a regular allowance for each month, which was an amount equivalent to the weekly holiday allowance. If, in this case, the Employer had paid wages by multiplying the actual working hours by the hourly wage rate without a monthly regular allowance, only adding a monthly bonus calculated for the annual 700% bonus, the Employer would have to pay all employees, including the Employee in this case, all unpaid weekly holiday allowances for the past three years.

⟨Case 3⟩ Whether Compensation Should be Given for Unused Annual Leave[217]

A certain company ("the Company") regulated in its rules of employment that it would not compensate for unused annual leave and instead would promote its use, which the Company did through individual emails to all personnel. Where the promotion of using annual leave has been done through email, the main point is whether or not the Company must give financial compensation for unused leave.

1. Current situations

The Company regulated in the rules of employment that it would not compensate for unused leave, and had informed personnel of the number of available annual leave days in the early part of the year, and sent similar emails again after six months to the employees to actively promote the use of annual leave. Then in October it notified each individual employee by email that he or she needed to use their remaining annual leave days by the end of the year, and if they did not, there would be no financial compensation for unused leave. In reality, the Company has not paid any allowance for unused annual leave so far.

---

[217] Jung, Bongsoo, "Whether Compensation should be given for Unused Annual Leave", 「Labor Law」, Jungang, August 2015.

5. 시사점

이번 진정사건에 있어 근로감독관은 시급제로 계산된 월급여가 지급되면서, 월 단위의 일정한 수당을 지급하였고, 이것이 주휴일수당에 상당하는 금액을 지급하였기 때문에 이번 사건의 경우 주휴수당이 지급되었다고 판단하였다. 만약, 이번 사건에서 회사가 월 일정한 수당지급 없이 일한 시간만큼 시급을 계산한 후, 연 700%의 보너스를 월 단위로 분배하여 지급하였다면 회사에서는 충분한 급여를 지급하였음에도 불구하고 주휴수당을 미급한 것이 되고, 이 근로자뿐만 아니라 다른 모든 근로자에 대해서도 3년 동안의 임금에 대해 미지급된 주휴수당을 추가로 지급하여야만 한다.

〈사례 3〉 미사용 연차수당 미지급 사건[217]

회사는 취업규칙(연차휴가 사용촉진)을 통해 근로자에게 미사용 연차휴가는 보상하지 않는다고 규정하고 있고, 이메일로 개인별 휴가사용을 적극적으로 권장하였다. 눈여겨볼 사항은 이러한 이메일상 휴가사용촉진조치를 한 경우, 사용자의 금전보상이 면제될 수 있는지 여부이다.

1. 현 실태

취업규칙에 '연차휴가 사용촉진' 규정을 두어 미사용 연차휴가는 보상을 하지 않는다고 명시하고 있고, 회사는 이메일을 통해 연초에 휴가 일수를 알려주었으며, 6개월이 지난 후에는 잔여일수를 알려주고 휴가사용을 적극 권장하였다. 그리고 매월 10월에는 휴가사용에 대해 개인별로 미사용휴가 일수를 이메일로 알려주었고, 휴가를 사용하지 않을 시에는 금전보상이 없음을 이미 통지하였다. 또한 실제로 휴가사용을 권장하는 등 수차례의 관련 이메일을 발송하였다. 실제로 회사는 미사용 연차휴가에 대한 수당을 한번도 지급한 사례가 없었다.

---

[217] 정봉수, "미사용 연차수당 미지급 사건", 「월간 노동법률」, 중앙경제사, 2015년 8월호

2. Related law and guideline regarding measures for promoting use of annual leave

(1) Regulation of the Labor Standards Act (LSA)

The current LSA regulates the provision of 'promoting the use of annual paid leave' in relation with 'annual paid leave'.[218]

(2) Related guidelines

The 'written document' mentioned in Article 61 of the LSA refers to a paper document. Electronic documents are only possible in exceptional cases where the company has handled every operation by means of electronic documents in the process of its drafting, obtaining approval and implementing through equipped electronic work-processing systems (Guideline Gunjung-1128, Feb. 7, 2012). Accordingly, informing by email in the course of promoting the use of annual leave cannot be regarded as notification by written document (Guideline Gujung-6488, Nov 1, 2013).

If the employee has submitted a vacation plan with stipulated dates of leave after the employer has promoted the use of annual leave, the stipulated dates of leave shall be regarded as the employee's declaration of intention to use their annual leave. Provided, in cases where the employee comes to work on the stipulated date of leave, if the employer received the employee's labor and did not express a rejection of their coming in to work, it shall be regarded that the employer has approved the labor service on the expected date of leave, and so the employer shall pay an unused leave allowance (Guideline Limjang-285, Oct 21, 2005).

---

[218] Article 60 (Annual Paid Leave) (1) An employer shall grant 15 days' paid leave to a worker who has registered not less than 80 percent attendance during one year.
  (2) An employer shall grant one day's paid leave per month to a worker whose consecutive service period is shorter than one year or whose attendance is less than 80 percent, if the worker has offered work without absence throughout one month.
  (4) After the first year of service, an employer shall grant one day's paid leave for each two years of consecutive service in addition to the leave prescribed in paragraph (1) to a worker who has worked consecutively for 3 years or more. In this case, the total number of leave days including the additional leave shall not exceed 25.
  (7) The leave referred to in paragraphs (1) through (4) shall be forfeited if not used within one year. However, this shall not apply in cases where the worker concerned has been prevented from using the leave due to any cause attributable to the employer.
  Article 61 (Promoting the Use of Annual Paid Leave) If a worker's leave has been forfeited for non-use pursuant to Article 60 (7) despite the fact that the employer has taken measures described in any of the following subparagraphs to promote the use of paid leave prescribed in Article 60 (1), (3) and (4), the employer shall have no obligation to compensate the worker for the unused leave, and shall not be deemed to have caused the non-use through reasons attributable to the employer's action(s) under the proviso of Article 60 (7):
  1. Within the first 10 days of the six months before unused leave is to be forfeited pursuant to Article 60 (7), an employer shall notify each worker of the number of their unused leave days and urge them in writing to decide when they will use the leave and to inform the employer of the decided leave period; and
  2. If a worker, despite the urging prescribed in subparagraph (1), has failed to decide when they will use whole or part of the unused leave and to inform the employer of the decided leave period within 10 days after they were urged, an employer shall decide when the worker uses the unused leave and notify the worker of the decided leave period in writing no later than 2 months before the unused leave is to be forfeited pursuant to Article 60 (7).

2. 연차휴가 사용촉진 조치에 대한 법규정과 행정해석

(1) 근로기준법 규정

현행 근로기준법상 연차휴가와 관련해 연차유급휴가의 사용촉진에 대해서는 규정을 두고 있다.[218]

(2) 행정해석

근로기준법 제61조의 서면은 종이로 된 문서를 의미하고 전자문서는 회사가 전자결제체계를 완비해 전자문서로 모든 업무의 기안, 결재, 시행과정을 관리하는 경우에만 예외적으로 가능하다(2012.2.7. 근정과-1128). 이에 연차유급휴가의 사용촉진조치와 관련해 이메일로 통보하는 것이 근로자 개인별로 서면촉구 또는 통보하는 것에 비해 도달 여부의 확인 등이 불명확한 경우 서면으로 촉구 또는 통보로 인정되기 어렵다(2013.11.01 근정과-6488).

휴가사용촉진조치에 의하여 근로자가 휴가사용시기를 정하여 사용자에게 휴가 사용계획서를 제출하였다면 그 지정된 시기에 연차유급휴가의 사용하겠다는 의사표시로 볼 수 있을 것이므로 휴가를 청구한 것으로 볼 수 있다. 다만, 근로자가 휴가사용시기를 지정하고도 출근한 경우 사용자가 노무수령 거부의 의사표시 없이 근로를 제공받았다면 휴가일 근로를 승낙한 것으로 보아야 하므로 연차유급휴가근로수당을 지급하여야 한다(2005.10.21. 임장팀-285).

---

[218] 제60조【연차 유급휴가】① 사용자는 1년간 80퍼센트 이상 출근한 근로자에게 15일의 유급휴가를 주어야 한다.
  ② 사용자는 계속하여 근로한 기간이 1년 미만인 근로자 또는 1년간 80퍼센트 근로자에게 1개월 개근 시 1일의 유급휴가를 주어야 한다.
  ④ 사용자는 3년 이상 계속하여 근로한 근로자에게는 제1항에 따른 휴가에 최초 1년을 초과하는 계속 근로 연수 매 2년에 대하여 1일을 가산한 유급휴가를 주어야 한다. 이 경우 가산휴가를 포함한 총 휴가 일수는 25일을 한도로 한다.
  ⑦ 제1항부터 제4항까지의 규정에 따른 휴가는 1년간 행사하지 아니하면 소멸된다. 다만, 사용자의 귀책사유로 사용하지 못한 경우에는 그러하지 아니하다.
제61조【연차 유급휴가의 사용 촉진】사용자가 유급휴가(제60조제1항·제3항 및 제4항)의 사용을 촉진하기 위하여 다음 각 호의 조치를 하였음에도 불구하고 근로자가 휴가를 사용하지 아니하여 소멸된 경우(제60조제7항: 1년간 휴가청구권의 소멸시효 기간의 경과)에는 사용자는 그 사용하지 아니한 휴가에 대하여 보상할 의무가 없고, 사용자의 귀책사유(제60조제7항 단서)에 해당하지 아니하는 것으로 본다.
첫째. 휴가청구권의 소멸시효기간(제60조제7항 본문)에 따른 기간이 끝나기 6개월 전을 기준으로 10일 이내에 사용자가 근로자별로 사용하지 아니한 휴가 일수를 알려주고, 근로자가 그 사용 시기를 정하여 사용자에게 통보하도록 서면으로 촉구할 것;
둘째. 제1호에 따른 촉구에도 불구하고 근로자가 촉구를 받은 때부터 10일 이내에 사용하지 아니한 휴가의 전부 또는 일부의 사용 시기를 정하여 사용자에게 통보하지 아니하면 휴가청구권의 소멸시효기간 (제60조제7항 본문)에 따른 기간이 끝나기 2개월 전까지 사용자가 사용하지 아니한 휴가의 사용 시기를 정하여 근로자에게 서면으로 통보할 것

3. The Company's countermeasures

The Company has promoted the use of annual leave through email, but has not done so through written documents. Also, the Company did not evidentially reject the provision of the employee's labor when the employee provided work on dates expected to be used as annual leave. Based upon these facts, the Company recognized that it had not taken measures promoting the use of leave as stipulated by the LSA, and then paid unused annual leave allowance for the past three years in the salary payment for June 2015.

The labor case herein is a very common case that can occur easily for companies. Regarding promotion of the use of annual leave, it is frequent for companies to take formal measures without assigning annual leave for definite working days to employees and in this way avoid paying allowance for the unused annual leave. That is, companies promote the use of annual leave by informing through email only. In cases where the employees come to work on days designated for annual leave, companies do not pay annual leave allowance for unused annual leave owing to their efforts to promote the use of annual leave. However, as this case shows, the Company did not provide the use of annual leave on the designated days, and employees could not use annual leave due to reasons attributable to the Company. The Company therefore had to pay an unused annual leave allowance.

3. 회사의 대응 및 처리결과

　회사는 이메일로 연차휴가 사용촉진조치를 하였지, 근로기준법에 따른 서면에 의한 사용촉진 조치를 하지 않았다. 또한 근로자가 휴가신청을 한 경우에도 불구하고 휴가신청기간에 근로를 제공한 경우에 근로거부 표시를 명확히 하지 않았다. 이러한 사실에 대해 회사는 근로기준법에 정한 휴가 사용촉진조치를 하지 않았다는 것을 인정하고, 2015년 6월 급여에서 전 직원의 최근 3년기간의 미사용 연차휴가수당을 모두 지급하였다.

　위에서 다루었던 사례는 기업에서 일상적으로 일어날 수 있는 사건이다. 사용자가 연차휴가 사용촉진조치에 대해 형식적 조치 만을 취하고 실질적으로 연차휴가를 부여하지 않으면서도 미사용 연차휴가수당을 지급하지 않는 경우가 많다. 즉, 연차휴가 사용촉진 조치를 이메일로 통보하면서, 휴가일자에 출근하여 근무를 하는 경우에 회사가 휴가사용촉진조치를 다하였기 때문에 미사용 연차수당을 지급하지 않아도 된다고 생각하는 경우가 많다. 하지만, 이러한 경우에 사용자가 휴가를 보장하지 않은 것이라 볼 수 있기 때문에 사용자의 귀책사유로 휴가를 사용하지 못한 것으로 간주하여 미사용 연차휴가수당을 지급해야 한다.

Chapter 5 Retirement Benefit Plan

Ⅰ. Severance Pay System
Ⅱ. The Retirement Pension Plan
Ⅲ. Severance Settlement-related Taxation Issues
Ⅳ. Key Issues: The Confusing Administrative Interpretation from the Ministry of Employment and Labor on Calculating Severance Pay
Ⅴ. Related Labor Cases
  〈Case 1〉 Failure to Pay Severance Pay to Foreign Teachers
  〈Case 2〉 Failure to Pay Severance Pay to Company Directors

제5장 퇴직급여제도

Ⅰ. 퇴직금제도
Ⅱ. 퇴직연금제도
Ⅲ. 퇴직합의금의 과세문제
Ⅳ. 주요쟁점: 이상한 퇴직금 계산법을 안내하는 고용노동부의 행정해석
Ⅴ. 실무사례

　〈사례 1〉 원어민 교사 퇴직금 미지급 사건
　〈사례 2〉 회사 임원 퇴직금 미지급 사건

Chapter 5 Retirement Benefit Plan

Ⅰ. Severance Pay System

Retirement benefit plans consist of the Severance Pay Plan, Defined Benefit Retirement Pension Plan, and Defined Contribution Retirement Pension Plan. These three plans are equivalent in value, and companies established since December 2005 are required to carry one or more of them.

As there is no provision on qualifying causes of retirement for entitlement to severance pay, an employer shall give severance pay in all cases of termination of the employment relationship, including due to the employee's resignation or death, the company's disorganization, completion of the work, their having reached the retirement age, or their being dismissed for disciplinary reasons.

1. Requirements for receipt of severance pay

(1) Those eligible for severance pay shall be employees under the Labor Standards Act.

① Whether to pay severance pay to an employee who was appointed as a company director

In cases where an employee was appointed as company director without terminating employment, the matters related to severance pay shall be evaluated as follows: ⓐ In cases where the director fulfills his duties with the authority of a representative director or executive director commissioned by the company by means of the Commercial Act and/or Civil Act and receives a service fee, the director cannot be deemed an employee under the Labor Standards Act. Therefore, his severance pay occurs from the time when he was appointed as director (on the date of employment termination according to the LSA). statue of limitations is also calculated from the same date. ⓑ In cases where, despite holding a director's title, he maintains subordinate relations to the employer and is actually in an employee position, the severance pay occurs from the time the director resigned from the company. statue of limitations is also calculated from the same date.[219]

② How to calculate severance pay for a person assigned to a regular position from that of a daily worker

Consecutive years of employment to calculate severance pay for an employee who worked for the company as a daily worker but was reemployed as a regular employee shall be considered collectively based on the concrete facts as follows: If a temporary employee quit his temporary position, the employer accepted it, and he followed employment procedures by applying for a regular position, his

---

[219] MOEL Guidelines: Wage 68200-814 2001.11.27.

Ⅰ. 퇴직금제도

 퇴직급여제도라 함은 퇴직금제도, 확정급여형퇴직연금, 확정기여형퇴직연금을 말한다. 세 가지 제도는 모두 동등한 가치를 갖는 것으로 간주되며, 2005년 12월 이후 신설되는 사업장은 세 제도 중 한 가지 이상의 제도를 설정하여야 한다. 퇴직의 사유는 제한이 없기 때문에 근로자의 사직, 사망 또는 기업의 소멸, 일의 완료, 정년의 도래 및 징계 해고 등 근로계약이 종료되는 모든 경우에 지급된다.

1. 퇴직금 지급요건

(1) 퇴직금 지급 대상자: 근로기준법상의 근로자여야 한다.
 ① 직원이 임원으로 선임된 경우 퇴직금 지급여부
  재직 중인 직원이 근무기간의 단절 없이 이사로 선임된 경우에 있어 퇴직금을 둘러싼 법률관계는 아래와 같이 판단하여야 한다. ㉠ 이사가 상법 및 민법에 따라 회사의 업무대표권 또는 집행권을 위임받아 업무를 수행하고, 보수를 받는 등 근로기준법상 근로자로 볼 수 없는 경우에는 임원으로 선임된 날(근로기준법상의 근로관계가 종료된 날)을 기준으로 퇴직금 지급청구권이 발생하고, 소멸시효 또한 이날부터 기산된다. ㉡ 명칭만 이사일 뿐 사용자와 여전히 고용종속관계를 유지하고 있는 등 사실상 근로기준법상의 근로자에 해당되는 경우에는 이사로서 퇴직한 날을 기준으로 퇴직금 지급청구권이 발생하고, 이날부터 소멸시효가 기산된다.[219]
 ② 일용직으로 근무하다가 정규직으로 전환된 경우의 퇴직금 산정방법
  동일한 사업장에서 일용직으로 입사하여 근무하다가 정규직으로 임용되어 계속 근로한 근로자의 퇴직금 계산을 위한 계속 근로연수 판단은 아래와 같이 구체적인 사실관계를 종합적으로 고려하여야 한다. 근로자의 자발적인 의사에 따라 일용직 사직의사 표시와 사용자의 사직수리가 이루어진 이후에 정규직으로의 전환을 위한 시험응시 등 임용절차를 거친 경우라면 이는 정규직 임용여부와는 관계없이 기왕의 일용직에 대한 근로관계는

---
[219] 행정해석: 임금 68200-814 2001.11.27

previous labor contract was terminated effectively regardless of the new employment. However, if the temporary employee was rehired to a regular position while maintaining temporary employment, this is only a transfer to a regular position from an irregular position and his employment cannot be deemed effectively terminated.[220]

③ When a retired employee is rehired by the same company, the employer cannot make a special contract that excuses the employer from severance pay obligations, as this violates a compulsory law. Such agreement becomes null and void.

When rehiring a retired employee, the company shall pay severance pay to the employee with a service period of at least one year after re-employment. Even though both parties agree there will be no severance pay, this agreement violates a compulsory law and becomes null and void.[221]

④ Whether a full-time lecturer at an entrance exam institute is entitled to severance pay

If a full-time lecturer registered as an individual service provider provided labor service to the employer under substantial employment relations, they can receive severance pay. Whether or not a person is an employee under the Labor Standards Act shall be determined by whether the employee provides labor service to the employer under subordinate relations for the purpose of wages in a business or workplace regardless of the contract type. Full-time lecturers at an institute worked every day (6 days per week), which was distinct from other part-time lecturers, received fixed wages, and observed service and personnel regulations such as starting time and finishing time. They are therefore employees who provide labor service under subordinate relations.[222]

⑤ If a person has continuously maintained daily employment formally as a daily employee, the Labor Standards Act shall apply to them and the employer shall pay severance pay to the daily employee who has served at least one year.

If a person has been a daily worker formally but maintained daily employment without cessation, they shall be considered a regular employee. It is not true that the continuity of employment shall be estimated by the employee providing an average of 25 days or more of work per month, but also by the employee providing 4 to 15 days on average every month. As the daily employees in this case provided labor service for 4 or 5 days every month without exception, they shall be considered continuously employed and the Labor Standards Act shall

---

[220] MOEL Guidelines: Wage 68207-581 2000.11.14.
[221] MOEL Guidelines: Kungi 68207-584 1999.03.12
[222] Seoul District Court ruling on Nov. 10, 2006, 2004Gadan69638.

유효하게 단절된 것으로 볼 수 있을 것이나, 일용직 근로관계를 계속 유지하고 있는 상태에서 정규직으로의 채용이 이루어진 경우라면 이는 일용직에서 정규직으로 전환된 것에 불과한 것이므로 근로관계가 유효하게 단절되었다고는 볼 수 없다.[220]

③ 정년퇴직자가 동일 사업장에 재고용 시 퇴직금 부지급은 강행법규 위반으로 무효이다.

정년퇴직한 근로자를 재고용하는 경우에도 재고용 시점부터 계속 근무한 기간이 1년 이상이면 퇴직금을 지급하여야 한다. 당사자 간에 이를 지급하지 않기로 합의하였다 하더라도 동 합의는 강행법규 위반으로 무효이다.[221]

④ 입시학원 종합반 전임강사가 퇴직 시 퇴직금을 받을 수 있는지 여부

개인사업자로 등재된 입시학원 종합반 전임강사가 실질적인 종속관계로 사용자에게 근로를 제공했다면 퇴직 시 퇴직금을 받을 수 있다. 근로기준법상 근로자에 해당 되는지 여부는 그 계약형식에 상관없이 실질에 있어 근로자가 사업 또는 사업장에 임금을 목적으로 종속적인 관계에서 사용자에게 근로를 제공했는지 여부에 따라 판단해야 한다. 원고들은 학원에서 재학생반 전임강사로 다른 시간강사 내지 단과반 강사들과 달리 매일(주 6일) 출근하며 고정적인 월급을 받았던 점, 출퇴근 시간 등 학원 강사들에 대한 복무규정과 인사규정이 시행됐던 점 등에 비추어 종속적인 관계에서 근로를 제공한 근로자로 봄이 상당하다.[222]

⑤ 형식상 일용근로자로 되어 있다 하더라도 일용관계가 계속되어온 경우, 상용근로자로 보아 근로기준법을 적용해야 하고 1년 이상 근로한 자에 대하여는 퇴직금을 지급해야 한다.

형식상으로는 비록 일용근로자로 되어 있다고 하더라도 일용관계가 중단되지 않고 계속되어 온 경우에는 상용근로자로 보아야 할 것이고, 또한 근로자가 월 평균 25일 이상 근무하여야만 근로관계의 계속성을 인정할 수 있는 것은 아니며, 매월 빠뜨리지 않고 4, 5일에서 15일 정도씩 계속하여 일해 온 경우에는 근로관계의 계속성이 인정된다 할 것인바, 원고들이 피고회사에서 일용근로자로 근무하는 동안 매월 빠뜨리지 않고 최소한

---

[220] 행정해석: 임금 68207-581, 2000.11.14.
[221] 행정해석: 근기 68207-584, 1999. 03.12
[222] 서울서부지방법원 2006.11.10 선고 2004가단69638 판결

apply to them.[223]

⑥ The Labor Standards Act also applies to illegal migrant employees, who are therefore entitled to severance pay.

The term "employee" used in Article 2 of the Labor Standards Act means a person, regardless of occupation, who offers work to a business or workplace for the purpose of earning wages. In Article 6 of the Act, an employer shall not take discriminatory action in relation to working conditions on the grounds of nationality. The Labor Standards Act is applicable to foreign migrant employees, unless there are special reasons otherwise. Accordingly, the rules of severance pay stipulated in the Labor Standards Act apply to illegal migrant employees.[224]

(2) Consecutive years of employment: The employee shall serve continuously for at least one year.

Years of continuous employment refer to the period from the time when the employee begins working for the company to the time when the employee resigns from the company.

① The period of disciplinary 'suspension from work' due to an employee's own reasons shall be included in the period of continuous employment, which is the basic data for calculating severance pay, if a person maintains subsidiary employment relations with his employer.[225]

According to Article 8(1) of the Employee Retirement Benefit Security Act, an employer shall pay severance pay equivalent to the average wage for thirty days or more for each one year of continuous employment. The period of continuous employment in this Act means "the period from establishment of a labor contract to its termination." The period in which the employee did not provide labor service, but remained under subordinate employment relations with an employer, shall be included into the period of continuous employment for calculating severance pay. Accordingly, the period of disciplinary 'suspension from work' due to the employee's own reasons shall be included in the period of continuous employment as the basic data for calculating severance pay, so long as an employee has maintained subsidiary employment relations with his employer.

② The consecutive years of employment to calculate severance pay shall include the total period of employment, excluding the period of time when the employer ordinarily hired fewer than five employees. (Effective until December 2010; after this period, this shall apply to all employers.) [226]

---

[223] Seoul District Court ruling on Apr. 19, 95Gahap11509.
[224] Supreme Court ruling on Aug. 26, 1997, 97Da18875.
[225] MOEL Guidelines: Retirement Benefit Security Team-1596.
[226] MOEL Guidelines: Retirement Benefit Security Team-2582, 2006.07.20.

4, 5일 이상 계속하여 근무해 온 사실을 인정할 수 있으므로 원고들에 대하여도 계속적 근로관계가 인정되어 근로기준법이 적용되어야 할 것이다.[223]
⑥ 불법체류외국인 근로자에게도 근로기준법상의 퇴직금 규정이 적용된다.
　　근로기준법 제2조에서 근로자란, 직업의 종류를 불문하고 사업 또는 사업장에 임금을 목적으로 근로를 제공하는 자를 말한다고 규정하고 있고, 또 같은 법 제6조에 의하면 사용자는 근로자에 대하여 국적을 이유로 근로조건에 대한 차별적 대우를 하지 못한다고 규정하고 있으므로 특별한 사정이 없는 한 외국인 근로자에 대하여도 근로기준법이 적용된다고 할 것이다. 따라서 불법체류외국인 근로자에게도 근로기준법상의 퇴직금 규정이 적용된다.[224]

(2) 계속근로연수: 1년 이상 계속 근로한 자라야 함.

계속근로연수는 원칙적으로 근로자가 입사한날부터 퇴직일까지의 기간을 말한다.

① 근로자의 귀책사유로 인한 징계정직기간의 경우 사용종속관계가 유지되고 있다면 퇴직금산정의 기초가 되는 계속근로기간에 포함하는 것이 타당하다.[225] 근로자퇴직급여보장법 제8조제1항에 의하면 퇴직금은 계속근로기간 1년에 대하여 30일분 이상의 평균임금을 지급하여야 한다. 동법에서 계속근로기간이란 「근로계약을 체결하여 해지될 때까지의 기간」을 의미하므로, 실제로 근로를 제공하지 않은 기간이라 하더라도 사용종속관계가 유지되고 있는 기간은 퇴직금 산정을 위한 계속근로연수 산정 시 포함하여야 한다. 따라서 근로자의 귀책사유로 인한 징계정직기간의 경우에도 사용종속관계가 유지되고 있다면 특별한 사정이 없는 한 그 기간은 퇴직금산정의 기초가 되는 계속근로기간에 포함하는 것이 타당할 것이다.

② 퇴직금계산을 위한 계속 근로연수는 전체 재직기간 중에서 상시근로자수가 5인 미만인 기간을 제외한 기간을 합산한 기간으로 해야 한다(2010년 12월 이전 기간 까지만 해당됨, 이 이후 전 근로자에 적용).[226]

---

[223] 서울지방법원 1996.04.19 선고 95가합 11509 판결
[224] 대법원 1997.08.26 선고 97다18875 판결
[225] 행정해석: 퇴직급여보장팀-1596 2006.05.11
[226] 행정해석: 퇴직급여보장팀-2582 2006.07.20

The severance pay according to Article 4 and 8 of the Employee Retirement Benefit Security Act applies to all businesses or workplaces in which no fewer than five employees are ordinarily employed. In cases where the company has maintained five or more ordinary number of employees for a long period of time, but the number of employees were reduced to fewer than five employees for a certain period of time, the consecutive years of employment to calculate severance pay shall include the total period of employment, excluding the period of time when the employer ordinarily hired fewer than five employees.

2. Calculation of severance pay

Severance pay shall be 30 days or more of average wage for each year of consecutive service. The period for continuous employment shall include suspensions from work, service as a full-time labor officer of a Labor Union, labor service as a daily employee, detention periods from a criminal case, probationary periods, periods of strike, periods of absence, periods of suspension of service, suspensions from work owing to personal illness, etc. However, military service periods shall not be included in continuous employment.

① 'Suspension period from work' due to the employee's personal reasons shall be included in the period for calculating average wages.

Average wage to calculate severance pay according to Article 2 of the Labor Standards Act means the amount calculated by dividing the total wages paid to a relevant employee during the three calendar months immediately before the day on which a cause for calculating his average wages occurred by the total number of calendar days during those three months. If the amount calculated in this method is lower than that of the ordinary wage of the employee concerned, the amount of the ordinary wage shall be deemed his average wages. In cases where the period of calculating average wages includes a period of time falling under any of Subparagraph 1 to 8 of Article 2(1) of the Enforcement Decree to the LSA, the period and wages paid for that period shall be deducted respectively from a basis period for the calculation of average wages and the total amount of average wage. However, the period in which the employee did not provide labor service due to his own reasons, such as absences for personal reasons, shall not be excluded from the basis period for the calculation of average wages. Accordingly, in cases where the employee did not provide labor service during the basis period to calculate severance pay due to personal reasons such as absences for personal reasons, the identical period shall be included into a basis period of average wages and calculated for severance pay[227].

② How to include bonuses paid through one year into the amount subject to the calculation of average wages.

---

[227] MOEL Guidelines: Wages 68207-132,2003.02.27.

근로자퇴직급여보장법 제4조 및 제8조의 규정에 의한 퇴직금은 상시 5인 이상의 근로자를 사용하는 사업(장)에 적용되고 있다. 사업장에서 상당기간동안 상시근로자수가 5인 이상을 유지하다가 5인 미만으로 감소되어 상당기간동안 유지되는 경우 퇴직금계산을 위한 계속근로연수는 전체 재직기간 중에서 상시근로자수가 5인 미만인 기간을 제외한 기간을 합산한 기간으로 한다.

2. 퇴직금 산정

퇴직금은 계속근로연수 1년에 대하여 30일분 이상의 평균임금으로 지급되어야 하며, 휴직기간, 노조전임기간, 일용근무기간, 형사사건구금기간, 수습시용기간, 쟁의행위기간, 결근기간, 개인질병 휴직기간 등은 근속기간에 포함되며, 군복무기간은 근속기간에서 제외된다.

① 휴직기간이 근로자 귀책사유에 해당되는 경우 평균임금산정 기준기간에 포함하여 평균임금을 산정하여야 한다.

퇴직금산정을 위한 평균임금은 근로기준법 제2조의 규정에 의거 이를 산정하여야 할 사유가 발생한 날 이전 3월간에 지급된 임금총액을 그 기간의 총일수로 나눈 금액을 말하며, 이러한 방법으로 산출된 평균임금액이 당해 근로자의 통상임금보다 저액일 경우에는 그 통상임금액을 평균임금으로 하도록 정하고 있다. 평균임금 산정기간 중에 같은 법 시행령 제2조 제1항 제1호 또는 제8호에 해당하는 기간이 있는 경우에는 그 기간과 그 기간 중에 지불된 임금은 평균임금 산정기준이 되는 기간과 임금의 총액에서 각각 공제하도록 규정되어 있다. 그러나 결근 등 근로자 귀책사유에 의하여 근로를 제공하지 못한 기간은 평균임금 산정기준이 되는 기간에서 공제하도록 규정되어 있지 아니하다. 만일 평균임금 산정기준이 되는 기간에 근로를 제공하지 못한 사유가 결근 등 근로자 귀책사유에 해당되는 경우에는 동기간도 평균임금산정 기준기간에 포함하여 평균임금을 산정하여야 한다.[227]

② 1년간 지급받은 상여금을 평균임금 대상금품에 산입하는 방법

---

[227] 행정해석: 임금 68207-132 2003.02.27

There are no regulations stipulated in labor law about the matters concerning payment of bonuses, but bonuses shall be deemed wages as remuneration for work when they are stipulated in the rules of employment for payment conditions, amount, and payment period, or when they have been paid so habitually to all employees that the employee may have natural expectations to receive a bonus as a matter of course. On the other hand, in cases where the payment rate of bonuses was established per year-unit and paid for the period exceeding one month, the total amount of bonuses paid for a certain month shall not be included in calculation of average wages. The bonuses shall be calculated by dividing the total amount of bonuses paid to the relevant employee during the twelve calendar months before the day on which a cause for calculating his average wages occurred by the total number of calendar months, which is 3/12 times the total amount of bonuses paid per year.[228]

③ In cases where the severance pay regulation has been revised justifiably in the middle of the consecutive work period, the severance pay regulation effective at the time of retirement shall apply in calculation of severance pay. The calculation shall not be applied differently by dividing the period before or after the revision of the severance pay regulation.[229]

3. Prohibition against systems discriminating in terms of severance pay

① Discriminating severance pay between full-time employees and part-time employees violates the principle of prohibition for different application.[230]

Article 34(2) of the Labor Standards Act prohibits establishment of different severance pay systems according to job classification, title, business classification, etc. in one workplace and requires one severance pay system. If a company differs in application of severance pay between full-time employees and part-time employees, this violates the principle of prohibition against discrimination. Even though the company hired full-time employees and part-time employees differently and applied them differently in hiring procedures, job characteristics, promotion/transfer, etc., discrimination in severance pay shall not be justified without reasonable cause.

② That the company included the amount equivalent to severance pay into the monthly wage for foreign pilots amounted to establishment of a different application between foreign employees and native employees.[231]

---

[228] MOEL Guidelines: Wages 68207-120.
[229] Supreme Court ruling on Sep. 10, 1996, 95Da15414.
[230] Seoul District Court ruling on Oct. 20, 2000, 2000Kahap8606.
[231] Supreme Court ruling on Mar. 27, 1998, 97Da19725.

상여금의 지급 등에 대하여는 노동관계법에 별도 규정되어 있지 아니하나, 취업규칙 등에 지급조건, 금액, 지급시기가 정해져 있거나 전 근로자에게 관례로 지급하여 사회통념상 근로자가 당연히 지급 받을 수 있다는 기대를 갖게 되는 경우에는 근로의 대상성을 갖는 임금으로 보고 있다. 한편 상여금의 지급률을 연간단위로 설정하여 1개월을 넘는 단위로 지급하고 있는 경우에는 이를 지급 받은 그 달의 임금으로 취급하여 일시에 전액을 평균임금에 산입하는 것이 아니며, 평균임금을 산정하여야 할 사유가 발생한 날 이전 12개월의 기간 동안에 지급 받은 상여금 전액을 근로월수로 분할 계산하여 즉, 3/12을 평균임금산정 기준 임금총액에 산입한다.[228]
③ 계속근무기간의 중간에 퇴직금규정이 유효하게 변경된 경우 퇴직금을 산출함에 있어서는 전체 근무기간에 대하여 퇴직당시에 유효한 퇴직금규정을 적용해야 하는 것이지 퇴직금규정 변경 전후의 기간을 나누어 변경 전 근무기간에 대해 변경전의 규정을 적용할 것은 아니다.[229]

3. 퇴직금 차등제도 금지

① 정규직 직원과 시간제 직원에 대해 차등의 퇴직금 제도를 두어 차별하는 것은 차등금지원칙에 위반된다.[230]
근로기준법 제34조 제2항은 하나의 사업 내에서 직종, 직위, 업종 등에 따라 차등의 퇴직금 제도를 두는 것을 금지하고 하나의 퇴직금 제도를 적용하도록 하는 것인 바, 피고회사가 정규직직원과 시간제직원에 대해 차등의 퇴직금 제도를 두어 차별하는 것은 위 차등금지원칙에 위반하는 것이라고 보아야 할 것이고, 정규직직원과 시간제직원 사이에 피고회사 주장과 같은 채용절차, 근로의 성격, 승급·전보조치의 유무 등에서 차이가 있다고 하더라도 이것이 위와 같은 차별을 정당화할 합리적인 이유가 된다고 할 수 없다.
② 외국인 조종사에 대하여는 월급여 속에 퇴직금 상당액을 포함시켜 지급하기로 한 것은 내국인 근로자와의 사이에 차등제도를 설정한 것이다.[231]

---

[228] 행정해석: 임금 68207-120
[229] 대법원 1996.9.10. 선고 95다15414 판결.
[230] 서울지방법원 2000.10.20 선고 2000가합8606 판결.

If a company agreed to include the amount equivalent to severance pay into the monthly wage for foreign pilots, it means that the company will not pay severance pay at the time of retirement to those foreign pilots. This is a different system of severance pay, prohibited by Article 28(2) of the previous Labor Standards Act, from that applied to native pilots who receive severance pay upon quitting. Therefore, foreign pilots can apply for severance pay by the rules of employment applying to the majority of employees.

③ If there are two different applications of severance pay, such as the rules of employment regulating a cumulative severance pay system for native employees and individual employment contracts regulating a singular severance pay system for foreign workers, this violates the regulation prohibiting different application of severance pay.[232]

4. How to pay severance pay

Interim severance pay is implemented only in cases where the employee demands it, but the employer does not have a duty to agree to the employee's demand. Even if there are relevant regulations regarding the interim severance pay system in the rules of employment or the collective bargaining agreement, individual employees must request it concretely and then it can be handled as an adjustment of interim severance pay.

① Whether it is possible to pay interim severance pay for all employees with the consent of the majority of employees[233]

Enforcement Decree (Article 3) of the Employee Retirement Pension Security Act (Reasons for Interim Severance Pay)

1. Where an employee who has not owned a house has purchased a house in their own name;
2. Where an employee who has not owned a house makes a key money deposit (according to Article 303 of the Civil Act) or a security deposit (according to Article 3-2 of the Housing Lease Protection Act) for the purpose of moving into a residence. In this case the employee can only apply for the retirement pension one time during employment in a company or business;
3. Where an employee, employee's spouse according to Article 50 (Paragraph 1) of the Income Tax Act, or their dependent family member has received

---

[232] Supreme Court ruling on Nov. 28, 1997, 97Da24511.
[233] MOEL Guidelines: Wages 68200-111, 2002.02.20.

외국인 조종사에 대하여는 월급여 속에 퇴직금 상당액을 포함시켜 지급하기로 합의하였다고 하더라도, 이는 결국 외국인 조종사에 대하여는 퇴직 시 퇴직금을 지급하지 않는다는 것이므로, 퇴직금을 지급받는 내국인 근로자와의 사이에 구 근로기준법 제28조 제2항이 금지하는 차등제도를 설정한 것이라 할 것이고, 따라서 원고는 피고에 대해 다수 근로자에 대한 퇴직금제도임이 분명한 피고의 취업규칙에 따른 퇴직금을 청구할 수 있다.
③ 퇴직금 지급에 관하여 누진제를 적용하도록 규정한 국내 직원에 대한 취업규칙과 달리 해외 기능공에 대해서는 개별 근로계약에 의해 단수제를 적용한 경우, 퇴직금 차등제도 금지 규정에 위반된다.[232]

4. 퇴직금 지급방법

근로자의 퇴직금 중간정산 요구가 있는 경우에 시행이 가능하나, 근로자의 요구에 사용자가 반드시 응해야 할 의무가 있는 것은 아니며, 취업규칙이나 단체협약에 퇴직금 중간정산제 실시를 위한 근거를 마련하고 있다 해도 개별 근로자의 별도의 구체적인 요구가 있어야만 유효한 퇴직금 중간정산으로 인정된다.
① 퇴직금 중간정산을 집단적 동의를 받아 시행할 수 있는지[233]

근로자퇴직급여보장 시행령 제3조(퇴직금의 중간정산 사유)
1. 무주택자인 근로자가 본인 명의로 주택을 구입하는 경우
2. 무주택자인 근로자가 주거를 목적으로 「민법」 제303조에 따른 전세금 또는 「주택임대차보호법」 제3조의2에 따른 보증금을 부담하는 경우. 이 경우 근로자가 하나의 사업 또는 사업장에 근로하는 동안 1회로 한정한다.
3. 근로자, 근로자의 배우자 또는 「소득세법」 제50조제1항에 따른 근로자 또는 근로자의 배우자와 생계를 같이하는 부양가족이 질병

---

[231] 대법원 1998.03.27 선고 97다19725 판결.
[232] 대법원 1997.11.28 선고 97다24511 판결
[233] 행정해석: 임금 68200-111 2002.02.20

> medical care for six months or more;
> 4. Where an employee has been declared bankrupt under the Debtor Rehabilitation and Bankruptcy Act within five years from the time of providing the retirement reserve as collateral;
> 5. Where an employee has received a decision for commencement of a rehabilitation proceeding under the Debtor Rehabilitation and Bankruptcy Act within five years from the time of providing the retirement reserve as collateral;
> 6. Where wages are decreasing due to the Wage Peak System according to rules from Paragraph 1 ~ 3 of Article 28 (1) of the Enforcement Decree to the Employment Insurance Act; and
> 7. Where other reasons and conditions prescribed by Ordinance of the Ministry of Employment and Labor, such as natural disasters, etc., are met.

According to Article 34 (3) of the Labor Standards Act, an employer may, upon request by an employee, even before his retirement, pay a severance pay calculated on the basis of consecutive years of employment. In this case, the number of consecutive years of employment for the calculation of a severance pay after such advance payment shall be reckoned anew from the moment of the latest adjustment of balances. The Employee Retirement Benefit Security Act, revised July 26, 2012, strengthened the Retirement Benefit Plan to ensure the retirement benefit is used as income during old age, rather than extra income before retirement. Interim severance payments are now restricted, and one of only seven reasons must exist.

② Even though the company has paid some amount as severance pay in the wages paid every month, it cannot be accepted as payment of severance pay.[234]

The severance pay stipulated in Article 34(1) of the Labor Standards Act occurs on the condition of termination of employment relations, and, in principle, will not occur during the middle of the labor contract. Even if the employer agreed with an employee on payment of a certain amount of money as severance pay inside wages paid every month, this cannot be valid as payment of severance pay stipulated in Article 34(1) of the Labor Standards Act.

---

[234] Supreme Court ruling on Mar. 11, 2005, 2005Do467.

> 또는 부상으로 6개월 이상 요양을 하는 경우
> 4. 퇴직금 중간정산을 신청하는 날부터 역산하여 5년 이내에 근로자가 「채무자 회생 및 파산에 관한 법률」에 따라 파산선고를 받은 경우
> 5. 퇴직금 중간정산을 신청하는 날부터 역산하여 5년 이내에 근로자가 「채무자 회생 및 파산에 관한 법률」에 따라 개인회생절차 개시 결정을 받은 경우
> 6. 「고용보험법 시행령」 제28조제1항제1호부터 제3호까지의 규정에 따른 임금피크제를 실시하여 임금이 줄어드는 경우
> 7. 그 밖에 천재지변 등으로 피해를 입는 등 고용고용노동부 장관이 정하여 고시하는 사유와 요건에 해당하는 경우

근로기준법 제34조 제3항의 규정에 의거 사용자는 근로자의 요구가 있는 경우에는 근로자가 퇴직하기 전에 당해 근로자가 계속 근로한 기간에 대한 퇴직금을 미리 정산하여 지급할 수 있으며, 이 경우 미리 정산하여 지급한 후의 퇴직금 산정을 위한 계속근로연수는 정산시점부터 새로이 기산하도록 정하고 있다. 다만, 2012년 7월 26일 개정된 근로자퇴직급여 보장법은 근로자의 퇴직급여가 생활자금으로 소모되지 않고 노후에 소득 재원으로 사용될 수 있도록 퇴직금 제도를 정비하였으며, 퇴직금 중간정산의 엄격한 제한이다. 즉, 퇴직금을 재직 중에 중간정산 할 수 있는 사유가 7가지로 제한된다.

② 근로관계가 계속되는 동안 매월 지급되는 임금 속에 퇴직금이라는 명목의 금원을 지급하였다고 하여도 퇴직금 지급으로서의 효력은 없다.[234]

근로기준법 제34조 제1항에서 규정한 퇴직금이란 퇴직이라는 근로관계의 종료를 요건으로 하여 비로소 발생하는 것으로 근로계약이 존속하는 동안에는 원칙적으로 퇴직금 지급의무는 발생할 여지가 없는 것이므로 사용자와 근로자들 사이에 매월 지급받는 임금 속에 퇴직금이란 명목으로 일정한 금원을 지급하기로 약정하고 사용자가 이를 지급하였다고 하여도 그것은 근로기준법 제34조 제1항에서 정하는 퇴직금 지급의 효력은 없다.

---

[234] 대법원 2005.3.11 선고 2005도467 판결.

③ A special contract giving up the right to request severance pay or not to launch a civil suit is null and void due to violation of the Labor Standards Act, even if signed by an employee.[235]

Severance pay is the remuneration characteristic of deferred wages to be paid in return for continuous employment to an employee who retires after serving a certain period of time. The concrete right to request severance pay occurs on condition of the fact of termination of continuous employment. If an employee previously signed a special contract giving up the employee's right to request severance pay at the time of retirement or to launch a civil suit, this is null and void due to violation of the Labor Standards Act's compulsory regulation.

II. The Retirement Pension Plan

Before December 2005, there were only two types of retirement payments stipulated in the Labor Standards Act: the Statutory Severance Pay Plan to be paid upon resignation and the Interim Severance Pay Plan which could be paid while the employee was still employed. However, in December 2005, the Employee Retirement Benefit Security Act (hereinafter referred to as the ERBS Act) was enacted and introduced something new: the Retirement Pension Plan, which can take the form of either a Severance Pay System or a Retirement Pension Plan. The Retirement Pension Plan is also further broken down into three types: the Defined Benefit Plan, the Defined Contribution Plan and the Individual Retirement Plan. Under these plans and upon retirement, employees can receive gains made from investment of their pension funds, either as a lump sum or monthly pension from an outside financial agency.

The ERBS Act, revised July 26, 2012, strengthened the Retirement Benefit Plan to ensure the retirement benefit is used as income during old age, rather than extra income before retirement. Interim severance payments are now restricted, and one of only seven reasons must exist.[236] The Individual Retirement Plan has also been

---

[235] Supreme Court ruling on Aug. 23, 2002, 2001Da41568.
[236] Enforcement Decree (Article 3) to the Employee Retirement Pension Security Act (Reasons for Interim Severance Pay)
  1. Where an employee who has not owned a house has purchased a house in their own name;
  2. Where an employee who has not owned a house makes a key money deposit (according to Article 303 of the Civil Act) or a security deposit (according to Article 3-2 of the Housing Lease Protection Act) for the purpose of moving into a residence. In this case the employee can only apply for the retirement pension one time during employment in a company or business;
  3. Where an employee, employee's spouse according to Article 50 (Paragraph 1) of the Income Tax

③ 퇴직금청구권을 포기하거나 민사소송을 제기하지 않겠다는 부제소특약은 근로기준법에 위반되어 무효이다.[235)]

퇴직금은 사용자가 일정기간을 계속하여 근로하고 퇴직하는 근로자에게 그 계속근로에 대한 대가로서 지급하는 후불적 임금의 성질을 띤 금원으로서 구체적인 퇴직금청구권은 계속근로가 끝나는 퇴직이라는 사실을 요건으로 하여 발생되는 것인 바, 최종 퇴직 시 발생하는 퇴직금청구권을 사전에 포기하거나 사전에 그에 대한 민사상 소송을 제기하지 않겠다는 부제소특약을 하는 것은 강행법규인 근로기준법에 위반되어 무효이다.

Ⅱ. 퇴직연금제도

2005년 12월 이전에는 근로기준법 퇴직금제도(근로자가 퇴사할 할 때 일시금으로 받는 법정 퇴직금제도와 근로자가 재직 중에 받을 수 있는 퇴직금 중간정산제도)만 존재하였으나, 2005년 12월 근로자퇴직급여보장법(근퇴법)이 제정되면서 퇴직연금제도가 도입되었다. 현행 퇴직급여제도는 퇴직금제도와 퇴직연금제도로 구성된다. 여기서 퇴직연금제도는 확정급여형(DB) 퇴직연금제도, 확정기여형(DC) 퇴직연금제도, 개인형 퇴직연금제도(IRP)로 3가지 형태로 구성된다. 퇴직연금제도는 회사가 근로자의 재직기간 동안 퇴직급여의 지급에 필요한 재원을 외부 금융기관에 적립하면, 근로자가 퇴직할 때 적립된 재원으로부터 연금 또는 일시금의 퇴직급여를 받아 노후생활에 사용할 수 있도록 하는 제도이다.

2012년 7월 26일 개정된 근퇴법은 근로자의 퇴직급여가 생활자금으로 소모되지 않고 노후에 소득재원으로 사용될 수 있도록 퇴직금 제도를 정비하였으며, 다음의 특징을 갖는다. 첫째, 퇴직금 중간정산의 엄격한 제한이다. 즉, 퇴직금을 재직 중에 중간정산할 수 있는 사유가 7가지로 제한된다.[236)]

---

235) 대법원 2002.8.23 선고 2001다41568 판결.
236) 근로자퇴직급여보장 시행령 제3조(퇴직금의 중간정산 사유)
   1. 무주택자인 근로자가 본인 명의로 주택을 구입하는 경우
   2. 무주택자인 근로자가 주거를 목적으로 「민법」 제303조에 따른 전세금 또는 「주택임대차보호법」 제3조의2에 따른 보증금을 부담하는 경우. 이 경우 근로자가 하나의 사업 또는 사업장에 근로하는

introduced. In cases where retirement pension holders resign before retirement, opening of an IRP is mandatory, and funds are transferred as a lump sum from the previous employer to either the new employer's pension plan, or an IRP account. The accumulated retirement benefit in this IRP account will, by law, be kept and managed until the employee is 55.

1. Differences between the Severance Pay System and the Retirement Pension Plan

The differences between the Retirement Pension Plan and the Severance Pay System are as follows:

① Under the Retirement Pension Plan, the company deposits the retirement contributions with an outside financial agency, and the employee receives a retirement benefit from the financial agency upon resignation. Under the Severance Pay System, the employer pays a pre-determined amount in severance pay upon employee resignation.

② The Defined Benefit Plan is the same as the severance pay system, with the amount calculated in the same way: multiplying the average wage for each of the most recent three months by the years of service. The Defined Contribution Plan requires a deposit of 1/12 of the employee's annual salary every year, with the individual retirement benefit varying according to performance of fund investments.

③ In cases where an employee receives a lump sum from the Retirement Pension Plan, they shall receive it into an IRP. However, under the Severance Pay System, the employee can still receive a lump sum as before, as there is no obligation to transfer to an IRP in the Severance Pay System. However, the employee can open an IRP account and receive payment there if they wishes.

④ The Retirement Pension Plan guarantees the principal funds contributed, as they are managed by an outside agency. Under the Defined Benefit Plan also, the principal deposited outside is guaranteed. However, the Severance Pay System has a weakness in that should the company go bankrupt and the funds become

---

Act, or their dependent family member has received medical care for six months or more;
4. Where an employee has been declared bankrupt under the Debtor Rehabilitation and Bankruptcy Act within five years from the time of providing the retirement reserve as collateral;
5. Where an employee has received a decision for commencement of a rehabilitation proceeding under the Debtor Rehabilitation and Bankruptcy Act within five years from the time of providing the retirement reserve as collateral;
6. Where wages are decreasing due to the Wage Peak System according to rules from Paragraph 1 ~ 3 of Article 28 (1) of the Enforcement Decree to the Employment Insurance Act; and
7. Where other reasons and conditions prescribed by Ordinance of the Ministry of Employment and Labor, such as natural disasters, etc., are met.

둘째, 개인형퇴직연금제도(IRP)를 도입이다. 이 IRP 제도는 퇴직연금제도에 가입한 근로자가 중도 퇴직하는 경우 의무적으로 가입하여야 하며, 이직 또는 조기 퇴직으로 인해 수령한 퇴직 일시금은 반드시 IRP계좌로 이전되며, 이 적립된 퇴직급여는 55세까지 의무적으로 보관, 운용할 수 있도록 한 제도이다.

1. 퇴직금제도와 퇴직연금제도 비교

퇴직금제도와 퇴직연금제도의 차이점을 비교하면 다음과 같다.
① 먼저 퇴직연금제도는 근무기간 중 일정금액의 퇴직급여를 금융기관에 사외 적립하고, 근로자 퇴직시점에 금융기관이 퇴직급여를 지급하는 방식으로 운영한다. 퇴직금제도에서는 근로자가 퇴직할 때 회사가 산정된 금액의 퇴직급여를 직접 지급한다.
② DB제도는 퇴직급여 산정방식이나 지급되는 금액 등이 퇴직금제도와 동일하다. 따라서 퇴직금 제도와 DB제도의 경우 퇴직 전 최근 3개월의 평균임금에 근속연수를 곱한 금액이 지급금액이 된다. 반면, DC제도에서는 연간 임금총액의 12분의 1 이상을 매년 적립하고, 가입자 개개인의 운용 성과에 따라 퇴직급여 수령액이 달라진다.
③ 지급방법은 퇴직연금제도에서는 퇴직 일시금을 지급받을 경우에 반드시 IRP로 수령해야 한다. 그러나 퇴직금제도에서는 퇴직급여의 IRP 강제이전 의무가 없기 때문에 기존방식처럼 일시금으로 퇴직급여를 지급하면 되고, 원하는 근로자는 별도로 IRP를 개설하여 퇴직급여를 수령할 수도 있다.
④ 퇴직연금제도는 사외적립방식이므로 사외적립된 비율만큼 수급권이 보호되며, DB제도 전액 적립 시 지급액 전액에 대하여 수급권이 보호된다. 반면 퇴직금제도의 경우 퇴직급여를 사내에 유보하므로 회사가 도산하면

　　동안 1회로 한정한다.
3. 근로자, 근로자의 배우자 또는 「소득세법」 제50조제1항에 따른 근로자 또는 근로자의 배우자와 생계를 같이하는 부양가족이 질병 또는 부상으로 6개월 이상 요양을 하는 경우
4. 퇴직금 중간정산을 신청하는 날부터 역산하여 5년 이내에 근로자가 「채무자 회생 및 파산에 관한 법률」에 따라 파산선고를 받은 경우
5. 퇴직금 중간정산을 신청하는 날부터 역산하여 5년 이내에 근로자가 「채무자 회생 및 파산에 관한 법률」에 따라 개인회생절차개시 결정을 받은 경우
6. 「고용보험법 시행령」 제28조제1항제1호부터 제3호까지의 규정에 따른 임금피크제를 실시하여 임금이 줄어드는 경우
7. 그 밖에 천재지변 등으로 피해를 입는 등 고용고용노동부 장관이 정하여 고시하는 사유와 요건에 해당하는 경우

unavailable, since they were deposited within the company.

⑤ The Retirement Pension Plan requires regular retirement contributions to an outside agency, which can reduce the company's financial burden as it does not have to pay out large amounts upon resignation, contrary to the severance pay system. As the severance pay should be paid in full as a lump sum upon retirement, the company will have a heavier financial burden.

2. Necessity for and Concept of the Retirement Pension Plan

(1) Necessity for the Retirement Pension Plan

From the employee's perspective, the reasons necessitating the Retirement Pension Plan are as follows: Firstly, it is necessary to supplement the social welfare system. Currently, most people depend on the National Pension only. However, this is not enough for necessities. With three levels of social security (National Pension, Retirement Pension, and Individual Pension), employees will be far better prepared. Secondly, it is necessary to protect the right for employees to secure their retirement benefits. If the company goes bankrupt, the employee will most likely not receive wages of any kind. To ensure benefits do not remain unpaid, companies shall deposit their contributions at an outside financial agency through the Retirement Pension Plan.

From the employer's perspective, the reasons necessitating the Retirement Pension Plan are as follows: Firstly, companies can reduce corporate tax through the Retirement Pension Plan. Only 20% of the retirement benefit reserve each year can be considered business expenses, and each year this percentage will be reduced 5% until 2016, when there will be no tax benefit at all. However, 100% of retirement reserve for the Retirement Pension Plan can be claimed as a tax deduction each year. Secondly, the Defined Benefit Plan aids in reducing company debt, as the retirement pension deposit is deducted from the retirement reserve. The Defined Contribution plan allows the total amount the company has paid into the retirement benefit each fiscal year to be regarded as actual retirement payout, thereby reducing company debt. Thirdly, companies introducing the Retirement Pension Plan can also save from a reduction in wage claim premiums: 50% of the premiums multiplied by the guaranteed rate covered by the Defined Contribution retirement benefit.

(2) Introduction of the Retirement Pension Plan

The employer shall establish pension regulations, obtain the consent of the

근로자가 퇴직급여를 못 받을 가능성이 크다.
⑤ 퇴직연금제도에서는 퇴직급여를 주기적으로 사외에 적립하여 비용 부담을 분산하고 있어 사용자의 재정부담이 경감되나 퇴직금제도에서는 근로자 퇴직 시 일시에 퇴직금을 지급해야 하므로 회사의 재정부담이 가중된다.

2. 퇴직연금제도 필요성 및 도입

(1) 퇴직연금제도 필요성

근로자의 입장에서 퇴직연금이 필요한 이유는 첫째, 사회보장제도의 보충효과를 위해서 필요하다. 현재 노후자금은 국민연금에만 의존하고 있는 경우가 대부분인데, 노후 대비를 국민연금만으로 하기에는 많이 부족하다. 따라서 국민연금, 퇴직연금, 개인연금의 3층 노후보장수단이 필요하다. 둘째, 퇴직금 수급권의 보장 차원에서 필요하다. 기업이 도산할 경우에 근로자는 퇴직금을 받을 수 없다. 이를 해결하기 위해서는 퇴직연금제도를 통해 퇴직급여를 사외 금융기관에 안전하게 예치할 필요가 있다.

사용자 입장에서 퇴직연금이 필요한 이유는 첫째, 법인세 절감 효과를 들 수 있다. 퇴직금제도로 사내적립을 한 경우 2012년을 기준으로 적립금 추계액의 20%만 손비로 인정되며, 매5%씩 감소하여 2016년에는 사내적립금에 대한 손비인정이 없어진다. 그러나 퇴직연금제도는 추계액 범위 내에서 기업 납입금의 100%가 비용으로 인정을 받는다. 둘째, 회사의 부채비율 개선효과가 있다. DB형 제도에 가입하게 되면 퇴직연금예치금을 퇴직급여충당금에서 차감형식으로 표시하여 기업의 부채비율 개선효과가 있고, DC형 제도로 가입했을 경우 당해 회계기간에 회사가 납부한 퇴직연금 부담금 전액을 퇴직급여(비용)로 인식하므로 기업의 퇴직금 부채가 소멸되는 효과가 있다. 셋째, 퇴직연금제도를 도입한 기업에 대해서는 임금채권부담금이 일정부분 경감되어 이를 통한 추가적인 비용절감을 할 수 있다. 경감 금액은 부담금의 50%에 퇴직연금제도로 지급 보장되는 비율을 곱한 금액이다.

(2) 퇴직연금제도 도입

퇴직연금을 도입하기 위해서는 사용자는 근로자 대표의 동의를 얻어 연금

employee representative, and permission from the Ministry of Employment & Labor before introducing the Retirement Pension Plan. Upon employee retirement, the financial agency shall pay out a lump sum or a regular pension from the retirement fund the employer deposited. The retirement pension company (trustee) will be a financial agency such as a bank, insurance company, or securities firm, and perform operational management and asset management. Operational management includes designing of the retirement pension, operational method of the assets, and administration. Asset management includes such tasks as depositing contributions and paying out retirement benefits, maintaining and managing assets, establishing and managing/operating the account.

3. Types of Retirement Pension Plan

(1) The Defined Benefit Retirement Plan (DB)

① Concept: Under the Defined Benefit plan the company deposits 60% or more of the retirement contributions expected for the year to an outside agency, and the financial agency pays 100% of the retirement benefit within its obligation to pay[237]. The Defined Benefit plan is characterized by a prior confirmation of the severance payment. This is calculated in the same way as in the existing Severance Pay System, and is equal to the final month's total wage. Severance pay is calculated by multiplying the average monthly wage (over the final 3 months) before resignation/retirement by the years of service.

② Characteristics: As the amount of retirement benefit is determined beforehand, plans for the retirement years are possible. As the company contributes to and manages the retirement reserve directly, the employee is free of those responsibilities. One disadvantage is that transferring the retirement deposits to another company is difficult. Depositing additional money or withdrawing money early is not allowed by law, but it is possible to borrow the money as a secured loan, for the following purposes: 1. First-time purchase of a house; 2. Medical treatment for 6 months or longer for the employee or their dependents; 3. Decision for commencement of a rehabilitation proceeding; 4. Bankruptcy; or 5. Other reasons and conditions such as natural disasters, etc., prescribed by Ordinance of the Ministry of Employment & Labor. The DB Plan is suitable for companies with job security, low turnover, and who provide high salary increases.

③ Conditions for eligibility: The employee receives retirement pension or lump

---

[237] The Minimum Reserve is the amount equivalent to 60% of the Standard Mandatory Reserve from July 26, 2012 to the end of 2013. After this period, the Minimum Reserve is to increase 10% every two years, becoming 70% of the Standard Mandatory Reserve from 2014 to the end of 2015, then 80% of the Standard Mandatory Reserve from 2016 to the end of 2017, and the rate stipulated by decree of the Minister of Employment & Labor from 2018 on.

규약을 작성하고 고용노동부의 승인을 받아야 한다. 퇴직연금사업자(금융기관)는 근로자 퇴직 시 기업이 적립한 퇴직급여를 퇴직근로자에게 일시금 또는 연금으로 지급한다. 퇴직연금사업자는 은행, 보험, 증권사 등의 금융기관이 있으며 운용관리와 자산관리의 업무를 수행한다. 운용관리 업무는 퇴직연금 제도설계, 자산의 운용방법 제시, 행정적 측면의 제도운영이 있고, 자산관리 업무는 부담금 수령 및 퇴직급여 지급, 자산의 보관 및 관리, 계좌의 설정 및 관리, 운용지시를 이행하는 일이다.

3. 퇴직연금제도 종류

(1) 확정급여(DB) 퇴직연금제도

① 개념: DB제도는 회사가 기준책임준비금의 60%이상을 사외 금융기관에 예치하고[237], 금융기관이 지급의무가 있는 범위의 100%를 지급하는 방식이다. 확정급여형은 근로자가 받을 퇴직금이 기존 퇴직금 제도와 동일하게 최종임금 수준에 따라 퇴직금이 결정된다. 퇴직금은 퇴직 시의 평균임금에 근속연수를 곱하여 산정하며 이 때 퇴직 시의 평균임금은 최종 3개월간의 평균임금이다.

② 특징: DB제도는 퇴직할 때 받을 급여수준이 확정되었기 때문에 안정적인 노후설계가 가능하며, 부담금 납입과 적립금 운영을 기업이 대신하므로 근로자의 부담이 없는 반면 직장 이동에 따른 연금의 이동성이 원활하지 못하다. 또한 추가납입이나 중도인출은 불가하고 법정 사유에 한해 담보대출만 가능하다. 그 법정사유는 무주택자의 주택구입, 본인 또는 부양가족의 6개월 이상 요양, 파산 선고, 개인회생절차 개시, 기타 천재사변 등으로 고용노동부장관이 인정하는 경우이다. 따라서 DB제도는 기업이 1) 안정적이고 이직률이 낮으며, 2) 임금상승률이 높은 경우에 적합한 제도이다.

③ 수급요건: 퇴직 시에 연금 또는 일시금으로 수령한다. 연금수령은 연금

---

[237] 사용자의 최소적립금은 2012년 7월 26일부터 2013년 말까지는 기준책임 준비금의 60%에 해당하는 금액이며, 그 후 매 2년 마다 10%씩 상승한다. 2014년부터 2015년 말까지는 최소적립금은 70%, 2016년부터 2017년 말까지는 기준책임준비금의 80%, 2018년 이후부터는 고용노동부령에서 정하는 비율을 적용한다.

sum allowance upon retirement. The retirement pension is eligible for those who are 55 years old or older and have subscribed to it for 10 years or more. In this case, the beneficiary period shall be 5 years or longer. The lump sum payment is paid to those who were not eligible for pension and who want to receive it as a lump sum payment. This lump sum payment means that the retirement benefit is transferred to the IRP account.

(2) The Defined Contribution Retirement Plan (DC)

① Concept: The level of contribution the employer and employee make is predetermined by pension law, with the employee's final retirement benefit determined by the company's contributions and the employee's investment gains. Investment outcomes are up to the employee and the final payment depends on the performance of his or her investments. The employer deposits 1/12 of the employee's annual salary every year. A retirement payment is deposited every month, like an interim severance payment. Final payout is determined by performance of the employee's investments. The employee's retirement benefit is equal to company contributions and investment returns.

② Characteristics: Employees can put additional money into this fund. As the fund is separately managed, it is easy to move it to another company, plus, payout can be higher than the Defined Benefit plan if the investment returns are good. However, management of the retirement funds is the responsibility of each employee, who is responsible for choosing appropriate investments. The companies that are more suited to the Defined Contribution plan are 1) Companies with lower salary increases and 2) Companies implementing an annual salary system.

③ Conditions for eligibility: The employer deposits 1/12 of the employee's annual salary every year. The employee manages the retirement fund, and will receive it as a monthly pension or lump sum payment upon retirement. Those who are 55 years old or older and have subscribed to it for 10 years or more are eligible. In this case, the beneficiary period shall be 5 years or longer. A lump sum is paid to those ineligible for the pension or who want to receive it as a lump sum payment. This lump sum payment means that the retirement benefit is transferred to the IRP account.

The Defined Contribution Plan holder can legally withdraw the deposit or borrow the money as a secured loan during employment for the following reasons: 1) First-time purchase of a house; 2) Medical treatment for 6 months or longer for the employee or their dependents; 3) Decision for commencement of a rehabilitation proceeding; 4) Bankruptcy; or 5) Other reasons and conditions such as natural

가입자가 55세 이상으로서 가입기간이 10년 이상, 이 경우 연금의 지급기간은 5년 이상이어야 한다. 일시금은 연금수급자격을 갖추지 못했거나 일시금 수령을 원하는 자에게 지급하며, 일시금은 IRP계좌로의 전환을 의미한다.

(2) 확정기여(DC) 퇴직연금제도

① 개념: DC제도는 기업의 퇴직급여 부담금 수준을 노사가 사전에 연금규약으로 확정하고 부담금을 납부하는 제도로 근로자의 최종 퇴직급여 수령액은 기업이 부담한 금액과 근로자 개인의 운용수익에 따라 결정된다. 사용자는 가입자의 연간임금총액의 12분의 1에 해당하는 금액을 퇴직급여의 부담금으로 납부하여야 한다. 매년 발생하는 퇴직급여를 개인별로 적립하는 점에서 매년 중간정산을 하는 것과 유사하다. 근로자 개인의 운용성과에 따라 향후 받을 퇴직급여 수령액이 달라질 수 있으며, 운용결과에 대한 책임은 근로자가 진다. 근로자가 받을 퇴직급여는 기업부담금과 운용수익을 합한 금액이다.

② 특징: DC 제도는 근로자 추가부담금 납입이 가능하며, 적립금이 개인별로 관리되므로 직장이동시 적립금의 이동성이 편리하며, 운용수익률 예상치가 급여상승률 보다 높을 경우 확정급여형보다 유리하다. 그러나, 적립금 운용을 위한 근로자 각자의 노력이 요구되고, 금융상품 선택과 운용에 따른 위험부담이 있다. DC제도가 적합한 기업은 1) 임금인상률이 낮은 기업, 2) 연봉제를 실시하는 기업 등이다.

③ 수급요건: 사용자가 매년 근로자 연간 임금총액의 1/12 이상을 근로자 계좌에 적립하면, 근로자가 직접 적립금을 운용하다가 퇴직 시 연금 또는 일시금의 형태로 받을 수 있다. 연금수령은 연금가입자가 55세 이상으로서 가입기간이 10년 이상, 이 경우 연금의 지급기간은 5년 이상이어야 한다. 일시금은 연금수급자격을 갖추지 못했거나 일시금 수령을 원하는 자에게 지급하며, 일시금은 IRP계좌로의 전환을 의미한다.

DC 제도에 있어 법정 사유에 한하여 적립금 담보대출 또는 중도인출이 가능하다. 그 법정사유는 무주택자의 주택구입, 본인 또는 부양가족의 6개월 이상 요양, 파산 선고, 개인회생절차 개시, 기타 천재사변 등으로

disasters, etc., prescribed by Ordinance of the Ministry of Employment and Labor.

(3) The Individual Retirement Plan (IRP)

① Concept: The Individual Retirement Plan can take the form of a Company IRP or an Individual IRP. The Company IRP is a retirement pension plan as described in the Employee Retirement Benefit Security Act and is acceptable as a retirement benefit scheme for companies that employ 9 or fewer employees. It operates in basically the same way as the Defined Contribution plan, but companies do not have to create the pension rules. In cases where the company later employs 10 or more employees, the Defined Contribution plan shall be adopted. The Individual IRP was designed for the employee to be able to manage his or her own retirement benefit until retirement or until receiving it if resignation occurs earlier.

② Characteristics/ Conditions for eligibility: Under the Retirement Pension Plan, when the employee resigns or retires, the retirement benefit shall be transferred to an IRP. Upon reaching the age of 55, the employee can receive a regular retirement pension or lump sum payment. The IRP reserve cannot be withdrawn earlier than the required age except for the legal reasons described in Article 2 of the Enforcement Decree of the ERBS Act: Reasons for Offering Right to Receive Benefits as Collateral. However, The Retirement Pension Plan (DB, DC, Company IRP) shall be transferred to the IRP except in the following situations: 1) The subscriber receives payment after age 55 upon retirement; 2) The subscriber returns the borrowed money with wage collateral; 3) The retirement fund is equal to 1.5 million won or less, as stipulated by the Minister of Employment & Labor.

4. Comments

Although the Retirement Pension plans were introduced in December 2005, they have not yet been widely used due to the existing severance pay system. However, recent revisions to related law restricts interim severance payment and provides many incentives to introduce the Retirement Pension plans, incentives which are expected to gradually increase use of those plans. Retirement benefits have often been used as an additional bonus to normal wages. However, they should be used as retirement benefits to supplement old-age security. Accordingly, these Retirement Pension plans should be encouraged further to help people have the funds they will need, through strategic government support. Employees also need to recognize that

고용노동부장관이 인정하는 경우이다.

(3) 개인형퇴직연금제도 (IRP)

① 개념: 개인형 퇴직연금제도는 기업형 IRP제도와 퇴직 후의 개인형 IRP 제도로 구분할 수 있다. 기업 IRP는 상시 근로자 10인 미만의 사업장인 경우 퇴직급여 제도로 인정된다. 기본적 운용구조는 DC제도와 동일하나, 퇴직연금규약 작성의무가 없다. 향후 근로자가 10인 이상이 될 경우 DC로 전환해야 한다. 개인형 IRP는 근로자가 이직 또는 조기 퇴직 시 수령한 퇴직급여를 은퇴할 때까지 보관, 운용할 수 있도록 한 제도이다.

② 특징/수급요건: 퇴직연금제도에서 퇴직 또는 이직하는 경우에는 퇴직급여를 반드시 개인형 IRP로 이전해야 한다. 이 경우, IRP 적립금은 55세 이후에 연금으로 수령하거나 일시금으로 수령할 수 있다. IRP의 적립금은 자유로이 인출할 수 없으며, 인출을 원하는 경우에는 법정사유(시행령 2조: 담보대출사유)에 해당되어야 한다. 다만, 퇴직연금제도(DB, DC, 기업IRP)에서 퇴직 시 개인 IRP로 강제이전이 제외되는 경우는 다음과 같다.(시행령 9조) 1) 가입자가 55세 이후에 퇴직하여 급여를 받는 경우; 2) 가입자가 퇴직급여를 담보로 대출받은 금액 등을 상환하기 위한 경우; 3) 퇴직급여액이 고용노동부장관이 정하는 금액(150만 원) 이하인 경우이다.

4. 시사점

2005년 12월 이후 도입된 퇴직연금제도가 기존의 퇴직금제도로 인해서 활성화 되지 못하였다. 그러나 최근 근로자퇴직급여보장법 개정으로 인해, 퇴직금의 중간정산을 엄격히 제한하고, 또한 퇴직연금제도에 많은 혜택을 부여하고 있어 점차 활성화될 것이라 예상된다. 퇴직급여가 퇴직을 위해서 사용되어야 함에도 불구하고 급여에 덧붙여진 보너스 형태로 사용된 부분이 많았다. 그러나 퇴직금은 그 용어와 같이 근로자의 퇴직을 위해서 노후보장용으로 사용되는 것이 원칙이라 할 수 있다. 따라서 앞으로 퇴직연금제도를 활성화하여 노후자금을 준비할 수 있는 자금 확보 수단으로 사용되어야 할 것이다. 이를 위해 퇴직연금제도에 대한 일관적인 정책적 지원과 기업과

the retirement benefit is not money to be spent on pre-retirement costs, but is to be saved as a matter of course to prepare for the golden years.

III. Severance Settlement-related Taxation Issues

1. Introduction

Unfair dismissals are often resolved through a severance settlement between the company and the dismissed worker, but new conflicts often arise over taxation issues. I recently handled a similar situation. On February 15, 2022, a case for unfair dismissal was filed on behalf of two dismissed employees. In this case, an oral proposal was developed between the company and the dismissed employees as an out-of-court settlement which included a severance payment equivalent to 8 months of salary. In response to this, the company's attorney wrote and sent an agreement which stated that 30% in earned income tax for wages would be deducted from the severance settlement. The employees objected to the company's tax decision and requested that the severance agreement be tax-free as consolation pay for termination of employment. The company asked its certified public accountant about the taxation method for a severance settlement. Accordingly, the certified public accountant contacted the National Tax Service about how to handle taxation on a severance settlement that is relief for unfair dismissal. The National Tax Service responded that if the amount was paid as a condition for withdrawing the lawsuit, it should be regarded as reward money, which would be taxed according to other income rules, which would mean it would be taxed at 22%. In response, the dismissed employees argued that the company treated it as other income because they wanted to avoid any sort of legal risk despite the fact that it could be non-taxable if the company handled it as compensation for forced termination, and negotiations between the two sides broke down. The company and employees attended a hearing on June 3, 2022 for the Labor Commission's decision. Judges at the Labor Commission understood that both parties, labor and management, had an intention to reach an agreement on this dismissal case, but that they could not reach one due to taxation issues. The judges did not render a decision on the hearing day and gave both parties an additional week to come to an agreement. During this period, the company made a final proposal that included 8.5 months' salary as compensation and applied for it to be taxed as retirement income. The employees accepted this proposal and an agreement was reached.[238]

근로자들의 퇴직금이 생활자금이 아닌 퇴직연금은 노후보장을 위한 저축이라는 인식의 전환이 필요하다고 하겠다.

Ⅲ. 퇴직합의금의 과세문제

1. 문제의 소재

부당해고사건에서 회사와 해고된 근로자 사이에 퇴직합의금을 통해 해고사건이 해결되는 경우가 많이 있지만, 이에 대한 과세 문제로 새로운 갈등이 발생하여 다투는 경우도 종종 본다. 최근 유사한 사건을 경험하였다. 지난 2022년 2월 15일 해고된 근로자 2명을 대리하여 부당해고구제신청 사건을 진행하였는데 이 사건은 회사와 해고된 근로자가 8개월의 퇴직합의금으로 퇴직사건을 종결하자는 구두합의가 이루어졌다. 이에 대해 회사측 대리인이 합의서를 작성해서 보내왔는데, 8개월분의 임금에 대해 30%의 근로소득세를 공제한다는 내용이었다. 이에 대해 근로자는 회사의 과세처리방식에 대해 이의를 제기하였고, 퇴직합의금을 퇴직위로금으로 하는 비과세 처리를 해줄 것을 요청하였다. 회사는 자문 공인회계사에게 퇴직합의금에 대한 과세방법을 문의하였다. 이에 공인회계사는 국세청에 '부당해고 구제신청 사건 종결합의금 과세방법'에 대해 질의를 하였고 국세청은 소송을 취하하는 조건으로 지급한 금액이라면 기타소득 사례금으로 보아야 한다 라는 답변을 주었다. 기타소득으로 처리할 경우 22% 과세처리가 된다. 이에 대해 해고근로자들은 회사가 퇴직위로금으로 처리할 경우 비과세로 처리할 수 있음에도 불구하고 회사의 체면을 위해서 기타소득으로 과세처리 한다고 주장하면서, 양측의 합의는 결렬되었다. 회사와 근로자는 노동위원회의 심판결정을 위해 2022년 6월 3일 심판회의에 참석하였다. 노동위원회의 공익위원들은 본 해고사건에 대해 노사간 합의 의사가 있었지만, 세금 때문에 합의를 못하고 있다고 판단하여 당일 판정을 하지 않고 이들의 합의를 위해 1주일동안 시간을 주었다. 이 기간에 회사는 최종적으로 8.5개월의 퇴직합의금을 퇴직소득으로 처리하겠다는 최종제안을 하였고,

Chapter 5 Retirement Benefit Plan

Here, I would like to examine the taxation methods for earned income, retirement income, other income, and when income related to a severance settlement is untaxable, and then look at related precedents to confirm which taxation method should apply.

2. Types of Taxation for Severance Settlements (Earned Income, Retirement Income, Other Income, Non-taxable)

(1) Earned income

Earned income refers to salary, money, remuneration, wages, bonuses, allowances, and payments of a similar nature received for providing work (Article 20, Paragraph 1, Item 1 of the Income Tax Act). Unlike business income, earned income is generally generated by those who provide work and receive payment in a subordinate position to others.[239] Regardless of the name, anything with a similar nature is taxed as earned income. The scope of earned income includes not only general wages, but also all income received by workers from employers, except for tax-free items and retirement income on the premise of retirement (Article 38 of the Enforcement Decree to the Income Tax Act).

> The tax base, excluding personal exceptions and various income deductions from wage and salary income, is applied as: ▲ 6% for up to KRW 12 million ▲ 15% for more than KRW 12 million and up to KRW 46 million ▲ 24% for more than KRW 46 million and up to KRW 88 million ▲ 35% for more than KRW 88 million and up to KRW 150 million ▲ 38% for more than KRW 150 million and up to KRW 300 million ▲ 40% for more than KRW 300 million and up to KRW 500 million ▲ 42% for more than KRW 500 million and up to KRW 1 billion won ▲ 45% for more than KRW 1 billion.[240]

For example, if the severance settlement is KRW 120 million, the total amount of tax due would be KRW 52,153,200, with KRW 47,412,000 being earned income tax and KRW 4,741,200 being 10% local income tax. The total tax bill comes to 43.4% of the total amount received, reducing the actual amount received to KRW 67,846,800.[241]

---

[238] Seoul Labor Commission decision on June 10, 2022, 2022buhae631.
[239] Lee, Changhee et al., 「Tax Law」, KNOU Press, 2017, p. 162.
[240] The Chosun Ilbo, Employee income tax has increased by 39% since the Moon Jae-in administration took office. Feb. 13, 2022.

근로자들이 이 조건을 수용하면서 원만히 합의가 이루어질 수 있었다.[238]

다음에서는 퇴직합의와 관련된 근로소득, 퇴직소득, 기타소득, 비과세의 과세방법에 대해 살펴보고 어떤 세율을 적용해야 하는지에 대한 대해 관련 판례를 통해 확인하고자 한다.

2. 퇴직합의금에 대한 과세처리 유형(근로소득, 퇴직소득, 기타소득, 비과세)

(1) 근로소득

근로소득세는 근로를 제공함으로써 받는 봉급, 급료, 보수, 임금, 상여, 수당 및 이와 유사한 성질의 급여를 말한다 (소득세법 제20조, 제1항 제1호). 근로소득은 사업소득과는 달리 일반적으로 타인에 대하여 종속적 지위에 서서 근로를 제공하고 그 대가를 받는 사람에게 발생한다.[239] 그리고 명칭과 상관없이 무엇이든 '유사한 성질'을 가진 것은 모두 근로소득으로 과세한다. 근로소득의 범위는 일반적인 급여 뿐만 아니라 근로자가 사용자로부터 받는 비과세 항목과 퇴직을 전제로 받는 퇴직소득을 제외하고는 모두 근로소득에 해당된다 (소득세법 시행령 제38조).

> 근로소득금액에서 인적공제와 각종 소득공제를 제외한 과세표준은 ▲1200만 원 이하는 6% ▲1200만 원 초과 - 4600만 원 이하는 15% ▲4600만 원 초과 - 8800만 원 이하는 24% ▲8800만 원 초과 - 1억5000만 원 이하는 35% ▲1억5000만 원 초과 - 3억원 이하는 38% ▲3억원 초과 - 5억원 이하는 40% ▲5억원 초과 - 10억원 이하는 42% ▲10억원 초과는 45%의 기본세율이 각각 적용된다.[240]

예를 들어, 퇴직합의금이 120,000,000원인 경우, 근로소득세 47,412,000원과 지방소득세 10%인 4,741,200원으로 납부세액은 총 52,153,200원이 된다. 이는 총 수령액의 43.4%가 과세되는 것이며 실수령액은 67,846,800원이 된다.[241]

---

[238] 서울지방노동위원회 결정, 2022.6.10. 서울2022부해631.
[239] 이창희 외 4인, 「세법」, KNOU Press, 2017, 162면.
[240] 조선일보, 직장인 근로소득세, 문재인정부 출범 후 39% 늘었다. 2022.2.13. 인터넷 근로소득세 검색

Chapter 5 Retirement Benefit Plan

(2) Retirement income

Retirement income refers to income paid by an employer to a worker due to that worker's retirement (Article 22, Paragraph 1, Item 2 of the Income Tax Act). This includes severance pay, honorary retirement pay and severance benefits as a result of corporate restructuring.[242]

Retirement income enjoys significant reductions in taxes owed as a way of protecting retirees' ability to provide for themselves in their old age. Retirement income tax varies depending on the number of years of service, but comes to a maximum of 24%. However, the retirement income deduction applies to the total amount of severance pay and retirement pay already paid, which becomes subject to taxation.

		Retirement income				(Number: KRW)	
	Severance settlement	KRW 50 million	Deduction(plus 10% resident tax)	KRW 150 million	Deduction(plus 10% resident tax)	KRW 300 million	Deduction(plus 10% resident tax)
Years	5 years	2,810,000	6.2%	23,320,000	17%	65,170,000	24%
	10 years	1,610,000	3.5%	12,740,000	9%	46,370,000	17%
	20 years	650,000	1.4%	6,420,000	5%	24,900,000	9%
	30 years	160,000	0.4%	4,030,000	3%	15,190,000	6%

For example, if the retirement allowance for an employee with five years of service is KRW 120 million, the actual tax on that retirement income would be KRW 12,342,500 plus 10% local income tax of KRW 1,234,750, for a total tax bill of KRW 13,576,750. This means that 11.3% of the total amount is deducted as Retirement Income tax, and so the actual amount to be paid is 106,423,250 won.[243]

(3) Other Income

Other income refers to income other than interest income, dividend income, business income, earned income, pension income, retirement income and capital gains (Article 21, Paragraph 1 of the Income Tax Act). If the employer pays the severance settlement in good faith to end the employment relationship early, it is regarded as reward money belonging to other income, and means a 22% tax bill. However, if the amount is paid as compensation for emotional or status damage, it is not taxed.[244]

---

[241] Refer to the KangNam Labor Law Firm app: Automatic calculation of Retirement Income tax: https://k-labor.co.kr/main/auto4.html
[242] Lee, Changhee et al., 「Tax Law」, KNOU Press, 2017, p. 168.
[243] Refer to the KangNam Labor Law Firm app: Automatic calculation of Retirement Income tax: https://k-labor.co.kr/main/auto4.html
[244] National Tax Service Administrative Guidelines, Income, Income Tax Division-1126, Nov. 8, 2010.

(2) 퇴직소득

퇴직소득은 사용자가 근로자에게 퇴직을 원인으로 하여 지급하는 소득을 말한다 (소득세법 제22조 제1항 제2호). 퇴직금 뿐만 아니라 회사의 구조조정에 따라 실시하는 명예퇴직이나 퇴직위로금도 퇴직소득으로 본다.[242]

퇴직소득은 근로자의 노후보장이나 퇴직후의 생활보장 차원에서 세액 계산에서 상당한 공제혜택을 제공하기 때문에 납부액이 근로소득에 비해 과세율이 훨씬 적다. 퇴직소득세는 근속연수에 따라 차이가 있으나 최대 24%이내에서 적용된다. 다만, 퇴직소득 공제는 퇴직합의금과 기 지급된 퇴직금을 합한 총 금액이 과세의 대상이 된다.

퇴 직 급 여 (숫자: 원)							
	퇴직합의금	5천만원	공제율(주민세 10% 포함)	1억 5천만원	공제율(주민세 10% 포함)	3억원	공제율(주민세 10% 포함)
계속 근로 기간	5년	2,810,000	6.2%	23,320,000	17%	65,170,000	24%
	10년	1,610,000	3.5%	12,740,000	9%	46,370,000	17%
	20년	650,000	1.4%	6,420,000	5%	24,900,000	9%
	30년	160,000	0.4%	4,030,000	3%	15,190,000	6%

예를 들어, 근속년수가 5년인 근로자의 퇴직위로금이 120,000,000원인 경우, 퇴직소득세는 실제 세금 12,342,500원과 지방소득세 10%인 1,234,750원으로 총 13,576,750원이 된다. 이는 총 수령액의 11.3%가 퇴직소득으로 공제되는 것이며, 실수령액은 106,423,250원이 된다.[243]

(3) 기타소득

기타소득은 이자소득, 배당소득, 사업소득, 근로소득, 연금소득, 퇴직소득 및 양도소득 외의 소득을 말한다 (소득세법 제21조 제1항). 퇴직합의금에 대해 사용자가 퇴직관계를 조기에 끝내기 위해서 선의로 지급하는 경우에는 기타소득에 속하는 사례금으로 간주하여 기타소득세 22%를 징수한다. 그러나 정신적 또는 신분상의 명예훼손 등에 대한 보상으로 지급하는 금액이면 과세 대상에서 제외된다.[244]

---

241) 강남노무법인 앱: 임금명세서 자동계산 https://k-labor.co.kr/main/auto0_view.html
242) 이창희 외 4인, 「세법」, KNOU Press, 2017, 168면.
243) 강남노무법인 앱, 퇴직소득세 자동계산: https://k-labor.co.kr/main/auto4.html
244) 국세청 행정해석, 소득, 소득세과-1126, 2010.11.8.

For example, if the retirement settlement amount is KRW 120 million, KRW 26,400,000, or 22%, is deducted as tax on other income, with the actual amount received totaling KRW 93,600,000.

(4) Non-taxable Income

Compensation received due to a breach or cancellation of a contract is considered other income (Article 21, Paragraph 1, Item 10 of the Income Tax Act). However, in relation to a severance settlement, the amount received as compensation for damages or consolation money for damage to the freedom or honor of another person or inflicting mental pain, etc., is not taxable.[245]

3. Major Cases on Taxation of Severance Settlements

One example of a case of unfair dismissal recognized the severance settlement as non-taxable, while another decided a 22% tax rate applied to a severance settlement as other income.

Judicial guidelines for the relevant cases:

> (1) If a settlement has been reached in a lawsuit, stating that the employer pays a certain amount to the worker, and that the worker gives up the rest of the claim during litigation, the amount paid should be viewed as dispute settlement money agreed to instead of giving up his/her claims. Even if the settlement amount was calculated by the employee's wages, it cannot be regarded as wages or severance pay.[246]
>
> (2) The reward money stipulated as other income in Article 21 (1) 17 of the Income Tax Act means money and goods paid as a courtesy in relation to handling office work or providing services, etc. The decision must be made after comprehensively considering the motive and purpose for seeking that money, the relationship with the other party, and the amount.[247]

---

[245] Song, Gae-dong, Damage Compensation and Tax Law, Tax Law Research, Nov. 2004, p. 82.
[246] Supreme Court ruling on Mar. 31, 2022, 2018da237237.
[247] Supreme Court ruling on Sep. 13, 2013, 2010du27288; Supreme Court ruling on Feb. 9, 2017, 2016du55247.

예를 들어 퇴직합의금이 120,000,000원인 경우, 기타소득세 22%인 22,400,000원이 공제되고 실수령액은 93,600,000원이 된다.

(4) 비과세

계약의 위약 또는 해약으로 인하여 받는 위약금과 배상금에는 기타소득을 적용한다 (소득세법 제21조 제1항 제10호). 그러나 퇴직합의금과 관련하여 이것이 타인의 신체의 자유 또는 명예를 해하거나 기타 정신상의 고통 등을 가한 것에 대한 손해배상 또는 위자료로 받는 금액은 과세 대상의 소득에 해당되지 아니한다.[245]

3. 퇴직합의금의 과세문제에 대한 주요 판례

부당해고를 다투는 사건에 있어 한 판례는 퇴직합의금을 비과세로 인정하였고, 다른 판례는 퇴직합의금을 사례비로 인정하여 기타소득 22%를 공제하였다. 이에 관련하여 판례와 그 판단기준은 어디에 있었는지 확인해보고자 한다.

관련한 판례의 논리는 다음과 같다.

> (1) 해고무효확인 소송의 계속 중 사용자가 근로자에게 일정 금액을 지급하되 근로자는 그 나머지 청구를 포기하기로 하는 내용의 소송상 화해가 이루어졌다면 이러한 화해금의 성질은 근로자가 해고무효확인 청구를 포기하는 대신 받기로 한 분쟁해결금으로 보아야 한다. 비록 그 화해금액을 산정함에 있어 근로자의 임금 등을 기초로 삼았다 하더라도 이를 임금 또는 퇴직금 등으로 볼 수는 없다.[246]
>
> (2) 소득세법 제21조제1항 제17호가 기타소득의 하나로 규정한 '사례금'은 사무처리 또는 역무의 제공 등과 관련하여 사례의 뜻으로 지급되는 금품을 의미하고, 여기에 해당하는지는 금품 수수의 동기·목적, 상대방과의 관계, 금액 등을 종합적으로 고려하여 판단하여야 한다.[247]

---

[245] 송개동, 손해배상과 세법, 조세법연구, 2004.11. 82면.
[246] 대법원 2022. 3. 31. 선고 2018다237237 판결.

Chapter 5 Retirement Benefit Plan

A. A case in which severance settlement was recognized as non-taxable[248]

(1) Facts

In December 2015, Director A, who was in charge of public relations for Qualcomm Korea, was fired for disclosing the contents of the Fair Trade Commission investigation into the company to the media without the company's prior approval. Accordingly, in March 2016, Director A filed a lawsuit against the company, claiming the dismissal was invalid. The court recommended that the company reconcile with Director A and pay an additional KRW 500 million to Director A. The company and Director A did not object to this, so reconciliation was finalized in October 2016. At the time of his dismissal, Director A was paid over KRW 200 million a year, and he had about 13 years left until retirement.

The company applied a tax rate of 22% to the reward money as other income without necessary expenses under the Income Tax Act. Of the KRW 500 million payment, KRW 110 million was withheld and KRW 390 million paid to Director A. Accordingly, Director A applied for a debt collection order to the court, saying that the collection of income tax and local income tax was unreasonable because the settlement amount was considered non-taxable income. The court accepted his argument.

(2) Understanding the judgment and related criteria

1) Reward money, defined as other income, means money and/or valuables paid as a courtesy in connection with handling office work or providing services (Article 21 (1) 17 of the Income Tax Act). Whether this falls under other income should be determined after comprehensively considering the motive and purpose for giving and receiving money or valuables, the relationship between the parties, and the amount of money.[249] In addition, even if the money and valuables seem to be paid out as administrative processing, etc., if they contain a nature that cannot be regarded as reward money in reality, none will be regarded as reward money.[250]

2) This judgment maintained the decision of the High Court during the original trial. The payment of reconciliation money to the plaintiff is only in accordance with the binding force of the decision to recommend reconciliation in this case, and it is difficult to see that the plaintiff should be made to express Thank you

---

[248] Supreme Court ruling on Mar. 31, 2022, 2018da237237.
[249] Supreme Court ruling on Sep. 13, 2013, 2010du27288. Supreme Court ruling on Feb. 9, 2017, 2016du55247.
[250] Supreme Court ruling on Jan. 15, 2015, 2013du3818.

A. 퇴직합의금을 비과세로 인정한 판례[248]

(1) 사실관계

한국퀄컴에서 2015년 12월 대관업무 담당 이사 A는 회사에 대한 공정거래위원회 조사 내용을 회사의 사전 승인없이 언론에 공개한 것을 이유로 해고되었다. 이에 A는 2016년 3월에 회사를 상대로 해고무효확인소송을 제기하였다. 법원은 회사에 화해금 5억원을 A에게 지급하라는 화해권고결정을 내렸고, 이에 대해 회사와 A가 이의를 제기하지 않아 화해권고가 2016년 10월 확정됐다. 해고 당시 A는 연2억원 이상의 급여를 지급받고 있었으며, 정년까지 13년 정도의 기간이 남은 상황이었다.

회사는 화해금이 소득세법 상 '필요경비 없는 기타소득'에 해당된다고 보아 22%의 세율을 적용하였다. 5억원 중 1.1억원을 원천징수 하고 3억 9000만 원만 A에게 지급하였다. 이에 A는 화해금은 비과세소득에 해당되므로 소득세와 지방소득세 징수는 부당하다고 법원에 채권 추심명령을 신청하였고, 법원은 이를 받아들였다.

(2) 판결내용과 그 판단기준 이해

1) 기타소득의 하나로 규정한 '사례금'은 사무처리 또는 역무의 제공 등과 관련하여 사례의 뜻으로 지급되는 금품을 의미한다 (소득세법 제21조제1항 제17호). 여기에 해당하는지는 금품 수수의 동기⋅목적, 상대방과의 관계, 금액 등을 종합적으로 고려하여 판단하여야 한다.[249] 또한 그 금품이 외견상 사무처리 등에 대한 사례의 뜻으로 지급되는 것처럼 보일지라도 그 중 실질적으로 사례금으로 볼 수 없는 성질을 갖는 것이 포함되어 있다면 그 전부를 '사례금'으로 볼 수 없다.[250]

2) 이 판결은 원심인 고등법원에의 판결을 그대로 유지하였다. 원고의 화해금의 지급은 이 사건 화해권고결정의 구속력에 따른 것일 뿐, 원고가 피고에 대하여 '분쟁의 조기 해결에 대한 고마운 뜻'을 표시하기 위하여 이루어진

---

247) 대법원 2013. 9. 13. 선고 2010두27288판결, 대법원 2017. 2. 9. 선고 2016두55247.
248) 대법원 2022. 3. 31. 선고 2018다237237 판결.
249) 대법원 2013. 9. 13. 선고 2010두27288판결, 대법원 2017. 2. 9. 선고 2016두55247.
250) 대법원 2015. 1. 15. 선고 2013두3818 판결 참조

for early resolution of this dispute to the defendant. The lawsuit was filed on March 7, 2016, and the decision to recommend reconciliation was made after the closing of pleadings and was finalized on October 22, 2016, so it is difficult to say that the dispute between the plaintiff and the defendant was resolved early.[251]

3) Therefore, the issue is whether or not the legal nature of this severance settlement is as reward money equivalent to other income. It may be other income if the employee agrees to a severance agreement to end the lawsuit, and the employer pays in return for this. However, in the process of the plaintiff arguing that his dismissal was unfair, the settlement money following the court's recommendation for mediation cannot be considered other income because it cannot be said to be an expression of appreciation by either party. Therefore, this severance settlement is tax-exempt as it is not earned income, retirement income, or other income.

B. A case in which severance settlement was recognized as reward money and other income[252]

(1) Facts

1) The worker was hired by STX Engine Co., Ltd. in Changwon on May 10, 2004, and was fired on February 28, 2014. The worker applied for remedy against unfair dismissal with the Labor Commission, but was rejected on April 28, 2014. The employee then appealed to the National Labor Commission, where a mediation by the judgment committee resulted in reconciliation between the worker and employer. The worker confirms that the employment relationship with the company has been effectively terminated as of February 28, 2014, and the company shall pay the worker KRW 25,302,000 (before tax), which is 6 months' salary, as a dispute settlement by August 22, 2014. The parties agree not to raise any civil, criminal or administrative claims in the future in relation to this case, and to keep the details of this settlement confidential and never to disclose it to outside parties.

2) On August 22, 2014, the company regarded the settlement money of KRW 25,302,000 as reward money under other income, and withheld 20% for income tax (KRW 5,060,400) and 2% for local income tax (KRW 506,040), for a total tax withholding of KRW 5,566,440. The balance of KRW 19,735,560 was paid

---
[251] Original ruling: Seoul High Court ruling on May 10, 2018, 2017na 2073137.
[252] Supreme Court ruling on July 20, 2018, 2016da17729.

것이라고 보기는 어렵다 (이 사건 해고무효확인소송은 2016년 3월 7일에 제기되었는데, 이 사건 화해권고결정은 그 변론종결 이후에 이루어져 2016년 10월 22일에 확정되었으므로, 원고와 피고의 분쟁이 조기에 해결되었다고 보기도 어렵다).[251]

3) 따라서 본 퇴직 합의금의 법적 성질이 기타소득에 해당되는 사례금인지의 여부가 쟁점이 된다. 사례금은 근로자가 소송을 끝내기 위해 퇴직 합의서에 동의하였고, 이에 대해 사용자가 그 답례로 지급하는 경우에는 사례금으로 기타소득이 될 수 있다. 그러나 부당해고 여부를 다투는 과정에서 법원의 화해권고에 따른 분쟁해결 화해금은 어느 일방의 감사의 표시라고 할 수 없기 때문에 기타소득이 될 수 없다. 그러면 퇴직합의금은 근로소득, 퇴직소득, 기타소득도 아니므로 비과세의 대상이 된다.

B. 퇴직합의금을 기타소득의 사례금으로 인정한 판례[252]

(1) 사실관계

1) 근로자는 창원에 있는 STX엔진 주식회사에 2004년 5월 10일 입사해서 근무하던 중 2014년 2월 28일날 해고 되었다. 근로자는 노동위원회에서 부당해고 구제신청을 하였으며, 노동위원회는 2014년 4월 28일 부당해고 구제신청을 기각하였다. 이에 근로자는 중앙노동위원회에 재심을 신청하여 다투는 중에 위원회의 중재로 근로자와 사용자 사이에 화해가 이루어졌다. 그 화해 내용은 다음과 같다. 근로자는 2014년 2월 28일자로 회사와의 고용관계가 유효하게 종료되었음을 확인하고, 회사는 근로자에게 2014년 8월 22일까지 이 사건 분쟁조정금으로 월 급여 기준 6개월분인 25,302,000원(세전 금액)을 지급한다. 양 당사자는 이 사건과 관련하여 향후 일체의 민형사 및 행정상 이의를 제기하지 아니하고, 화해내용을 기밀로 하고 외부에 절대 발설하지 않기로 한다.

2) 회사는 2014년 8월 22일에 이 사건의 화해금 25,302,000원을 기타소득 중 사례금으로 보고 위 금원에 대하여 소득세(20%) 5,060,400원, 지방소득세

---
[251] 해당 항소심 판결: 서울고등법원 2018. 5. 10 선고 2017나2073137 판결.
[252] 대법원 2018. 7. 20. 선고 2016다17729 판결

Chapter 5 Retirement Benefit Plan

to the worker.
3) The worker filed a lawsuit arguing that the settlement money in this case was not subject to taxation.

(2) Understanding the details of the judgment and the related criteria

1) In the settlement of this case, it was confirmed that the employment relationship with the company was effectively terminated as of February 28, 2014, the date of dismissal of the employee, and the nature of the settlement money in this case is specified as dispute settlement money and in this case is only received on the premise that the dismissal dispute has been resolved due to mutual agreement, and cannot be said to be earned income paid on the premise that the employment relationship continues. However, the company is paying the settlement money in this case as an example of helping to resolve the dispute regarding unfair dismissal claims quickly and amicably, such as by giving up on reinstatement and salary claims and not raising any objections in the future. So, the settlement money in this case is considered reward money under other income in Article 21 (1) No. 17 of the Income Tax Act.

2) The original trial court in this case said, It cannot be said that the reconciliation money paid by one party while making mutual concessions and compromises in the course of a fierce legal dispute is not a gift to be paid as an expression of gratitude.[253] However, the Supreme Court regarded the severance settlement in this case as dispute settlement money and determined it as other income. In this case, there is criticism that the Supreme Court did not provide clear criteria for determining the severance settlement amount.[254]

4. Conclusion

In legal disputes, such as relief applications against an employer for unfair dismissal or a lawsuit to confirm the invalidity of a dismissal, the employer pays the employee a severance settlement and the employee withdraws the application for relief in return. If this severance settlement is paid as compensation for emotional damage, it can be regarded as dispute settlement money and excluded from taxation.

---

[253] Changwon Regional Court ruling on Mar. 24, 2016, 2015na9657.
[254] Kang, Jihyeon, Review of the 2018 Framework Act on National Tax and Income Tax Act, Tax Law Research (25-1), Apr. 2019, p. 258.

(2%) 506,040원의 합계 5,566,440원을 원천징수한 후 잔액 19,735,560원을 근로자에게 지급하였다.
3) 근로자는 이 사건 화해금은 비과세 대상이라고 주장하면서 소송을 제기하였다.

(2) 판결내용과 그 기준 이해

1) 이 사건 화해에서 근로자에 대한 해고일인 2014년 2월 28일자로 회사와의 고용관계가 유효하게 종료되었음을 확인하고 이 사건 화해금의 성격을 분쟁조정금으로 명시하고 있다. 이 사건 화해금은 해고의 분쟁이 해소되었음을 전제로 지급된 합의금일 뿐, 근로관계가 존속되고 있음을 전제로 지급된 근로소득이라고 할 수 없다. 그러나 회사는 근로자가 복직 및 급여청구 등을 포기하고 향후 일체의 이의를 제기하지 않기로 하는 등 부당해고 구제신청과 관련한 분쟁을 신속하고 원만히 해결할 수 있도록 협조하여 준 것에 대한 사례의 뜻으로 이 사건 화해금을 지급한 것으로 봄이 타당하므로, 이 사건 화해금은 소득세법 제21조 제1항 제17호에서 기타소득으로 정한 '사례금'에 해당한다고 보았다.

2) 이 사건의 원심은 치열한 법적 분쟁 과정에서 상호 양보하고 절충하여 해결하면서 일방이 지급하는 화해금을 고마운 뜻의 표현으로 지급하는 선물이라고 할 수 없다. 고 판시하였다.[253] 그러나 대법원은 본 사건의 퇴직합의금을 분쟁화해금으로 간주하여 기타소득으로 판단하였다. 이 사건은 대법원이 퇴직 합의금에 대해 명확한 판단기준을 제시하지 못했다는 비판이 있다.[254]

4. 시사점

근로자가 사용자를 상대로한 부당해고구제신청이나 해고무효확인소송 등의 법률적 분쟁에서 사용자가 근로자에게 퇴직합의금을 지급하고, 그 대신 근로자가 구제신청 등을 취하하는 경우가 많이 있다. 이 퇴직합의금이 정신적 손해에

---

253) 창원지방법원 2016.3.24. 선고 2015나9657 판결.
254) 강지현, 2018년 국세기본법 및 소득세법 판례회고, 조세법연구(25-1), 2019.4.258면.

However, in many cases, the National Tax Service considers severance settlements as other income (reward money) under the Income Tax Act when the lawsuit is withdrawn by agreement between the two parties to the dispute.[255]

The actual amount a worker receives of a severance settlement depends largely on which taxation method the employer applies. Assuming that an employee with 10 years of service was dismissed and could receive KRW 100 million as a severance settlement, the employee expects that KRW 100 million will be deposited into his or her bank account. However, as a withholding agent, the employer must deduct tax and pay it to the National Tax Service. If the tax item is treated as earned income, the employee will receive only KRW 58,158,200 after KRW 41,841,800, or 42% is deducted for tax. However, if the settlement money is treated as other income, the employee will receive KRW 78 million after KRW 22 million (22%) is deducted for tax. If this part is treated as retirement income, only KRW 5,024,523, or 5%, is deducted for tax, and the employee will receive KRW 94,975,477.[256] If the termination settlement agreement is paid as compensation for emotional damage, it is not taxed. Therefore, even though an agreement is reached in a dispute over dismissal, another potential source of conflict appears regarding what tax is applicable. In this regard, when drafting a settlement agreement, one way of avoiding this potential dispute is for both parties to agree on the actual amount of the settlement money that will be deposited into the employee's bank account.

VI. Key Issues: The Confusing Administrative Interpretation from the Ministry of Employment and Labor on Calculating Severance Pay

1. Introduction

The recent administrative interpretation of severance pay calculations by the

---

[255] National Tax Service Administrative Guidelines, Income, Withholding Tax Division-152, Mar. 26, 2012; Income, Income Tax Division-1126, Nov. 8, 2010; Choi, Jinsoo, Jeon, Youngjun, HR and TAX, Labor Law, May 2014, pp. 87-88.
[256] App of KangNam Labor Law Firm: automatic calculation of severance income tax at https://k-labor.co.kr/main/auto4.html

대한 보상으로 지급하는 것이면 이를 분쟁합의금으로 보아 과세대상에서 제외할 수 있다. 그러나 국세청에서는 법원이나 노동위원회의 조정으로 합의하여 소송을 취하하는 경우 퇴직합의금을 소득세법 상 기타소득 (사례금)으로 판단하는 경우가 많다.[255]

퇴직합의금에 대해 사용자가 어떤 과세 방식을 적용하는가에 따라 근로자의 실수령액에는 많은 차이가 있다. 근속년수 10년인 근로자가 부당해고를 당했고, 퇴직합의서를 작성하면서 1억원을 해고합의금으로 지급받는다고 가정하면, 근로자는 본인의 통장에 1억원이 퇴직합의금으로 입금 될 것으로 예상한다. 그러나 사용자는 원천징수의무자로서 세금을 공제하여 국세청에 납부해야 한다. 세목을 근로소득세로 처리하면, 세금으로 42%인 41,841,800원이 공제된 58,158,200원만 입금된다. 그렇지만 퇴직합의금을 기타소득으로 처리한다면, 세금은 (1억원의 22%인) 22,000,000원이 공제된 78,000,000원이 된다. 만일, 이 부분을 퇴직소득으로 처리한다면 세금은 5%인 5,024,523원 만을 공제하게 되므로 최종 94,975,477원이 근로자에게 지급된다.[256] 그리고 퇴직합의금을 정신적 손해에 대한 보상으로 지급하게 되면 이는 과세대상에서 제외된다. 따라서 부당해고 구제신청 사건에 있어 합의를 할 경우, 어떤 세목을 적용할 것인가가 주요 갈등의 요인으로 작용하고 있다. 이에 대해 퇴직합의서를 작성할 때, 실제 지급액을 기준으로 판단하는 것이 분쟁해결의 한 방법이라고 할 수 있겠다.

VI. 주요 쟁점 : 이상한 퇴직금 계산법을 안내하는 고용노동부의 행정해석

1. 문제의 소재

최근 고용노동부의 퇴직금 계산에 관한 행정해석은 많은 기업에 혼란을 주고

---

[255] 국세청 행정해석, 소득, 원천세과-152, 2012.3.26; 소득, 소득세과-1126, 2010.11.8; 최진수/전영준, HR과 TAX, 노동법률 2014.5. 87-88면.
[256] 강남노무법인 앱: 퇴직소득세 자동계산 https://k-labor.co.kr/main/auto4.html

Ministry of Employment and Labor (MOEL) is causing confusion in many companies.[257] If a worker who receives 2 million won per month in fixed wage has worked for one year and resigns, he must receive 2 million won in severance pay (total wage for 3 months: 6 million won/90 days x 30 days average wage). However, the MOEL guidance says it should be 2,296,650 won and is ordering companies to be punished if they do not pay the additional 296,650 won. In the case of ordinary wages, if the monthly salary, 2 million won, is divided by 209 monthly contractual working hours, the hourly ordinary wage is obtained (2 million won/209 hours). If this hourly ordinary wage is multiplied by 8 hours, which is the contractual working hours in a day, the normal wage for one day is calculated (hourly wage 9,569 won x 8 hours = 76,555 won). Since the daily ordinary wage is higher than the daily average wage, multiplying the daily ordinary wage by 90 days becomes 2,296,650 won (76,555 x 90 days of daily ordinary wage). This recent administrative interpretation states that, citing Article 2 (2) of the Labor Standards Act (LSA), if the hourly average wage of a worker is lower than the hourly ordinary wage, that hourly ordinary wage shall replace the hourly average wage.

However, this administrative interpretation violates the method for calculating severance pay under the current Employee Retirement Benefit Guarantee Act (the ERBG Act) and does not fit the interpretation of the law by the courts. The ERBG Act states that the principle of calculating severance pay is based on the average wage, and in particular, 1/12 of the total wage for the defined contribution (DC) retirement pension is specified. Court rulings also state that, in calculating average wage, the basic principle is to use the ordinary living wage of workers.[258]

Hereby, I would like to look at where the contradictions in the MOEL's administrative interpretation occur, and also examine in detail whether it is appropriate to use ordinary wage rather than average wage in the calculation of severance pay.

2. Reasons Why Ordinary Wage is Higher than Average Wage

(1) Reduction of statutory working hours

What is at issue here is that Article 2 (2) of the Labor Standards Act states that if the average wage is lower than the ordinary wage, the ordinary wage shall be the average wage. This provision did not change even when, on March 29, 1989, the

---

[257] Han Kyung-hee, Is the higher ordinary wage more often used than the average wage in calculating severance pay? Korea Apartment Daily, Sep. 15, 2020; Goh Hee-kyung, Disputes in calculating severance pay at an apartment workplace due to ordinary wage being higher than average wage... Why? Apartment Management Newspaper, July 24, 2020.

[258] Supreme Court ruling on Nov. 12, 1999: 98da49357.

있다.[257] 월 200만 원을 고정급으로 받는 근로자가 1년간 근무하고 퇴직하는 경우 당연히 퇴직금으로 200만 원을 받아야 한다 (3개월간 임금총액 600만 원 / 90일 × 30일의 평균임금). 그러나 고용노동부는 회사측에 2,296,650원으로 안내하면서 추가로 296,650원을 지급하지 않으면 처벌하겠다고 지도하고 있다. 그런데 통상임금은 월 급여 200만 원을 월 소정근로시간인 209로 나누면 시간급 통상임금이 나온다 (200만 원/209시간). 이 시간급 통상임금에 하루 소정근로시간인 8시간을 곱하면, 1일의 통상임금이 계산된다 (시간급 9,569원 × 8시간=76,555원). 이 1일의 통상임금이 평균임금보다 높기 때문에 1일의 통상임금에 30일을 곱하면 2,296,650원이 산출된다 (1일 통상임금 76,555×30일). 고용노동부의 행정해석은 근로기준법(근기법) 제2조 제2항을 인용하면서 근로자의 일급 평균임금이 일급 통상임금보다 적으면 그 일급 통상임금액을 일급 평균임금으로 본다는 내용이다.

그러나 고용노동부의 행정해석은 현행 근로자퇴직급여보장법(근퇴법)의 퇴직금 계산법을 위반하고 있고, 판례의 법해석에도 맞지 않기 때문에 폐기되어야 한다. 근퇴법은 퇴직금 계산의 원칙이 평균임금이라는 계산식과 특히 확정기여형의 임금총액의 12분의 1로 명시되어 있다. 판례도 평균임금을 계산함에 있어 근로자의 통상 생활임금을 사실대로 산정하는 것을 기본 원칙으로 하고 있다.[258]

따라서, 고용노동부의 행정해석상 모순점이 어디에서 발생했는지 확인해보고, 퇴직금 계산에서 평균임금이 아닌 통상임금으로 계산하는 것이 타당한지 구체적으로 살펴보고자 한다.

2. 통상임금이 평균임금보다 높게 된 원인

(1) 법정 근로시간의 축소

여기서 문제가 되는 것은 근로기준법 제2조 제2항은 평균임금이 통상임금보다 저액일 경우에는 통상임금을 평균임금으로 한다는 내용이다. 이 조항은 1989년 3월 29일 기존의 1주 법정근로시간이 48시간에서 44시간제로 단축된

---

[257] 한경희, 어려운 퇴직금 계산기준 평균임금보다 통상임금이 많다?, 한국아파트신문, 2020. 9. 15.; 고희경, '퇴직금 부족하다' 잇단 요구에 아파트 퇴직금 산정 혼돈왜, 아파트 관리신문, 2020. 7. 24.
[258] 대법원 1999. 11. 12. 선고 98다49357 판결.

existing statutory working hours per week were reduced from 48 hours to 44 hours per week. And on September 15, 2003, the statutory working hours per week were reduced to 40 hours, but there was no change to the provision. That is, the contractual monthly working hours are 240 hours in the 48-hour workweek system, 226 hours in the 44-hour week system, and 209 hours in the current 40-hour week system. Therefore, at the present time, contrary to the purpose of this article, the average wage must be lower than ordinary wage.[259] In other words, the average wage obtained by dividing the total wage by 30 days is actually lower than the ordinary wage, as the ordinary wage becomes the amount obtained by dividing the wage for 20 days by 30. On the other hand, since the ordinary wage is 6 days a week including the weekly holiday allowance, the monthly ordinary wage is divided by 25 days. In this way, the ordinary wage is always higher than the average wage.

(2) Changes in the wage structure

In December 2013, the Supreme Court ruled on a very important case related to ordinary wage that regular annual bonuses and various monthly allowances were included.[260]

As a result of this ruling, the annual fixed bonus system, which was the basic framework of Korean company wage structures, was abolished in 2014. The ruling simplifies wage structures. In other words, Korea's wage structure has come to consist of basic wages, legal allowances, and incentives since then, which increased the level of ordinary wages greatly.

3. Method for Calculating Statutory Severance Pay and Problems with Recent MOEL Guidelines on Calculating Severance Pay

(1) How to calculate statutory retirement pay

The ERBG Act stipulates that severance pay is calculated as average wage equivalent to 30 days for each year of the relevant worker's continuous service. In the defined benefit (DB) pension system, an amount calculated as the average wage of 30 days for each year of continuous service is deposited into the retirement pension account. In the defined contribution (DC) retirement pension system, 1/12 of the total annual wage is deposited into the retirement pension account. This is equivalent to 8.3% of the annual salary. Because a defined contribution (DC) retirement pension system pays a fixed amount each year, it cannot be recalculated later because the ordinary wage is higher than the average wage.[261] As such, it can

---

[259] Koo Kunseo, Strange severance pay calculation, Korea Economy Daily, Jan. 16, 2022.
[260] Supreme Court ruling on Dec. 18, 2013: 2012da89399, 2012da94643.

때에도 변경되지 않았다. 그리고 2003년 9월 15일 1주 법정근로시간이 40시간으로 단축되었음에도 불구하고 변경되지 않았다. 즉, 1주 48시간제에서 월 소정근로시간이 240시간, 1주 44시간제도에서 월 소정근로시간이 226시간, 현재 1주 40시간제에서 월 소정근로시간은 209시간이 된다. 따라서 현시점에서는 이 조항의 목적과 다르게 평균임금이 통상임금보다 저액일 수밖에 없다.[259] 즉, 임금총액을 30일로 나누는 평균임금은 실제로 20일치 임금을 30으로 나눈 금액이다. 이에 반해 통상임금은 주휴수당까지 포함하여 1주일에 6일이 되므로, 월 통상임금을 25일로 나누게 된다. 이렇게 하면 통상임금이 항상 평균임금보다 많게 된다.

(2) 임금구조의 변경

2013년 12월 통상임금에 대한 대법원합의체는 매년 고정적으로 지급하는 정기상여금과 매월 고정적 지급하는 각종수당은 모두 통상임금에 포함된다고 판결하였다.[260] 이 판결의 결과, 2014년부터는 우리나라 기업의 임금구조에서 기본골격 이었던 연간 고정상여금제도가 폐지되었다. 이 판결은 기업의 임금구조를 단순화시켰다. 즉, 기본급, 법정수당, 인센티브로 구성하게 하여, 통상임금의 수준을 대거 올렸다.

3. 법정 퇴직금 계산방법과 고용노동부의 퇴직금 계산 지침의 문제점

(1) 법정 퇴직금 계산방법

근퇴법에서 퇴직금은 근로자의 계속근로연수 1년에 대해 30일분의 평균임금으로 지급한다고 규정하고 있다. 확정급여(DB) 연금제도도 근로자의 계속근로연수 1년에 대해 30일분의 평균임금으로 계산한 금액을 퇴직연금 통장에 적립한다. 확정기여(DC) 퇴직연금은 연간임금총액의 12분의 1만큼 퇴직연금 계좌에 적립한다. 이는 연봉 대비 8.3%에 해당하는 금액이다. 확정기여(DC) 퇴직연금제도는 매년 확정된 금액을 지급하는 것이므로 나중에 평균임금 보다 통상임금이 더 높다는 이유로 다시 산정할 수 없다.[261] 이와 같이 근퇴법에서

---

[259] 구건서, 이상한 퇴직금 계산법, 한국경제신문 기고문, 2022. 1. 16.
[260] 대법원 2013. 12. 18. 선고, 2012다89399 판결, 2012다94643 판결
[261] 대법원 2021. 1. 14 선고 2020다207444 판결.

be said that severance pay is clarified by calculating the average wage, which is the total wage, in the ERBG Act.

In this way, severance pay and retirement pension are calculated with the average wage, which is the total wage. The reason for calculating and paying the average wage is to protect the living wage of workers and to match a certain wage level in terms of severance pay or accident compensation. The Labor Standards Act provides three ways to protect the level of average wage. First, if the average wage is lower than the ordinary wage, it is stipulated that the ordinary wage shall be the average wage (Article 2, Paragraph 2). Second, the calculations of average wage exclude the probationary period of workers, periods of absence due to reasons attributable to the employer, periods of maternity leave, periods of recovery from work-related illnesses or accidents, periods of childcare leave, periods of legal industrial action, etc. This is an exception to the calculation of average wage, and is a limited enumeration provision to prevent the average wage from being unreasonably low in special cases for workers.[262] Third, despite the exceptions to the above Enforcement Regulation to the Labor Standards Act, if the average wage fluctuates significantly due to the worker's accidental circumstances, the notice on special cases for calculating the average wage determined by the MOEL (Article 4 of the Enforcement Decree to the LSA) is applied.[263]

(2) Problems in using ordinary wage when calculating severance pay

Currently, the MOEL is saying that severance pay should be calculated using ordinary wage when the average wage is lower than ordinary wage.[264] However, in principle, severance pay should be based on calculations using the average wage, and ordinary wage should help to prevent a decrease in severance pay if average wage is lower. Currently, the severance pay and defined benefit (DB) retirement pension plan under the ERBG Act are calculated as the average wage of 30 days for each year of continuous service. One-twelfth of the total annual wage for defined contribution (DC) retirement pension plans is taken as a reserve fund. According to this guideline, all calculations of retirement benefits that currently reflect average wages should be converted to reflect ordinary wages (Article 12 of the ERBG Act). If this happens, the calculation system of the ERPG Act will be broken, resulting in chaos. In other words, the administrative interpretation of the MOEL is not in line with the interpreted purpose of this Act, as it results in the use of the ordinary wage as a supplement to the average wage used in the

---

[261] Supreme Court ruling on Jan. 14, 2021: 2020da207444.
[262] Supreme Court ruling on July 25, 2003: 2001da12669.
[263] Supreme Court ruling on June 25, 2020: 2018da292418.
[264] MOEL Guidelines: Labor Standards-3405, Aug. 25, 2020.

퇴직금 계산은 임금총액인 평균임금으로 계산한다는 것을 명확히 한 것이라 할 수 있다.

이렇게 퇴직금과 퇴직연금은 임금총액인 평균임금으로 계산한다. 평균임금으로 계산하여 지급하는 이유는 근로자의 생활임금 수준을 보호하여 퇴직금이나 재해보상에 있어 일정한 급여수준을 보장해 주기 위한 취지이다. 따라서 근로기준법은 평균임금의 수준을 보호하기 위해서 다음 3가지 방법을 제시하고 있다. 첫째, 평균임금이 통상임금 보다 저액일 경우에는 그 통상임금액을 평균임금으로 한다고 규정하고 있다(제2조 제2항). 둘째, 근로자의 수습기간, 사용자의 귀책 사유로 인한 휴업기간, 출산휴가기간, 업무상 질병이나 사고로 요양한 기간, 육아휴직기간, 정당한 쟁의행위기간 등의 경우에는 그 기간을 제외하고 평균임금을 계산하게 된다. 이는 평균임금 산정의 예외로 근로자의 특별한 경우에 평균임금이 부당히 낮게 산정되는 것을 막기 위한 제한적 열거규정이다.[262] 셋째, 위의 근로기준법 시행령의 예외에도 불구하고 근로자의 우연한 사정으로 평균임금의 변동이 심한 경우에는 고용노동부가 정하는 평균임금산정 특례 고시에 따른다 (근기법 시행령 제4조)[263].

(2) 퇴직금 계산시에 통상임금을 사용하는 경우의 문제점

현재, 고용노동부는 평균임금이 통상임금보다 적은 경우에 통상임금으로 퇴직금을 계산하여야 한다고 지도를 하고 있다.[264] 그러나 이 지침은 퇴직금 산정을 평균임금으로 계산하는 것이 원칙임에도 불구하고 평균임금의 저하를 막기 위해서 보충적 역할을 하는 통상임금으로 계산하자는 것이다. 현재, 퇴직급여보장법의 퇴직금이나 확정급여(DB) 퇴직연금제도의 급여가 계속 근로기간 1년에 대해 30일분의 평균임금으로 계산한 금액과 확정기여(DC) 퇴직연금제도는 임금총액의 12분의 1을 적립금으로 하고 있다. 이 지침에 따르면, 평균임금 반영을 모두 통상임금으로 전환해야 한다는 결론에 이르게 된다(근퇴법 제12조). 이렇게 되면 법의 체계가 무너지기 때문에 대혼란이 온다. 즉, 고용노동부의 행정해석은 퇴직금 계산에 있어 보충적으로 사용하는 통상임금을 평균임금으로 대체하여 사용하는 결과를 낳고 있기 때문에 이는

---
[262] 대법원 2003. 7. 25. 선고 2001다12669 판결.
[263] 대법원 2020. 6. 25 선고 2018다292418 판결.
[264] 행정해석: 근로기준정책과-3405, 2020. 8. 25.

calculation of severance pay.

4. Purpose of Average Wage in Calculating Severance Pay and the Clause to Use Ordinary Wage in Exceptions

(1) Purpose of using average wage in calculating severance pay

The severance pay system was introduced to ensure that companies can guarantee an income for their workers in their old age when there was no old-age pension in Korea. Therefore, the calculation of severance pay using average wage, which is the total amount of wages, was prepared in consideration of the fact that there is no disadvantage by reflecting the ordinary living wage of workers.[265] Since the total wage is the average wage, it has always been higher than ordinary wage, which reflects only fixed and regular wages. For this reason, Article 46 of the Labor Standards Act stipulates that 70% of the average wage or 100% of the ordinary wage must be paid as leave of absence allowance for periods attributable to the employer. This is because the use of average wages is the basis for severance pay regulations and accident compensation for workers. However, ordinary wage is calculated for the purpose of calculating hourly wage, and so such ordinary wage is used when calculating paid allowances stipulated in the Labor Standards Act, such as overtime pay and unused annual allowance under the Labor Standards Act. Because ordinary wages refer to fixed and pre-promised wages paid for the contractual working hours when a labor contract is drawn up, while the average wage is paid according to the rate of attendance at work, it does not decrease.

(2) Reasons for placing the clause to use ordinary wage in exceptions when calculating severance pay

The basic principle of average wage is to calculate the ordinary living wage of workers as a matter of fact. Severance pay is based on the average wage for the same reason.[266] According to Article 2 (2) of the Labor Standards Act, if the total wage decreases due to abnormal work, the average wage will be lower than the normal wage, so then the ordinary wage is used.[267] The precedent also stipulates that if the amount calculated as the average wage is lower than the ordinary wage of the worker concerned, the ordinary wage shall be the average wage in Article 2

---

[265] Supreme Court ruling on April 12, 1994: 92da20309; Supreme Court ruling on Nov. 12,1999: 98da49357.
[266] Supreme Court ruling on Nov. 12, 1999: 98da49357.
[267] Gwangju Appellate Court ruling on Dec. 22, 2015: 2004nu1062.

법 해석의 취지에 맞지 않는다.

4. 평균임금을 이용한 퇴직금 계산 취지와 통상임금 단서 조항 이해

(1) 퇴직금 계산을 위한 평균임금의 취지

퇴직금제도는 우리나라의 노령연금이 없던 시절에 기업에 근로자의 노후를 보장할 수 있도록 하기 위해 도입된 제도이다. 따라서 퇴직금 계산을 임금총액인 평균임금으로 계산하고 있는 것은 근로자의 통상의 생활임금을 사실대로 반영하여 불이익이 없도록 배려하는 차원에서 마련되었다.[265] 임금총액이 평균임금이기 때문에 고정적이고 정기적인 임금만 반영하는 통상임금보다 항상 높게 나온다. 이러한 이유로 근기법 제46조의 사용자의 귀책사유로 휴업한 기간에 대한 휴업수당도 평균임금의 70%나 통상임금의 100%를 지급해야 한다고 규정하고 있다. 이는 평균임금의 사용이 근로자 보호를 위한 퇴직금 규정과 재해보상의 근거가 되기 때문이다. 그러나 통상임금은 시간급 계산을 목적으로 계산되고, 근로기준법상 연장근로 수당, 미사용 연차수당 등 근로기준법에 정한 유급수당을 계산하는 경우에 통상임금을 활용한다. 왜냐하면, 통상임금은 근로계약 작성시 소정근로시간에 지급하는 고정적이고 사전에 약속된 임금을 말하므로, 출근율에 따라 실제로 지급받는 평균임금과 달리 저하되지 않는다.

(2) 퇴직금 계산 시 통상임금 단서 조항을 두는 이유

평균임금은 근로자의 통상 생활임금을 사실대로 산정하는 것을 기본원리로 하고 있다. 퇴직금도 그러한 이유로 인해 평균임금을 기준으로 산정하고 있다.[266] 근로기준법 제2조 제2항은 비정상적인 근무로 인하여 임금총액이 저하될 경우 평균임금이 통상임금 보다 낮아지는데, 이 경우 근로자 보호를 위하여 사용된다.[267] 판례도 근로기준법 제2조제2항은 평균임금으로 산출된금액이 당해 근로자의 통상임금보다 저액일 경우에는 그 통상임금액을 평균임금으로 한다고 규정하고 있다. 그 취지는 평균임금 산정사유가 발생하기 전 3개월 동안

---

[265] 대법원 1994. 4. 12 선고 92다20309; 대법원 1999. 11. 12. 선고 98다49357 판결.
[266] 대법원 1999. 11. 12. 선고 98다49357 판결.
[267] 광주고등법원 2015. 12. 22. 선고 2004누1062 판결.

Paragraph 2 of the Labor Standards Act. The purpose for this is to guarantee the minimum average wage in case the wage is significantly lower than in normal cases due to reasons attributable to the worker or an inability to work normally due to reasons attributable to the worker during the three months prior to the occurrence of the reason for calculating the average wage.[268] Here, ordinary wages refer to fixed wages in advance that are set to be paid regularly and uniformly regardless of the actual provision of work. For this reason, Article 2 (2) of the Labor Standards Act is used in cases where the average wage falls short of the ordinary wage.[269]

5. Conclusion

Severance pay is the wage calculated as the average wage of 30 days per year of a worker's continuous service. Here, the average wage falls short of the ordinary wage in situations in which workers are not protected by law, such as for absenteeism or personal leaves. At present, the ordinary wage is often higher than the average wage even in general cases, not just in special cases. This is because the standard calculation formula for ordinary wages is calculated on the basis of 6 days (including weekly holidays) in the 40-hour work week system, while average wage is calculated on the basis of 7 days a week. Accordingly, the provision in Article 2 (2) of the Labor Standards Act shall be added as a supplement when the average wage is lower than the ordinary wage, because the average wage shall be applied in accordance with the purpose of the Act. This is because, as can be seen with the MOEL's recent administrative interpretation, if the formula for calculating severance pay with ordinary wages is established, the severance pay systems in the Retirement Benefit Guarantee Act must be revised completely.

VII. Related Labor Cases

⟨Case 1⟩ Unpaid Severance Pay to Foreign Teachers[270]

---

[268] Seoul Administrative Court ruling on July 1, 1999: 98gu19789.
[269] Supreme Court ruling on June 28, 1991: 90daka14758; Supreme Court ruling on Dec. 26, 1990: 90daka12493.
[270] Jung, Bongsoo, "Unpaid Severance Pay for Foreign Teachers", 「Labor Law」, Jungang, Feb 2009

근로자의 귀책 사유로 인하여 휴업하거나 정상적인 근로를 하지 못하여 통상의 경우보다 임금이 현저히 낮아지는 경우에 대비하여 평균임금을 최대한 보장하려는데 있다고 판시하고 있다.[268] 여기서 통상임금은 실제 근로제공과 상관없이 정기적, 일률적으로 지급하기로 정하여진 사전적 고정급 임금을 의미한다. 이러한 이유로 근로기준법 제2조 제2항은 평균임금이 저하되어 통상임금에 미치지 못하는 경우에 사용된다.[269]

5. 시사점

퇴직금은 근로자의 계속근로연수 1년에 30일분의 평균임금으로 계산되는 임금이다. 여기서 평균임금이 통상임금에 미치지 못하는 경우는 근로자가 예외적인 결근이나 개인 휴직 등 법령에서 보호받지 못하는 그러한 상황에서 발생한다. 현재 이러한 특별한 경우가 아닌 일반적인 경우에도 통상임금이 평균임금보다 높은 경우가 많다. 왜냐하면, 통상임금에 대한 기준계산 수식은 1주일에 40시간제도에서 주휴일을 포함한 6일을 기준으로 해서 계산되지만, 평균임금은 1주일을 7일을 기준으로 해서 계산되기 때문이다. 따라서 근로기준법 제2조 제2항에서 평균임금이 통상임금보다 낮은 경우에는 통상임금을 평균임금으로 한다라는 규정은 그 법 취지에 맞추어 적용해야 한다. 왜냐하면, 고용노동부의 행정해석과 같이 퇴직금 계산을 통상임금으로 계산하게 되면, 퇴직급여보장법의 퇴직금 제도를 전면 수정해야 하기 때문이다.

Ⅶ. 실무사례

〈사례 1〉 원어민 교사 퇴직금 미지급 사건[270]

---

[268] 서울행정법원 1999. 7. 1. 선고 98구19789 판결.
[269] 대법원 1991. 6. 28. 선고 90다카14758 판결; 1990.12.26. 선고, 90다카 12493 판결
[270] 정봉수, "퇴직금 진정사건", 「월간 노동법률」, 중앙경제사, 2009년 2월호

Chapter 5 Retirement Benefit Plan

1. Summary

International School A (hereafter refer to as 'the School') established in 1999 in accordance with the Elementary, Middle and High School Act has regular curricula for kindergarten, elementary and middle school. Every year, the school renews employment contracts with foreign teachers for 10 months which does not include the summer vacation period. When the foreign teachers stopped working at the school, the school did not pay them severance pay. As a result, 7 foreign teachers (hereinafter refer to as "the Teachers") who resigned in July 2008 visited Kangnam Labor Law Firm to seek legal assistance in claiming unpaid severance pay on the grounds that they had been providing their labor service continuously for at least a year to the school but the school had not paid them the severance pay to which they were entitled.

2. The School's claim

Every year, the school begins a new academic year in August and finishes it in June of the following year. In order to be in line with such an educational schedule, the employment period was therefore contracted for 10 months from August each year to June of the following year, where summer vacation from July to August was not considered as an employment period. Every year, the school discussed such employment contracts with the teachers, and the new employment contracts took effect only with their agreement. In the two months following the end of each annual employment contract, no wages were paid to the teachers. In the School's opinion, as their employment ended properly and as the employment terms were contracted according to their free will, severance pay was therefore not paid.

3. Teachers' Claim

In the Teachers' opinion, however, as they have been renewing their annual contracts in the capacity as employees and as they have also been continuously working for at least a year, the school should be paying them severance pay in accordance with the law.

Every year, they sign a 10 month contract with the school in their capacity as teachers, and except for the summer vacation period, they continuously provided labor service As the teachers are short-term contract employees, the Private Teachers' Pension Act is not applicable to them. The awarding of severance pay to

1. 사건 개요

A 국제외국인학교 (이하'학교'라 함)는 '초중등교육법'에 의거 1999년에 설립된 외국인학교로, 유치원, 초등학교 및 중학교의 정규과정을 두고 있다. 학교는 원어민 교사들과 방학기간을 제외한10개월 단위로 매년 근로계약을 갱신하여 고용하고 있었으며, 원어민 교사들이 학교를 그만둘 때 퇴직금은 따로 지급하지 않았다. 이에 2008년 7월 학교를 그만 둔 원어민 교사 7명 (이하 '교사'라 함)은 본 노무법인을 찾아와 "본인들은 근로자로 1년 이상 계속 근로를 제공하였는데, 학교는 퇴직금을 지급하지 않았다"며 퇴직금지급청구를 의뢰하였다.

2. 외국인학교 주장

학교는 매년 8월경에 새 학년을 시작하여 다음해 6월 중순에 수업을 마감한다. 따라서 학교는 이 같은 학사일정에 맞추어 방학기간을 제외하고 매년 8월부터 익년 6월까지 10개월 가량의 계약기간을 정하여 교사들과 근로계약서를 작성해 왔다. 이 근로계약은 매년 교사들과 면담을 통해 교사들이 원할 때 마다 새로 작성되어왔다. 계약기간이 끝난 2개월 동안에는 임금을 전혀 지급하지 않았다. 따라서 학교는 정당하게 근로관계를 종결하고 자유의사에 의거하여 원어민 교사를 새롭게 채용한 것이므로, 퇴직금은 발생하지 않는다.

3. 근로자 주장

교사들은 근로자의 신분으로 매년 계약을 갱신하여 1년 이상 계속 근무하였기 때문에 학교는 법정퇴직금을 지급해야 한다.

교사들은 본 학교에서 10개월 단위로 매년 기간제 교사로 계약을 체결하여 방학기간을 제외한 기간 동안 계속 근로를 제공해 왔다. 교사들은 '사립학교연금법'에 적용을 받지 않는 기간제 교사의 지위를 갖는 자들로서 퇴직금에 관해서는 '근로자퇴직급여보장법'상의 보호를 받아야 하는 근로자에 해당한다. 근무시간은 월요일부터 금요일까지 매일 오전 7시45분부터 오후 3시30분

persons holding the position of teacher should duly be in accordance with any employees receiving due protection from the Employee Retirement Benefit Security Act. The teachers' working hour started at 7:45 in the morning and finished at 3:30 in the afternoon from Monday to Friday, and they receive a fixed wage, comprising of basic pay and a performance incentive. It appears that the objective for the school to make a 10-months employment contract that is annually renewable is to evade their obligation to pay severance pay. On average, each teacher participating in the appeal has worked for four years, and unless there is an apparent drop in their abilities, the school continues to renew the contracts. The contents of these contracts have been the same every year except for wage increases wages and the academic level of which each teacher is in charge.

4. Analysis of Related Administrative Interpretations

(1) Standard governing length of continuous employment service of a short-term contract teacher (Jun. 1, 2001, Kungi 68207-1780)
With the exception of vacation period where there is no class, if a short-term contract employee has repeated working periods, their previous employment period may be deemed as part of continuous work. However, the vacation period when the teacher did not provide any labor service shall be excluded from the calculation of continuous employment service.

(2) With the exclusion of vacation period, repeated employment period also may be deemed as continuous work but vacation period where no actual work is provided may not be included in the computation of severance pay. (Jun. 7, 2004, Kungi-2811)
A school has been hiring temporary teachers and has repeatedly employed them except during vacation periods. With the exception of vacation period, previous employment period in repeated employment periods may be deemed continuous work in the computation of severance pay.

5. Opinion

In conclusion, the Labor Office, based on the above mentioned administration interpretations, instructed that the school would have to pay the teachers severance pay.

〈Case 2〉 Unpaid Severance Pay to Company Directors[271]

---

[271] Jung, Bongsoo, "Unpaid Severance Pay for Directors", 「Labor Law」, Jungang, February 2009.

까지이며, 급여는 기본급과 능률급을 포함하여 일정금액을 지급받았다.

학교는 퇴직금 지급 의무를 회피할 목적으로 10개월 단위의 근로계약을 체결하고, 매년 반복 갱신 해 왔다. 진정한 교사들의 평균근속연수는 4년이고, 학교에서는 교직 수행능력이 현저히 떨어지는 경우가 아니면 계속 근로계약을 갱신하여 왔다. 근로계약의 내용에 있어서도 급여와 담당 학년을 제외하고 매년 동일했다.

4. 관련 행정해석

(1) 기간제교원의 계속근로연수 판단기준 (2001.06.01, 근기 68207-1780)
수업이 없는 방학기간을 제외하고 반복적인 기간을 정하여 근무해 온 경우 반복적으로 임용한 전기간을 계속근로로 인정할 수 있으며, 다만 실제 근로를 제공하지 않은 방학기간은 계속근로연수 산정 시 제외될 수 있다.
(2) 방학기간을 제외하고 반복적으로 임용한 기간도 계속근로로 인정할 수 있으나, 실제 근로를 제공하지 아니한 방학기간은 퇴직금 산정 시 제외할 수도 있다. (2004.06.07. 근로기준과-2811)
학교에서 기간제 교사를 고용함에 있어서 수업이 없는 방학기간을 제외하고 임용하는 것을 반복한 경우, 방학기간을 제외하고 반복적으로 임용한 기간을 포함한 전 기간을 퇴직금 산정을 위한 계속근로로 인정할 수 있다.

5. 이 사건의 결과

이 사건에 대해 노동부는 앞서 언급한 행정해석에 근거하여 학교가 진정 교사들에게 법정 퇴직금을 지급하여야 한다고 지급명령을 내렸다.

〈사례 2〉 회사 임원 퇴직금 미지급 사건[271]

---

271) 정봉수, "퇴직금 진정사건", 「월간 노동법률」, 중앙경제사, 2009년 2월호

Chapter 5 Retirement Benefit Plan

1. Summary

Company D ("the Company") introduced an annual salary system for all its directors in January 2000 and paid interim severance pay for their service provided until that time. Thereafter, the Company did not pay any severance pay in accordance with the annual salary contract which clearly includes severance pay for each year of service. When three retired directors ("the Directors") of the company recently heard of a related judicial ruling that severance pay shall not be paid together with monthly wages, they visited Kangnam Labor Law Firm and commissioned us to file a legal claim for the severance pay they did not receive.

2. Company D's Claim

When the Directors became directors, the Company paid an interim adjustment of severance pay as a formality to confirm that they no longer held the status of employee. Employees up to Bujang (department head level) are subordinate to the employer's direction and supervision, but when an employee becomes a director, they receives assignment from the Company within a certain work scope and takes initiative and leadership in handling such work scope. In addition, a director also carries the name card of a "director" and, in the capacity as a person in-charge of "business development", represents the Company in external associations or organizations. In particular, the director can attend executive meetings while Bujang or lower positions are not allowed to do so. Even in the aspect of welfare, directors are different from employees, as the directors receive director's welfare systems with subsidies for comprehensive medical exams and car maintenance allowances. Directors can also use the corporate card for their expenses. Therefore, as company directors cannot be regarded as employees, the Company has no obligation to pay severance pay to its directors.

3. Directors' Claim

When Directors A and B were working as directors around Jan 2000, the Company, of its own accord, instructed payment of interim severance pay and also drew up annual salary contracts with severance pay included therein. For Director A, although he was working as a director of the research institute, which is equivalent to a company executive director, he was actually working in subordination to the company president's direction and supervision. He resigned on notification by the Vice President of the cancellation of his employment contract in

1. 사건개요

D 기업은 2000년 1월 경 모든 임원에 대해 연봉제를 도입하면서 임원 전원에 대하여 퇴직금중간정산을 실시하였다. 이후 근속기간에 대한 퇴직금은 연봉에 합산되어 있다는 연봉계약서 내용에 따라 퇴직금은 별도로 지급하지 않았다. D 기업의 퇴직 임원 3명은 퇴직금이 임금에 포함되어 지급해서는 안 된다는 최근 판례에 대한 보도를 접하고, 본 노무법인을 방문하여 퇴직금 지급 청구를 의뢰하였다.

2. 회사의 주장

회사는 직원이 임원이 되었을 때, 퇴직금 중간정산을 실시하는 것은 당해 직원이 더 이상 근로자 신분이 아니라는 것을 확인하는 절차이다. 부장까지는 경영진의 지휘 감독을 받는 사용종속관계에 놓여있었지만, 임원이 된 이후로는 회사로부터 위임 받은 업무 범위 내에서는 주도적으로 업무를 처리했고 대외적으로는 협회나 외부단체에 '임원명함'을 사용하여 사업경영담당자로서 활동한다. 특히 '임원회의'는 부장 이하가 참석할 수 없으나 이에 참석하였으며 복리후생면에서는 있어서는 '종합검진 지원, 차량유지비 혜택'이 임원 기준에 따라 직원과 다른 기준으로 보장되었으며, 경비사용의 경우 임원 선임 후 '법인카드'를 사용할 수 있었다. 따라서 회사의 임원은 근로자로 볼 수 없으므로 임원에게는 퇴직금을 지급할 의무가 없다.

3. 근로자의 주장

근로자 A와 B는 이사로 근무 중 2000년 1월경 회사의 일방적 지시에 의해 퇴직금 중간정산을 실시하였고, 회사는 퇴직금이 합산된 연봉계약서를 작성하였다. 근로자 A는 연구소 소장인 상무급 임원으로 근무하였지만, 대표이사의 지시를 받아 사용종속관계에서 일하다가 2006년 6월 부사장으로부터 계약해지 통보를 받고 사직하였다. 근로자 B는 D 기업의 사업본부장으로 업무를 하면서, 회사의 지시에 의거하여 D 기업의 자회사 부사장으로 등기가 되었으며, 급여도

June 2006. As for Director B, while he was working as General Manager of Company D, he was registered as a Vice President of the Company's subsidiary under the direction of Company D, and he received salary paid by that subsidiary. However, in actual fact, he had been working under the direction and supervision of Company D until his resignation in March 2006.

In the case of Director C, he held the position of Bujang in Company D before being promoted to Senior Director in April 2004. At the request of the Company, he then accepted interim severance pay and went on to conclude an annual salary contract which included severance pay. Employee C resigned in January 2007.

4. Related Judicial Rulings

Persons who provide specific service under the direction and supervision of others such as directors and who receive a fixed pay as remuneration can be regarded as employees defined by the Labor Standards Act. (Supreme Court, 2002 da 64681)
Whether it is appropriate to regard a director as an employee defined by the Labor Standards Act has nothing to do with the manner in which the contract is made but should be judged based on whether the director was paid to provide a service that requires him to be in subordination. Regardless of whether they holds the position or title of company director or auditor in the real sense or just in name, as long as they receives remuneration as compensation for providing a specific labor service under the direction and supervision of the employer or receives remuneration as compensation for taking charge of specific labor service under the direction and supervision of persons such as the representative director in addition to the duties assigned to him/her by the company, such director can be regarded as an employee as defined by the Labor Standards Act.

Even if the company pays, as part of the employment contract, a severance pay in advance with annual salary, such payment does not have the same effect as the lawful severance pay stipulated in Article 34 of the Labor Standards Act. (Daegu District Court, 2006 kadan 2947)

5. Opinion

The labor inspector interviewed the Company and the Directors who filed for the appeal. It was concluded that Directors A and C were employees. However, Director B was judged as not an employee because he was a registered director of a subsidiary and received salary from the subsidiary. Following this, it was concluded that the Company must pay severance pay to Directors A and C.

자회사로부터 받았다. 실질적으로는 D 기업의 사용종속 관계에서 근로를 제공하다가 2006년 3월에 퇴직하였다.

근로자 C는 D 기업 부장으로 재직하다가 2004년 4월에 상무로 승진하여 임원이 되었다. 회사의 요청에 의거하여 퇴직금 중간정산을 실시하였으며, 이후 퇴직금은 연봉에 합산되어 있다는 연봉계약서를 체결하였다. 근로자 C는 2007년 1월에 퇴사하였다.

4. 관련 판례 내용

대표이사 등의 지휘·감독 아래 일정한 노무를 담당하고 그 대가로 일정한 보수를 지급받아 왔다면 그러한 임원은 근로기준법상의 근로자에 해당한다 (대법 2002다 64681)

근로기준법의 적용을 받는 근로자에 해당하는지의 여부는 계약의 형식에 관계없이 그 실질에 있어서 임금을 목적으로 종속적 관계에서 사용자에게 근로를 제공하였는지 여부에 따라 판단하여야 할 것이므로, 회사의 이사 또는 감사 등 임원이라고 하더라도 그 지위 또는 명칭이 형식적·명목적인 것이고 사용자의 지휘·감독 아래 일정한 근로를 제공하면서 그 대가로 보수를 받는 관계에 있다거나 또는 회사로부터 위임받은 사무를 처리하는 외에 대표이사 등의 지휘·감독 아래 일정한 노무를 담당하고 그 대가로 일정한 보수를 지급받아 왔다면 그러한 임원은 근로기준법상의 근로자에 해당한다.

근로계약에서 퇴직금을 미리 연봉 속에 포함시켜 지급하였다 하더라도 이는 근로기준법 제34조에서 정하는 법정 퇴직금 지급의 효력이 없다(대구지법 2006가단2947)

5. 시사점

근로감독관은 회사와 진정한 근로자들을 조사하여 근로자 A와 C는 근로자로 인정하였다. 그러나 근로자 B는 자회사의 등기임원이고 자회사로부터 임금을 받았기 때문에, 근로자가 아닌 것으로 판단하였다. 이에 따라 회사는 근로자 A와 C에 대해서만 퇴직금을 지급하고 이 사건을 종결하였다.

Chapter 6 Premiums for the Social Insurances

Ⅰ. Social Insurances

    1. Industrial Accident Compensation Insurance

    2. Employment Insurance

    3. National Health Insurance

    4. National Pension

Ⅱ. Social Insurances for Foreign Migrant Workers

Ⅲ. Insurances Exclusive to Foreign Migrant Workers

제6장 사회보험료

I. 사회보험
   1. 산업재해보상보험
   2. 고용보험
   3. 국민건강보험과 노인장기요양보험
   4. 국민연금

II. 외국인근로자의 사회보험

III. 외국인근로자의 전용보험

Chapter 6 Premiums for the Social Insurances

I. Social Insurances

1. Industrial Accident Compensation Insurance (IACI)

(1) Concept

IACI is a social insurance system in which the government provides, under the Labor Standards Act, an employee (who has been injured or become ill at a workplace), with compensation paid by their employer. Types of IACI benefits include for medical care, suspension, disability, nursing care, survivor, injury compensation pension, funeral expenses, and vocational rehabilitation. The term 'medical care benefit' refers to an insurance benefit paid to a worker for medical treatment if the worker is injured or sick due to work-related reasons. It should be noted, however, that if the injury or illness can be cured through medical treatment within 3 days, the medical care benefit will not be paid. In order to receive the medical care benefits, the person who suffered the industrial accident (or a family member) should claim the cause as an industrial accident, and the medical doctor of the Workers' Compensation and Welfare Service (WCWS) should recognize that it was an industrial accident.

(2) Industrial Accident Compensation Insurance Premium[272]

IACI premiums that an employer must pay are calculated by multiplying the sum of the individual total income of workers engaged in the business run by the employer with the accident insurance premium rate. The rate of industrial accident compensation premiums is determined by the Ministry of Employment and Labor based on the ratio of the total amount of compensation for industrial accident compensation insurance for the past three years as of June 30 of each year depending on the risk of the business sector.

1) General Premium

A single premium shall be applied within the same workplace. In a workplace that operates more than two businesses at different rates, the business that determines the applicable rate shall be as follows:
① The business with the larger number of employees
② If there is an equal number of employees, or the number of employees

---

[272] Korea Labor Welfare Corporation, "Handbook of Workers' Compensation and Employment Insurance in 2023"

Ⅰ. 사회보험

1. 산업재해보상보험[272]

(1) 개념

산재보험은 근로자가 업무상 사유로 부상을 당하거나 질병에 걸리는 경우 근로기준법상 사업주가 부담해야 할 보상책임을 국가가 대신하여 수행하는 사회보험제도이다. 산재보험 급여의 종류에는 요양급여, 휴업급여, 장해급여, 간병급여, 유족급여, 상병보상연금, 장의비, 직업재활급여 등이 있다. '요양급여'는 근로자가 업무상의 사유로 부상을 당하거나 질병에 걸린 경우 그 근로자에게 치료비 명목으로 지급되는 보험급여를 말한다. 다만 부상 또는 질병이 3일 이내의 요양으로 치유될 수 있으면 요양급여를 지급하지 않음에 유의해야 한다. 요양급여를 받기 위해서는 산재를 당한 환자나 그 가족이 산재라는 것을 주장하고, 사용자가 산재임을 인정하며, 처음 진료를 한 의사가 산재라는 소견을 갖고, 근로복지공단의 의사가 산재라고 판정해야 한다.

(2) 산재보험료율

사업주가 전액 부담하여야 하는 산재보험료는 원칙적으로 그 사업주가 경영하는 사업에 종사하는 근로자의 개인별 보수총액에 산재보험료율을 곱한 금액을 합한 금액으로 계산한다. 업무상 재해에 관한 산재보험료율은 사업 업종의 위험여부에 따라 매년 6월 30일 현재 과거 3년 동안의 보수총액에 대한 산재보험 급여총액의 비율을 기초로 사업 종류별로 구분하여 고용노동부령으로 정한다.

1) 일반적인 산재보험료율

하나의 적용사업장에 대하여는 하나의 보험요율을 적용한다. 하나의 사업장 안에서 보험요율이 다른 2종이상의 사업이 행해지는경우 다음 순서에 따라 주된 사업을 결정하여 적용한다.
① 근로자수가 많은 사업
② 근로자수가 동일하거나 그 수를 파악할 수 없는 경우는 임금총액이

---

[272] 근로복지공단, "2023년 산재·고용보험 가입 및 부과업무 실무편람"

cannot be determined, the business with the higher total wages: or

③ If it is impossible to determine the principal business by 1) or 2) above, the rate shall be determined according to the business with the higher sales of manufactured products or services.

2) Adjustment of Premiums in Exceptional Cases

Applying the same rate for identical industries is designed to create a balance between employers taking significant steps to avoid occupational accidents and employers who do not. In cases where the insurance benefits paid during the previous three years exceeds 85%, or is less than 75%, of the premiums for the same years, the applicable rate for that industry shall be adjusted up or down by a maximum of 50%. This new rate will be applied at the beginning of the following year.

(ⅰ) **Application of the Premium**

This special premium rate applies to companies that hire 30 employees or more, excluding the construction and logging industries. However, as of July 30, which is the period when the premiums for individual companies are calculated, if the type of industry to which the premiums apply has changed within the previous three years, this special premium application shall not be reflected.

(ⅱ) **Method of Calculation**

① Ratio of benefits vs. premiums = total insurance benefits paid during the previous three years / total premiums paid during the previous three years × 100

② The insurance benefits paid for unavoidable reasons due to occupational accidents by a third party, natural disasters, power outages, etc. shall be excluded in calculation.

(ⅲ) **Date of Application** : within 10 days after determination of the general premium rate.

2. Employment Insurance[273]

(1) Concept

Employment insurance includes the traditional social security insurance that provides unemployment benefits to unemployed employees, in addition to employment security insurance, which promotes re-employment through government vocational guidance, which exists to improve employee job security, the employment structure, employee vocational skills development, etc.

---

[273] Korea Labor Welfare Corporation, "Handbook of Workers' Compensation and Employment Insurance in 2023"

많은 사업

③ 상기 방법에 의하여 주된 사업을 결정할 수 없는 경우에는 매출액이 많은 사업을 주된 사업으로 결정

2) 산재보험료율 적용의 특례

동일사업의 보험료율을 적용함에 있어서 재해방지를 위해 노력한 사업주와 그렇지 못한 사업주간에 형평의 원칙을 실현하기 위해 과거3년간의 보험급여 금액의 85%를 넘거나 75%이하인 경우 그 사업에 적용되는 보험료율을 50% 범위 안에서 사업의 규모를 결정해서 인상 또는 인하하여 그 사업에 대한 다음 사업연도의 산재보험료율로 적용한다.

(i) 보험료율 적용

건설업 및 벌목업을 제외한 사업으로서 상시 근로자수가 30인 이상인 사업에 적용한다.

개별실적요율의 기준보험연도의 6월 30일 이전 3년의 기간 중에 산재보험료율 적용사업 종류가 변경된 경우 개별실적요율 적용 제외한다.

(ii) 산정방법

① 수지율 = 3년간의 보험급여총액 / 3년간의 보험료총액 × 100
② 제3자의 행위에 의한 재해나 천재지변·정전 등 불가항력적인 사유로 지급된 보험 급여액은 보험급여액에서 제외한다.

(iii) 결정시기 : 일반요율결정 후 10일 이내에 결정한다.

2. 고용보험[273]

(1) 개념

고용보험이란 실직근로자에게 실업급여를 지급하는 전통적 의미의 실업보험사업 외에 취업알선을 통한 재취업의 촉진과 근로자의 직업안정 및 고용구조 개선을 위한 고용안정사업, 근로자의 능력개발사업 등을 상호 연계하여 시행하는 사회보험제도이다.

---

[273] 근로복지공단, "2023년 산재·고용보험 가입 및 부과업무 실무편람"

(2) Employment Insurance Premium

Premium is charged according to the unemployment benefits premium rate and the employment security & vocational ability development premium rate. The unemployment benefits premium is shared equally between employee and employer, whereas the employment security and vocational skills development premiums are charged only to the employer.

Division		Employee	Employer
Unemployment benefits		0.9%	0.9%
Employment Security & Vocational Skill Development projects	Fewer than 150 employees		0.25%
	150 employees or more (see "Preferred Companies" below)		0.45%
	150 employees ~ fewer than 1000 employees		0.65%
	More than 1000 employees		0.85%

Preferred Companies: ① Mining industry: 300 employees or fewer; ② manufacturing industry: 500 employees or fewer; ③ construction industry: 300 employees or fewer; or ④ transportation, storage and communication: 300 employees or few

3. National Health Insurance[274]

(1) Concept

The National Health Insurance Program is designed to improve national health and promote social security by implementing insurance benefits for the prevention, diagnosis, and treatment of, and rehabilitation from, disease or injury, care before and during and recovery from childbirth and the overall promotion of health. Health insurance is a mandatory insurance combining both corporate and local membership, with 97% of the entire population enrolled, while others are covered by the Medical Care Assistance Act, which supports recipients of medical benefits under the National Basic Living Security Act.[275] Those excluded from corporate insurance coverage are ① those who are self-employed and do not employ any workers; ② daily workers employed for less than one month; ③ workers or employees working at seasonal or temporary jobs; and ④ irregular workers or part-timers (who work less than 60 hours per month) who do not attend a work place regularly.

---

[274] National Health Insurance Corporation, "Handbook of National Health Insurance in 2023"
[275] Lee, Chulwoo, 『Study on Migrant Residents』, Kyungin Printing, 2017, p 299.

(2) 고용보험료

고용보험 비용은 실업급여 보험료와 고용안정·직업능력개발사업의 보험료로 구분·부과되는데, 실업급여 보험료는 근로자와 사용자가 각 1/2씩 부담하고 고용안정·직업능력개발사업 비용은 사용자가 부담한다.

구 분		근로자	사업주
실업급여		0.9%	0.9%
고용안정, 직업능력 개발사업	150인 미만 기업		0.25%
	150인 이상(우선지원대상기업)		0.45%
	150인 이상~1000인 미만기업		0.65%
	1000인 이상 기업		0.85%

* 참고: 우선지원대상기업
① 광업 : 300인 이하; ② 제조업 : 500인 이하; ③ 건설업 : 300인 이하;
④ 운수, 창고 및 통신업 : 300인 이하

3. 국민건강보험[274]

(1) 개념

국민건강보험은 국민의 질병이나 부상에 대한 예방, 진단, 치료, 재활과 출산, 사망 그리고 건강증진에 대하여 보험급여를 실시함으로써 국민보건을 향상시키고 사회보장을 증진하기 위함을 목적으로 한다. 우리나라의 경우 현재 전체 국민의 약 97%가 국민건강보험의 적용을 받고 있으며, 그 외에 기초생활보장수급자 등에 속하는 국민은 의료급여법에 의하여 의료서비스를 제공받고 있다.[275] 국민건강보험은 직장가입자와 지역가입자로 구분되는 의무보험이다. 직장가입자에서 제외되는 경우는 근로자를 채용하지 않은 자영업자, 1월 미만의 기간 동안 고용되는 일용근로자, 비상근 근로자, 1개월간의 소정근로시간이 60시간 미만인 시간제 근로자 등이다.

---

[274] 국민건강보험공단, "2023년 건강보험 가입 및 부과업무 실무편람"
[275] 이철우 외, 『이주민법연구』, 경인문화사, 2017, 299면.

Chapter 6 Premiums for the Social Insurances

Long-term care insurance is automatically granted upon subscription to the National Health Insurance Program. Long-term care insurance is designed to ease the burden on families of caring for the elderly with chronic conditions such as dementia or stroke. It encompasses a broad range of assistance needed for a prolonged period of time by older people with chronic disabilities, such as with bathing, dressing, eating, etc.

(2) National Health Insurance Premium

The premium is calculated by multiplying the premium rate by the standard monthly wage. The premium calculated is shared equally by the employee and the employer.

Employee's premium = National Health Insurance Premium(①) + Long-Term Care Insurance Premium(②)

① National Health Insurance Premium = (Total income − non-taxable income) × 3.545%

② Long-Term Care Insurance Premium = ① × 12.81%

---

1) National Health Insurance Premium
- Monthly income (monthly average income) = Yearly total income (Total income − non-taxable income) ÷ Number of months served
- Premium: 7.09% (3.545% for employer; 3.545% for employee)
- In cases where the employee receives wages from two different companies, the monthly premium shall be calculated based on each company's income and paid separately.

2) Long-Term Care Insurance Premium

Long-Term Care Insurance Premium = National Health Insurance Premium × 12.81% (Long-Term Care Insurance Premium)

4. National Pension[276]

(1) Concept

The National Pension System is designed to provide a pension for employees who reach a certain age, and to provide a pension to help support surviving family members after the sudden death or injury of an employee. All persons residing in the country who are between the ages of 18 and 60 are subject to subscription to the National Pension. However, civil servants, soldiers, employees of private schools, and other employees described by Presidential Decree are ineligible for the pension

---

[276] National Pension Corporation, "Handbook of National Pension in 2023,"

노인장기요양보험은 국민건강보험 가입자가 보험 가입과 동시에 가입이 된다. 고령이나 치매 및 중풍 등의 노인성 질병으로 혼자서는 거동이 불편한 노인에게 세수, 목욕, 식사, 배변처리, 간호 등에 필요한 요양서비스를 제공하는 것을 말한다.

(2) 건강보험료율

직장가입자의 보험료는 표준 보수월액에 보험료율을 곱한 금액이 되며, 여기서 산출된 금액에 근로자와 사용자가 각각 50%씩 부담한다.

```
건강보험료 근로자 부담액 = 건강보험료(①) + 노인장기요양보험료(②)
① 건강보험료     = (총급여 - 비과세급여) × 3.545%
② 노인장기요양보험료 = ① × 12.81%
```

1) 건강보험료
- 보수월액(월평균보수) = 연간 총보수액(총급여 - 비과세소득) ÷ 근무월수
- 보험료율 : 7.09%(사용자 3.545%, 종업원 3.545%)
- 직장가입자가 2이상 적용사업장에서 보수를 받고 있는 경우에는 각 사업장에서 받고 있는 보수를 기준으로 각각 보수월액을 결정한다.

2) 노인장기요양보험료
노인장기요양보험료 = 건강보험료 × 12.81% (노인장기요양보험료율)

4. 국민연금[276]

(1) 개념

국민연금제도는 국민이 납부한 연금보험료를 가지고, 해당 국민이 일정한 연령에 이르렀을 때 노령연금을 지급하거나, 연금가입자가 장애 또는 사망한 경우에 그 가족의 생계를 위해 연금을 지급하는 제도를 말한다. 국내에 거주하는 만 18세 이상 만 60세 미만의 국민은 국민연금의 가입대상이 된다. 다만,

---

[276] 국민연금공단, "2023년 국민연금 가입 및 부과업무 실무편람"

under the Civil Servants' Pension Act, the Veteran's Pension Act, or the Private School Teachers Pension Act.

The scope of application is divided between the company and the individual. For companies ordinarily hiring one or more workers, enrollment in the national pension plan is mandatory. Those excluded from corporate insurance coverage are ① the self-employed who do not hire any workers; ② daily workers employed for less than one month; ③ workers or employees working at seasonal or temporary jobs; and ④ irregular workers or part-timers (who work less than 60 hours per month) who do not attend a work place regularly.

(2) National Pension Premium

The National Pension premium is shared equally by the employee and the employer, in proportion to the employee's income.

Standard monthly income = Annual total income (Total income − non-taxable income) ÷ Number of months worked

Premium: 9% (4.5% for employer; 4.5% for employee)

Total (100%)	Employee's burden (50% of premium)	Employer's burden (50% of premium)
9% of employee income	4.5% of employee income	4.5% of *actual* employee income

Range of standard monthly income		
Less than 370,000 won	= 370,000 × 4.5%	= 370,000 × 4.5%
370,000 won or more ~ 5.9 million won	= standard monthly income × 4.5%	= standard monthly income × 4.5%
More than 5.9million won	= 5.9 million × 4.5%	= 5.9 million × 4.5%

II. Social Insurances for Foreign Migrant Workers

There are four major insurances: Industrial Accident Compensation Insurance, Employment Insurance, National Health Insurance, and the National Pension Plan. (i)

공무원연금법, 군인연금법 및 사립학교연금법의 적용을 받는 공무원과 군인 및 사립학교 직원은 가입대상에서 제외된다.

국민연금 가입대상자는 사업장가입자와 지역가입자로 구분되는데, 상시 1인 이상의 근로자를 사용하는 사업장은 당연적용 사업장이 된다. 사업장가입자에서 적용이 제외되는 경우에는 근로자를 채용하지 않은 자영업자, 1월 미만의 기간 동안 고용되는 일용직 근로자, 비상근 근로자, 1개월간의 소정근로시간이 60시간 미만인 시간제 근로자 등이 있다.

(2) 국민연금보험료율

연금보험료는 국민의 소득에 비례하여 근로자와 사용자가 각각 50%씩 부담한다.

기준소득월액 = 연간 총보수액(총급여 - 비과세소득) ÷ 근무월수
보험료율 : 9%(사용자 4.5%, 종업원 4.5%)

계	종업원부담	사용자부담
9(100%)%	4.5(50%)%	4.5(50%)%

기준소득월액 범위		
37만 원 미만	= 37만 원×4.5%	= 37만 원×4.5%
37만 원이상~590만 원	= 기준소득원액×4.5%	= 기준소득원액×4.5%
590만 원 초과	= 590만 원×4.5%	= 590만 원×4.5%

Ⅱ. 외국인근로자의 사회보험

사회보험은 산업재해보상보험, 고용보험, 국민건강보험, 국민연금이라는 4대보험으로 구성되며, 보험의 내용에 따라 적용을 달리하는 특징이 있다.

Industrial Accident Compensation Insurance applies to foreigners as well, but the remaining social insurances vary in application. (ii) Regarding Employment Insurance, most foreign workers stay in Korea temporarily, so it is often optional. (iii) National Health Insurance is naturally applicable if a foreign worker is employed at a workplace. (iv) National Pension is naturally applied in principle, but the principle of reciprocity means it varies in accordance with relations with each foreign country.

<Social Insurances and their Application to Foreign Workers>

		Non-professional foreign workers (E-9)	Oversea Koreans H-2, F-4	Professional foreign workers E-1~E-7	Illegal workers
Industrial Accident Compensation Insurance		Applied	Applied	Applied	Applied
Employment Insurance	Unemployment allowance	Optional	Optional	Optional	Not applied
	Vocational development, Job security	Applied	Applied	Applied	Not applied
National Health Insurance		Applied	Applied	Applied (exceptions allowed)	Not applied
Long-term Care Insurance		Excluded	Visiting & Working: excluded; Overseas Korea: Applied	Applied (exceptions allowed)	Not applied
National Pension		Applied	Applied	Applied (Reciprocal)	Not applied

1. Industrial Accident Compensation Insurance (IACI)

Since the IACI Act stipulates in Article 1 (Purpose) that its purpose is to compensate workers for work-related accidents promptly, foreign workers must be protected. Regardless of their eligibility for working visas, all are covered by the IACI Act. If a foreigner is injured while providing work, whether he or she is an industrial trainee or an illegal foreign worker, the accident will be compensated for as an industrial accident. This has been confirmed by a Supreme Court case.[277] Workers are subject to workers' compensation in the event of a work injury,

---
[277] Supreme Court ruling Sep. 15, 1995: 94 noo 12067 (Withdrawal of decision on disapproval of medical treatment)

(i) 산업재해보상보험은 외국인도 당연히 적용되지만, 나머지 사회보험은 적용상 차이가 있다. (ii) 고용보험의 경우 외국인근로자는 한국에서 일시 체류하는 경우가 대부분이므로 본인의 선택에 의해 가입여부를 임의 적용으로 하는 경우가 많다. (iii) 국민건강보험은 외국인근로자가 고용을 전제로 사업장에 채용된 경우에는 당연 가입대상이 된다. (iv) 국민연금도 당연가입이 원칙이지만 외국 국가와의 관계에 따른 상호주의 원칙이 적용되고 있다.

<외국인근로자의 체류자격에 따른 사회보험 적용현황>

구분		외국인근로자 E-9(비전문)	동포근로자 H-2(방문취업) F-4(재외동포)	전문외국인력 E-1(교수)~E-7(특정활동)	불법체류 근로자
산재보험		적용	적용	적용	적용
고용보험	실업급여	임의가입	임의가입	임의가입	미적용
고용보험	직업능력 고용안정	적용	적용	적용	미적용
국민건강보험		적용	적용	적용 (예외인정)	미적용
노인장기요양보험		제외	방문취업: 제외 재외동포: 적용	적용 (예외인정)	미적용
국민연금		적용	적용	적용 (상호주의)	미적용

1. 산업재해보상보험(산재보험)

산재보험법 제1조(목적)에서 "근로자의 업무상 재해를 신속히 보상하고"라고 규정하여 보호대상을 근로자로 설정하여 두고 있으므로, 외국인근로자는 체류자격과 무관하게 모두 산재보험법을 적용받는다. 외국인 신분이 산업연수생이든지 불법체류 신분이든지 근로를 제공하다가 다친 경우에는 산업재해로 인정하게 되었다. 이는 대법원의 판례에서도 이를 확인하고 있다.[277] 산재보험은 국민여부 또는 불법체류 여부와 상관없이 업무상 재해를 당한

---
277) 대법원 1995. 9. 15. 선고 94누12067 판결 (요양불승인처분취소).

regardless of whether they are Korean citizens or illegal workers. The Supreme Court has made it clear that illegal stays are subject to crackdowns, but that illegal residents should also be covered by industrial accident insurance in the sense that workers must be protected by labor law for labor already provided.

The IACI Act is a social insurance system in which the State carries out compensation on behalf of the employer under the Labor Standards Act if a worker is injured or ill from work. Accident compensation is applied to all businesses or workplaces using workers, taking into account the risk, size and place of business. The following types of work are not covered by the IACI Act (Article 6): ① construction with a total construction cost of less than 20 million won, ② construction by a non-housing business or non-contractor, construction of buildings with a total floor area of ??less than 100 square meters (200 square meters for waterline construction), ③ household service ④ businesses with fewer than five workers in agriculture, forestry, fishing and hunting.[278] Therefore, in the event a business or workplace is not covered by the IACI Act and has an industrial accident requiring medical treatment for three days or less, the Labor Standards Act requires the employer to compensate for the work injury/illness.[279]

2. Employment Insurance Act (EIA)

Employment insurance grants benefits to eligible people to prevent undue hardship from unemployment, promote employment, develop the vocational skills of workers, and promote job-seeking activities. It thereby contributes to the economic and social development of the nation (Article 1 of the EIA). Employment insurance applies to all businesses or workplaces in principle, with exceptions in consideration of the size of business. It applies to all workers because its main purpose is to provide stability for unemployed persons, so does not apply if those persons do not need help or are protected by other insurance. Those excluded from employment insurance are: ① 65 years of age or older, ② Those working fewer than 60 hours a month (15 hours a week), ③ Civil servants under the National Civil Service and Local Public Service Act, ④ Those to whom the Private School Teachers Pension Act applies, ⑤ Sailors under the Seafarers Act, ⑥ Foreign workers who are not eligible for residency. However, foreigners with status of residence may subscribe and benefit.

---

[278] Enforcement Decree to the IACI Act, Article 2 (Exclusion of Application of Law), Paragraph 6.
[279] Korea Labor Welfare Corporation, Handbook of Workers' Compensation and Employment Insurance in 2023 and Employment, pp. 7-8.

경우에 산재보상의 대상이 된다. 대법원은 불법체류는 단속의 대상임을 명백히 하고 있지만, 이미 제공된 사실적 행위의 노동에 대해서는 노동법의 보호가 있어야 한다는 취지에서 불법체류자도 산재보험이 적용된다고 판결하였다.

산재보험법은 근로자가 업무상 사유로 부상을 당하거나 질병에 걸리는 경우 근로기준법상 사업주가 부담해야 할 보상책임을 국가가 대신하여 수행하는 사회보험제도이다. 산재보험은 근로자를 사용하는 모든 사업 또는 사업장에서 적용되는 것을 원칙으로 하면서, 사업의 위험률, 규모 및 사업장소 등을 참작하며 다음 사업은 예외로 산재보험법의 적용을 받지 않는다(산재법 제6조). 제외되는 사업장은 "① 가사서비스업, ② 농업, 임업, 어업, 수렵업 중 상시 5인 미만의 근로자를 사용하는 사업"이다.[278] 따라서 산재보험법에서 적용되지 않는 사업이나 사업장의 경우와 3일 이하의 요양을 필요로 하는 산업재해의 경우에는 근로기준법에 따라 사용자가 업무상 재해에 대한 보상을 하여야 한다.[279]

2. 고용보험

고용보험은 실업의 예방, 고용의 촉진 및 근로자의 직업능력의 개발과 향상을 꾀하고, 근로자가 실업한 경우에 생활에 필요한 급여를 실시하여 근로자의 생활안정과 구직 활동을 촉진함을 목적으로 마련된 사회보험이다(법 제1조). 고용보험은 근로자 입장에서 실업급여를 받는 것이 주 목적이므로 모든 근로자에게 적용되는 것이 원칙이지만, 실업급여의 도움이 필요하지 않거나 다른 보험에서 보호되는 경우에는 적용되지 않는다. 고용보험이 적용 제외 되는 근로자는 ① 65세 이상인 자, ② 1월간 소정근로시간이 60시간(1주간 15시간)미만인 자, ③ 국가공무원법 및 지방공무원법에 의한 공무원, ④ 사립학교교원연금법의 적용을 받는 자, ⑤ 선원법에 의한 선원, ⑥ 거주자격이 없는 외국인근로자 등이다. 다만, 체류자격을 가진 외국인은 임의가입이 가능하다.

실업급여 보험료는 노사가 절반씩 납부하고, 고용안정사업과 직업능력개발

---

[278] 산재법 시행령 제2조(법의 적용 제외 사업) 제6호.
[279] 근로복지공단, "2023년 산재.고용보험 가입 및 부과업무 실무편람", 7-8면.

Chapter 6 Premiums for the Social Insurances

Unemployment benefits of course include unemployment benefits, but also maternity leave allowances and childcare leave benefits. Therefore, foreigners cannot receive maternity leave benefits and childcare leave benefits as well as unemployment benefits if they do not have employment insurance. If a foreign worker who is staying for employment in Korea does not intend to receive unemployment benefits, he or she may not subscribe.

<Foreign Worker Eligibility for Employment Insurance>

Status of Sojourn	Application	Status of Sojourn	Application
A-1 (Diplomat)	×	E-1 (Professor)	△ (Optional)
A-2 (Government official)	×	E-2 (Foreign language instructor)	△ (Optional)
A-3 (Agreement)	×	E-3 (Research)	△ (Optional)
B-1 (Visa exemption)	×	E-4 (Technology transfer)	△ (Optional)
B-2 (Tourist/transit)	×	E-5 (Professional employment)	△ (Optional)
C-1 (Temporary news coverage)	×	E-6 (Artistic performer)	△ (Optional)
C-3 (Short-term visit)	×	E-7 (Designated activities)	△ (Optional)
C-4 (Short-term employee)	△ Optional	E-9 (Non-professional employment)	△ (Optional)
D-1 (Artist)	×	E-10 (Crew employee)	△ (Optional)
D-2 (Student)	×	F-1 (Visiting or joining family)	×
D-3 (Industrial trainee)	×	F-2 (Resident)	○ (Compulsory)
D-4 (General trainee)	×	F-3 (Accompanying spouse/child)	×
D-5 (Journalism)	×	F-4 (Overseas Korean)	△ (Optional)
D-6 (Religion)	×	F-5 (Permanent resident)	○ (Compulsory)
D-7 (Supervisor)	▲Reciprocal	F-6 (Marriage to Korean Citizen)	○ (Compulsory)
D-8 (Corporate investor)	▲Reciprocal	G-1 (Miscellaneous)	×
D-9 (International trade)	▲Reciprocal	H-1 (Working holiday)	×
D-10 (Job Seeking)	×	H-2 (Working visit)	△ (Optional)

Source: Korea Labor Welfare Corporation, Working Guide for Workers and Workers' Compensation and Employment Insurance 2023, p. 18.

* 'x' denotes those foreigners ineligible for employment insurance.

사업 보험료는 사업주가 전액 부담한다. 실업급여 부분은 실업수당과 산전산후 휴가수당 및 육아휴직 급여의 재원이 된다. 외국인이 고용보험을 가입하지 않으면 실업수당뿐만 아니라 산전산후 휴가수당과 육아휴직 급여를 받을 수 없다. 한국에서 취업을 목적으로 체류하는 외국인근로자중 실업급여를 받을 의도가 없는 경우에는 가입을 하지 않을 수도 있다.

<외국인의 체류자격별 고용보험 적용 여부>

체류자격	고용보험 적용	체류자격	고용보험 적용
1. 외 교(A-1)	×	19. 교 수(E-1)	△(임의)
2. 공 무(A-2)	×	20. 회화지도(E-2)	△(임의)
3. 협 정(A-3)	×	21. 연 구(E-3)	△(임의)
4. 사증면제(B-1)	×	22. 기술지도(E-4)	△(임의)
5. 관광통과(B-2)	×	23. 전문직업(E-5)	△(임의)
6. 일시취재(C-1)	×	24. 예술흥행(E-6)	△(임의)
7. 단기종합(C-3)	×	25. 특정활동(E-7)	△(임의)
8. 단기취업(C-4)	△(임의)	26. 비전문취업(E-9)	△(임의)
9. 문화예술(D-1)	×	27. 선원취업(E-10)	△(임의)
10. 유 학(D-2)	×	28. 방문동거(F-1)	×
11. 산업연수(D-3)	×	29. 거 주(F-2)	○(강제)
12. 일반연수(D-4)	×	30. 동 반(F-3)	×
13. 취 재(D-5)	×	31. 재외동포(F-4)	△(임의)
14. 종 교(D-6)	×	32. 영 주(F-5)	○(강제)
15. 주 재(D-7)	▲(상호주의)	33. 영 주(F-6)	○(강제)
16. 기업투자(D-8)	▲(상호주의)	34. 기 타(G-1)	×
17. 무역경영(D-9)	▲(상호주의)	35. 관광취업(H-1)	×
18. 구직(D-10)	×	36. 방문취업(H-2)	△(임의)

출처 : 근로복지공단, "2023년 산재·고용보험 가입 및 부과업무 실무편람", 18면.
※ ×로 표시된 경우에는 임의가입도 불가함에 유의

3. National Health Insurance (NHIA)

All business and local subscribers covered by National Health Insurance are required to pay premiums. However, foreign workers (E-9) and visiting Korean workers (H-2) under the employment permit system in the Foreign Employment Act and in Article 7 (4) of the Long-Term Care Insurance Act can be exempted through a separate application process through a nursing care insurance subscriber. All other foreign workers who do not have a basis for exemption are automatically subscribed to long-term care insurance and pay the premium along with the health insurance premium.

4. National Pension (NPA)

Foreigners working in workplaces are subject to the National Pension Act (Article 126) and foreign nationals residing in Korea shall, of course, become business or regional subscribers. However, if the law equivalent to Korea's NPA in the foreigner's country of citizenship does not apply to Republic of Korea nationals living there, the national pension system in Korea corresponding to the national pension shall be taken as the principle of a reciprocity with foreign countries Those not covered by the National Pension Scheme are those here on temporary stay visas or without income.[280]

National Pension applies to foreign nationals when they are employed at a workplace that must subscribe to it. To receive the pension benefit, the foreign national must have paid into the national pension for at least 10 years and reach the age of 60. This is not easy for most foreign workers to do. In this case, a lump-sum refund will be given, which will be handled in accordance with the social security agreement Korea has with that national's country of citizenship. In addition, the National Pension Act was amended in January 2015 in accordance with the decision of the Constitutional Court in recognition of the property value of national pensions (Article 126 of the NPA).[281]

5. Opinion

---

[280] Excluded foreigners: (1) Those who have stayed without permission to extend their stay in accordance with Article 25 of the Immigration Control Act; (2) A person who has not registered as an alien under Article 31 of the Immigration Control Act or who has been issued an order of forced eviction under Article 59 (2) of the same Act; (3) Status of residence (D-1), Study abroad (D-2), Technical training (D-3), General training (D-4), Religion (D-6), Visiting living (F- 1) Person with companion (F-3) and others (G-1).

[281] Constitutional Court of Korea decision Jun. 29, 2000: 99 Hunba 289; Constitutional Court of Korea decision on May 28, 2009: 2005 Hunba 20

3. 국민건강보험

국민건강보험이 적용되는 모든 사업장가입자나 지역가입자 모두 당연 적용되어 보험료를 납부한다. 다만 「노인장기요양보험법」 제7조 제4항에 따라 외국인고용법의 고용허가제에 속하는 외국인근로자(E-9)와 방문취업 동포근로자(H-2)는 별도의 적용제외 신청절차를 통해 장기요양보험 가입자에서 제외를 받을 수 있다. 제외신청의 근거가 없는 다른 외국인근로자들은 모두 장기요양보험에 자동 가입되어 보험료를 건강보험료와 함께 납부한다.

4. 국민연금

국민연금법 제126조에 따라 사업장에 사용되는 외국인과 국내에 거주하는 외국인은 당연히 사업장가입자 또는 지역가입자가 된다. 다만, 그 국민연금에 상응하는 연금제도를 그 외국인의 본국법이 대한민국 국민에게 적용되지 아니하면 해당 외국인에게도 국민연금을 적용하지 않는다는 상호주의의 입장을 취하고 있다. 그리고 국민연금의 가입 적용대상에서 제외되는 외국인은 일시적으로 체류하거나 소득이 없는 외국인이다.[280]

국민연금은 외국인근로자가 국민연금 사업장에 취업한 경우 당연가입 조건으로 적용되는데 노령연금을 수급하기 위해서는 10년 이상 국민연금에 가입하고 60세의 연령에 도달하여야 한다. 외국인근로자가 이를 충족하기는 쉽지 않다. 이 경우 반환일시금을 수령하는데, 이는 출신국과의 사회보장협정에 따라 기 납부한 국민연금 보험료를 일시반환 받을 수 있다. 2015년 1월 국민연금법이 개정되어, 국민연금에 상응하는 연금제도가 없는 국가의 외국인 경우에는 국민연금의 가입자에서 제외되었다(동법 제126조).[281]

5. 시사점

---

[280] 제외되는 외국인: ① 출입국관리법 제25조에 따라 체류기간연장허가를 받지 아니하고 체류하는 자, ② 출입국관리법 제31조에 따른 외국인등록을 하지 아니하거나 같은 법 제59조 제2항에 따라 강제퇴거명령서가 발급된 자, ③ 체류자격이 문화예술(D-1), 유학(D-2), 기술연수(D-3), 일반연수(D-4), 종교(D-6), 방문동거(F-1), 동반(F-3), 기타(G-1)인 자이다.

[281] 헌법재판소 2000.6.29.선고 99헌바289 결정; 헌법재판소 2009.5.28.선고 2005헌바20 결정.

Chapter 6 Premiums for the Social Insurances

The four main insurances for foreign workers are granted natural benefits. With Industrial Accident Compensation Insurance, there is insufficient compensation to workers injured/ill from industrial accidents at workplaces hiring fewer than five workers in rural areas. If Employment Insurance is voluntary and foreign workers become unemployed or find another job, most will be excluded from maternity leave or parental leave. Illegal residents are excluded from National Health Insurance coverage. Paying into the National Pension Scheme is mandatory for non-professional foreign workers (E-9), even though it is impossible, under the short-term visa system, for them to stay long enough to be eligible for the benefits. which is another burden that the employer should pay as the employer's burden in premiums. So, the National Pension should be excluded from the mandatory social insurances.

Ⅲ. Insurances Exclusive to Foreign Migrant Workers

Employers are obliged to subscribe to Departure Maturity Insurance, Guaranty Insurance for unpaid wages, Foreign Workers' Care Insurance and Return-Expense Insurance.[282] When an employer re-employs a foreign worker, they shall extend the existing insurance coverage period of the Departure Maturity Insurance and Guaranty Insurance for unpaid wages (Article 13 of the FEA).[283]

1. Departure Severance Insurance

Departure Maturity Insurance replaces severance pay but accumulates at the same rate. It is payable when the foreign worker leaves the country(Article 13 of the Foreign Employment Act: FEA). The employer must pay a monthly premium of 8.3% of a worker's monthly ordinary wage stated in the employment permit system (EPS). This is to prevent late payment of severance pay and is limited to non-professional employment (E-9) and visiting overseas Korean workers (H-2) in

---

[282] If they do not subscribe, they will be fined up to 5 million won.
[283] Korea Industrial Labor Corporation, "2023 Foreign Worker Exclusive Insurance Guide"

외국인근로자에 대한 4대 보험은 당연가입으로 처리되고 있다. 산재보험의 경우 농어촌 지역의 5인 이내 사업장에서 산업재해를 당한 경우 제대로 재해보상이 이루어지지 않고 있어 개선이 요구된다. 고용보험이 임의보험으로 외국인근로자가 실업이나 타사업장으로 이전할 경우, 출산휴가나 육아휴직의 경우 미가입에 따른 고용보험의 보호를 받지 못한다. 국민건강보험의 경우 불법체류자 신분은 적용제외가 됨으로 인해 가장 중요한 건강보호에 미흡한 면이 많다. 국민연금은 단순기능 외국인근로자(E-9)의 경우 단기순환제로 장기체류가 불가능한 대상인데도 국민연금이 강제가입 대상으로 하고 있어 국민연금 보험료에 대해 사업주에 대해 추가 부담을 줄 수 있기 때문에 4대 사회보험중 국민연금이 제외되는 것이 필요하다.

Ⅲ. 외국인근로자의 전용보험

사용자는 출국만기보험 및 임금체불 보증보험, 외국인근로자는 상해보험 및 귀국비용보험에 의무적으로 가입해야 한다.[282] 사용자가 외국인근로자를 재고용시에는 출국만기보험과 보증보험의 기존 보험가입기간을 연장하여야 한다(외국인고용법 제13조).[283]

1. 출국만기보험

출국만기보험은 퇴직금에 갈음하여 퇴직금에 해당하는 금액을 적립하는 것으로 외국인근로자가 퇴직할 경우 퇴직금에 갈음하여 수령한다(외고법 제13조). 사용자는 납입보험료로 고용허가제에 기재된 월 통상임금의 8.3%를 매월 납부하여야 한다. 이는 퇴직금의 체불을 예방하기 위한 것으로 고용허가제의 비전문취업(E-9)과 방문취업(H-2) 근로자에 한정된다.[284] 출국만기보험은 근로자가 퇴직급여보장법상 퇴직금을 대신하여 운영하는 보험으로

---
[282] 미가입시 500만 원 이하의 벌금 또는 과태료가 부과된다.
[283] 한국산업인력공단, "2023년 외국인근로자 전용보험 안내서"
[284] 이하룡, 「외국인근로자와 외국적 동포」, 박문각, 2014, 475-476면; 하갑래, 「근로기준법」, 1031-1032면.

the EPS.[284] Departure Maturity Insurance is operated in lieu of the retirement allowance under the Retirement Benefit Security Act (RBSA), with the benefits paid to foreign workers when their employment relations end and only if they have worked for at least one year at the same workplace. This second stipulation means that the departure maturity insurance is paid on the premise that the foreign worker is leaving Korea. The Constitutional Court decided that payment of severance pay when leaving Korea would be in line with the purpose of the Foreign Employment Act, even if retirement benefits were paid on the basis of departure, rather than on the premise of terminated employment relations.[285]

If a foreign worker has worked for less than one year after the Departure Maturity Insurance is purchased, the insurance will not be paid to the foreign worker but return to the employer instead. insurance benefit will be returned to the. Since the departure maturity insurance is paid in lieu of retirement allowance, it must be paid within 14 days after employment relations end in accordance with Article 36 of the Labor Standards Act.

2. Guaranty Insurance for unpaid wages

The employer is obliged to purchase Guaranty Insurance against late payment of wages for their foreign workers (Article 23). Since this Guaranty Insurance is paid to the foreign workers in lieu of the unpaid wages, the insurance company pays the unpaid wages first, then charges the company for the amount equivalent to the paid arrears. Foreign workers whose wages have been unpaid must first report the fact to the Labor Office of the Ministry of Employment and Labor. However, there is a maximum payout of 2 million won. The amount of wages outstanding will be billed directly to the employer or processed in the same way as for Koreans who have not been paid their wages.

---

[284] Lee, Ha-Ryong, Foreign Workers and Oversea Koreans, Park Moon Gak, 2014, pp. 475-476; Ha, Gae-Rae, Labor Standards Act, pp. 1031-1032.
[285] Constitutional Court of Korea ruling Mar. 31, 2016: 2014 Hunma 367 (Departure maturity insurance accepted as constitutional).

사업장에서 이탈하지 않고 1년 이상 근무한 경우에 한해 외국인근로자가 퇴직시 보험금이 지급 된다. 다만, 1년 이상 사업장에 근무한 외국인근로자가 사업장을 이탈한 때에는 보험금을 수령할 수 없다. 왜냐하면 출국만기보험의 성격상 출국을 전제로 퇴직금이 지급되기 때문이다. 헌법재판소는 불법체류의 예방목적을 위해 예외적으로 퇴직을 전제로 하는 것이 아닌 출국을 전제로 퇴직급여를 지급해도 외국인고용법의 취지에 맞는다고 하여 합헌을 결정하였다.[285]

출국만기보험 가입 후 외국인근로자가 1년 미만 근무한 경우에는 해당 외국인근로자에게는 보험금이 지급되지 않는다. 외국인근로자가 동일한 사업장에서 1년 미만으로 근무하거나 이탈하는 경우에는 사용자에게 보험금이 반환된다. 출국만기보험이 퇴직금에 갈음하여 지급되므로 근로기준법 제36조에 따라 퇴직 후 14일 이내에 지급하도록 되어 있지만, 외국인근로자 특성상 반드시 출국 되도록 공항의 출국심사를 마친 경우 곧바로 지급하도록 하고 있다. 외국인 전용보험 중 출국만기 보험의 경우에는 불법체류를 방지하기 위해 외국인근로자가 퇴직하고 본국으로 귀국할 때 공항에서 수령하거나 귀국 후 수령할 수 있도록 하고 있다.

2. 임금체불 보증보험

사용자는 외국인근로자의 임금체불에 대비하여 보증보험에 의무적으로 가입해야 한다(외고법 제23조). 이 보증보험은 사용자의 임금체불시 대신 외국인근로자에게 지급하는 것이므로 보험회사가 체불임금을 먼저 지급하고, 보험회사는 기지급된 체불임금에 상당하는 금액을 회사에 청구하게 된다. 임금체불시 외국인근로자는 먼저 고용노동부 지방노동청 근로감독과에 체불사실을 신고하고, 임금체불확인서를 발급받은 경우에라야 보험금을 지급받을 수 있다. 다만, 임금체불금액이 보증금액 한도인 200만 원을 초과할 경우에는 보증금액 한도 내에서 외국인근로자에게 체불임금을 지급해야 한다. 나머지 임금체불금액은 사용자에게 직접 청구하거나 일반 체불임금 처리절차와 같게 진행한다.

---

[285] 헌법재판소 2016.3.31. 선고 2014헌마367 결정(출국만기보험 위헌심사 청구에 합헌)

Chapter 6 Premiums for the Social Insurances

<Insurances Exclusive to Foreign Migrant Workers>

	Departure Maturity Insurance	Guaranty Insurance for unpaid wages	Return-Expense Insurance	Accident Insurance
Purpose	Reduce the burden of severance pay	Preparation against non-payment of wages	Remove the burden of purchasing a return-home ticket before departure	Death, disability or disease not related to work
Sources	Article 13, Enforcement Decree 21	Article 23, Enforcement Decree 27	Article 15, Enforcement Decree 22	Article 23, Enforcement Decree 28
Insurer	Employer	Employer	Foreign worker	Foreign worker
Joining time	Within 15 days from the effective date of the labor contract	Within 15 days from the effective date of the labor contract	Within 3 months from the effective date of the labor contract	Within 15 days from the effective date of the labor contract
Premiums	Monthly deposit: 8.3% of monthly ordinary wages	One-time payment: 15,000 won / 1 year	Lump sum / 3 installments (400,000-600,000 won); varies by country	One-time payment: 20,000 won / 1 year (differs by age and gender)
Paying the premiums	Insured amount, but if the payment is insufficient, the employer pays the difference.	Unpaid wages are subsidized, up to a maximum 2 million won.	Deposit amount, (if the deposited amount is held for more than 30 months, interest will be paid).	-Death: 30 million won -Disability: 30 million won -Disease (death, disability): 15 million won
Benefits paid	When the foreign worker departs after working for at least one year.	When an employer delays payment of wages.	When the foreign worker leaves the country (except for temporary departures).	Upon death of a foreign worker, or occurrence of disability or disease.

Source: Korea Industrial Labor Corporation, "2023 Foreign Worker Exclusive Insurance Guide" pp 5-17.

3. Return Expense Insurance

Return Expense Insurance is mandatory to reduce illegal stays by encouraging

<외국인근로자 전용보험>

구 분	출국만기보험	임금체불 보증보험	귀국비용보험	상해보험
도입 목적	중소기업의 퇴직금 일시지급 부담 완화	임금체불에 대한 대비	귀국시 필요한 항공권구입 비용 충당	업무상 재해 이외의 사망·질병대비
근거	법 제13조, 시행령 제21조	법 제23조, 시행령 제27조	법 제15조, 시행령 제22조	법 제23조, 시행령 제28조
가입 대상	사용자	사용자	외국인근로자	외국인근로자
가입 시기	근로계약 효력발생일부터 15일 이내	근로계약 효력발생일부터 15일 이내	근로계약 효력 발생일부터 3개월 이내	근로계약 효력 발생일부터 15일 이내
보험료 납부 방법	매월 적립 - 월 통상임금의 8.3%	일시금 1년/15,000원	일시금/3회분납 (40만-60만 원) 국가별 차이	일시금 1년 / 2만 원 (연령,성별에 따라 차등)
보험금	적립금액 지급(차액지급), 단 지급요건 불충분시 사업주 귀속	200만 원 한도 내에서 체불임금만큼 지급	적립금액 지급(30개월 이상시 이자)	-사망:3천만 원 -장해:3천만 원, -질병(사망·장해):1,500만 원
보험금 지급 사유	1년 이상 근무한 외국인근로자의 출국	사용자의 임금체불 발생	외국인근로자 출국(일시 출국 제외)	외국인근로자 사망 또는 질병

출처 : 한국산업인력공단, "2023년 외국인근로자 전용보험 안내서"1-17면.

3. 귀국비용보험

귀국비용보험은 외국인근로자가 체류기간 만료 도래시 출국을 유도하고,

foreign workers to leave the country when their period of stay expires and to help them have the money necessary for returning home (Article 15 of the Foreign Employment Act). Payment of insurance premiums must be made within 80 days of the date of entry (E-9 Non-professional Foreigners) or the start of the labor contract (H-2 Visiting overseas Korean Workers). The benefit shall not be paid for temporary departures, but only if the foreign worker leaves the country due to expiration of the employment contract or expiration of the status of residence.

4. Accident Insurance

Foreign workers (E-9, H-2 status of residence) must be registered for Accident Insurance within 15 days of the effective date of the labor contract in preparation for death, disability or illness unrelated to work (Article 23). Accident insurance premiums vary depending on gender and age. As insurance premiums are low, insurance benefits are limited. A maximum of 30 million won is paid if a foreign worker dies or acquires a disability, and 15 million won for illness. In other words, if you are hospitalized for a personal illness and receive surgery or long-term care, the benefits from this insurance are not enough to cover such large medical expenses.

불법체류를 방지하기 위해 귀국시 필요한 비용을 대비하고자 외국인근로자가 의무적으로 가입해야 하는 보험이다(외고법 제15조). 보험금은 체류 기간 만료시 귀국에 필요한 항공료를 지원하기 위한 용도로 사용된다. 보험료 납입은 입국일(E-9 단순기능외국인) 또는 근로계약 개시일(H-2 방문취업 동포근로자)로부터 80일 이내에 이루어져야 한다. 이 보험료는 그 취지에 따라 일시적인 출국에는 지급하지 않고, 외국인근로자가 근로계약 만료 또는 체류자격 만료로 출국하는 경우에만 지급된다.

4. 상해보험

상해보험은 외국인근로자(E-9, H-2 체류자격)가 업무상 재해 이외의 상해 또는 질병사고 등에 대비하여 근로계약 효력 발생일부터 15일 이내에 가입해야 한다(외고법 제23조). 상해보험 보험료 성별, 연령에 따라 차이가 있으나 3년 가입시 2만 원 정도이다. 상해보험은 보험료가 낮은 만큼 보험료 수령액도 제한적이다. 외국인근로자가 사망하거나 후유장해가 있는 경우에 한해 최대 3000만 원, 질병사망인 경우에는 1500만 원이 지급된다.

Chapter 7 Wage-related Personnel Systems

Ⅰ. Motivation Systems

Ⅱ. Gain Sharing System

Ⅲ. Welfare System Operation

제7장 부록: 임금관련 인사제도

I. 동기부여제도
II. 성과배분제도
III. 복리후생제도

Chapter 7 Wage-related Personnel Systems

Ⅰ. Motivation Systems[286]

1. Concept of Motivation

A company can hire skilled employees and develop their abilities; however, the endeavor does not always result in satisfactory performance. This means that the employees' performance is autonomous and affected by their inclination to perform the job. Performance, ability, and motivation are functionally interrelated as follows:

$$\text{Performance} = f\ (\text{ability, motivation})$$

To acquire optimal performance, the employees shall not only exhibit ability but also strive to achieve the company's goals and contribute to attaining them. There are substantial differences in the level of employee motivation. According to psychologists, performance result is differentiated ±30% based upon employee motivation level among those who possess the same capabilities to perform the job.

2. Combining the Interests of Employees and Company

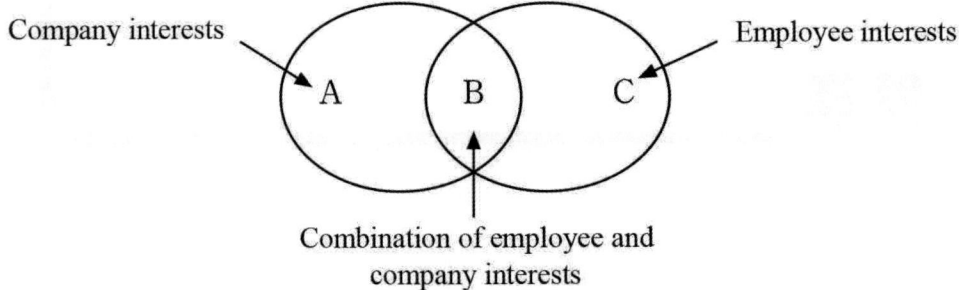

Employees have their own interests, as do companies. Conflicts arise when the

---

[286] Park, KyeongKyu, 「New Human Resources Management」, 7th ed., Hongmoonsa, 2019; Kim, Youngjae, 「New HR Workforce Management」 4th ed., Topbooks; and Lim, Changhee, 「Organizational Behaviors」, 6th ed., B&Books, 2018.

Ⅰ. 동기부여제도[286]

1. 모티베이션의 의의

기업에서는 우수한 능력을 갖춘 사람들을 고용하여 이들의 능력을 향상시킬 수 있지만 이러한 노력이 항상 만족할 만한 성과로 이어지지는 않는다. 종업원의 성과는 종업원이 직무를 얼마나 잘 수행하고자 하는지의 자발적인 의욕에 달려 있다. 성과와 능력 및 모티베이션과의 관계를 함수관계로 나타내면 다음과 같다.

$$성과 = f(능력, 모티베이션)$$

종업원들이 만족할 만한 성과를 가져오기 위해서는 능력 이외에도 종업원들 스스로 기업이 추구하는 목표에 동조하고 목표달성을 위해 공헌하도록 하는 노력이 필요하다. 종업원들이 어떤 수준의 모티베이션을 갖고 업무를 수행하느냐에 따라 성과는 상당한 차이를 가져올 수 있다. 심리학자들은 같은 능력을 갖춘 종업원들이 일을 하였을 때 그들이 갖고 있는 모티베이션에 따라 성과가 ±30% 정도 차이가 있다고 주장하고 있다.

2. 종업원과 조직 이해관계의 통합

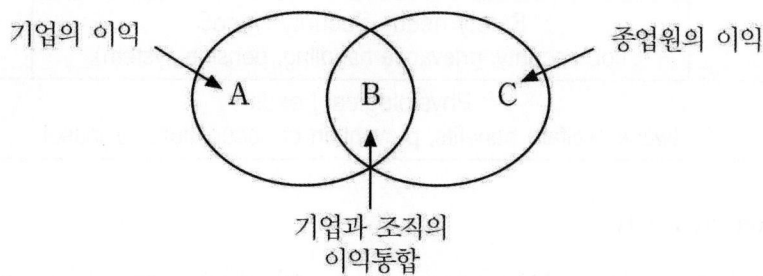

종업원은 자신들 나름대로 욕구를 가지고 있으며, 이 욕구와 기업이 추구하는 목표가 일치하지 않을 때 갈등이 일어나게 된다. 따라서 조직은 기업의

---

[286] 박경규,「신인사관리」제7판, 홍문사, 2019; 김영재외 2,「신인적자원관리」, 제4판, 탑북스, 2019; 임창희「조직행동」제6판, 비엔엠북스, 2018

employees' desires do not match the company's pursuits. Accordingly, the company shall provide more benefits to those yielding to the company's pursuits far above other pursuits. For this type of incentive reward, a structured reward system must be developed so as to combine employee and company interests.

3. Motivation Theory

It is necessary to understand how employees behave in order to satisfy individual desires and improve company performance at the same time. Thus, the company needs to understand employee motives, their causes, and their development.

(1) Level of desires (Maslow)

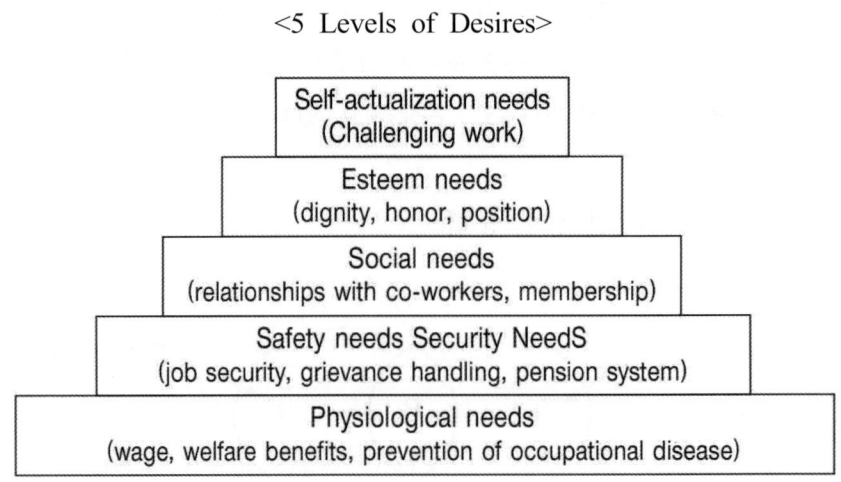

<5 Levels of Desires>

1) Physiological needs

Physiological needs include sleep, food and drink, etc. They are basic and influential. Survival needs in the company are wages, welfare, etc.

2) Safety and security needs

In addition to survival needs are safety and security needs, which include security from danger, accident, disease, violence, crime, cold, heat, etc. The company takes

목표달성을 위해 조직의 목표에 기여한 종업원들에게 더 큰 보상을 하여 종업원들에게 동기부여를 시켜주어야 한다. 이러한 동기부여 보상체계를 위하여 종업원의 이익과 회사의 이익이 통합될 수 있는 보상체계가 필요하다고 하겠다.

3. 모티베이션 이론

종업원 개인의 욕구충족과 기업의 성과향상을 위하여 종업원들의 행동이 어떻게 변화되는지를 이해할 필요가 있다. 이를 위해서는 우선 종업원들이 어떤 동기를 가지고 어떤 과정을 거쳐 동기가 유발되어 행동으로 나타나는지를 파악해야 한다.

(1) 욕구단계설(매슬로우(Maslow))

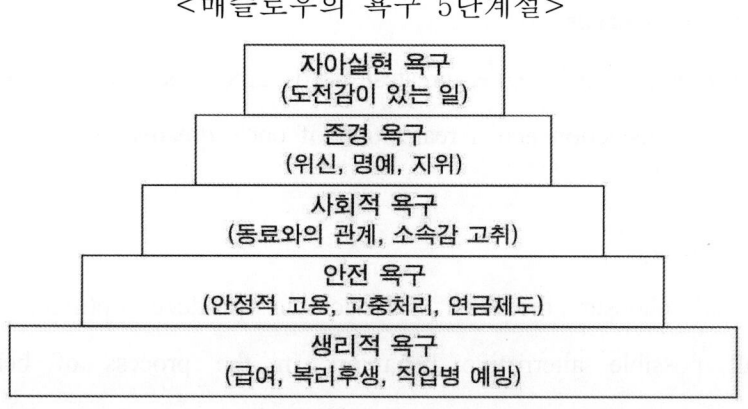

<매슬로우의 욕구 5단계설>

1) 생리적 욕구

기본적인 생리적 욕구(Physiological Needs)는 의식주, 수면, 갈증 등에 대한 욕구로서 모든 욕구 가운데 가장 기본적인 것이면서 가장 강력하다. 기업에서 생리적 욕구를 충족시키기 위한 조치로서는 급여, 복리후생 등이 해당된다.

2) 안전의 욕구

생리적 욕구가 충족된 이후 나타나는 것이 안전의 욕구(Safety and

measures to fulfill safety and security needs through job security, pension system (or severance pay), etc.

3) Social needs

Social needs are desired when survival needs and safety and security needs have been met. Social needs include friendship, affection, membership, etc. with other people or groups. For these needs, the company should encourage a friendly atmosphere among its employees and promote collegiality.

4) Esteem needs

Esteem needs are desires of people for recognition in society, desires to maintain self-esteem and self-respect, and to earn respect from others. Esteem can be identified with feelings of dignity, high social standing, self-esteem, etc. Thus, the company shall strive to appoint a job appropriate to employee age and assign positions after proper career development.

5) Self-Actualization needs

Self-Actualization needs are the greatest needs among all human needs. They are needs for self-satisfaction and a realization of one's dreams.

(2) Expectation theory

An individual chooses the best behavior to produce optimum results after evaluating all possible alternative behaviors in the process of behavior-related decision-making. In this case, motivation is affected by three factors.

First, expectancy is a person's reliability factor to bring about specific results in certain activities. Secondly, instrumentality presents rewards when one establishes a certain level of results. Lastly, valence is the intensity of preference concerning specific rewards.

For instance, when a student prepares for a test, they may expect to get a higher score if he studies hard for it (expectancy). The student also believes that they may qualify for a scholarship if they receives a high score on the test (instrumentality).

security Needs)이다. 안전의 욕구는 위험, 사고, 전쟁, 질병, 폭행, 범죄, 매우 춥거나 더운 기온 등으로부터 벗어나 안전해지고 싶은 욕구이다. 기업에서 안전의 욕구를 충족시킬 수 있는 조치로서는 고용의 안정성, 연금제도(또는 퇴직금) 등이 있다.

3) 사회적 욕구

생리적 욕구와 안전의 욕구가 충족되면 사회적 욕구(Social Needs)가 중요하게 나타나는데, 이는 다른 사람이나 집단과의 우정, 애정, 소속감 등에 대한 욕구이다. 이에 대해 기업에서는 동료와의 관계를 돈독히 할 기회를 마련하고 소속감을 고취시키는 노력이 필요하다.

4) 자아존중의 욕구

자아존중의 욕구(Esteem Needs)는 사람들이 사회생활을 통해 자신의 능력을 높게 평가받고 자신을 존중하고 자존심을 지니며 다른 사람으로부터 존경받기를 원하는 욕구이다. 위신이나 지위욕, 자긍심 등이 이 욕구와 관련된다. 이에 대해 기업에서는 적절한 경력개발을 통해 종업원의 나이나 지위에 걸맞은 직급을 보유하도록 노력해야 한다.

5) 자아실현의 욕구

마지막으로 인간의 욕구 가운데 최상층에 위치해 있는 것이 자아실현의 욕구(Self-Actualization Needs)이다. 이는 자기충족 및 성취에 대한 욕구로 자기가 가지고 있는 능력을 실현시키고자 하는 욕구이다.

(2) 기대이론

개인은 자신의 행동 결정 과정에서 여러 가지 가능한 행동 대안을 평가하여 자기 자신에게 가장 중요시하는 결과를 가져오리라고 믿는 행동 대안을 선택한다. 이 경우에 모티베이션은 3가지 요소에 의해 영향을 받는다.

첫 번째는 기대감(expectancy)으로, 어떤 활동이 특정 결과를 가져오리라고 믿는 가능성을 말한다. 두 번째는 수단성(instrumentality)으로 어떤 특정한 수준의 성과를 달성하면 바람직한 보상이 주어지리라고 믿는 정도이다. 그리고 마지막으로 유의성(valence)으로 특정 보상에 대해 갖는 선호의 강도이다.

예를 들어 학생이 시험준비를 할 때, 시험준비를 열심히 하면 좋은 성적을 받을 수 있다고 판단될 때(기대감), 높은 시험성적을 받으면 장학금을 받는

Thus, when the student sees that the test score and scholarship are important (valence), they is motivated to study harder.

(3) Reinforcement theory

According to the reinforcement theory, desirable behaviors cannot persist and will gradually disappear unless there is continuous reinforcement. That is, rewarded behaviors have a greater tendency to be repeated. Therefore, when an employee performs excellent work or improves productivity substantially, or suggests a contributing idea, such behaviors can be maintained with rewards. However, absence of rewards lowers the expectancy of the recurrence of such behaviors. This means higher performance can be least expected if the employee's performance or contributions are not reinforced.

4. Methods of Motivation

(1) Tangible rewards

A powerful incentive to promote higher performance is offering tangible rewards such as additional wages and welfare. Monetary rewards are especially effective to those employees who are especially concerned about survival needs on account of their living status. Nevertheless, such tangible rewards are limited since they can degrade the company's market competition due to excessive private expenditures.

(2) Intangible rewards
1) Job designing

Employees are often discouraged from work due to simplicity of the work, weariness, boredom, etc. or on account of extreme job standardization. The company can overcome this problem through job rotation, job enlargement, job substantiality, job crossing, semi-autonomous work groups, working hours adjustment, etc.

2) Job security

Maslow's theory on the safety and security needs is applied.

다고 믿을 때(수단성), 그리고 시험성적과 장학금이 학생에 있어 중요할 때 (유의성) 학생은 열심히 공부할 의욕을 갖게 된다고 한다.

(3) 강화이론

강화(reinforcement)이론은 강화가 이루어지지 않으면 새로운 행동은 지속되지 못하고 사라지게 된다. 즉 보상받는 행동은 반복되는 경향을 보인다. 그러므로 종업원들이 작업을 훌륭하게 수행했거나 생산성을 획기적으로 높였다든지, 창의적인 제안을 했을 경우, 이에 대해 보상을 함으로써 이러한 행동은 계속해서 일어날 수 있지만, 반대로 보상받지 못했을 경우에는 이러한 행동이 계속적으로 일어나기를 기대할 수 없다. 즉, 종업원의 성과나 공헌이 지속적으로 인정되지 않는다면 종업원들이 높은 성과를 보이리라는 기대를 할 수 없다.

4. 기업의 동기부여 방법

(1) 경제적(실체적) 보상

종업원의 근로 의욕을 높일 수 있는 강력한 도구는 바로 경제적 보상이다. 경제적 보상은 임금과 복리후생으로 구성되어 있다. 경제적 보상은 종업원의 생계와 직접 관련되기 때문에 생리적 욕구가 강한 종업원에게는 그 효과가 크다. 그러나 경제적 보상은 인건비 상승으로 기업의 경쟁력을 약화시킬 수 있으므로 제한적일 수밖에 없다.

(2) 비경제적(비실체적) 보상
1) 직무설계

종업원들이 지나친 직무표준화로 인해서 단조로움, 권태, 지루함 등으로 의욕상실이 나타나게 되는데 이를 극복하기 위한 방법으로는 직무순환, 직무확대, 직무충실, 직무교차, 준자율적 작업집단, 근로시간의 조정 등이 있다.

2) 직무의 안정성

이는 매슬로우가 제시한 욕구 가운데 안전욕구에서 언급되는 사항이다.

3) Working conditions

Employee desires for safe and comfortable working conditions are attributable to their safety needs. The employer cannot expect the employees to be enthusiastic about work if they are working under poor conditions.

4) Fair leadership

An employer's outstanding leadership not only promotes effective work performance but also contributes to the company's overall performance.

5) Company culture

The employees are affected greatly by the values upheld by their company and the amount of autonomy and decision-making authority bestowed upon them. Successful companies emphasize creativity and active participation. Employees of such companies tend to work harder.

(3) Human-relation systems

1) Counseling

Counseling from psychologists with professional knowledge assists employees with problems they cannot handle alone. Accordingly, it reduces the number of conflicts among employees, helps them maintain a positive attitude, and addresses many personal issues.

2) Participation system

This system is designed to motivate the employees to work by providing an opportunity to participate in management.

3) Grievance handling system

A mature society has the social power and ability to disclose potential conflicts and solve problems through discussion. Although not all conflicts can be solved, many can be mitigated through disclosures. Thus, the employer shall prepare certain procedures to fairly handle the complaints or grievances of the employees.

3) 근로조건

근로자들이 편안하고 안전한 근로조건을 원하는 것은 안전에 대한 욕구에서 나오는 것이다. 불편하고 열악한 환경하에서 종업원들의 근로의욕이 솟아나기를 기대하기는 어렵다.

4) 공정한 리더십

관리자의 훌륭한 리더십은 종업원이 효과적으로 업무를 수행하는 것을 도와줄 뿐만 아니라 기업의 성과향상으로도 이어지게 된다.

5) 기업문화

종업원이 속해 있는 기업이 어떤 가치를 중시하며 자율권과 재량권을 어느 정도 부여하느냐가 종업원의 동기부여에 많은 영향을 미친다. 우수한 기업은 창의성, 적극적인 참여 등을 강조하는 경향이 있는데 이런 기업에 속해 있는 종업원들은 그렇지 못한 기업에 있을 때보다 열심히 일할 것으로 기대할 수 있다.

(3) 인간관계 제도

1) 카운슬링

카운슬링에 전문적 지식을 갖춘 심리치료사들이 관여하게 되는데 종업원이 다룰 수 없는 수준의 문제일 때 상당한 도움이 될 수 있다. 카운슬링은 종업원이 갖고 있는 갈등을 줄이고 긍정적인 태도를 계속 지속하도록 만들며, 이해관계를 통합시키는 가장 효과적인 방법 중의 하나이다.

2) 참여제도의 도입

종업원들이 경영에 참여할 수 있는 길을 열어 놓음으로써 종업원들의 근로의욕을 북돋우기 위함이다. 제안제도 등이 대표적인 예이다.

3) 불만 처리제도

성숙한 조직일수록 잠재된 갈등을 표면화시켜 토론을 통해 갈등 해결을 도모하려는 의지와 능력을 갖추고 있다. 물론 모든 갈등이 몇몇 수단에 의해 완전히 제거될 수는 없다고 하더라도 갈등을 표면화시키고 감소시키는 데 크게 기여할 수 있을 것이다. 이를 위해서는 종업원들이 갖고 있는 불만이나 고충(grievance)을 공정하게 처리할 수 있는 절차를 구비하는 것이 필요하다.

II. Gain Sharing System[287]

1. Concept of Gain Sharing System

Recently, there has been a gradual increase in the expectations of employees to participate in management. This trend will continue with the sharp increase of employee intellectual levels and transfer of labor-management relations from that of rivals to cooperative and collectively-fated relations. As active counter-measures to cope with this prospect, the company can introduce a 'Gain Sharing System' and take control of employee wishes to participate in management.

The Gain Sharing System is introduced in group-centered sharing. It is a method by which the employer pays the employees a bonus for high achievement shown in a major organizational unit such as the overall organization, plant, or business section, etc.

2. Methods of the Gain Sharing System

High performance recognized by a Gain Sharing System can be measured mainly by profit, production, total sales, or by a mixed index. Of these, measuring by profit is most common. The amount of Gain Sharing is calculated by the sharing rate for high performance results exceeding the company target as follow:

Amount of Gain Sharing = (good result - the target) × sharing rate

When Gain Sharing is rendered as a bonus, the bonus rate is:

(1) Increasing: Pays the amount calculated by multiplying the bonus rate of Gain Sharing with the individual base pay
(2) Stair: Pays a 50% bonus for 90~100% target achievement, 70% bonus for 100~120% target achievement, etc.
(3) Flat: Simply pays 00% for target achievement
   In general, companies in Korea use the flat-type or stair-type and give payments once or twice a year. The total amount paid as Gain Sharing is approximately 12% on average.

---

[287] Park, KyeongKyu, 「New Human Resources Management」, 7th ed., Hongmoonsa, 2019; Kim, Youngjae, 「New HR Workforce Management」 4th ed., Topbooks; and Lim, Changhee, 「Organizational Behaviors」, 6th ed., B&Books, 2018.

Ⅱ. 성과배분제도[287]

1. 성과배분의 의의

최근 근로자들의 경영참가에 대한 기대는 점차 증대되고 있으며 이러한 추세는 근로자들의 의식수준 향상과 대립적 노사관계에서 협력적·공동체적 노사관계 중심으로 이행에 따라 향후에는 더욱 가속화될 전망이다. 이러한 전망에 대응한 적극적인 대처수단으로서 성과배분제도를 도입하여 증대되는 직원들의 경영참가 욕구를 해소할 수 있다.

집단 중심의 균등배분이 가장 뚜렷하게 나타나는 것이 성과배분(Gain Sharing)이다. 성과배분제도는 전체 조직체 또는 공장이나 사업부 등 주요 조직 단위의 성과를 구성원들에게 상여금 형태로 추가 임금을 지불하는 방법이다.

2. 성과배분의 방법

성과배분제도에서 성과는 주로 이익, 생산량, 매출액 또는 이들의 복합적인 지수가 사용되는데 그 중 이익이 가장 많이 사용된다. 그리고 성과배분액은 다음과 같이 성과목표를 초과한 성과업적에 배분율을 곱하면 산출된다.

성과배분액 = (성과업적 - 성과목표) × 배분율

성과배분을 상여금으로 지불하는 경우 상여금의 비율은
(1) 연속형 : 성과배분액을 기본금 총액을 나누어 산출된 상여금 비율을 개별 기본급에 곱하여 지급
(2) 계단형 : 90~100% 성과달성에는 보너스 50%, 100~120% 성과달성에는 보너스 70% 등 계단식으로 계산
(3) 평면형 : 성과목표를 달성하는 경우에 ○○%를 지급하는 단순한 방법
우리나라 기업에서 대체로 평면형과 계단형이 많이 사용되고 있고, 연 1~2회 지급되며, 성과배분액이 차지하는 비중은 평균 12% 정도이다.

---

[287] 박경규, 「신인사관리」 제7판, 홍문사, 2019; 김영재외 2, 「신인적자원관리」, 제4판, 탑북스, 2019; 임창희 「조직행동」 제6판, 비엔엠북스, 2018

3. Effects and Problems of the Gain Sharing System

(1) Effects

The Gain Sharing System brings positive results such as improvement of productivity, increase of work concentration, reduction of extended work avoidance, cultivation of labor-management cooperation, ease of collective negotiation on wages, etc.

(2) Problems

1) Many companies do not apply a single formula to the Gain Sharing System and resort to convenient methods according to the situation.
   Thus, when organizational members do not understand the target index clearly, the Gain Sharing System fails to maximize their target awareness and motivation.
2) The amount paid in the Gain Sharing System is greatly influenced by the level of the company's targets. Accordingly, conflicts may arise between two parties given that the company prefers higher targets, whereas the employees prefer lower targets.

III. Welfare System Operation[288]

1. Purpose of Welfare Systems

Welfare, which means additional benefits other than wages, can motivate employees to higher performance. It not only helps maintain physical and mental wellbeing in performing their duties, but prospective employees are also attracted to an advantageous work environment. Given that the system builds strong commitment to the company, it serves as an effective means to reduce absences and resignations. Moreover, the company can agree to a welfare program prior to any union demands by advocating them in advance.

---

[288] Park, KyeongKyu, 「New Human Resources Management」, 7th ed., Hongmoonsa, 2019; Kim, Youngjae, 「New HR Workforce Management」 4th ed., Topbooks; and Lim, Changhee, 「Organizational Behaviors」, 6th ed., B&Books, 2018.

3. 성과배분제도의 효과와 문제점

(1) 성과배분의 효과
성과배분제도는 대체로 생산성 향상, 근무 집중도의 증가, 잔업회피태도의 감소, 노사협조 분위기의 조성, 수월한 임금교섭 등의 긍정적 효과를 가져 온다.

(2) 성과배분의 문제점
1) 많은 기업체에서 성과배분에 정확한 공식을 일관성 있게 적용하지 않고 상황에 따라 편의적인 방법으로 성과배분을 하고 있다. 따라서 조직구성원들이 성과지표를 정확하게 알지 못함으로써 그들의 목표의식과 동기부여를 극대화시키지 못하고 있다.
2) 성과배분액은 성과목표를 어느 수준에 정하느냐에 따라서 많은 영향을 받는다. 따라서 성과목표를 높게 설정하려는 경영층과 이를 낮게 설정하려는 구성원들 간에 많은 갈등을 야기할 수 있다.

Ⅲ. 복리후생제도[288]

1. 복리후생제도의 의의

복리후생은 임금 외에 추가적으로 얻는 보상이기 때문에 이로 인해 종업원의 사기가 높아져 성과향상으로 연결될 수 있다. 또한 복리후생은 현직 종업원의 신체적·정신적 성과창출능력을 유지하는 데 도움을 주며 노동시장에서 보다 유리한 입장에 서서 신규 인력을 확보할 수 있게 해준다. 뿐만 아니라 현직 종업원에게 기업에 대한 소속감을 높여 주기 때문에 결근율을 줄이고 이직을 방지하는 데 매우 효과적이다. 또한 노동조합이 있는 경우 노동조합이 요구하기 전에 복리후생 프로그램을 도입함으로써 노조의 요구를 사전에 배제할 수 있다.

---
[288] 박경규, 「신인사관리」 제7판, 홍문사, 2019; 김영재외 2, 「신인적자원관리」, 제4판, 탑북스, 2019; 임창희 「조직행동」 제6판, 비엔엠북스, 2018

Chapter 7 Wage-related Personnel Systems

2. Considerations in Introducing a Company Welfare Program

(1) On the company side

1) How much the company can set aside for welfare costs from the total personnel costs when introducing the welfare program needs to be considered. This is reviewed in relation to the wages the company pays its employees. That is, when the company increases welfare expenses, it is likely to bring a negative effect to wages.

2) The company shall also weigh welfare costs and benefits. Here, the benefits are measured by the company's accomplishments from introducing the welfare program.

3) The company shall consider the level of its competitors' welfare systems. This includes external equity in welfare costs and decision-making about maintaining the welfare gap between the company and its competitors.

There are three given strategies: Raising the level of the company's welfare so that it is higher than its competitors ("market leader strategy"); raising it to the same level ("competitive strategy"); and lowering it ("market lagging strategy").

4) The company shall consider legal requirements first. Then, the welfare program it introduces shall more than meet the requirements.

(2) On the employee side

1) How well the employees accept the level of welfare as equity is important. Equity is assessed by looking at past welfare programs offered by the company, the level of current welfare programs introduced by its competitors, and the size of the current welfare benefits the company distributes to an individual.

2) The company shall consider employee statistics. Welfare programs are usually selected differently according to age, gender, marital status, and the number of dependents. For example, senior employees prefer pensions, severance pay, educational support for their children, etc. whereas younger employees prefer

2. 기업의 복리후생 결정시 고려사항

(1) 기업측
1) 복리후생 프로그램을 도입함에 있어서 기업이 부담하게 되는 복리후생비가 전체 인건비 범위 내에서 어느 정도 허용될 수 있느냐 이다. 이것은 기업이 종업원에 대해 지불하는 임금과의 관계에서 검토된다. 즉 기업이 복리후생비를 늘릴 경우 아무래도 이것은 임금상승에 부정적인 영향을 미치지 않을 수 없다.
2) 투입된 복리후생비와 이로 인해 창출된 편익과의 관계가 고려되어야 한다. 여기서 편익은 바로 기업이 복리후생 프로그램을 도입하는 목적이 어느 정도 달성되느냐에 관한 것이다.
3) 경쟁기업의 복리후생 수준이다. 이것은 복리후생비에 대한 외부공정과 관련되는 것으로서 경쟁기업의 복리후생 수준과 해당 기업의 그것 간에 어느 정도 수준을 유지하느냐에 대한 정책결정이다. 이에 대해서는 세 가지 전략이 있는데 해당기업의 복리후생 수준을 경쟁기업의 그것보다 높이는 선도전략, 경쟁기업의 수준과 비슷하게 하는 경쟁전략, 그리고 경쟁기업 수준보다 낮게 하는 추종전략이 있다.
4) 법적 요구사항이다. 기업이 도입하는 복리후생 프로그램에 대해 국가 법정 요구사항 이상으로 하여야 한다.

(2) 종업원측
1) 복리후생의 수준에 대해 종업원이 어느 정도 공정한 것(equity)으로 지각하고 있느냐이다. 공정한 지각의 기준은 해당 기업에서 도입되었던 과거의 복리후생 수준, 현재 타 기업에서 도입하고 있는 복리후생 수준 그리고 현재 해당기업 내 종업원 개인에게 배분되고 있는 복리후생 혜택의 크기가 된다.
2) 종업원의 인구 통계적 특성이다. 해당기업 종업원의 연령구조, 성별, 결혼 여부 그리고 부양가족 수에 따라 선호하는 복리후생 프로그램이 다르기 때문이다. 예를 들면, 연령이 높은 종업원은 연금이나 퇴직금 또는 자녀 학비 지원 등의 복리후생을 선호하는 반면 연령이 낮은 종업원은 유급휴가,

paid leaves, training opportunities, etc., and employees with a large number of dependents tend to prefer medical support programs.

3. Welfare Programs

(1) Living facilities

Under this welfare program, the employee may be provided with housing facilities, dining facilities, etc.

Living facilities benefit the employee with housing security, reduce commute time, and increase actual income, but costs the company a lot of money. If there is a shortage of facilities, conflicts may arise concerning the distribution of benefits.

Dining facilities are an important part of the welfare program because they are closely related to the maintenance of employee health and can be costly for the company.

(2) Financial and convenience facilities

Financial and convenience facilities include snack shops, a lending system, etc. Internal facilities, such as a snack shop, help increase actual wages by providing quality products at cheaper prices. A lending system is a system in which the company provides loans to its employees at a lower interest rate.

(3) Health facilities

Health facilities refer to general facilities that promote health for the employees and their dependents. They include medical treatment facilities, recreation facilities, health facilities, etc. Concerning medical treatment facilities, the company can directly operate a medical treatment center or a hospital, or provide health examinations or medical treatment services or medical consultation through a designated hospital. In addition, the company can directly run recreational facilities or provide employees with outside recreational facilities affiliated with the company. The company may provide the employees partial or full coverage of recreational fees. Health facilities include a sauna, barbershop, beauty shop, etc.

교육훈련 기회를 더 선호할 것이다. 또한 부양가족 수가 많은 종업원은 그렇지 않은 종업원보다 의료비지원 프로그램을 더 선호한다.

3. 복리후생 프로그램

(1) 생활시설

기업이 근로자에게 제공하는 생활시설과 관련되는 복리후생 프로그램은 주택시설, 급식시설 등이 있다.

기업의 주택시설 지원은 종업원에게 생활의 안정, 통근시간의 단축, 실질소득의 상승효과를 가져다준다는 장점이 있지만 주택시설을 건축하는 데 막대한 비용이 발생하며, 주택시설이 충분하지 못할 경우, 종업원에 대한 혜택의 배분 관련 갈등이 유발될 수 있다.

급식시설은 종업원의 건강유지와 밀접한 관계가 있으며 이를 위한 지출비용 또한 크기 때문에 중요한 복리후생 프로그램에 해당한다.

(2) 경제시설

경제시설과 관련되는 복리후생 프로그램은 매점, 대여금제도 등이 있다. 매점으로 불리는 구내시설은 종업원에게 양질의 일용품을 저렴하게 공급함으로써 실질임금을 높여주는 역할을 한다. 대여제도는 종업원들이 생활에 자금이 필요할 때 낮은 이자로 자금을 빌려주는 제도이다.

(3) 보건위생시설

보건위생시설은 종업원 및 그 가족의 보건위생을 위한 제 시설로서 진료시설, 휴양시설, 보건시설 등이 있다. 진료시설을 통한 서비스는 기업이 직접 진료소나 병원을 운영할 수 있으며 혹은 지정병원을 통한 건강진단 및 진료서비스의 제공 그리고 건강상담을 할 수 있게 해 준다. 휴양시설은 기업이 휴양소를 직영하거나 외부기관과 계약을 체결하여 종업원을 이용하게 할 수 있다. 또는 기업이 종업원에게 휴양비의 전부 혹은 일부를 부담하는 경우도 있다. 보건시설에는 목욕탕, 이발관, 미용실 등이 있다.

(4) Education, sports, and recreation facilities

The company provides educational or cultural opportunities through educational facilities, libraries etc. Sports and recreation facilities are designed to promote the physical and mental development of the employees so they can make the most of their leisure, recreation, etc. These include gymnasiums, playgrounds, tennis courts, volleyball courts, swimming pools, etc.

4. "Cafeteria" Style Welfare Programs

(1) There are two types of "cafeteria" style welfare programs: a standard benefits package and a flexible benefits package. The standard benefits package does not give employees options but is pre-selected and applied. In this case, employees are obliged to accept it whether or not the package is suited to their needs. Accordingly, the standard benefits package can be less effective if employees do not fully appreciate the benefits offered to them. In order to avoid such problems and maximize employee satisfaction, the company can introduce a flexible benefits package to better meet employee needs.

(2) The flexible benefits package offers various welfare programs the employees can select from. Accordingly, the plan is referred to as a "cafeteria" style program from the idea that people select their own items at a cafeteria.

(4) 교육·체육·오락시설

기업은 교육시설을 통해 종업원들의 교양을 높이거나 특정 분야의 교육 기회를 제공한다. 또한 이와 관련하여 기업 내 도서실을 운영하기도 한다. 체육 및 오락시설은 종업원의 건전한 심신 발달, 여가의 이용, 오락 등을 목적으로 한다. 예를 들면 체육관, 운동장, 테니스장, 배구장, 수영장 등이 있다.

4. 카페테리아식 복리후생

(1) 복리후생 프로그램의 선택과 관련하여 표준적 복리후생 프로그램(standard benefits package)과 선택적 복리후생 프로그램(flexible benefit package)이 있다. 전자는 복리후생 프로그램에 대해 종업원에게 선택의 기회를 주지 않고 기업이 일방적으로 설계하고 이를 적용시키는 것을 말한다. 이 경우 종업원은 기업이 제공하는 복리후생이 자기들의 욕구구조와 일치하든 그렇지 않든 수용하지 않을 수 없다.

따라서 표준적 복리후생 프로그램의 경우 기업이 많은 복지비를 지출하였음에도 불구하고 이를 받아들이는 종업원이 별로 고맙게 생각하지 않는다면 문제이다. 바로 이러한 문제점을 극복하여 기업이 제공하는 복리후생에 대한 종업원의 만족도를 극대화하기 위해 기업은 종업원의 욕구에 맞는 복리후생 프로그램으로 선택적 복리후생 프로그램을 도입하고 있다.

(2) 선택적 복리후생 프로그램은 기업이 다양한 복리후생 프로그램을 제시하고 이 중 종업원이 원하는 것을 그들 스스로 선택할 수 있게 하는 것이다. 선택적 복리후생 프로그램을 보통 카페테리아식(cafeteria style)이라고 부른다. 카페테리아식 식당에서 사람들이 자기가 원하는 음식을 자유로이 선택하는 데에서 비롯된 것이다.

Wage Manual
임금매뉴얼(제2개정판)

발 행 일 : 2019년 12월 1일 초판발행
발 행 일 : 2023년 10월 10일 2개정판
지 은 이 : 정 봉 수
펴 낸 이 : 정 봉 수
펴 낸 곳 : 강남노무법인 출판부 (K-Labor Press)
편집·디자인 : 정 영 철
주   소 : 서울시 강남구 대치동 테헤란로 406 A-1501 (대치동, 샹제리제센터)
전   화 : 02-539-0098
팩   스 : 02-539-4167
홈페이지 : www.k-labor.com
출판등록 : 강남, 바00177
I S B N : 979-11-85290-27-0
정   가 : 30,000원

■ 이 책자는 저작권법에 따라 보호받는 저작물이므로 무단전재와 복제를 금합니다.